Social Web Evolution:
Integrating Semantic Applications and Web 2.0 Technologies

Miltiadis D. Lytras
Athens University of Economics & Business, Greece

Patricia Ordóñez de Pablos
University of Oviedo, Spain

INFORMATION SCIENCE REFERENCE

Hershey · New York

Director of Editorial Content:	Kristin Klinger
Senior Managing Editor:	Jamie Snavely
Managing Editor:	Jeff Ash
Assistant Managing Editor:	Carole Coulson
Typesetter:	Sean Woznicki
Cover Design:	Lisa Tosheff
Printed at:	Yurchak Printing Inc.

Published in the United States of America by
Information Science Reference (an imprint of IGI Global)
701 E. Chocolate Avenue, Suite 200
Hershey PA 17033
Tel: 717-533-8845
Fax: 717-533-8661
E-mail: cust@igi-global.com
Web site: http://www.igi-global.com/reference

and in the United Kingdom by
Information Science Reference (an imprint of IGI Global)
3 Henrietta Street
Covent Garden
London WC2E 8LU
Tel: 44 20 7240 0856
Fax: 44 20 7379 0609
Web site: http://www.eurospanbookstore.com

Library of Congress Cataloging-in-Publication Data

Social web evolution : integrating semantic applications and Web 2.0 technologies / Miltiadis D. Lytras and Patricia Ordonez de Pablos, editors.

p. cm.

Includes bibliographical references and index.
Summary: "This book explores the potential of Web 2.0 and its synergies with the Semantic Web and provides state-of-the-art theoretical foundations and technological applications"--Provided by publisher.

ISBN 978-1-60566-272-5 (hardcover) -- ISBN 978-1-60566-273-2 (ebook) 1. Organizational learning. 2. Knowledge management. 3. Online social networks. 4. Semantic Web. 5. Web 2.0. I. Lytras, Miltiadis D., 1973- II. Pablos, Patricia Ordonez de.

HD58.82.S66 2009
025.042'7--dc22
                    2008047729

British Cataloguing in Publication Data
A Cataloguing in Publication record for this book is available from the British Library.

All work contributed to this book is new, previously-unpublished material. The views expressed in this book are those of the authors, but not necessarily of the publisher.

Social Web Evolution: Integrating Semantic Applications and Web 2.0 Technologies is part of the IGI Global series named Advances in *Semantic Web and Information Systems (ASWIS)* Series, ISBN: 1935-3626

To the smiling longskater
- Patricia

Editorial Advisory Board

Table of Contents

Detailed Table of Contents

Chapter I

Exploring a Professional Social Network System to Support Learning in the Workplace.................... 1

    Anthony "Skip" Basiel, Middlesex University – IWBL, UK

    Paul Coyne, Emerald Group Publishing Ltd, UK

The authors of this chapter explore how professionals can network, collaborate and capture informal learning in an online work-based environment. It addresses the pedagogical approaches that underpin emerging Web 2.0 technological trends and provide recommendations for future use of such online environments.

Chapter II

Knowledge Producing Megamachines: The Biggest Web 2.0 Communities of the Future 17

    Laszlo Z. Karvalics, University of Szeged, Hungary

This chapter addresses the control crisis of science whose resolution requires radical social innovation. The only possible way for achieving this is the partial fusion of certain portions of scientific activity with the system of public education, by means of organizing scientists, teachers, as well as middle and highschool students into hybrid, knowledge producing mega-machines. The authors of the chapter subsequently argue that doing so will at the same time bring about a pragmatic shift in public education, for which professionals in the field of pedagogy have long been ready in principle and in theory.

Chapter III

Web 2.0 Driven Sustainability Reporting 31

    Daniel Süpke, Carl von Ossietzky Universität Oldenburg, Germany

    Jorge Marx Gómez, Carl von Ossietzky Universität Oldenburg, Germany

    Ralf Isenmann, Fraunhofer Institute for Systems and Innovation Research Karlsruhe, Germany

Web 2.0 driven sustainability reporting describes an emerging digital approach powered through Web 2.0 technologies for companies communicating sustainability issues. Such a computer-based application of semantics overcomes the limitations of orthodox methods and provides an array of specific capabilities to improve sustainability communication both, for companies (reporters), and their various stakeholders (report readers), that is, along interactivity, customisation ,and reporting à la carte, stakeholder dialogue, and participation. This chapter gives an outline on this up-and-coming sustainability reporting approach along three categories: (i) Media-specific trends in sustainability reporting are observed. (ii) New opportunities Web 2.0 technologies are offering for corporate sustainability reporting are identified. (iii) The concept and implementation of a software tool for sustainability reporting à la carte is presented making clear the movement away from early reporting stages towards the advanced one of a Web 2.0 driven approach.

Sergio Fernández, Fundación CTIC, Spain
Diego Berrueta, Fundación CTIC, Spain
Lian Shi, Fundación CTIC, Spain
Jose E. Labra, University of Oviedo, Spain
Patricia Ordóñez de Pablos, University of Oviedo, Spain

Electronic Mailing lists are a key part of the Internet. They have enabled the development of social communities who share and exchange knowledge in specialized and general domains. In this chapter the authors describe methods to capture some of that knowledge which will enable the development of new datasets using Semantic Web technologies. In particular, the authors present the SWAML project, which collects data from mailing lists. The authors also describe smushing techniques that normalize RDF datasets capturing different resources that identify the same one. They have applied those techniques to identify persons through the mailing lists of open source communities. These techniques have been tested using a dataset automatically extracted from several online open source communities.

D. Sandy Staples, Queens University, Canada

This chapter describes one of the Web 2.0 technologies, Social Networking Sites (SNS). A definition of SNS is offered, as is a short history of these sites. The existing research is reviewed and organized to summarize what we know about SNS usage (from the perspectives of student use, general population use and organizational use), and what people know about the antecedents and outcomes of SNS use. The chapter concludes with discussion of new developments, challenges and opportunities. There are many opportunities for future research and organizational applications of SNS as SNS adoption grows at incredible rates.

Jingyuan Zhao, Harbin Institute of Technology, China

Knowledge is taken as core competitive power in the current society. The teacher as an educational operator often touch much knowledge, if they could manage knowledge efficiently, the work efficiency will be increased greatly. To mine knowledge and make tacit knowledge explicit, teachers should manage personal knowledge. By the survey of teachers' personal knowledge management in China, the study finds some problems in terms of Chinese teachers' personal knowledge management, especially many Chinese teachers are not good at making use of Web technologies to assist them on managing knowledge and communicating with other teachers. One studying focus of Web 2.0 technologies is personal knowledge management, and Web 2.0 provides a series of effective tools and platforms for personal knowledge management. The chapter discusses on the concept of teachers' personal knowledge management, and presents the strategies of teachers' personal knowledge management based Web 2.0 technologies, using for reference for teachers' personal knowledge management practice.

Chapter VII

Ángel García-Crespo, Universidad Carlos III de Madrid, Spain
Ricardo Colomo-Palacios, Universidad Carlos III de Madrid, Spain
Myriam Mencke, Universidad Carlos III de Madrid, Spain
Juan M. Gómez-Berbís, Universidad Carlos III de Madrid, Spain

The current chapter introduces CUSENT, a tool for semantics-enhanced sentiment analysis of customer opinions expressed in corporate blogs. The research work presents the examination of emotions and sentiments from the perspective of information systems, and, in particular, provides a review of the principal efforts for the conceptualization of emotions and sentiments in texts. Subsequently, a description of the proposed architecture of the platform is outlined. The authors aim to contribute a solution which automates the analysis of customer opinions in company blogs that relies on existing techniques, but further exploits these methods to store and reuse customer feedback. The novel combination of opinion mining with an ontology of emotions can thus be used in organizational creation and innovation processes, which characterize the new forms of communication derived from the institutional and commercial use of Web 2.0.

Chapter VIII

Irene Samanta, Technological Education Institute of Piraeus, Greece

This chapter is to define the firm's innovative core and create frameworks to integrate innovation throughout the management of knowledge by generating implementing ideas, strategies and plans applied that cultivate a thinking organization aims to associate innovation with business targets. It argues that companies which manage and transform the knowledge effectively reap the rewards of scientific and technological achievement in order to adopt innovation concept in their operation. Furthermore, the author hope that firms understanding the information received from the current global business world and transmit it to reap the rewards of scientific achievement will increase their competitiveness competition not only for sales, but also for technical know – how and skills. At the company level depends on the speed with which new products can be brought to the market place and on the importance of achieving new cost – saving improvements.

Archives have a key role to play in underpinning learning in its broadest sense, both as a formal activity within an institution and informally within the community. This is becoming especially important in an increasingly KM-based environment. This chapter provides an overview of technologies that can be applied to archival knowledge management. Furthermore, it assesses their actual or potential contribution to the basic processes of knowledge sharing within archival organizations, with a focus on lifelong learning. The scope of the first section (the screens) is to identify new developments that seem to be significant and to relate them to technology research in the archival field. The second section (the frames) discusses the concepts supporting digital collections by integrating collections of digitized archival resources to create new services and infrastructures. The third section (the agendas) analyses-from the educational perspective of lifelong learning-important social benefits, both quantitatively and qualitatively, of developing new infrastructures for accessing and using archival resources.

Chapter X

In clinical training, students plan, implement and evaluate their learning activities by themselves. They apply theories and concepts in a real clinical environment and learn through social interaction and reflective thinking to experience, conceptualize, apply and create new knowledge to solve clinical problems. Since students are sent to different clinical locations for training and are mentored on a one-to-one basis, it is difficult for students to share their knowledge, make enquiries or interact with their peers and mentors for social and reflective learning. Web 2.0 provides a collaborative and social interactive platform that allows learners to exchange, share, acquire, codify, distribute, and disseminate knowledge. Its functions and features are able to construct a virtual and distributed environment for learners to gather, filter and update the knowledge over different internet sources. This paper thus aims to discuss the functions and features of Web 2.0 technology and its applications to clinical training.

Folksonomies offer an easy method to organize information in the current Web. This fact and their collaborative features have derived in an extensive involvement in many Social Web projects. However they present important drawbacks regarding their limited exploring and searching capabilities, in contrast with other methods as taxonomies, thesauruses and ontologies. One of these drawbacks is an effect of its flexibility for tagging, producing frequently multiple syntactic variations of a same tag. In this chapter we study the application of two classical pattern matching techniques, Levenshtein distance for the imperfect string matching and Hamming distance for the perfect string matching, to identify syntactic variations of tags.

    Katia Sycara, Carnegie Mellon University, USA
    Paul Scerri, Carnegie Mellon University, USA
    Anton Chechetka, Carnegie Mellon University, USA

The chapter explores the use of evolutionary game theory (EGT) to model the dynamics of adaptive opponent strategies for a large population of players. In particular, it explores effects of information propagation through social networks in evolutionary games. The key underlying phenomenon that the information diffusion aims to capture is that reasoning about the experiences of acquaintances can dramatically impact the dynamics of a society. The chapter presents experimental results from agent-based simulations that show the impact of diffusion through social networks on the player strategies of an evolutionary game and the sensitivity of the dynamics to features of the social network.

    Jaehun Joo, Dongguk University, Korea
    Sang M. Lee, University of Nebraska – Lincoln, USA
    Yongil Jeong, Saltlux, Inc., Korea

This chapter introduces an application of the Semantic Web based on ontology to the tourism business. Tourism business is one promising area for Semantic Web applications. To realize the potential of the Semantic Web, we need to find a killer application of the Semantic Web in the knowledge management (KM) area. The ontology as a key enabler is deigned and implemented under a framework of the Semantic-Web-driven KM system in a tourism domain. Finally, we discussed the relationship between the Semantic Web and KM processes.

    Miranda Mowbray, HP Laboratories Bristol, UK

This chapter is concerned with how to design an online learning community in such a way as to encourage cooperation, and to discourage uncooperative or antisocial behavior. Rather than restricting design to visual and interface issues, the author takes a wide view, touching on aspects of the governance, social structure, moderation practices, and technical architecture of online learning communities. The first half of the chapter discusses why people behave antisocially in online learning communities, and ways to discourage this through design. The second half discusses why on the other hand people behave cooperatively in online learning communities, and ways to encourage this through user-centered design, applying some results of experiments in social psychology. The chapter is intended to be of practical use to designers of online learning communities.

This chapter introduces the concept of virtual learning communities and discusses and further enhances the theory and definitions presented in related literature. A model comprising four criteria essential to virtual learning communities is presented and discussed in detail. Theory and case studies relating to the impact of virtual learning communities on distance education and students from diverse cultural groups are also examined. In addition, this chapter investigates the enabling technologies and facilitation that is required to build virtual learning communities. Other case studies are used to illustrate the process of building virtual learning communities. Emerging technologies such as Wikis and video lectures are also analysed to determine the effects they have on building and sustaining effective virtual learning communities.

Using a case study approach, this chapter examines the role of organizational networks in the success and failure of information and communications technology projects. Within a framework informed by the literature of information systems failure, the diffusion of innovation and social network analysis; it argues that information systems projects must take into account the social context in which they are implemented. To be successful such networks require a mix of extended and locally based support networks, because they provide access to much needed resources, including innovations, strategic advice, training, and support at the appropriate level. It further argues that the people who are working in a regional setting felt themselves to be in an extremely disadvantageous situation because they typically lacked support from similar networks. The author hopes that highlighting the importance of such support networks will lead to a better understanding of systems failure and success, and will contribute to improved policy formulation and practice.

The chapter investigates an actionable context of knowledge networking, from the perspective of sustainable development which should accommodate the building of communities in cyberspace so much exemplified in today's Internet and World Wide Web. The premise of this exploration is that members, or participants, in any community are engaged in learning that is critical to the survival and reproduction of that community. Through community participation, learners find and acquire models and have the opportunity themselves to become models and apprentices of others. This investigation provides a basis for thinking about the possibilities of a virtual community and the dynamics of its construction across a variety of computer-based contexts. The design and refinement of technology as the conduit for extending and enhancing the possibilities of virtual community building is an essential issue, but the role of the individuals as participants in such a community is as important. The idea of sustainable knowledge networking is to bring about continual learning and change for the community in need. The emergent challenge of such a mission is to demarginalize many of the non-technical issues of building virtual communities for knowledge transfer and learning. The chapter concludes by reiterating the challenge of expositing what it means to create an appropriate context of knowledge networking through which purposeful actions can be supported with the elaboration of suitable information technologies.

Changqing Li, National University of Singapore, Singapore
Tok Wang Ling, National University of Singapore, Singapore

This chapter introduces how to effectively organize ontology languages and ontologies and how to efficiently process semantic information based on ontologies. In this chapter the authors propose the hierarchies to organize ontology languages and ontologies. Based on the hierarchy of ontology languages, the ontology designers need not bear in mind which ontology language the primitives exactly come from, also we can automatically and seamlessly use the ontologies defined with different ontology languages in an integrated environment. Based on the hierarchy of ontologies, the conflicts in different ontologies are resolved, thus the semantics in different ontologies are clear without ambiguities. Also, these semantic-clear ontologies can be used to efficiently process the semantic information in Semantic Web and E-Business.

Ben K. Daniel, University of Saskatchewan, Canada
David O'Brien, University of Saskatchewan, Canada
Asit Sarkar, University of Saskatchewan, Canada

This chapter aims to introduce user-centered design and its basic concepts associated with online learning communities. Another aim is to search for guidelines to ensure quality in online learning. Human-computer interaction for education provides the missing holistic approach for online learning. Functioning in a sociotechnical framework, online learning communities combine information and knowledge stores situated in shared social spaces using social learning software. In recent years, educational technologists linked theory and systems design in education. However, several disciplines combine in online learning. User-centered design provides the cross-disciplinary approach that appears to be essential for quality in online learning design and engineering. Thus, seven guidelines for experts' evaluation are proposed as signposts: intention, information, interactivity, real-time evaluation, visibility, control, and support.

Preface

As semantic technologies prove their value with targeted applications, there are increasing opportunities to consider their application in social contexts for knowledge, learning, and human development.

Semantic Web and Knowledge Management has been accepted as a critical enabler aiming to increase knowledge-related performance by better use of intellectual assets, in addition to which many governments are forced to increasingly deal with knowledge services that form larger parts of the global economy and society.

Thus there are recent examples of applications of semantics for empowering knowledge management or better supporting knowledge services for social networks. In this edited book we explore the potential of Web 2.0 and its synergies with Semantic Web, and we provide the state of the art in theoretical foundations and technological applications. In the context of Social Web Evolution, social and human issues are of equal if not higher importance than the technical issues that have tended to receive the bulk of attention in the past. Consequently, chapters that touch these aspects, or those that extend technical and domain knowledge to social and human issues are especially sought. This is intended to initiate a dialog between the social, psychological, and technical views of the field.

Web 2.0 is one of the hottest topics in Information Systems. Currently, the main discussion is emphasized on technologies while there is a great demand for editions that will analyze the business models and business perspectives of the new generation Web. This book is one of the first attempts to discuss in an integrated way the business implications of Web 2.0 and its linkage to business value.

Web 2.0, refers to a perceived or proposed second generation of Internet-based services—such as social networking sites, Wikis, communication tools, mashups and folksonomies—that emphasize on online collaboration and sharing among users.

Additionally we also include further readings of a complimentary nature to the contents of the rest of our publication. As an added value to our readers, the further readings are to provide additional related data in support of the book's comprehensive concepts, principles and results, as well as studies that build upon the appeal of this publication as a one-stop reference source.

We do not want to miss this opportunity to say thanks to IGI Global, and in particular to Jan Travers and Kristin M. Klinger for giving us the opportunity to develop this book. Also thanks to all authors of chapters, for their interest in collaborating in this book.

Miltiadis D. Lytras
Athens, Greece, October 2008

Patricia Ordóñez de Pablos
Gijón, Spain, October 2008

Chapter I
Exploring a Professional Social Network System to Support Learning in the Workplace

Anthony "Skip" Basiel
Middlesex University – IWBL, UK

Paul Coyne
Emerald Group Publishing Ltd, UK

ABSTRACT

This chapter sets out to explore how professionals can network, collaborate and capture informal learning in an online work-based environment. It addresses the pedagogical approaches that underpin emerging Web 2.0 technological trends and provide recommendations for future use of such online environments. Existing Virtual Learning Environments (VLEs) are primarily content driven with little provision for social engagement and stakeholder-generated material. Similarly, many organisations have little or no structure for facilitating online interaction in a work based learning context. Since 2006 Emerald Group Publishing and the Middlesex Centre for Excellence in Work Based Learning have been partnering to develop, test and implement an online platform that will support collaborative, interactive learning. This link between Industry and Higher Education is critically reviewed. The InTouch (2008) platform was incorporated into the syllabus for MCEWBL's work-based Professional Practice BA Honours programme in 2007 to support newly trained professionals as they worked through a professional development work based learning programme. The pedagogical underpinning of the course was reflective, self-directed learning and the blog, Wiki and profiling tools provided had the potential to either contribute to this aim or become a major part of how students construct their understanding of themselves in their professional practice. Emerald and MCEWBL have been monitoring the adoption, use and challenges associated with using Web 2.0 technology to support work based learning in order make recommendations about future pedagogical frameworks and approaches. This platform and related online pedagogic principles fills the gap between informal, free tools that provide little security or structure and heavyweight VLEs that offer tutor-made content, but do not naturally support social interaction for learning. The chapter provides some ideas and strategic options about implementing similar tools in other organisational settings and provides frameworks to evaluate these options in line with existing resources and capabilities. It concludes with an in-progress web-based learning design or ePedagogy that unifies the threads of the online learning experience.

INTRODUCTION

Middlesex University work based learning (WBL) has been operating for over ten years at the time of this writing. Its original distance learning design was a paper-based correspondence model which relied heavily on the content in the handbooks and one-to-one (1-2-1) tutorial support from WBL Learning Development Tutors predominantly through email and phone feedback. Over the past few years there has been a steady transition into the use of a commercial virtual learning environment (VLE) in the form of Blackboard/WebCT.

At first this system matched the WBL teaching and learning design since there was a strong reliance on the course handbook for information and guidance. However, as student numbers increased the student-teacher ratio meant this model was not sustainable for the future. The 1-2-1 pedagogic model would need to expand into a triad that would promote and support peer involvement. Students were growing in their ICT confidence and capability with the increased use of Web 2.0 social network systems such as Facebook and YouTube. This was evidenced by student representatives at the WBL Board of Studies sighting the need to continue to improve the VLE for the future (BOS, 2007).

Cohorts of WBL candidates identified the need for a shift from a content-driven eLearning system to one which could support the type of peer review that WBL was growing into. The WBL programme structure has three main stages. First, students construct a portfolio of their prior professional knowledge. This Recognition of Accredited learning (RAL or a.k.a. Accreditation of Prior Experiential Learning (APEL)) stage benefited by candidates sharing professional experiences in constructing their areas of learning claims (Armsby, 2006). Next, WBL students would formulate an individual learning agreement that would guide the construction of the degree programme based on how much Higher Education (HE) credit was attained in the RAL stage. In conjunction with this activity they would learn about methods of conducting research in the workplace which would prepare them for the final stage of the degree. Lastly, research systems would be carried out in the workplace to amass enough credit to complete the programme. The nature of this learner-managed-learning approach to WBL meant that as the candidate progressed through the programme peer-support became increasingly beneficial (Stephenson, 2007).

In a work based learning context, then, there can be both a *formal* and *informal learning* scenarios. The traditional formal learning setting might be one of the blended learning tutorial sessions for WBL candidate getting an induction on how to compose a prior learning accreditation portfolio. Here the training pedagogy would be teacher-led and supported by on/offline discussions. But it could be argued that the 'real learning' transpired informally after the 'taught session'. Informally the students may meet to debrief with each other at the café over coffee. There they would compare their interpretation of the learning event which would lead to the formation of learning partnerships. This learning support network would communicate to provide peer-review of draft work for the portfolio. An online system was needed to facilitate this evolving professional social network for practitioner researchers.

It was at a conference at University College London (2006) that a dialogue opened between the MU-WBL group and the Emerald Publishing InTouch contingent. The open source Elgg Social Network platform being developed by Emerald would be the new approach to address these needs.

A university / industry partnership association was also a positive deliverable of this network collaboration. Emerald Publishing had a good test bed and source of evaluation data in the WBL pilot case study group. This is discussed in detail later in the chapter. The Institute for Work Based Learning benefited by having a professional social network to support its learners. Additionally, both groups collaborated in scholarly activity. Co-authored research system proposals were written for JISC (2008) in the UK and the FP7 European Commission (2008).

Another joint effort was seen in international conference publications and poster-demo presentations. The 7th European Conference on e-Learning (2008) held in Cyprus gave both organisations the opportunity to get feedback from the eLearning community and share the services they provide to potential clients. Future collaborations are currently being investigated.

A PROFESSIONAL SOCIAL NETWORK (PSN) APPROACH

A variation of social networking focuses on a professional context which demonstrates how an innovative combination of existing technologies and interoperability standards can be harnessed to support the learning paradigm shift taking place from learning by knowledge transfer to learning by knowledge construction. This next section of the chapter discusses a European Commission (FP7, 2008) project proposal.

The PSN group brings together a range of extant and emerging standards and technologies to provide a next generation platform for Technology Enhanced Learning that will have a significant impact on learning outcomes.

The PSN enables:

- Faster and more effective learning, acquisition of knowledge, competences and skills.
- Unlocking people's and organisations' ability to master knowledge and apply it.
- Increased knowledge worker productivity.
- More efficient organisational learning processes.

System Outcomes

The motivating factor for the technology objectives is not the technology itself but the comprehension and application of specific technology in the service of learning and development.

Our semantically rich PSN platform promotes networked learning by connecting stakeholders in real-time through an agent or 'mentor-help' system. This can be achieved through a combination of technologies and standards, including the Elgg server, RDF (Resource Description Framework), SKOS (Simple Knowledge Organisation System) and FOAF (Friend of a Friend). Interoperability with existing services and standards ensures the long term sustainability of the system. Therefore the PSN, where possible, offers users the ability to search across currently popular network sites using a web services approach – e.g. OpenSocial, OpenID, FaceBook, and Explode.us.

Social and Organisational Learning Objectives

Our initial proposition is that effective learning in a networked society includes the natural discovery of learning resources, contextualised support services (i.e. Mentor-Help) and the mining of personal profiles, opinions and social networks, wherever they are located. Specifically, the system aims to develop a deep understanding of the pedagogies and technologies required to exploit the strategic learning opportunities that a richly connected society offers European businesses, government agencies and academic organisations.

The system also aims to advance the collective understanding of the issues involved in deploying and integrating PSNs in organisational learning infrastructures. This work uncovers reasons for success or failure and asks if these outcomes are related to culture, technology or something else entirely. The findings help inform non-technological strategies for organisations attempting to exploit these new tools to achieve and sustain EU competitive advantages regardless of industry or sector. As such, the system models are scalable and flexible for re-use.

System design should allow for scalability in the provision of adding languages to the system database:

- This would allow real-time text communication in a trans-national fashion.
- Support system can be accessed via mobile interfaces via text and/or voice.
- Feedback from the support system will factor in psychological considerations to match appropriate levels of help to the user making the query.

An intelligent and adaptive support system provides end-users with the resources to engage confidently with the network members and maintain motivation within the online community.

Technology Objectives

The PSN group are developing a next-generation multi-modal, multi-lingual professional social networking platform with the following characteristics:

- **Organisational Design:** Structurally neutral to allow a generic PSN to be deployed to academic, corporate or government organisations.
- **Simple System Design:** Scaleable and portable and easy to deploy technology that requires little or no overhead to existing IT investments.
- **Plug-in Technology Architecture:** Can be flexed in a number of directions to support content and services supporting many subjects/disciplines and industry sectors through the addition or removal of plug-in software modules.
- **Open Standards Compliant:** SKOS, SIOC, FOAF, OpenID, OpenSocial.

Progress Beyond the State-of-the-Art

We can form a common ground of understanding that the '**state of the art**' is *the current stage of development of a practical or technological subject; freq. (esp. in attrib. use) implying the use of the latest techniques in a product or activity* (OED Definition 2008).

In this section we broadly define the 'State of the art' for the key technical and infrastructural and pedagogical components of the system. We refer to both the theory and practice surrounding:

- Social networks
- Semantic web
- Organisational learning models of European SMEs
- Mobile and Multimodal interfaces for social and professional activities via web platforms

Once the state of the art has been defined we proceed to describe how the PSN system moves beyond what is currently the state of the art in order to achieve the goals of the system.

In an attempt to understand the current state of the art, as it relates to the strands of development of the PSN we have carried out an extensive literature and patent review.

Social Networking and the Semantic Web

Social networking web sites fostering the development of explicit ties between individuals as "friends" began to appear in 2002. Sites such as Friendster, Tribe, Flickr the Facebook and LinkedIn were early examples. Less explicitly based on fostering relationships than, say, online dating sites, these sites nonetheless sought to develop networks or "social circles" of individuals of mutual interest. LinkedIn, for example, seeks to connect potential business partners or prospective employers with potential employers. Flickr connects people according to their mutual interest in photography. And numerous sites offer dating or matchmaking services. Emerald InTouch connects researchers, academics and practitioners concerned with, amongst other things, management theory and practice, publishing, learning and research.

The semantic web, as originally conceived by Tim Berners-Lee, "provides a common framework that allows data to be shared and reused across application, enterprise, and community boundaries" (W3C, 2001). Developed using the resource description framework (RDF), it consists of an interlocking set of statements (known as "triples"). "Information is given well-defined meaning, better enabling computers and people to work in cooperation" (Berners-Lee et al., 2001). The semantic web is therefore, a network of statements about resources.

Outside professional and academic circles, arguably the most widespread adoption of the semantic web has been in the use of RSS. RSS, known variously as rich site summary, RDF site summary or really simple syndication, was devised by Netscape in order to allow content publishers to syndicate their content, in the form of headlines and short introductory descriptions, on its My Netscape web site (Downes, 2000). The use of RSS has increased exponentially, and now RSS descriptions (or its closely related cousin, Atom) are used to summarise the contents of hundreds of newspapers and journals, weblogs (including the roughly eight million weblogs hosted collectively by Emerald InTouch, Blogger, Typepad, LiveJournal and Userland), Wikis and more.

Initiatives to represent information about people in RDF or XML have been fewer and demonstrably much less widely used. The HR-XML (Human Resources XML) Consortium has developed a library of schemas "define the data elements for particular HR transactions, as well as options and constraints governing the use of those elements" (HR-XML Consortium, 2005). Customer Information Quality TC, an OASIS specification, remains in formative stages (OASIS, 2005). And the IMS learner information package specification restricts itself to educational use (IMS, 2005). It is probably safe to say that there is no commonly accepted and widely used specification for the description of people and personal information. As suggested above, developments in the semantic web have addressed themselves almost entirely to the description of resources, and in particular, documents.

Outside the professional and academic circles, there have been efforts to represent the relations between persons found in social networks explicitly in XML and RDF. Probably the best known of these is the Friend of a Friend (FOAF) specification (Dumbill, 2002). Explicitly RDF, a FOAF description will include data elements for personal information, such as one's name, e-mail address, web site, and even one's nearest airport. FOAF also allows a person to list in the same document a set of "friends" to whom the individual feels connected. A similar initiative is the XHTML Friends Network (XFN) (GPMG, 2003). XFM involves the use of "rel" attributes within links contained in a blogroll (a "blogroll" is a list of web sites the owner of a Blog will post to indicate readership).

Currently there is little in the way of personal description in the semantic web. The vast majority of XML and RDF specifications identify per-sons (authors, editors, and the like) with a string rather than with a reference to a resource. And such strings are ambiguous; such strings do not uniquely identify a person (after all, how many people named John Smith are there?) and they do not identify a location where more information may be found (with the result that many speci-fications require that additional information be contained in the resource description, resulting in, for example, the embedding of VCard infor-mation in LOM files).

The Learning Organisation and Networks

A recent benchmark study from Nemertes Re-search (2007) showed that 83 percent of organi-

Figure 1. Current mechanisms for social network interactions and interactive media for organisational learning. ©2008 Basiel & Coyne. Used with permission.

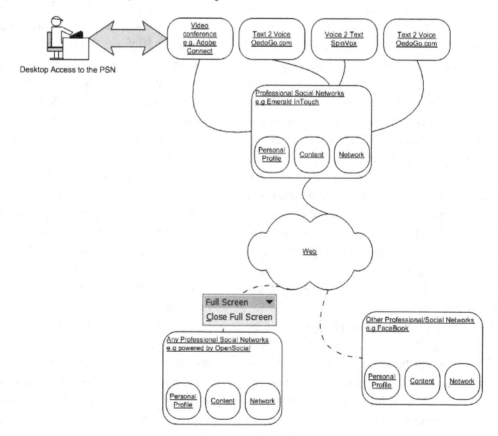

sations now consider themselves to be "virtual" with workgroups spread across multiple locations and geographies. The workforce is increasingly mobile. According to Nemertes, fully 91% of company employees do at least some work outside of traditional headquarter locations, and 96 percent use some form of real-time collaboration tools (e.g. IM, Web or audio/video conferencing).

But Nemertes also found that only 43% of global organisations had a mobility strategy (with another 26% currently developing one). Among US and EU based companies, only 35% had a strategy, with another 16% having one in development; thus, almost half of US and EU enterprises have no organisation-wide strategy for supporting the needs of the mobile workforce. Even more noteworthy, only 15% of all organisations interviewed had a specific mobility budget.

Although collaboration is an increasingly vital feature of business life, companies often promote collaboration indiscriminately. Directive mandates to "just collaborate" create confusion and bottlenecks, diminishing organisational effectiveness (Cross et al., 2004). Creating a business case for exploring and creating cooperative workplaces seems to be more fitting. The word cooperative is defined as the engagement in joint economic activity. It also suggests an enterprise may be operated jointly by those who use its facilities or services.

Table 1. Mobile social networks

Dodgeball	Veeker
ZingKu	Zemble
Groovr	Socialight
Friendstribe	Hobnobster
JuiceCaster	Flagr
Rabble	Twitter
Moblabber	Jambo
Wadja	Nakama
Treemo	

It is also clear however from the following research, and from Nemertes, that the competitive advantages that can be created through the networked relationships formed in the pursuit of learning and training is uneven.

However, co-operation between organisations within markets has long been identified as a factor in economic success and networking between organisations can contribute to stability and reduce uncertainty (Porter, 1990). These networks can evolve over time as 'natural' clustering's of enterprises, or can be 'induced' artificially as a result of interventions like the development of business or science parks.

Mobile and MultiModal/MultiLingual Social Networks for Organisational Learning

A key design requirement of a Professional Social Network is that is should be able to support multiple languages and modalities.

A brief survey of Social Professional networking sites that exhibit mobile characteristics produced list shown in Table 1.

Many of these sites and services offer a simplified location-based service for connecting with friends and groups to coordinate activities and stay in touch and have little impact or relevance to issues of work based or organisational learning.

However new developments centred on the convergence of location based services, social networking and semantic web are underway. Artilium (2008), a US based provider of enhanced mobile communications is leading the way on next generation context-aware services, presence and personalisation in the mobile networking arena and their expertise in this area is acknowledge. The PSN team however believe that many of the characteristics of the Artilium offer can be provided through the applied combination and improved interoperability of the component parts the PSN team bring to the system.

Table 2. Patent summary

Patent registers of the EU, Europe and the US				
'Learning Social Network'	'Learning Social Network'	'Organisational Learning'	Interactive social network'	'Semantic Social Network'
No results	No results	SYSTEM FOR SUPPORTING A VIRTUAL COMMUNITY Inventor: SCHLACK JULIE W (US) Applicant: COMMUNISPACE CORP (US) EC: ☒ IPC: G06F3/14; G06F3/14 Publication info: US2007226628 - 2007-09-27	SYSTEM AND METHOD FOR DYNAMICALLY GENERATING AND MANAGING AN ONLINE CONTEXT-DRIVEN INTERACTIVE SOCIAL NETWORK Inventor: REICH ROBERT (US); NEWCOMB PETER (US) Applicant: EC: IPC: G06F15/173; G06F15/16 Publication info: US2007192461 - 2007-08-16	Knowledge discovery agent system and method Inventor: ESTES TIMOTHY W (US) Applicant: EC: ☒ G06N5/02K IPC: G06E1/00; G06E1/00 Publication info: US2006112029 - 2006-05-25
			SOCIAL NETWORK-ENABLED INTERACTIVE MEDIA PLAYER Inventor: CRULL ROBERT WAYNE (US); MILLER BILL CODY (US); (+2) Applicant: CATALOG COM INC (US); CRULL ROBERT WAYNE (US); (+3) EC: H04L29/06S8B IPC: G06F15/16; G06F15/16 Publication info: WO2007076072 - 2007-07-05	

Additional searches through the patent registers of the EU, Europe and the US highlighted some basic work in this area from the private sector.

Standards and Interoperability

The Social Networking phenomenon, as described in the previous section began to appear in 2002. Sites such as Friendster, Tribe, Flickr the Facebook and LinkedIn were early examples. Recently there has emerged a move towards the standardisation of Social Network Profiles in an attempt to manage Access and Identity Management (AIM) and provide more opportunities to connect across networks from LinkedIn, Google, FaceBook and so on. Such a development is often referred to as OpenAPI.

Open API (often referred to as OpenAPI) is a word used to describe sets of technologies that enable websites to interact with each other by using SOAP, JavaScript any other web technology. While its possibilities aren't limited to web-based applications, it's becoming an increasing trend in so-called Web 2.0 applications including social and professional networks. The term API stands for Application programming interface. With the advent of the Facebook Platform, launched June 1st 2007, Facebook incorporated an OpenAPI into its business model.

OpenSocial is currently being developed by Google in conjunction with MySpace and other social networks including Bebo.com Engage. com, Friendster, hi5, Hyves, imeem, LinkedIn, MySpace, Ning, Oracle, orkut, Plaxo, Salesforce. com, Six Apart, Tianji, Viadeo, and XING. The ultimate goal is for any social website to be able to implement the APIs and host 3rd party social applications. Explode.US is the OpenAPI of the Emerald InTouch platform.

Beyond State of the Art?

The previous section reviewed developments and current capabilities in:

- Social & professional networks
- Semantic web
- Organisational learning
- Mobile and Multimodal Interfaces to social networks
- Standards and interoperability

We identified the key technologies, trends and theories that one should be aware of in any discussion of professional networks, interoperability and organisational learning as seen in Table 3.

Development of a Semantic Web Capability within a Mainstreamed and Practical Platform for Organisational Learning

The links found in the web pages of social networks are instances of what are known as "weak ties". Weak ties are acquaintances that are not part of your closest social circle, and as such have the power to act as a bridge between your social cluster and someone else's (Cervini, 2005).

As matters currently stand, if I conducted a search for "social networking" then probability dictates that I would most likely land on the pages of Tony Karrer, since he is cited in most places I am likely to find through a random search. But Karrer's organisational affiliation and location may be very different from mine; it may also be preferable to find a resource authored by someone who shares my own perspective more closely or is, geographically more convenient. Therefore, it is reasonable to suppose that if I were to search for a resource based on both the properties of the resource and the properties of the author, I would be more likely to find a resource than were I to search for a random author.

Such a search, however, is impossible unless the properties of the author are available in some form (something like a FOAF RDF file), and also importantly, that the properties of the author are connected in an unambiguous way to the resources being sought.

The explicit conjunction of personal information and resource information within the context of a single distributed search system will facilitate much more fine-grained searches and levels of rich interactivity than either system considered separately.

A convergence of these disparate technologies brought together in a unified and applied format represents a true step beyond the current state of the art in Professional Social Networks for learning.

Figure 2 presents a simplified schematic of the PSN. With reference to Figure 1, it is now possible

Table 3. Professional networks summary

Current State of the Art	Beyond State of the Art
• Social & professional networks • Semantic Web	[1] Development of a Semantic Web capability within a mainstreamed and practical platform for Organisational Learning
• Mobile and Multimodal Interfaces to Social Networks	[2] Multimodal access to a PSN
• Standards and Interoperability	[3] Standards and Interoperability

Figure 2. The PSN Architecture. ©2008 Basiel & Coyne. Used with permission.

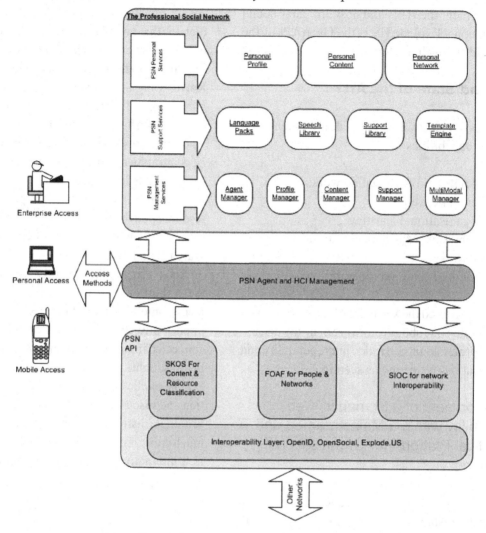

to perceive the step forward in interoperability and the concomitant benefits for personal and organisational learning that the PSN offers.

Mobile and MultiModal Interfaces to Social Networks: The PSN Agent

The PSN agent provides a natural language style interface to the people and resources of the site. By employing 'Call-Centre-like technology' any user will be able to call the PSN and submit a re-quest to the agent facilitating a natural, although remote, interaction with the PSN to discover network human resources and content.

The agent and the PSN platform interact with each other as a direct benefit from the newly developed semantic profiling work provided through the FOAF module and the inclusion of a SKOS conformant ontology. Such interactions allow for complex queries to be made in a natural and lan-guage neutral fashion. We believe this represents a step forward in multilingual and Multimodal access to professional social networks.

Figure 3. New Media captioned web video

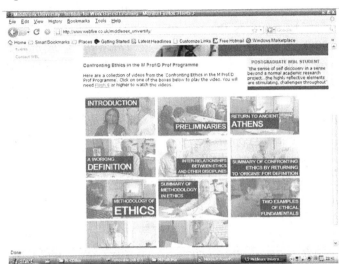

Adoption and Support

The biggest threat to the system is that we have a well designed online Professional Social Network that no one uses. Our answer to this challenge is addressed by our New Media Induction design. First, state of the art of induction and training applies a marketing approach. The pedagogic design of the induction is closer to a movie trailer or television advertisement than the traditional instructional design. Information is provided in smaller chunks with an emphasis on building personal connections as much as learning how to use the system. Next, our blended approach to dissemination is taken to this induction process. A face-to-face session is sandwiched between online sessions to strengthen motivation. Figure 3 shows a collection of short 10 minute digital videos that are used to reinforce the issues addressed in the induction process.

The innovative PSN induction pedagogic design builds on the members' prior knowledge of ICT systems and human networks to apply to our new eLearning environment. Just-in-time/case pedagogic design appeals to the full-time workplace based learner in our busy knowledge economy.

Standards and Interoperability: The PSN API

The current methods of accessing disparate social and professional networks are limited. However, as mentioned in the previous section, there is much work underway to develop an OpenAPI approach to network connectedness. Mobile and Multimodal access is developing at a variable rate but is limited to leisure and social networks.

The work of the PSN team seeks to build upon the work of the SIOC, SKOS and FOAF working groups and in addition seek to incorporate the work of the OpenSocial and OpenID movements to ensure the long term sustainability and interoperability of the PSN.

The PSN API and in particular the documentation supporting the architectural development work will we believe provide other groups with a solid basis for extending and creating professional and social sites which will be quite different from the PSN but backwards and forwards compatible dues to the adoption and integration of multiple and non-proprietary standards.

CASE STUDY

The following case study explores the use of Emerald InTouch (2008) social network environment where the programme tutor, Alan Durrant, shared his experience:

... I thought about how to use Web 2.0 technology as part of my teaching (and) considered the requirements of learners coming onto the Professional Practice BA Hons. programme. The course is for professional performing arts students (i.e. dancers, musicians or actors) where training has been very hands-on and directed. I wanted to give these students a higher education experience counter to this approach, where they would have to take much more autonomous control over their programme of study. The pedagogical underpinning of this method is reflective, self-directed learning. I wanted to help students develop their career management, critical and reflective skills in order to pursue their career more effectively.

The biggest challenge for the pilot study was that of adoption. Although it was one of the course requirements to use Emerald InTouch, there were mixed levels of usage. Some students regularly posted blogs and updated their profiles, whereas others did not log-on since the induction sessions. Durrant said he "*adopted an approach of strong encouragement*". As he points out:

there are always going to be questions about how a system like InTouch fits into an academic programme. My feeling is that students are often busy people who may not take time to reflect and will simply do what they need to do to complete the course. So if we want to develop them as reflective practitioners then we have to create situations where they are forced to reflect.

One of the ways to do this would be by replacing assignments with assessment of the effective-

ness of a students' contribution to the collective discussions on the blog or the wiki:

This approach may be something we consider at Middlesex, but at present we are starting by creating situations where students must record reflections via InTouch without the assessment imperative. At the start of the course this was very tutor-driven but we are now seeing more peer-to-peer interaction as compared with a lot of e-learning systems. InTouch is very intuitive. However, like any system, you need to use it often enough to feel confident on it. We have found that the students that did not attend the induction session took a long time to understand the system. Next year it will be essential for students to attend the (face-to-face or online) induction where we will carry out a more in-depth introduction to this platform.

Alan's conclusions highlight the importance of a well designed new media induction resource. If you want to use this type of social network system, it is important to identify the value of the new media system induction that can be designed to engage the stakeholders of the Professional Social Network (PSN) System.

As well as student usage, it has also been important to ensure that there are protocols in place for the tutors. Durrant acknowledges that he also had to do some work to ensure complete familiarity with the platform and also to regularly check InTouch for comments and new blog posts as, he asserted, "*There was nothing more demoralising than posting a comment and your tutor does not respond to because they have long since stopped checking the site.*" In response the Emerald technical team have added an 'alert tool' to email when changes are made to the system.

Basiel (1999) refers to this accessibility issue as a 'push-pull learning preference'. Some online learners like to go to a website or learning system to engage with the learning resources or

Table 4. Media literacy spectrum summary

eLearning events	*'Offline students'*	'Millennials' networked learners
Synchronicity	*Asynchronous*	'Live interaction'
Learner age profile	*Mature learner*	Millennium kids
Learning style	*Reflective*	Spontaneous
Learning design	Just-in-case	*Just-in-time*
Learning platform	*Local hard drive*	Server-side & client-side web browser
Mobile applications	*'off network games'*	Bluetooth & Broad band wireless social online games & simulations
Historic perspective	*'90's multimedia stand alone resources'*	'00's new media streaming '
Content source	*Expert generated Content focus*	'Stakeholder generated' Process focus
Revise content	*Slower turn-around on revised materials*	Online revisions more quickly achieved
Push-pull preference	*Tend to go to sources of knowledge*	Tend to have up-to-the-minute information sent

communication / collaboration tools. They 'pull' their learning from the system. Others prefer to have prompts sent to them. This may take the form of an email alert or a text SMS message to their phone. This preference may differ for the various functionalities of the VLE. For example, the learner may want to have a text message sent when a new meeting is posted in the online diary, but not get an alert every time someone enters a message on the text discussion board.

This 'media literacy spectrum', as coined by Basiel et. al. (2008) can be observed when developing the learners' profile. Some attributes are summarised in Table 4.

A functionality of the platform was the profiling tool which connected students through shared interests, research areas, courses or via a simple keyword search. According to Durrant, *"(this) tool was extremely helpful because students would be coming onto the programme largely, if not completely working at a distance. Keyword linking made instant connections between people with the same interests, a great icebreaker."* Campus based induction focused on the profiling tool to allow students to become familiar with the system. Many of the students were already using

social software such as Facebook and were more comfortable about uploading information about themselves rather than starting off with some sort of course-related or professional blog.

An instantiation of the success behind the pedagogic design of the system to develop an online community was demonstrated by one of the distant (off-campus) German students inviting a UK colleague to visit over the Christmas holiday. This comradery was fostered through the InTouch online social system design.

SUMMARY DISCUSSION

This chapter has addressed some interesting issues about the evolution of learning from an individual face-to-face context to one of an online professional social network model. We have stressed the importance of examining the underpinning pedagogic designs of the learning systems to guide the appropriate choice of online support tools.

In summary now we provide a critical discourse in the current 'gap in state of the art'. The main issues concerning social networks that are flourishing on the web now focus on the Web 2.0

semantic web design. Present tagging conventions are not adequate to progress the value of the systems forward. Accessibility to multimodal interfaces is improving with mobile systems, but there is a need to adapt and apply pedagogic design principles from this chapter to improve mobile performance. Standards and interoperability is in its early stages with web 1.0 content. More work is needed to synthesise these guidelines to professional social network system.

The case study offered in this chapter provided us with a grounded experience of using a professional social network. Both barriers and lessons learnt are now highlighted.

Barriers to professional social networks:

- **Adoption:** How can we get full-time working professionals to use a PSN? No evidence has emerged in this chapter to suggest that a 'silent member' of the PSN is not learning. Further studies are needed to challenge this possible misconception.
- **Induction design:** To address the concern about active participation through to the completion of the eLearning event the value of new media design was emphasised. Traditional instructional design training strategies should be challenged in this new PSN context.

Lessons learnt from the case study:

- **Protocols:** Communication and collaboration guidelines are needed to be made explicit in a PSN system. A mix of top-down (managers) and bottom-up (learners) approaches should be taken to get feedback from PSN stakeholders. These protocols are negotiable over time and will continue to adapt with the flexibility of the system.
- **Evaluation:** The PSN must have in place an evaluation strategy and associated technical system. Through the constant collection

and analysis of data from PSN stakeholders the natural evolution of the system can continue.

The closing thoughts for our chapter on professional social networks offer some recommendations to those readers that may want to venture into this area of organisational eLearning:

- **Establish learner's profiles:** Profiles of the PSN members should be done at several levels. First, a feasibility study will show the needs identified by the stakeholders. Next, personal Web 2.0 profiles identify learning styles and preferences.
- **Define the type of VLE (online pedagogy):** Will the eLearning model be content driven with a strong set of digital resources? Or, will the focus be on the communication and support needed to network and collaborate?
- **Define the tools to use (eg: blogs, Wikis, etc.) and the deployment strategy (eg: how many and at what stage):** Appropriate eLearning toolsets should be mapped over from the PSN member profiles.
- **Design induction pedagogy and new media presentation:** Get good initial motivation to promote a culture of change to adopt regular use of the PSN. By getting its use to be part of the daily routine you can address drop out prevention.
- **Explore organisational learning for your context:** Can you progress individual learning to a networked context? What system changes will be needed to adjust for this scalability?
- **Plan a shift to a professional network context:** How can you adapt existing eLearning protocols and systems to a PSN context? Or, will it be easier to start over fresh with a new system?
- **Decide on the appropriate online support model for your PSN:** The range of support

may range from a static FAQ to mobile web bot agent model. From your feasibility study data pick an appropriate set of tools to provide academic, technical and administrative help in the media and mobile platform that the learner's need.

- **Formative feedback:** In the annual review strategy be sure to have systems in place to act on the changes needed to keep the PSN current to the learner's needs.

If you are a member of a professional organisation then this chapter has critically discussed some issues to take you forward into the 21st century learning society. The Web 2.0 pedagogic models, tool sets and protocols have been offered to provide a framework by which you will be able to open and establish the communication needed to help your organisation progress.

REFERENCES

7th European Conference on e-Learning (2008). Retrieved June 27, 2008 from http://academic-conferences.org/ecel/ecel2008/ecel08-abstracts.htm

Armsby, P., Costley, C., Garnett, J. (2006). The legitimisation of knowledge: a work-based learning perspective of APEL. *Lifelong Learning and Education, 25*(4), 369-83. Retrieved June 27, 2008, from www.emeraldinsight.com/.../published/emeraldfulltextarticle/pdf/0860190301_ref.html

Artilium (2008). Educational technology—a long look back. *BJET, 39*(4), 234-236. Published online.

Basiel (1999). Retrieved June 27, 2008. *Paper*: http://www.elearning.mdx.ac.uk/research/push-pull/pushpull/Push&Pull.htm. *Toolkit*: http://www.elearning.mdx.ac.uk/research/pushpull/pushpull/PROFILE.HTM

Basiel A., Commins R., & Howarth M. (2008). Retrieved June 27, 2008 from http://www.elearning.mdx.ac.uk/research/index.htm.#digital_literacy

Berners-Lee et al. (2001). The Semantic Web. *Scientific American*. Retrieved from http://www-personal.si.umich.edu/~rfrost/courses/SI110/readings/In_Out_and_Beyond/Semantic_Web.pdf

BOS (2007). Retrieved June 27, 2008 from http://oasisplus.mdx.ac.uk/webct/urw/lc4831306002.tp4831347002/CourseContentDispatch.dowebct?tab=view&displayinfo=47723305021

Cervini (2005). Semantic networks and social networks. *The Learning Organization, 12*(5).

Cross et al. (2004). *An informal history of eLearning*. Retrieved from http://www.emeraldinsight.com/Insight/viewContentItem.do?contentType=Article&hdAction=lnkpdf&contentId=839895

Downs S. (2006). E-Learning 2.0. *National Research Council of Canada*. Retrieved from, www.elearningmag.org/subpage.cmf?section=articles&article=29-1

Dumbill, E. (2002). *Finding Friends with XML and RDF, XMLWatch*. Retrieved June 27, 2008 from http://www-106.ibm.com/developerworks/xml/library/x-foaf.html

Emerald InTouch (2008). Retrieved June 27, 2008 from http://info.emeraldinsight.com/products/intouch/index.htm

Facebook (2008). Retrieved June 27, 2008 from http://www.facebook.com/

FP7 (2008). Retrieved June 27, 2008 from http://www.elearning.mdx.ac.uk/research/index.htm.#4_April_

FP7 European Commission (2008). Retrieved June 27, 2008 from http://cordis.europa.eu/fp7/

GPMG (2003) *XHTML Friends Network (XFN)*. Retrieved from, http://gmpg.org/xfn/ and http://www.downes.ca/cgi-bin/page.cgi?post=31624 and http://www.emeraldinsight.com/Insight/ViewContentServlet;jsessionid=0672AB01BCFD4DC910E9F3D12B123297?Filename=Published/EmeraldFullTextArticle/Pdf/1190120502_ref.html

HR-XML Consortium (2005). Retrieved from, http://www.hrcertify.org/index.php

IMS Global Learning Consortium. (2005). *IMS Learner Information Package Specification.* Available at: www.imsglobal.org/profiles/

InTouch (2008). Retrieved June 27, 2008 from http://intouch.emeraldinsight.com/

JISC (2008). Retrieved June 27, 2008 from www.jisc.ac.uk/

Nemertes Research (2007). *Supporting mobile worker networks: components for effective workplaces.* Retrieved June 27, 2008 from http://www.emeraldinsight.com/Insight/ViewContentServlet?Filename=Published/EmeraldFullTextArticle/Articles/3120090303.html

OASIS (2005). *Customer Information Quality TC*, available at: www.oasis-open.org/committees/ciq/charter.php

OED Definition (2008). Retrieved June 27, 2008 from http://www.oed.com/

Porter (1990). Retrieved June 27, 2008 from http://books.google.co.uk/books?hl=en&lr=&id=TT596zcGF0oC&oi=fnd&pg=PT454&dq=Porter,+1990&ots=Wl4aMVx-NL&sig=MAonDDTcOBsSLJR31MnGmXxGTu8

Stephenson J. & Young D. (2007) *The Use of an Interactive Learning Environment to Support Learning Through Work, in Work-based Learning Futures.* Young D & Garnett, J, University Vocational Awards Council, Bolton. June 27, 2008 from http://www.johnstephenson.net/jsfullcv.htm

University College London (2006). Retrieved June 27, 2008 from http://www.publishing.ucl.ac.uk/events.html

W3C (2001). Retrieved June 27, 2008 from www.w3.org/

YouTube (2008) Retrieved June 27, 2008 from www.YouTube.co.uk

Chapter II
Knowledge Producing Megamachines:
The Biggest Web 2.0 Communities of the Future

Laszlo Z. Karvalics
University of Szeged, Hungary

ABSTRACT

In the present study, the authors point of departure is the control crisis of science whose resolution requires radical social innovation. The author then shows that the only possible way for achieving this is the partial fusion of certain portions of scientific activity with the system of public education, by means of organizing scientists, teachers, as well as middle and high-school students into hybrid, knowledge producing mega-machines. The author shall subsequently argue that doing so will at the same time bring about a pragmatic shift in public education, for which professionals in the field of pedagogy have long been ready in principle and in theory. As a final result we shall see the emergence of science and public instruction tailored to the global system level, within the framework of the information society.

INTRODUCTION

The best way to predict the future is to invent it.
(Alan Kay)

The two perhaps most important sub-systems of the Information Society, Science and Public Education, are confronting a social innovation process of staggering force. Even though the re-search workshops of particular countries produce sensational results day by day, and the national systems of public education undergo continuing renewal, nonetheless in terms of their interest structures, their institutional mechanisms, and their financing, both science and public education have up to the present day continued to carry the imprint of the industrial era. For that reason, their functional disturbances can be managed ever less effectively by short lived pseudo-reforms of purely transitional impact.

The information technology background systems of modern sciences produce an incredible quantity of output signals. For many of the sciences (primarily genetics, oceanography, meteorology/climatology, environmental sciences, nuclear physics, pharmacology, archeology, and, first of all, astronomy) it is more and more problematic to manage the content of their permanently swelling background stores Beside financial resources the "human agent", human infrastructure, is becoming one of the bottlenecks. If we need brains in a "pre-digestive" process, it can easily find them where the task is exactly to make these brains able to do (even) scientific work: in the school benches. With the pupils socialized in the adequate community scope, involving resources and learning basic knowledge to satisfy their sateless desire to know and with their teachers an alliance may be created, and the biggest human GRID (the biggest Web 2.0. community) will be composed from these hybrid online clusters – the new type of knowledge producing and learning communities.

This process will, however, not run its course automatically. It requires efforts aligned with the same orientation, over several decades, by scientists from the various specialized fields, coordinators of instruction, political decision makers, teachers, social researchers, and information technological system developers. The final result guided by a vision, and the broad sweep of the project that builds the path leading to that goal, make for social innovation of a scope and importance whose like has never before been formulated either by the sociology of science, by the philosophy of education, or by research in futurology.

At this point our assertions concerning the future are hypotheses. Our aim is to elaborate scenarios ripened in a series of debates and work toward consensus-based conceptual structures, all of which will make it possible to initiate effective and soundly based social action and coordination, if and when the vision gains acceptance.

THE CONTROL CRISIS OF SCIENCE AND THE INEVITABLE CONTROL REVOLUTION

In the relevant literature there is a general acceptance of statements such as that the globalization of science has accelerated, that modes of knowledge production are emerging which follow new patterns, or that the rapid build-out of the new cyber-infrastructure of science introduces radical changes in methodologies of numerous scientific fields. There is, however, a considerable divergence of opinions concerning the depth of the challenge facing science and what the most comprehensive framework might be for interpreting the respective changes.

Beniger

On my part, I consider the model introduced by James Beniger in his epochal work, The Control Revolution (Beniger, 1986), to be the most fertile theoretical approximation. I hold so because the current situation of science can be elegantly interpreted using Beniger's category of a control crisis while also convincingly revealing the defining features of the incubating control revolution.

Shortly after the publication of his book, Beniger himself attempted to summarize in an independent study how his model might be extended to global science (Beniger, 1988).

The control revolution was the successful answer given to the lightning-fast process of industrialization which evolved during the century following the 1830's. Beside reining in speed and energy, adequate answers were successfully found to governance and enterprise management through technological innovations supporting the flow and elaboration of information, together with the social innovation of modern bureaucracy. Beniger's attention is drawn early to the double role in this process played by telematics, the increasingly interwoven world of information and communication systems. With its innovations, telematics supports the broad establishment of new and effective control structures. Yet in so far as the very processes whereby information is interpreted and evaluated for control purposes, are not successfully subjected to regulation over and over again by use of adequate methods, the feedback weakens and the system runs into new forms of control crisis.

When Beniger applies this to science, as a system constructed par excellence from the streaming of information flows, he perceives almost everywhere the indications of a growing control crisis. He finds the primary threat in the large-scale startup of new systems of telematics which disturb, or with their excessive radicalism—because they abandon a paper-based world—even disorganize, the accustomed flow patterns of already produced knowledge. Thereby they further weaken the functioning of the most important feedback mechanism, the citation system.

It is strange how completely Beniger (1988:26) is mistaken when he has fears for scientific reports, the publishing of specialized journals, or the publication of conference proceedings in their capacity as feedback mechanisms, on account of their exposure to information challenges. *"Telematics threatens global science ... [with] ... a crisis of control. Many involved with the computerization of information systems have predicted—some gleefully—a decline in the formal scientific paper, a blurring of the distinction between research notes and papers and between papers and the response to them by others, an increase in multiple authorship by scores or even hundreds who participate in a telematic discussion, and the decline of formal journals, editors, and the gatekeeping function more generally."* (Commenting on Beniger's work, Gerhard Fröhlich shares this anxiety (Fröchlich, 1996)

Surely, the last two short decades have brought a control revolution precisely from this point of view, with the creation of the new environment of digitalization, web-browsing, or full-text search capability. (For a summary of this point of view, see (Nentwich, 2005). And yet, at the same time Beniger's general model is more relevant than ever. The current control crisis of science cannot be found along the obstacles of accessibility to results; it has shifted to the scenes of new knowledge creation. By to-day the lack of feedback can already be attributed primarily and principally to system-level constraints on the interpretation of knowledge and of raw information and data.

Revolution in Sign Production, Shortage in Brains

Modern sciences, with their up-to-date information technology parks, are producing output data in quantities already so staggering as to make these incapable of being overviewed in a properly interpretive manner by the scientific community—which, to make things worse, is continually perfecting its capacity of producing and storing even more new information and data. *"New data – whole new types of data – are accumulating faster than researchers can make sense of them. The result is something like an optical illusion"* (Hugh Kieffer, cited by Norton, 2004). Those sciences which have high levels of demand for raw data and their interpretation—genetics, oceanography, meteorology/climatology, environmental sciences, atomic physics, pharmacology and above all astronomy—are currently undergoing the cyber-infrastructure revolution with their GRIDs, their enormous capacities for calculation, simulation and visualization, their more and more intelligent agents and work-flow devices.

Yet the scientists are aware of the control crisis. They all have the bitter experience that their efforts of building new models and coming up with pioneering connections and hypotheses are constrained by the small capacity of the analytic personnel available for handling lower-level, supportive transformational tasks. These tasks include surveys of measurement data, of elementary objects, or of relevant singular events; the testing of map structures; or the confirmation/verification of masses of elementary correlations. Any successes achieved in automating or computerizing the analysis of the raw data will only reproduce at the next higher analytic level the experience of support personnel being unable to cope with the mass of transformational tasks.

In the past, scientists had met this experience only when surveying the specialized literature and running into the limits of the library services or the reference/abstract/search systems. Yet by now the capacity limit shows up in relation to the output of each scientist's own data—a control crisis that cannot be managed by traditional approaches. This is because until now the preferred tool of control revolutions was the automation/computerization of the kind of human intellectual effort that could be translated into appropriate algorithms, just as the computer itself had replaced human computations done by pencil and paper. (Grier, 2005)

Wherever this algorithmic translation can be continued—as in the case of robot librarians or the "robot scientist" used in gene sequencing—the impact of the control crisis can be moderated. As A. M. Weinberg says, *"extreme automation may be appropriate for those activities that are time constrained, it may lead to clogged information channels for those scientific activities for which time is less important than depth of understanding."* (Weinberg, 1989). Thus the scientific community has come step by step to the recognition that the bottleneck is in the areas of knowledge and insight that cannot be reduced to algorithms; the process of knowledge production is constrained by human brains capable of interpreting, placing in context, and thereby counterbalancing the sheer mass of raw data being generated. Therefore the new scientific control revolution can only arise from the human infrastructure, it can only be a human revolution—and as such calls not for technological but for social innovation.

PRELUDE TO THE KNOWLEDGE PRODUCING MEGA-MACHINES

During the past three decades the science establishment has tried to ease the intensifying pressure with three parallel minor innovations:

1. Organizational and institutional solutions facilitating the optimal use of the available capacities and numbers of human brains (*intensification*).
2. Interconnection of existing research staffs into virtual communities of ever growing size (*concentration*).
3. Attempted massive mobilization of new brains capable of being involved in the solution of scientific problems (*extensive growth*).

Each of these solutions yielded some temporary and partial results—but these results paradoxically ended up by reinforcing the basic problem, because of the increased demand for data production stimulated precisely by the successful feedback. We shall show below, one by one, why neither of the three approaches can be expected to promise further advance. Yet each of these three attempts has made a significant contribution to identifying the feasible path toward the real control revolution.

Intensification has time as its equivalent. When the staff of research assistants suddenly increases, this also means that we have to discover a way of reassigning the precious time of leading scientists to activities that yield higher added value. Sophisticated bibliographic software is meant to serve the same objective. And scientists gather into problem-centered invisible colleges which are arising in parallel with the hierarchies of traditional authority, in order to make sure that the time required to arrive at new insights will be shortened by means of an intensive exchange of knowledge. The fundamental constraint on such ways of intensification arises from the ever smaller part of the aggregate knowledge in a given area of science that has come to be represented as the personal knowledge of any one individual. As formulated close to forty years ago by an outstanding Hungarian economist, Ferenc Jánossy, *"Precisely this is why we have to beware of tugging by sheer force at the net of individual knowledge, trying to cover all of the increased area, until the meshes are torn and only large holes remain instead of the dense coverage of the net."* (Jánossy, 1975). This recognition opens the way to the search for more decentralized and democratic knowledge production models.

Concentration is embodied in ever larger cooperating communities of researchers. The pioneering Human Genome Project has been followed by several similar research undertakings whose common element is the allocation of human resources required by such extensive research tasks, on the basis of novel principles.

Precursors

At the end of 2006 more than 100 thousand scientists from more than 175 countries have taken part in the **Innocentive initiative.** The website (http://www.innocentive.com) organizes the cooperation of world-level researchers as *problem solvers,* and companies wishing to solve their development questions focusing on science, as *seekers.* It is effective primarily in the search for innovative answers given to complex challenges, mainly in the fields of pharmacology, biotechnology, chemistry, food industry and plastics industry, with financial awards often exceeding $ 100,000.

The **Academici** website offers a search framework constructed for facilitating any emerging scientific cooperative initiatives and has thereby made it possible for scientists and researchers anywhere in the world to share their experiences at any time without limits and restrictions or to discuss any questions, proposals, suggestions,

or problems. On www.academici.com those interested can search according to several criteria, such as research field or scientific interest. In this way educational or scientific institutions located at the greatest world distances from each other can mutually get in touch in a matter of minutes.

The **DILIGENT project** of the European Union develops safe, coordinated, dynamic and cost effective test beds for virtual scientific communities, to facilitate the sharing of knowledge and cooperation. Involving the website (http://www.diligentproject.org/), experiments are proceeding in two real-time application fields, an environmental sustainability project and a cultural-heritage preservation topic, by combining the Grid and the DL (digital library) technologies. It is readily apparent that from the point of view of control structures, the size constraint is given by the maximal number of the scientists who can be meaningfully interconnected. Meanwhile, the cooperative forms, workflow solutions, software systems, and online cooperative cultures created for several tens of thousands of participants are already paving the way for making possible the operations and organization of research communities of several-million-members which are expected to emerge in the course of the control revolution.

The Advent of Participatory Citizen Science

Extensive growth comes from drawing into science some social groups that had earlier, to some extent consciously, been excluded. The orientations of citizen science and participatory research (Irwin, 1995, Park et al., 1993) do not fight for the renaissance of amateur science but for the integration of knowledge created outside the scientific establishment, into the scientific problem solving processes. Typical examples, often with the spirit of movements, come into being and evolve in order to support the scientific emancipation of indigenous knowledge, that is, knowledge concerning the local environment, weather, therapies, animals or plants.

There exists, however an even more comprehensive context, the aspect of "open science" which fights, on theoretical and historical grounds, for breaking down the walls between Science and Non-science (Dasgupta and David, 1994). Open science, in the spirit of a new ethos (actually, one harking back to the 17th century) and fired by powerful economic arguments, carries the banner for a program of broadly spreading out such knowledge as already exists, and hopes from this — among other things — for a growth in the number of persons involving themselves in the cultivation of science. The attraction of new brains has been started in several ways, based not upon theoretical but rather very practical considerations, by drawing participants primarily into problems of the environment and sustainability, because of their personal exposure and ready competency. The projects with the broadest participation are, however, connected to space research where millions of amateur astronomers have even earlier been able to get into the scientific establishment with their observations and results. In the highly computation-intensive SETI@home project only the redundant computer time was lent by more than four million people, but in the Stardust@home project voluntary brains were already also being needed, in order to act as virtual microscopes in the identification of collected micro-particles. (The *Johnson Space Center*, with the help of the *Planetary Society* and the *University of California at Berkeley*, has performed a high-resolution scan of the so called aerogel used for capturing spatial dust. The scanned micro-images are available in 700,000 movie-length segments via the Internet, containing less than 50 expected micro-particles scattered like needles in a vast haystack. Results obtained in interpreting the images by voluntary scientific participants joining in from the public, if proven reliable by tests, will help in finding and isolating individual micro-particles. These will be named by their discoverers (http://plan-etary.org/programs/projects/stardustathome/). This monotonous and tiring work required what amounts almost to a hunt for volunteers, who were permitted to join the search after successfully passing a test.

Practices of bringing new brains into science, undertaken so far, clearly demonstrate that in selected cases this may lead to success; it does, however, not provide a system-level solution to the problem of the missing human infrastructure. Voluntarism and contingency cannot be reconciled with a systemic revolution of control. And yet, we owe a lot to these projects, because they are proving day by day they that it is possible both to imagine and to operate problem solving communities of never seen size, and to boot, with outsiders. In the public discourse, they strengthen narratives relating to the decentralization, democratization and massive expansion of science, and thereby they open up the door to the real control revolution—the creation of knowledge producing mega-machines.

PLAN OF A MEGA-MACHINE

The mega-machine is Lewis Mumford's noted category (Mumford, 1967, 1970). Studies in the history of technology often refer to it as the term for a large and hierarchically organized task community—from the pyramid builders to the many armies of history. Mumford intended, however, to convey more than a simple metaphor. He was in part also interested in how the human components of a mechanism cooperate with the tool components, the mega-technics; how a few large cities which attain a central role in communications, labeled megalopolis, become the scenes of these events; how social control of technology emerges; and how communities of this size can be described with the terminology of cybernetics. Mumford (1967:191-192) was interested in how "... *to turn a random collection of human beings...into a mechanized group that could be manipulated at command. The secret of mechanical control was to have a single mind with a well-defined aim at the head of the organization, and a method of passing messages... (to) the smallest unit.".*

We can even consider the information society itself, in its most comprehensive sense, as a mega-machine (May, 2000). Yet we find the expression especially useful when we are looking for a name to designate the kind of knowledge-producing communities that will be able to exceed the largest present scales of scientific cooperation perhaps a hundredfold. And since we have seen the short-comings of current efforts aimed at increasing the number of brains participating in scientific research tasks, the conditions outlining the criteria that future scientific mega-machines will have to fulfill have become quite clear:

- Guarantee of staffs of sufficient size.
- Guarantee of staff availability.
- Professional-methodological quality assurance of activities.
- Accountability, dedicated areas of responsibility, deadlines met and capable of being met, clear project scenarios, and professional management.
- Organized transfer of or instruction in the knowledge minimally necessary to join a project.
- Facilitation of tasks, continuous mediation among individual participants of the system.
- Flexible, many-sided online system management service, oriented to facilitating horizontal as well as vertical interactions.

But where could the many tens of millions of brains be found for this? How could communities of this size be made manageable and operable in line with the above expectations?

According to a rough but conservative extrapolation based on UNESCO data for the year 2004 (http://gmr.uis.unesco.org/ViewTable.aspx), by 2007 there were approximately *800 million*

students in the 12-18 age cohort, supervised in an orderly and structured manner by some *40 million teachers*. Public education is a human mega-machine that is already at hand, striving, to boot, toward a fully online existence at astonishing speed. It appears to be perfectly suitable, while radically renewing its current functioning, to become at the same time also a mega-machine for research, thereby solving the control crisis of science. Or put in a different way, other than the hundreds of millions who are now articulated into the national systems of public education, we can find no social group on earth or in heaven that would so completely satisfy our prior expectations concerning size, availability and organization.

Why is it then that this statement, when we first come upon it, should nevertheless feel so startling, bizarre, and utopian? Indeed, once we realize that it is necessary, we only have to convince ourselves that it is possible. If we accept the goal — to plan and put in motion the new mega-machines built on public education — then we can take our time pondering the details of the path that will lead us there. So the challenge does not lie in listing all the steps that are indispensable for implementing the initiative but rather, in figuring out how to make the vision itself realistic. Can it possibly be sustained as a hypothesis? Is a mega-machine conceptualized in this way at all imaginable? Is it outlandish in relation to the institutional and functional order of public education or to the contrary, is it wonderfully adaptable to that order? But above all, why do we find it so hard to throw ourselves enthusiastically into listing the fantastic functional consequences that we hope will flow from the birth of the new mega-machine?

Perhaps it sounds strange at first but it is impossible to find a single serious and objective counter-argument. Yet acceptance of the vision is all the more impeded by hardened views, mistakes, preconceptions, misunderstandings and optical illusions, which must be brought into the open, exhibited, and demolished before we can once again take a searching look at the vision itself.

As it usually happens, when seeking to define the outlines of the Future, we run into the attitudinal roadblocks of the Past.

EDUCATION: THE SPIRIT OF THE INDUSTRIAL ERA, OR THE DELAYED CENTURY OF THE CHILD

Ellen Karolina Sofia Key wrote her emblematic book entitled The Century of the Child in 1900 (Key, 1900), a polemic discourse in which she attempted a showdown with the shadows of the 19th Century. Ellen Key envisaged a radically new 20th Century built on a positive child image, in which the schools would no longer deliberately freeze but rather set free the intellectual and spiritual energies hiding in the child. Sadly, the Swedish author was mistaken. Despite all the emancipatory, promising initiatives of that century, the real turnaround is still waiting in the wings. The school as an institution has shown an appalling lack of change ever since the end of the 19th Century. Its objective function pursues social and labor market integration, its image of the child is paternalistic, and its pattern of knowledge flow is determinedly one-way. The school decants the necessary abilities, skills and knowledge into the child's head with the help of the teachers and the material of instruction, while keeping the child's time budget, comportment, and knowledge organization under strict control, standardizing the required minimal levels of knowledge. The reason why the tired commonplaces of the so-called world crisis of education never mature into an interpretation as a control crisis, is simply that the school is actually experiencing no crisis at all, it is fulfilling its task, the feedbacks are working — just so long as the fundamental assumptions and criteria of success continue to be those of the industrial era. Likewise, the science of the industrial era is not in crisis, either, because the processes of selection for the replacement of its cadre of scientists are continuing smoothly without any hitch. (And of course the alarm bells are immediately rung as soon as the process begins to falter somewhere, with particular disciplines attracting insufficient interest on the part of the relevant age groups.)

But let us now replace the out-of-date objective function with that of the information era. From the point of view of up-to-date knowledge asset management, is the school getting a suitable return from the brains committed to its care? Does it deal with the knowledge carried by the students on the basis of an appropriate valuation, does it regard such knowledge as a capital asset, does it make an effort to integrate that knowledge in a truly transformative fashion as much as possible with the total mass of knowledge?

If we measure the school's quality of functioning by how well it creates a foundation for the holistic image of the human essence as one of life-long learning, then it is immediately apparent that we are in deep trouble. The crucial question therefore becomes whether a totally and essentially industrial-era mega-machine might be capable of renewing itself by assimilation to the demands of the information age, or whether the imperative of change must necessarily aim at dismembering the mega-machine itself. Ivan Illich's answer was clear, definite and scandalizing: the school as an institution was itself the chief obstacle to renewal.

The current search for new educational funnels must be reversed into the search for their institutional inverse: educational webs which heighten the opportunity for each one to transform each moment of his living into one of learning, sharing, and caring. (Illich, 1970)

In my personal opinion, a process of creative destruction leads to far more difficulties than the re-planning and re-engineering of the mega-machine of public education. The school has changed much, to its advantage. For a long time, pedagogical theory has also been knocking on the door with a set of claims that it delineates normatively in connection with the school, the teaching/learning processes, and the children of the information age. Specifically:

- Education should move away from authoritarian orthodoxy toward a world of horizontal communications and of cooperating, problem solving teen-age student communities.
- Let us teach each child from an early age to think critically, thereby supporting the development of a facility that allows pondering problems from different perspectives and, even independently, with a thoroughness maturing toward the scientific level.
- The teacher should be an animator, not a device for the recitation of instruction material. The teacher should smartly direct the independent knowledge operations of the students that also make use of library and Internet resources, intervening only at critical points.
- Wherever possible, the principle of learning by doing and getting the children to make their own discoveries should replace mindless cramming.
- Education should build on children as self-confident and smart users of the world of information-technology devices and systems who are already on the brink of absorbing this experience and knowledge at the same time as their mother tongue.

If we want to build a pragmatic pedagogical program on the above theoretical expectations, we could nowhere find a better option than to involve teen-age students and their teachers by the millions into the suitably prepared and well-organized problem-solving processes, involving network communications and cooperative work, that are emerging in a number of scientific areas.

The spirit of the out-of-date industrial era is left with just one position it can take to save it from retreat. That is to call into question the suitability of the 12-18 age group for active and creative participation in scientific group work.

Mini-Einsteins versus Intellectual Immigrants

It may seem gratifying to collect a colorful posy of the latest acts of student geniuses. How a Hungarian high-school student living in Calgary, with two weeks' work, succeeded in proving Albrecht Dürer's five-hundred-year old geometric conjecture which had earlier resisted the mathematical community's best efforts? How a fifteen-year-old boy, jointly with his world famous co-author, published an excitingly original astrophysical hypothesis? How teen-age girls were involved in choosing the optimal landing point for the Mars terrain exploration robot?

Yet, what needs proof is not that talented teen-age students are at times capable of producing results comparable to those of grey-haired professors. We lose our way if we try to look for economy-size scientists among 12-18 year old children; the mega-machine demands something entirely different. The students, with the help of their teachers, must be capable of and suitable for appropriately undertaking massive partial tasks, typically of a low level of abstraction, yet still calling for natural intelligence. Let us replace one single research assistant with a hundred children and four teachers, and we will begin approaching realistic proportions. And ten thousand children with four hundred teachers may well provide us with as much problem-solving power for a scientific program as a research staff of one hundred. Of course, what we should expect from a student is, accordingly, one hundredth of what we may expect from an adult scientific researcher.

All this is well known by all those who had tried their hand at on-site scientific work jointly with massive groups of students. Where research programs, because of their very nature or a lack of support, have to make do without sufficient human resources, they increasingly turn to teenagers under the whip of necessity. Our space limitations preclude displaying the variety of color and the richness of form of currently running efforts of this kind. Tens of thousands of students are becoming articulated into research programs of great vitality, in the course of which they undertake full-valued ornithological observations, ecological surveys and measurements, or data collection efforts pertaining to local history. The exacting database of Estonian trees has been compiled by the student participants of the Tiger Leap program of the Estonian Schoolnet. The SG@ Schools project in Singapore is being planned with reliance, in part, on the efforts of students in gene sequencing, animation tasks, and complex financial calculations.

The screenagers, representatives of today's generation that had grown up on television and the computer, are adapting to the new cognitive environment—according to Douglas Rushkoff's apt remark (Rushkoff, 1996),—as naturally and flexibly as the children of immigrants learn the language of the recipient country, faster and more effectively than their parents. And it is hard to imagine that the digital kids, who effortlessly cope with directing the traffic of the Chicago airport on a simulation game, who are daily managing extended online contact networks, and who can smartly transform information from one complex format into another, were not to be destined to accomplish even more. Would they not be suitable for administering questions in sociological surveys — perhaps concerning precisely their own age group? Or to read original sources and abstract their contents? Or to translate professional texts with their teachers' help? Or to answer questions, even by the thousand, put to them by scientists about what they find digging deep into their individually assigned little fields of inquiry? Or to try aggregating their partial bits of knowledge within flexible ad hoc communities? Of course they would. It would take no more than looking at them and seeing them in this particular way.

Still, many think that scientific activities are not for teenagers, that it is better to keep science at the level of illustrations meant just to awaken their interest, in order to make them disposed to learn. Their situation is therefore powerfully illuminated by the results of comparative educational surveys which show that if we integrate a broad collection of scientific problem solving methods, approaches, and philosophies into educational practice from an early age, we find an abrupt increase in children's disposition to learn as well as in their learning performance. Pedagogical action research has also shown that just as the acquisition of computer skills creates no particular problems, in the same way neither are there cultural, linguistic, religious or social obstacles to the acquisition of skills in undertaking activities of a scientific type. By transforming the public education system in a way that integrates information and science literacy into education from a very early age, we can promote an equality of opportunities more effectively than in any other way.

The children stand ready to become parts of the knowledge producing mega-machines. It is only the scientists, education-policy leaders, parents, and teachers who will have to come to believe this.

The Architecture of the Mega-Machine and its Impacts

In the coming years or decades, a series of research projects and experimental programs will put together and give precise shape to the basic structure and to the thousands of small details of the operation of knowledge producing mega-machines. In the discussion below I wish to survey, without any pretense to completeness, some of the fundamental aspects and characteristics that will almost certainly be relevant to the future system:

- Mega-machines will organize as hybrids of researchers, teachers and students which are multiply articulated in depth and in which assignments are distinguished as a function of the time requirement, profundity, and scope of each task.

- The age, experience, interests and earlier project involvements of each teen-age student will point to many differing roles. The representatives of science are also bound to arrive at specific divisions of labor amongst themselves. The ones facing, however, the largest shift in their identities are the teachers. At an earlier stage of their careers they had to choose between scientific work and the teaching profession which offers a lower social prestige. Yet as knowedge brokers, directors, and coordinators of bona fide research sub-projects, they will move into a totally new, inspiring professional and motivational environment, in their role as essential cogwheels in the functioning of the mega-machines. Beside this, the continuing role of exposition will also remain part of their responsibility — the awakening of interest, the nurturing of essential basic skills, and the incubation of the ability of students for participation in scientific group work.

- The disciplines currently experiencing the deepest control crises are the ones most likely to take the lead in building up their problem-solving clusters. These include genetics, biotechnology, and the environmental sciences as one set of fields; space research and astronomy as another; and finally, from among the social sciences, history and archeology.

- The inclusion of students in building project organizations can begin above the ages of ten or twelve. It seems to be obvious that there will be a particular system level that includes all students as parts of large, long-term undertakings aimed at structuring vast masses of raw information. This will involve the continuous follow-up of modular objects tailored to the capabilities of individuals (or of elementary research communities) and the steady enrichment of the knowledge pertaining to these objects (heavenly bodies, particular gene sequences, archaeological specimens, or historical sources), together with the mobilization, as required, of such knowledge. From here, not everyone's way necessarily leads to problem solutions at higher system levels, but all will remain members of this elementary problem community where one can continue doing one's modest partial task as long as attending school or even beyond, life-long.

- Within the mega-machine, dynamic cluster formation will necessarily get going along the typical attributes of the scientific problems under study. And since the unit topics, if they are well chosen, are likely to be multi-dimensional and complex, the students, in their capacity as individual owner/managers of particular dedicated problem objects, can be members of three, four, or even more problem communities organizing around particular attributes.

- The representatives of science are present in the system in part as clients who, on the basis of jointly agreed criteria, define the tasks to be undertaken. The tasks then tend to spread out within the mega-machine, possibly with benign, multiple overlaps. The scientists are also present within the problem field continuously and interactively, with responsibility for quality assurance, the creation of professional-methodological standards, and enforcement of the latter. The system harbors the possibility of competition and choice; the potential topics compete for resources, and individual clusters are relatively autonomous in choosing the focus of their activities. The results obtained thanks to the mega-machines will be the shared treasure of humankind.

- Other than maintaining the national language in scientific work, the force field guiding the operation of the mega-machine is basically a global one. The clusters are kept in motion by horizontal contacts among students of diverse nationalities, languages, cultures and religions, and through such an interconnectivity a new, global consciousness emerges in a meaningful way.
- This is closely connected with global problems that have so far called for consciousness raising in part as a challenge to education. The school of the future—in James Martin's words—will also be a civilization school, since it demands that the basic knowledge necessary for the survival of civilization be introduced into the curricula urgently and in their full range. "Education for survivability—the most important subject we can teach." (Martin, 2006). A work of similar outlook and message but with richer development of the topic is (Adams and Carfagna, 2006).
- Yet all this will be perceived as more organic and credible once everyone gets a share in laying a scientific foundation for the solution.
- For several reasons, the necessary lingua franca of the mega machine can only be English. (It is not impossible, though, that over the long run the torch will be taken over by an artificial language developed especially for this purpose.)
- Even though the research activities of the students are tied to practical reality by the objects of study individually assigned to them, the online work management systems nevertheless are taking on a key role in the process. It is an important question whether the open platform of the Internet is suitable for handling interactive efforts by several million participants, requiring work management systems of never seen dimensions.

In any case, it is worth paying increased attention to software developments based on pioneering principles that promise solutions of entirely new levels of effectiveness. (We consider the Croquet project, www. opencroquet.org, as one of these.)
- Finally, it is important to emphasize that being a part of the scientific mega-machine will only be one side or one function of school life; there will be no total change of the guard compared to earlier solutions of instruction and subject matter, only an internal reorganization of proportions.

POLICY IMPLICATIONS

James Beniger notes correctly that in the case of large-scale social innovations it is always politics that has the decisive word: " ... *the information society does not spring spontaneously from advanced industrialization. Technological possibilities for control present societal choices, which are themselves subject to political control*" (Beniger, 1988:22). And if innovation is global, as is the case with the future hybrid mega-machine of science and public education, then as an inevitable complication, two political system levels get in each other's way. Beside national education and science policies, the international organizations representing the global level are also very much concerned, since the mega-machine can only be coordinated in a transnational space. And although UNESCO's profile (science, education, infocommunication) would predestine the organization to lead such an important innovation program, looking at its current planning and operational system it is hard to imagine that it would be able to fulfill the task. It is more probable that the professional world organization of one of the scientific disciplines might come to a consensus about building a smaller pilot prototype of the mega-machine. And similarly, within the strategic-political decision space of the nation state it is hard to expect that a vision, no matter how realistic it may be, will gain priority, let alone support, solely on the basis of its projection of a future that is highly attractive in many ways. It is much more probable that the growing control crisis — whose spectacularly visible aspect is the increasing lack of financial and human resources compared with what would really be needed—will sooner or later inherently enforce the search for solutions. When national science policies see no other way, they will out of sheer necessity reach for the possibilities offered by the mega-machines.

It is especially difficult to realize and accept that in a global social innovation of such scope the expected benefits will not accrue in the form of traditional competitive advantages.

Why should the United States wish to turn in this direction, given that its leading position attained in science is sure to be safe for a long time to come, even without the upheaval of the mega-machines? When does the moment of epiphany arrive, insisting that the value of new knowledge produced by the mega-machine is becoming clearly measurable even under conventional budgetary criteria? How will the truth get to the point where it can be grasped—once again from a budgetary or national security perspective—that common actions organized in favor of common scientific aims reduce to insignificance or overwrite the traditional forms of international conflict? Let us not forget, it is part of the vision that the educational systems of the world's zones of conflict will also be integrated into the mega-machine. In the 21st century which offers little chance for religious, cultural or political convergence, could precisely science not become one kind of common language?

And what about the smaller countries? Is there any point for them to get going with their own mini-scale mega-machines? For example, on the basis of their recent educational and science-policy accomplishments, mentioned earlier, Finland,

Estonia, and Singapore would without further ado be suitable and mature enough to experiment with sciences, themes, clusters—mobilizing in their entirety their teenage student cadres of hundreds of thousands. And what stands in the way of the possibility of these countries starting to build a mega-machine in cooperation with an ambitious country like Chile, with one of the Chinese or Indian provinces, or with one of the smaller American federal states?

Even the longest journey begins with the first step. Are we standing ready to initiate a discourse?

ACKNOWLEDGMENT

For the help I have received in preparing the final verson of this chapter, I wish to express my sincere thanks eminently to *Thomas Vietorisz* (Cornell University) and to *Adam Tolnay* (Stanford University), *Nicholas Vonortas* (George Washington University), *Gabor Agoston* (Georgetown University).

REFERENCES

Adams, J. M., & Carfagna, A. (2006). *Coming of Age in a Globalized World: The Next Generation Kumarian Press* (See especially the section titled: Global Education: Schooling World Citizen).

Beniger, J. R. (1986). *The Control Revolution. Technological and Economic Origins of the Information Society.* Harvard University Press

Beniger, J. R. (1988). Information Society and Global Science. In Telescience: Scientific Communication in the Information Age. *Annals of the American Academy of Political and Social Science, 1,* 14-28. The study was republished in Dunlop and Kling (1991)

Dasgupta, P., & David, P. A. (1994). Toward a New Economy of Science. *Research Policy, 23,* 487-521.

Dunlop, C., & Kling, R. (Eds) (1991). *Computerization and Controversy: Value Conflicts and Social Choices.* San Diego: Academic Press

Fröchlich, G. (1996). The (Surplus) Values of Scientific Communication. *Review of Information Science, 2.* http://www.inf-wiss.uni-konstanz.de/RIS/1996iss02_01/articles01/02.html

Grier, D. A. (2005). *When computers were human.* Princeton University Press

Illich, I. (1970). *Deschooling Society.* New York: Harper and Row

Irwin, A. (1995) *Citizen Science: A Study of People, Expertise and Sustainable Development (Environment and Society).*

Jánossy F. (1975). *A gazdasági fejlödés trendvonaláról* (On the trendline of economic development) (2. enlarged edition, Magvető, Budapest. (English version: The end of the economic miracle; Appearance and reality in economic development International Arts and Sciences Press (1971)

Key, E. (1900). *The Century of the Child.* In English it was first published in 1909, following the German translation of 1902.

Martin, J. (2006). *The Meaning of the 21st Century. A vital blueprint for ensuring our future.* Riverhead Books

May, C. (2000). The Information Society as Mega-Machine. The Continuing Relevance of Lewis Mumford. *Information, Communication and Society, 2,* 241-265.

Mumford, L. (1967). *The Myth of the Machine, 1: Technics and Human Development.* New York: Harcourt Brace Jovanovich. The Myth of the Machine, vol. 2: The Pentagon of Power. New York: Harcourt Brace Jovanovich, 1970.

Nentwich, M. (2005). Cyberscience: modelling ICT-induced changes of the scholarly communication system. *Information, Communication and Society, 4,* 542-560.

Norton, O (2004). Planet Ice. Mars revisited. *National Geographic, 1*(9).

Park, P., Brydon-Miller, M., Hall, B., & Jackson, T. (1993) *Voices of Change: Participatory Research in the United States and Canada.*

Rushkoff, D. (1996). *Playing the Future. What We Can Learn from Digital Kids.* Riverhead Books, New York

Weinberg, A. M. (1989). Science, government, and information: 1988 perspective. *Bull. Med. Libr. Assoc., 1,* 1–7.

Chapter III
Web 2.0 Driven Sustainability Reporting

Daniel Süpke
Carl von Ossietzky Universität Oldenburg, Germany

Jorge Marx Gómez
Carl von Ossietzky Universität Oldenburg, Germany

Ralf Isenmann
Fraunhofer Institute for Systems and Innovation Research Karlsruhe, Germany

ABSTRACT

Web 2.0 driven sustainability reporting describes an emerging digital approach powered through Web 2.0 technologies for companies communicating sustainability issues. Such a computer-based application of semantics overcomes the limitations of orthodox methods and provides an array of specific capabilities to improve sustainability communication both, for companies (reporters), and their various stakeholders (report readers), that is along interactivity, customisation, and reporting à la carte, stakeholder dialogue, and participation. This chapter gives an outline on this up-and-coming sustainability reporting approach along three categories: (i) Media-specific trends in sustainability reporting are observed. (ii) New opportunities Web 2.0 technologies are offering for corporate sustainability reporting are identified. (iii) The concept and implementation of a software tool for sustainability reporting à la carte is presented making clear the movement away from early reporting stages towards the advanced one of a Web 2.0 driven approach.

FROM ISOLATED REPORTING TO SUSTAINABILITY REPORTING

Corporate sustainability reporting has its roots both in environmental and in non-financial reporting (IISD et al., 1992; DTTI et al., 1993; UNEP and SustainAbility, 1994). It follows a development path towards a concept of balanced reporting, usually communicating the three pillars of environmental, social, and economic performance and its mutual interrelations, in business terms often called the triple bottom line approach (Elkington, 1997). Sometimes, this approach is put in popular terms like "making values count" (ACCA, 1998), or "linking values with value" (KPMG, 2000), or described as "creating value and optimising prosperity according to the Triple P bottom line" (SER, 2001). The latter is understood as combining shareholder value, eco-efficiency, and corporate citizenship, or being part of corporate social responsibility (CSR Europe, 2000).

In the 10 years since sustainability reporting first became a topic of broader interest in academia, business, and government, it has rapidly grown to a field of research with increasing relevance for companies (Kolk, 2004) and capital markets (Flatz, 2003), even in the eyes of investors (Australian Government, 2003). At present, sustainability reporting seems to become part of companies' daily affairs, even entering (to a certain extent) the business mainstream. Hence, for a growing number, not just for some pioneering companies, the question is now how to report on sustainability issues, and no longer whether to report at all (Marshall and Brown, 2003).

Regardless of nationality or other differences in country results, this is not only true for leading edge companies in corporate sustainability and few sector leaders, but also for global players and multinationals (KPMG, 2005), stock-quoted and publicly traded companies (Raar, 2002), as well as for a number of medium-sized (Clausen et al., 2001) or small companies (EC, 2002). This trend is evidently a worldwide phenomenon (Kolk,

2004), with North America and Europe coming first, followed by the Asia-Pacific region, and even spreading to Africa (Visser, 2002).

While the field is still evolving, as sustainability reporting matures and practice develops into a more sophisticated stage, companies have to realise that the "honeymoon period" (DTTI et al., 1993) in which comprehensive non-financial reports received media and public attention just for the fact that they publish reports at all rather than for what was disclosed is over. Nowadays, a substantial amount of information is required. However, further to the relevance of contents, issues of communication style also become of greater importance (Beattie and Pratt, 2003; Hund et al., 2004; ACCA, 2004), in particular interactivity (Teo et al., 2003; Isenmann and Kim, 2006), target group tailoring (Jensen and Xiao, 2001; Isenmann and Marx Gómez, 2004), and stakeholder dialogue (WBCSD, 2002; Unerman and Bennett, 2004). Due to cross media availability and other innovative opportunities offered by the internet and its associated technologies and services, companies are entering a new transitional stage of online reporting (SustainAbility and UNEP, 1999; Clarke, 2001; Wheeler and Elkington, 2001).

In this chapter, we provide an outline of how to benefit from Web 2.0 technologies for communicating sustainability issues, while developing from early sustainability reporting stages towards a more sophisticated digital approach. Using Web 2.0 technologies, however, companies and stakeholders can overcome the current limited and rather monological reporting approach and develop practice towards more social interaction.

As the overall aim, this chapter attempts to bridge the gap between the business-driven field of sustainability reporting and its different facets on the one hand and on the other, the technology-intensive area of online information systems, software tools and information management harnessing for Web 2.0 technologies and semantics. Although research in both domains is still quite disparate, recent progress in social web evolution enables an array of unique capabilities to be employed for closing this gap. In particular semantic technologies, services, and markup languages like XML (eXtensible Markup Language, e.g. W3C, 2004; Glushko and McGrath, 2005), XBRL (eXtensible Business Reporting Language, e.g. DiPiazza and Eccles, 2002) and EML (Environmental Markup Language, e.g. Arndt and Günther, 2000) provide powerful tools, to the benefit of all groups involved in or affected by sustainability reporting (GRI, 2006), be they managers, accountants, employees, members of the financial community, customers, suppliers, local authorities, non-governmental institutions, pressure groups, or organisations focused on benchmarking, rating and ranking.

ISSUES OF CURRENT SUSTAINABILITY REPORTING

While sustainability reports are a comprehensive way of corporate communication and hence being regarded as flagship instruments, the way information is distributed and directed is still far from ideal, e.g. in terms of stakeholder dialogue, interactivity, and participation. This becomes apparent due to a) report content not being tailored to the specific needs of its different, unique readers and b) the direction of communication is going strictly from the company to the stakeholders; a

dialogue driven process is not provided. From four possible ways of exchanging information between the actors, only one is applied currently, while the other three are mostly ignored (see Figure 1).

The four ways, information about the content of a sustainability report (or the content itself) can be exchanged, are:

a. *From the company to stakeholders*: This is the basis of all communication in this context. The company creates a sustainability report and makes it available to all its stakeholders, e.g. over the web. All other forms of exchange are based on this report.

b. *From stakeholders to stakeholders:* This level of communication is reached, once stakeholders are given the opportunity to discuss the content provided by the company amongst themselves. Exchange of information between readers is also the basis for building an active community.

c. *From stakeholders to the company:* If stakeholders are enabled to give feedback about the report, the information flow is changing from strict one-way direction of communication to a bidirectional process, allowing readers to participate in the evaluation of data, and giving companies the opportunity to establish direct contact with its stakeholders.

d. *From companies to companies:* This possibility describes a form of communication,

Figure 1. Four ways of communication. ©2008, Daniel Süpke. Used with permission.

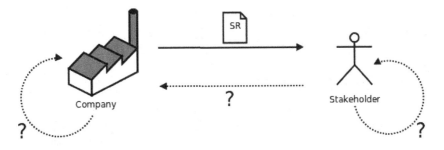

where different companies are exchanging information about their sustainability performance with each other, e.g. for comparison or to evaluate the collaboration of different companies among a production chain.

Corresponding to target group tailoring, the core element emphasised here is stakeholder dialogue. When providing stakeholder dialogue, companies can demonstrate openness and honesty in reporting, especially if communication with participating parties is meaningful, open, and fair. Such communication makes clear that reporters take readers' needs and preferences into account, e.g. through feedback loops or other mechanisms for learning, finally linking to the management as an important input for reflection.

Following the guidebook on sustainability communication and stakeholder involvement (WBCSD 2002; Hund et al. 2004), stakeholder dialogues can take every form of a continuum, from passive and non-participatory to active and fully participatory; put in business terms, the spectrum includes: information, consultation, involvement, collaboration, and empowerment.

Within this chapter, three ways of stakeholder engagement and dialogue are discussed and ideas given, on how to improve the communication flow, or to establish it at all: The way, information within a report is presented to its readers (a) can be improved, compared to the status quo. The main focus lies on b) and c), describing how

to enable discussion between stakeholders and the possibility of feedback. The communication among different companies (d), can be enabled e.g. by establishing sustainability networks, but will not be covered within this chapter.

IMPROVING USABILITY WITH TAILORED REPORTS

A major problem of current sustainability reporting practise is the (static) way reports are presented, whereas content of most reports is inflexible and not adapted for different stakeholders. This is a result of the way information is being delivered: A report is created, and then presented as either a print document or online, in HTML, or PDF. While there is no way to modify print documents, online platforms can potentially provide the ability to change design and content for different stakeholders on the fly, and to add additional, hyperlinked multimedia elements, given a sophisticated information management layer (Isenmann, Gómez 2004, ACCA 2001). To classify different levels of user modelling, the following taxonomy is suitable (Figure 2):

Systems can be classified according to their degree of user modelling and their degree of system adaption. The former differentiates between stereotyped (not regarding different users), individualised (addressing different user types), and personalised systems (addressing different, unique persons). The latter differentiates the way,

Figure 2. Classification of target group tailoring (based on Lenz 2003). ©2008, Daniel Süpke. Used with permission.

Degree of user modelling	personalised			
	individualised		Best practise	
	stereotyped	Status quo	O$_2$	
		adapted	adaptable	adaptive

Degree of system adaption

information is provided: Adapted systems only allow changing the information at the time of implementation, while possible modification of information during run time is expressed by the term adaptable. Adaptive systems finally are able to estimate by themselves, what information the current user could be interested in, without any explicit configuration.

Currently, most sustainability reports accessible over the web are to be described as stereotyped and adapted. Their content is only defined once and then delivered in this form to readers without any opportunity of tailoring specific information needs and individual preferences. This disregard of different personalities, while being the easiest implementation for companies, comprises a number of problems. Comprehensive sustainability reports can be very large; thus the amount of information provided can also be very large (especially compared to e.g. environmental reports), while the information processing capabilities of its readers remain the same, bearing some issues:

- Readers might not be able to separate relevant from irrelevant information:
  o High effort for finding specific information.
  o Relevant information might not be recognised at all.
- Especially casual readers might want a short overview instead of details.

This situation is changing only very slowly. One company going beyond this static approach is the telecommunications provider O_2. On the company's website, readers are able to define the content of their sustainability report by selecting articles with functionality similar to shopping carts. Using this, they can choose from different parts of a full report, and put them in the cart, for examples specific indicators about environmental performance like water withdrawal (see Figure 3). Finally, a report can be downloaded in HTML

or PDF, with content based solely on the content of the cart. This approach demonstrates that the use of information and communication technologies (ICT) helps handling the growing amount of information, or is indeed even necessary (see DiPiazza and Eccles, 2002).

While O_2's solution is one step ahead of other reporting systems available, it still is not able to support different stakeholder groups efficiently. The creation of a tailored report, while possible, has to be done from scratch, without any suggestions or help from the system. It can be assumed that a casual visitor of the web page is not willing to spend a lot of time to create the "perfect" report and thus might not see all relevant information, or make an effort at all.

Solving the problem of unguided compilation of report content was the first step towards a more flexible, user-oriented system. The authors developed a software system (Süpke et al., 2008) that is based on the idea of a shopping cart allowing readers to change content (e.g. performance indicators) at any time, but added an important feature:

1. In a preceding step, readers can assign themselves to the closest target group reflecting their general interests. These are based on the most common stakeholder groups in technical literature (e.g. employees, customers, press, environmental groups ...).

2. Based on the selection in step 1, the content of the shopping cart will be preselected, fitting to the typical informational needs of the chosen group. This way, a visitor is able to download a tailored report very fast, while still being able to readjust the content at any time.

3. Finally, the report can be downloaded in HTML, PDF, Postscript and XML. This way, the report is suitable for instant view in the web browser, for resending and printing, and for further, automated computation.

Figure 3. Customising an O₂ report. ©2008, Daniel Süpke. Used with permission.

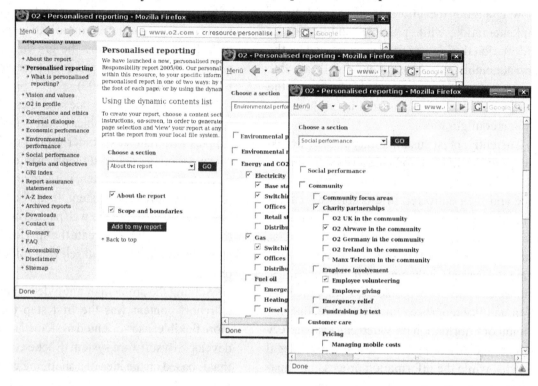

This first step of flexible reporting is based on static profiles. It is considerably more efficient and suitable for a large number of different stakeholder groups, but yet far from the potential benefit, computer guided report generation could provide.

Ultimately, the ideal reporting system should be adaptive and personalised; such a system would be able to differentiate different unique persons and present exactly the information that is currently needed. Furthermore, it would be able to recognise the content of a sustainability report automatically, with as little data provided by the reader as possible. This way, a user friendly, efficient, and tailored reporting process would be enabled. Today, there is no reporting system in existence, which is able to determine a reader's preferences on its own. The question remains, how such an adaptive system could be realised. Overall, the current way of sustainability reporting has the following major problems:

a. Communications are only going a single direction, from companies to stakeholders.
b. Report content is not suggested "on the fly" according to the reader's current selection.
c. Conversion of report data into digital format is very complex.

The authors suggest using the potentials of Web 2.0 ideas to solve problems a) and b). There are a number of websites that provide a new type of functionality that could be adapted for sustainability reporting and lift it to a new level of user interaction. To identify these features, there has to be a definition of what Web 2.0 in this context actually means. There are many different interpretations for this term (O'Reilly, 2007). Yet, there is one concept standing out: stakeholders are to be involved directly into the communication process to improve the quality of a website the more of them are actively involved. On many websites, this is even going as far as the content

Figure 4. Example of a Recommender engine. ©2008, Daniel Süpke. Used with permission.

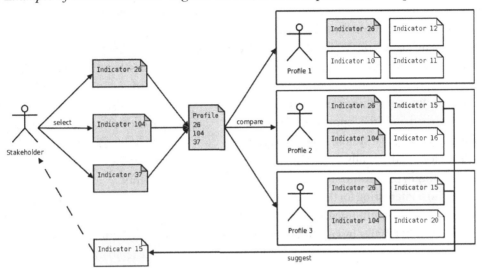

itself being delivered no more by the operator of the page, but by the users themselves. Prominent examples are e.g. YouTube or MySpace. This can not be applied directly to sustainability reporting, as the report content still has to be about, and thus, from the company itself. Therefore, the following definition is suggested for Web 2.0 in the context of sustainability reporting:

(Sustainability) Pages based on Web 2.0 allow a steady improvement of the provided content by enabling a linked communication for users, with the goal of a user-driven, targeted and interactive processing of content.

Using this definition, successful web sites can be analysed for their services and features, and how these can be applied to sustainability reporting. This analysis is yet to be finished, but some examples will show the benefit of this approach.

Suggesting Report Content Based on a Recommender Engine

Overall, a Recommender engine is required, that is able to identify content suitable for a user based on his current selection of content. There are examples of Web 2.0 sites which demonstrate the success and feasibility of a Recommender engine. Probably the most prominent example for this is last.fm, a page where users provide the songs they are listening to on their computer. This list is used to generate a profile of the user's music taste. By matching this against other users' profiles, new suggestions for similar bands, songs, and music styles can be provided. This example of a Recommender engine can be applied to sustainability reporting, whereas profiles of a user's self-compiled report can be created and used to match against other profiles.

When a user selects some articles/indicators for the cart, a profile based on this selection can be created in the background. This profile can be matched against others. If similarities are found, new indicators can be suggested to the user, helping him to find relevant content. For example, user A chooses indicators 26, 104, and 37 (see Figure 4). A profile is created for that selection and matched against existing profiles 1-3. The stakeholder from profiles 2 and 3 also did select indicators 26 and 104 and thus are deemed similar. Because both of these also put indicator 15 in their cart, there is a high probability that user A might be interested in this and thus, the indicator is suggested for use by him.

This is a typical example of improved sustainability reporting based on Web 2.0: The more stakeholders read and customise a report, the more profiles can be created. More profiles present in the system lead to finer matching results. In the end, it is easier for readers of the report to find relevant information, because of a system supporting them in their selection. Additionally, companies can use e.g. data mining in the profiles to evaluate, what projects are most interesting for their stakeholders and how to improve communications or specific sections of business. Finally, by generating profiles on the fly, new suggestions to similar, relevant content can be given, negating the need for static, pre-defined profiles and allow self-adapting suggestions, based on empirical data.

Improving Report Content and Stakeholder Relations with Discussion Platforms

Another example for prominent Web 2.0 features, which can and should be applied to sustainability reporting, can be found on YouTube. While the main aspect, providing user generated content (videos), is certainly not feasible, there are still many aspects to be considered. On YouTube, every video can be rated and commented by users. This aspect of evaluating content can be applied e.g. for different performance indicators or projects within a sustainability report. Furthermore, it gives companies the possibility to establish direct contact to stakeholders, taking influence on discussion that might otherwise happen outside of a companies focus. It may even help to undertake surveys regarding certain aspects of a company's strategy. Enabling readers to discuss and exchange opinions about the report in general, or even specific parts, is the basis of all feedback-enabled sustainability reporting systems.

Of course, feedback given by stakeholders might not necessarily be positive towards the

company in general. Still, the possible advantages might outweigh this problem:

- Stakeholders that have the possibility to express their thoughts might increase loyalty towards a company; giving stakeholders the opportunity to participate, and showing reaction to this, will show more consideration of stakeholder's desires than "ignoring" their demands by not allowing them to express thoughts.
- Marketing research can be accomplished much easier when a company is able to directly communicate with its stakeholders and react to their feedback. Analysis of user profiles and comments can lead to valuable information.
- If a company enables its stakeholders to participate in evaluation of content and another one does not, the latter might be suspected of not wanting to discuss their performance.

CONCLUSION

Web 2.0 sustainability reporting opens up a host of new questions, e.g. with respect to the target groups addressed and those actually reached. Among technical aspects of online communication and matters of efficient information management, a credible effort in Web 2.0 sustainability reporting will have to address issues such as the digital divide, restricted access etc. On both ends of the communication link appropriate ICT infrastructure is needed; not just with the companies communicating, but more importantly with the stakeholders that need to be actually reached. ACCA (2001) compiled some "cardinal sins" of online reporting in order to make its limitations clear.

Yet, communication processes are clearly evolving and changes have to be met. New forms of social interaction, going along with the spreading of broadband connection, will enable more and more stakeholders to participate in the process of opinion making. Companies not considering this will fall behind in taking influence on the discussion and evaluation of their performance, especially with regards to the increasing attention towards sustainability aspects.

On the other hand, utilising the potentials of modern web platforms will not only help stakeholders to participate in shaping a modern business, but will ultimately help the companies themselves, by providing new terms of dialogue, market research and increasing customer loyalty. Summarised, the evolution towards web 2.0 based communities and the possibilities this new form of social interaction includes will change the ways of communication fundamentally and should especially be considered in areas, where communication is of the essence, like corporate sustainability reporting.

REFERENCES

Arndt, H-K., & Günther, O. (Eds.). (2000). Environmental Markup Language (EML). *First Workshop, Berlin 1999*. Metropolis: Marburg.

Association of Chartered Certified Accountants (ACCA). (1998). *Making Values Count: Contemporary Experience in Social and Ethical Accounting, Auditing, and Reporting*. London: The Certified Accountants Educational Trust.

Association of Chartered Certified Accountants (ACCA). (2001). *Environmental, Social and Sustainability Reporting on the World Wide Web: A Guide to Best Practice*. London: ACCA, (pp. 18-21).

Association of Chartered Certified Accountants (ACCA). (2004). *Towards Transparency: Progress on Global Sustainability Reporting 2004*. London: Certified Accountants Educational Trust.

Australian Government Department of the Environment and Heritage. (2003). *Corporate Sustainability – An Investor Perspective. The Mays Report*. Canberra: Environmental Protection Branch. Department of the Environment and Heritage. http://deh.gov.au/industry/finance/publications/index.html [22 March 2004].

Beattie, V., & Pratt, K. (2003). Issues concerning web-based business reporting: An analysis of the views of interested parties. *The British Accounting Review, 35*(2), 155-187.

Clarke, T. (2001). Balancing the triple bottom line: Financial, social and environmental performance. *Journal of General Management, 26*(4), 16-27.

Clausen, J., Loew, T., Klaffke, K., Raupach, M., & Schoenheit, I. (2001). *The INEM Sustainability Reporting Guide – A Manual on Practical and Convincing Communication for Future-Oriented Companies*. International Network for Environmental Management (INEM): Hamburg. http://www.inem.org/free_downloads [22 March 2002].

Corporate Social Responsibility (CSR) Europe. (2000). *Communicating Corporate Social Responsibility. Transparency, Reporting and Accountability. Recommendations for CSR Reporting*. CSR Europe: Brussels.

Deloitte Touche Tohmatsu International (DTTI). International Institute for Sustainable Development (IISD), SustainAbility Ltd. (1993). *Coming Clean - Corporate Environmental Reporting, Opening up for Sustainable Development*. DTTI: London.

DiPiazza, S. A., & Eccles, R.G. (2002). *Building Corporate Trust. The Future of Corporate Reporting*. Wiley: New York, (p. 127).

Elkington, J. (1997). *Cannibals With Forks: The Triple Bottom Line of 21st Century Business*. Capstone: Oxford.

Flatz, A. (2003). Screening for sustainability. A case study of the Dow Jones Sustainability Index. In S. Waage (Ed.), *Ants, Galileo, and Gandhi. Designing the Future of Business Through Nature, Genius, and Compassion* (pp. 144-168). Greenleaf: Sheffield.

Global Reporting Initiative (GRI) (2006). *G3 Sustainability Reporting Guidelines.* Amsterdam: GRI

Glushko, R. J., & McGrath, T. (2005). *Document Engineering. Analyzing and Designing Documents for Business Informatics and Web Services.* MIT: Cambridge, London.

GRI (2006). *G3 - Leitfaden zur Nachhaltigkeitsberichterstattung.* Amsterdam: Global Reporting Initiative.

Hund, G., Engel-Cox, J., & Fowler, K. (2004). *A Communications Guide for Sustainable Development. How Interested Parties Become Partners.* Battelle: Columbus.

International Institute for Sustainable Development (IISD). Deloitte & Touche, Business Council for Sustainable Development. (1992). *Business Strategy for Sustainable Development. Leadership and Accountability for the 90'.* IISD: Winnipeg.

Isenmann, R., & Kim, K. (2006). Interactive sustainability reporting. Developing clear target group tailoring and stimulating stakeholder dialogue. In S. Schaltegger, M. Bennett, & R. Burritt (Eds.), *Sustainability Accounting and Reporting* (pp. 533-555). Springer: Berlin.

Isenmann, R., & Marx Gómez, J. (2004). How to provide customized environmental reports properly. In A. Scharl (Ed.), *Environmental Online Communication* (pp. 173-182). Springer: London.

Jensen, R. E., & Xiao, J. Z. (2001). Customized financial reporting, networked databases, and distributed file sharing. *Accounting Horizons, 15*(3), 209-222.

Kolk, A. (2004). A decade of sustainability reporting: developments and significance. *International Journal of Environment and Sustainable Development, 3*(1), 51–64.

KPMG. (2000). *Beyond the Numbers: How Leading Organisations are Linking Values with Value to Gain Competitive Advantage.* KPMG's Assurance & Advisory Services Center (AASC): KPMG.

KPMG. (2005). *KPMG International Survey of Corporate Responsibility Reporting 2005.* University of Amsterdam (The Netherlands), KPMG global sustainability service. KPMG: Amsterdam.

Lenz, Ch. (2003). *Empfängerorientierte Unternehmenskommunikation. – Einsatz der Internet-Technologie am Beispiel der Umweltberichterstattung.* Eul: KölnEul, J. (p. 212).

Marshall, S. R., & Brown, D. (2003). Corporate environmental reporting: What's in a metric? *Business Strategy and the Environment, 12*(2), 87-106.

O'Reilly, T. (2007). What is Web 2.0: Design Patterns and Business Models for the Next Generation of Software. *Communications & Strategies, 1,* 17

Raar, J. (2002). Environmental initiatives: Towards triple-bottom line reporting. *Corporate Communications, 7*(3), 169-183.

Sociaal Economische Raad (SER). (2001). *Corporate Social Responsibility. A Dutch Approach.* Koninklijke: Assen.

Süpke, D., Marx Gómez, J., & Isenmann, R. (2008). Concept and implementation of a flexible and differentiated shopping cart functionality for creating personalised sustainability report. *IEEE Proceedings 3rd International Conference on Information & Communication Technologies: from*

Theory to Applications (ICTTA-2008) – Section Very Large Business Applications, Damascus, (pp. 963-964).

SustainAbility Ltd, United Nations Environment Programme (UNEP). (1999). *Engaging Stakeholders 1999. The Internet Reporting Report*. Beacon Press: London.

Teo, H-H., Oh, L. B., Liu, C., & Wei, K. K. (2003). An empirical study of the effects of interactivity on web user attitude. *International Journal of Human-Computer Studies, 58*(3), 281-305.

Unerman, J., & Bennett, M. (2004). Increased stakeholder dialogue and the internet: Towards greater corporate accountability or reinforcing capitalist hegemony? *Accounting, Organziations and Society, 29*(7), 685-707.

United Nations Environment Programme Industry and Environment (UNEP), Sustainability Ltd.

(1994). *Company Environmental Reporting. A Measure of the Progress of Business and Industry Towards Sustainable Development*. Technical Report 24. UNEP: Paris.

Visser, W. (2002). Sustainability reporting in South Africa. *Corporate Environmental Strategy, 9*(1), 79-85.

Wheeler, D., & Elkington, J. (2001). The end of the corporate environmental report? Or the advent of cybernetic sustainability reporting and communication. *Business Strategy and the Environment, 10*(1), 1-14.

World Business Council for Sustainable Development (WBCSD). (2002). *Communications and Stakeholder Involvement Guidebook for Cement Facilities*. Report prepared by the Battelle Memorial Institute and Environmental Resources Management. http://www.wbcsdcement.org/pdf/final_report1_2.pdf [18 September 2003].

Chapter IV
Mailing Lists and Social Semantic Web

Sergio Fernández
Fundación CTIC, Spain

Diego Berrueta
Fundación CTIC, Spain

Lian Shi
Fundación CTIC, Spain

Jose E. Labra
University of Oviedo, Spain

Patricia Ordóñez de Pablos
University of Oviedo, Spain

ABSTRACT

Electronic Mailing lists are a key part of the Internet. They have enabled the development of social communities who share and exchange knowledge in specialized and general domains. In this chapter the auhtors describe methods to capture some of that knowledge which will enable the development of new datasets using Semantic Web technologies. In particular, the authors present the SWAML project, which collects data from mailing lists. They also describe smushing techniques that normalize RDF datasets capturing different resources that identify the same one. They have applied those techniques to identify persons through the mailing lists of open source communities. These techniques have been tested using a dataset automatically extracted from several online open source communities.

INTRODUCTION

Early forms of electronic mailing lists were invented almost as soon as electronic Mail (e-Mail) and are a cornerstone of Internet, allowing a lot of people to keep up to date on news related with their interests. Besides direct messaging between individuals, mailing lists exist as private or public forums for information exchange in communities with shared interests. Mailing list archives are compilations of the previously posted messages that are often converted into static HTML pages for their publication on the web. They represent a noteworthy portion of the contents that are indexed by web search engines, and they capture an impressive body of knowledge that, however, is difficult to locate and browse.

The reason for this difficulty can be traced back to the translation procedure that run to transform the e-mail messages into static HTML pages. This task is fulfilled by scripts that create static HTML pages for each message in the archive. In addition, some indexes (by date, by author, by thread) are generated and usually split by date ranges to avoid excessive growth.

On the one hand, this fixed structure reduces the flexibility when users explore the mailing list archives using their web browsers. On the other hand, most of the meta-data that were associated to each e-mail message are lost when the message is rendered as HTML for presentational purposes.

We propose to use an ontology and RDF (Resource Description Framework, Klyne 2004) to publish the mailing list archives into the (Semantic) Web, retaining the meta-data that were present in the messages. Additionally, by doing so, the information can be merged and linked to other vocabularies, such as FOAF (Brickley and Miller, 2005).

The rest of the chapter is organized as follows: in section 2 we describe the main developments of Social Semantic Web related with mailing lists. In section 3, we explain several techniques to collect RDF datasets from mailing lists and other social sources. Section 4 contains a description of the SWAML project that collects those RDF datasets from mailing lists. In section 5, we describe several applications that consume that data. In section 6, we discuss some experiments that we have done over those datasets. Finally, in section 7 we present some conclusions and future work.

SOCIAL SEMANTIC WEB

The Semantic Web vision tries to develop new ways to integrate and reuse the information published on the web. To that end, the W3C has developed several technologies, like RDF, which enable to add metadata descriptions that contain meaningful values and global properties to resources. The resulting metadata forms a graph model which can be easily linked with other graphs (Berners-Lee, 2006) incrementing the knowledge represented by the original graph. Those values and properties formalize the knowledge of a particular. In 2004, the W3C consortium developed OWL (Patel-Schneider et al, 2004), a web ontology language which facilitates the definition of those formalizations, called ontologies. Based on description logics, OWL has been adopted as the standard ontology language with several available editors, reasoners and tools. There have been also a number of ontologies developed in OWL for different purposes and with different level of detail, from generic to domain-specific ones.

On the other hand, in the last years, the concept of Web 2.0 has attracted a lot of interest. One of the key aspects of Web 2.0 applications is the social part of the web. Users are not considered as mere consumers of information, but also as producers. People want to share knowledge, establish relationships, and even work together using web environments. It is necessary to develop people-oriented web technologies which can represent people interests and that enable the integration and reuse of people related information in the same way that the semantic web vision advocates. These technologies can be seen as social semantic web and we expect that there will be more and more applications making use of them.

One of the first developments is the FOAF vocabulary, which represents basic properties of people, like their name, homepage, etc. as well as the people they know. FOAF descriptions are very flexible and can be extended to other domains.

There are already web portals which export their user profiles in FOAF format and the number of FOAF applications is increasing.

Apart from FOAF, there are other ontologies related to the social semantic web. In particular, SIOC (Semantically-Interlinked Online Communities), provides a vocabulary to interconnect different discussion methods such as blogs, web-based forums and mailing lists (Breslin 2005, Breslin 2006). Although we will apply mainly SIOC to mailing-lists, it has a wider scope than just mailing lists, and generalizes all kinds of online discussion primitives in the more abstract `sioc:Forum` concept. Each forum represents an online community of people that communicate and share a common interest. The goal of SIOC is to interconnect these online communities.

Other relevant concepts of the ontology are `sioc:User` and `sioc:Post`, which model respectively the members of the communities and the content they produce. Instances of these three classes (forums, users and posts) can be linked together using several properties.

The SIOC ontology was designed to express the information contained both explicitly and implicitly in Internet discussion methods. Several software applications, usually deployed as plug-ins, are already available to export SIOC data from some popular blogging platforms and content management systems. The effort, however, is focused on web-based communities (blogs, discussion forums), while little has been done so far to extend the coverage to legacy non-web communities, such as mailing lists and Usenet groups.

SIOC classes and properties are defined in OWL, and their instances can be expressed in RDF. Therefore, they can be easily linked to other ontologies. The obvious choice here is FOAF, which provides powerful means to describe the personal data of the members of a community.

Mailing lists can be easily described by instantiation of the SIOC classes and properties. Each mailing list can be represented by an instance of `sioc:Forum` (a subclass of Forum might be used instead, although it is not required). Messages sent to the list and their replies become instances of `sioc:Post`.

Finally, people involved into the list are instances of `sioc:User`. The SIOC ontology provides a property to link forums and users, namely `sioc:has_subscriber`. We argue that being subscribed to a mailing list is just one of the roles a user can play with respect to a forum. Moreover, the list of subscribers is often available only to the system administrator for privacy reasons. On the other hand, it is easy to collect the set of people who post to the list, i.e., the people actively involved in the forum. Depending on the settings, the latter may be a subset of the former, in particular in those mailing lists that forbid posting privileges to non-subscribers. Ideally, these two different semantics would be captured using new properties. However, for practical reasons, and to avoid privacy issues, we consider just the already existent `sioc:has_subscriber` property, and we populate it with the set of active members of a forum. Consequently, inactive members of the forum remain hidden, but this does not represent a problem due to the open world assumption.

Additionally, the Dublin Core (Dublin Core Metadata Element Set, Version 1.1, 2006) and Dublin Core Terms vocabularies are used to capture meta-data such as the message date (`dcterms:created`) and title (`dc:title`).

Given the distributed nature of RDF, it is expected that there will be different RDF datasets describing aspects of the same resources. The term *smushing* has been defined as the process of normalizing an RDF dataset in order to unify *a priori* different RDF resources which actually represent the same thing. The application which executes a *data smushing* process is called a *smusher*. The process comprises two stages:

First, redundant resources are identified; then, the dataset is updated to reflect the recently acquired knowledge. The latter is usually achieved by adding new triples to the model to relate the pairs of redundant resources. The OWL property `owl:sameAs` is often used for this purpose, although other properties without built-in logic interpretations can be used as well (e.g.: ex:has-SimilarName). Redundant resources can be spotted using a number of techniques. In this chapter, we explore two of them: (1) using logic inference and (2) comparing labels.

COLLECTING DATA INTO THE SOCIAL SEMANTIC WEB

Since SIOC is a recent specification, its adoption is still low, and only a few sites export SIOC data. There exist a number of techniques that can be used to bootstrap a network of semantic descriptions from current social web sites. We classify them in two main categories: intrusive and non-intrusive techniques.

On the one hand, methods which require direct access to the underlying database behind the social web site are **intrusive** techniques. The web application acts as the controller and publishes different views of the model in formats such as HTML and RSS. In terms of this pattern, publishing SIOC data is as simple as adding a new view. From a functional point of view, this is the most powerful scenario, because it allows a lossless publication due to the direct access to the back-end database. The SIOC community has contributed a number of plugins for some popular web community-building applications, such as Drupal, WordPress and PhpBB2. Mailing lists are also covered by SWAML, which is described in the next section. There is, however, a major blocker for this approach. All these software components need a deployment in the server side (where the database is). This is a burden for system administrators, who are often unwilling to make a move that would make it more difficult to maintain, keep secure and upgrade their systems. This is particularly true when there is no obvious immediate benefit of exporting SIOC data.

On the other hand, methods which do not require direct access to the database and can operate on resources already published on the web are **non-intrusive**. One technique is the use of cooked HTML views of the information, the same ones that are rendered by web browsers for human consumption. An example could be RSS/Atom feeds, which have become very popular in the recent years. They can be easily translated into SIOC instances using XSLT stylesheets (for XML-based feeds) or SPARQL queries (for RSS 1.0, which is actually RDF). Unfortunately, these feeds often contain just partial descriptions. Another technique is the use of public APIs. The Web 2.0 trend has pushed some social web sites to export (part of) their functionality through APIs in order to enable their consumption by third-party mash-ups and applications. Where available, these APIs offer an excellent opportunity to create RDF views of the data. A shared aspect of these sources is their ubiquitous availability through web protocols and languages, such as HTTP and XML. Therefore, they can be consumed anywhere, and thus system administrators are freed of taking care of any additional deployment. In contrast, they cannot compete with the intrusive approaches in terms of information quality, as their access to the data is not primary.

SWAML PROJECT

SWAML (Fernández et al, 2008) is a Python tool that reads mailing list archives in raw format, typically stored in a "mailbox" (or "mbox"), as defined in RFC 4155 (Hall 2005). It parses mailboxes and outputs RDF descriptions of the messages, mailing lists and users as instances of the SIOC ontology. Internally, it re-constructs the structure of the conversations in a tree structure, and it exploits this structure to produce links between the posts. This script is highly configurable and non-interactive, and has been designed to be invoked by the system task scheduler. This low-coupling with the software that runs the mailing list eases its portability and deployment.

SWAML could be classified as an intrusive technique because it requires access to the primary data source, even if in this case it is not a relational database but a text file (for instance, the approach followed by mle (Michael Hausenblas at al., 2007) is considered completely non-intrusive). Anyway, it is worth mentioning that some servers publish these text files (mailboxes) through HTTP. Therefore, sometimes it is possible to retrieve the mailbox and build a perfect replica of the primary database in another box. In such cases, SWAML can be used without the participation of the system administration of the original web server.

There are many ways in which a mailing list message might be related with other messages. However, we consider just two scenarios. The first one links a post with its replies (`sioc: has_reply`). Actually, due to sequential layout of the messages in the most widely used format to store mailing list archives (mailbox), it is easier to generate the inverse property (`sioc: reply_of`). Anyway, the `has_reply` property can be generated either by a description logics reasoner or by performing two passes over the sequence.

The second link among messages is established between a post and its immediate successor (or predecessor) in chronological order. It is worth to note that this link is not strictly necessary, because the following (or preceding) message can be obtained by sorting by date the sequence of posts. However, this is a rather expensive operation, because the whole set of posts is required in order to perform the sorting. The open world assumption makes this query even more challenging. Therefore, considering that browsing to the previous or next message is a common use case, and the complete set of posts can be very large or even unavailable, we introduced two new properties, `next_by_date` and `prev_by_date`. These properties where eventually accepted into the SIOC ontology. An RDF representation of a sample message is shown in Figure 1.

SWAML is essentially a mailbox parser and translator implemented in Python. Its output is a number of SIOC instances (`Forum`, `Posts` and `Users`) in a set of RDF files. SWAML can be invoked by the system task scheduler.

Parsing the mailbox and rebuilding the discussion threads may be sometimes tricky. Although each mail message has a supposedly unique identifier in its header, the `Message-ID`,

Figure 1. SIOC post example in RDF/XML

```
<rdf:RDF
  xmlns:dcterms='http://purl.org/dc/terms/'
  xmlns:sioc='http://rdfs.org/sioc/ns#'
  xmlns:rdf='http://www.w3.org/1999/02/22-rdf-syntax-ns#'
  xmlns:dc='http://purl.org/dc/elements/1.1/'
  xml:base='http://example.org/swaml-devel/'>
  <sioc:Post rdf:about="2006-Sep/post-52">
    <dc:title>Re: [swaml-devel] Changing SWAML ontology</dc:title>
    <sioc:has_creator rdf:resource="subscriber/s10"/>
    <dcterms:created>Wed, 6 Sep 2006 20:14:44 +0200</dcterms:created>
    <sioc:content><!-- ommitted --></sioc:content>
    <sioc:has_reply rdf:resource="2006-Sep/post-69"/>
    <sioc:previous_by_date rdf:resource="2006-Sep/post-51"/>
    <sioc:next_by_date rdf:resource="2006-Sep/post-53"/>
  </sioc:Post>
</rdf:RDF>
```

Figure 2. Buxon is an end-user application that consumes sioc:Forum instances, which in turn can be generated from mailboxes using SWAML.

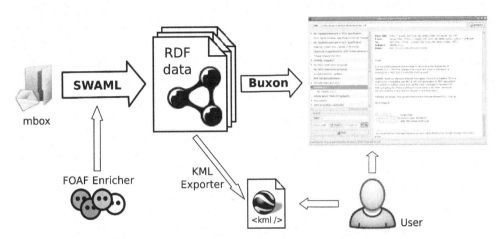

defined by RFC 2822 (Resnick, 2001), in practice its uniqueness cannot be taken for granted. Actually, we have found some messages with repeated identifiers in some mailing lists, probably due to non-RFC compliant or ill-configured mail transport agents. Therefore, SWAML assumes that any reference to a message (such as those created by the In-Reply-To header) is in fact a reference to the most recent message with that ID in the mailbox (obviously, only previous messages are

considered). Using this rule of thumb, SWAML builds an in-memory tree representation of the conversation threads, so sioc:Posts can be properly linked.

Actually, SWAML goes further than just a format-translation tool. A dedicated subroutine that runs as part of the batch execution but may be also separately invoked on any sioc:Forum, tries to find a FOAF description for each sioc: User.

Figure 3. A sample htaccess configuration file for Apache generated by SWAML. These two rules redirect the request to the proper file based on the content negotiation field of the HTTP request. Some lines have been wrapped for readability.

```
RewriteEngine On
RewriteBase /demos/swaml-devel/
AddType application/rdf+xml .rdf
Options -MultiViews

RewriteCond %{HTTP_ACCEPT} text/html [OR]
RewriteCond %{HTTP_ACCEPT} application/xhtml\+xml [OR]
RewriteCond %{HTTP_USER_AGENT} ^Mozilla/.*
RewriteRule ^/([0-9]{4})-([A-Za-z]+)/post-([0-9]+)$
            $1-$2/post-$3.xhtml [R=303]

RewriteCond %{HTTP_ACCEPT} application/rdf\+xml
RewriteRule ^/([0-9]{4})-([A-Za-z]+)/post-([0-9]+)$
            $1-$2/post-$3.rdf [R=303]
```

One important requirement of the semantic web is to be an extension (and not a replacement) of the current document-based web. Ideally, each user agent must be able to retrieve the information in their format of choice. For instance, current web browsers prefer (X)HTML documents, because they can be rendered and presented to the end user. However, semantic web agents require information to be available in a serialized RDF format, such as RDF/XML or N3. Furthermore, different representations of the same information resource should share a unique URI. Fortunately, the HTTP protocol supports this feature by using "content-negotiation". Clients of the protocol can declare their preferred formats in the headers of an HTTP request using the `Accept` header. Web servers will deliver the information in the most suited available format, using the `Content-type` header of the HTTP response to specify the actual format of the returned delivered content. MIME types such as `text/html` and `application/rdf+xml` are used as identifiers of the requested and available formats.

Setting up the content negotiation in the server-side usually requires some tuning of the web server configuration. It also depends on some choices made by the publisher of the information, such as the namespace scheme for the URIs or the fragmentation of the information. In (Miles et al, 2006) there is a list of some common scenarios, which are described to great detail, and configuration examples for the Apache web server are provided. The most suitable scenarios (or recipes, as they are called) to publish mailing list metadata

are the fifth and sixth, i.e., multiple documents available both in HTML and RDF.

The fifth scenario is extensively described in the referred source, and it has been implemented in SWAML. At the same time RDF and HTML files are written, SWAML also produces `htaccess` local configuration files for Apache. One of these configuration file is shown in Figure 3, while a sample request/response negotiation is depicted in Figure 4.

RDF metadata generated by SWAML can grow to a large size for lists with a high traffic and several years of operation, where there are tens of thousands of messages. The partition of the information might be an issue in such cases. On the one hand, information chunks are preferred to be small so any conceivable use case can be satisfied without retrieving a significant overload of unneeded information. However, scattering the metadata across a myriad of small files has some disadvantages. For instance, the number of resources that must be retrieved to fulfill a single query is greatly increased. Therefore, storing the RDF graph in a specialized database is an appealing alternative.

Fortunately, a common protocol to access semantic repositories using SPARQL as the query language is available (Clark 2006) and is gaining support by the RDF databases. This protocol exposes a simple API to execute and retrieve the results of SPARQL queries (at the present moment, SPARQL is a read-only query language, although there are proposals to extend it with full CRUD capabilities such as those of SQL). This abstract

Figure 4. An HTTP dialog with content negotiation

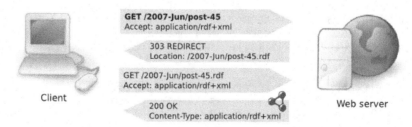

Figure 5. Sample Apache web server rewrite rule to translate HTTP request into SPARQL queries using a Sesame RDF repository. The last line has been wrapped for readability.

```
RewriteEngine On
RewriteBase /lists/archives

RewriteCond %{HTTP_ACCEPT} application/rdf\+xml
RewriteRule ^mylist/(.+)
        http://internal-server/sesame-server/repositories/mylist-rep/
        ?query=CONSTRUCT+{<http://example.org/lists/mylist/$1>+?y+?z}
        +WHERE+{<http://example.org/lists/mylist/$1>+?y+?z}
        &queryLn=sparql [R=303]
```

Figure 6. A single message rendered as XHTML code with RDFa and GRDDL markup by SWAML.

```
<html xmlns='http://www.w3.org/1999/xhtml'
      xmlns:dcterms='http://purl.org/dc/terms/'
      xmlns:sioc='http://rdfs.org/sioc/ns#'
      xmlns:dc='http://purl.org/dc/elements/1.1/'>
  <head profile='http://www.w3.org/2003/g/data-view'>
  <link href='http://www-sop.inria.fr/acacia/soft/RDFa2RDFXML.xsl'
        rel='transformation' />
  <title>[swaml-devel] CfP: FEWS2007</title>
  </head>
  <body>
    <div about='http://example.org/swaml/post/2007-May/5'
         typeof='sioc:Post'>
      <h1 property='dc:title'>[swaml-devel] CfP: FEWS2007</h1>
      <p>strong>From: </strong>
        <a href='http://example.org/swaml/subscriber/s2'
           rel='sioc:has_creator'>Diego Berrueta</a>
      </p>
      <p><strong>To: </strong>
        <a href='http://example.org/swaml/forum'
           rel='sioc:has_container'>SWAML Devel</a>
      </p>
      <p><strong>Date: </strong>
        <span property='dcterms:created'>
        Tue, 15 May 2007 19:24:49
        </span>
      </p>
      <pre property='sioc:content'><!-- omitted --></pre>
      <p>Previous by Date:
        <a href='http://example.org/swaml/post/2006-Sep/4'
           rel='sioc:previous_by_date'>previous</a>
      </p>
      <p>Next by Date:
        <a href='http://example.org/swaml/post/2007-Mar/6'
           rel='sioc:next_by_date'>next</a>
      </p>
    </div>
  </body>
</html>
```

query API may be realized by different means, such as SOAP bindings (described by a WSDL 2.0 interface) and HTTP bindings. The former enables interoperability with web service frameworks, while the latter can be exploited without the full-blown web service machinery.

Web service endpoints which implement the SPARQL protocol are sprouting on the web, some of them pouring huge amounts of data into the semantic web. We argue that metadata of large mailing lists can be conveniently exposed as SPARQL endpoints. That means to effectively translate the decision on data selection to the client (Pan 2006), and therefore minimizing the number of requests and the data overload. For instance, the client agent can retrieve all the headers of the messages in a given date range, but skip the body of the messages, saving a considerable amount of bandwidth.

However, non SPARQL-aware agents still need to access the information. This is the scenario of the sixth scenario (recipe) of the above cited document, but unfortunately this one is still being discussed. We propose a simple solution based on URL rewriting of the requests in order to translate conventional HTTP requests

for resources into SPARQL queries that dynamically generate an RDF subgraph that contains the requested information about the resource. The rewriting mechanism, the SPARQL query and even the presence of a data repository instead of static files is kept completely hidden to the client. At the same time, by avoiding the undesirable data replication, this technique helps to keep the information consistent. The most representative feature of our proposal is that it does not require any kind of server side script or application to translate the queries, because the data repository can serve the information directly in the format desired by the client.

We have implemented this technique using the Apache web server and Sesame 2.0 RDF repository (Broekstra et al, 2002). Figure 6 reproduces the hand-made htaccess file (as opposed to the ones that are automatically produced by SWAML). Unfortunately, Of course, the rewrite rule must be fired only when RDF data is requested, while requests for HTML must go through it.

We note, however, that our proposal presents some security-related issues. In particular, it is easily vulnerable to SPARQL-injection. Therefore, we strongly discourage the use of this technique

Figure 7. Buxon browsing SIOC-Dev mailing list.

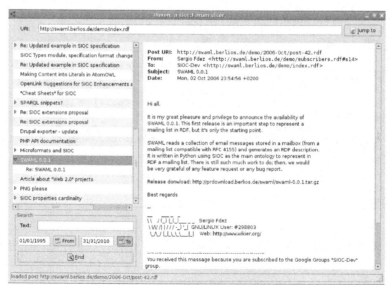

in production environments. Nevertheless, some changes in the regular expressions are possible in order to prevent this kind of attack.

There is another different approach to publishing metadata: to embed it into the HTML content. W3C is pushing two complementary technologies, RDFa (Adida & Birbeck, 2007) and GRDDL (Connolly, 2007), which respectively encode into, and extract RDF data from XHTML documents. We have also explored this path. SWAML generates simple XHTML pages for each message to illustrate the usage of both RDFa and GRDDL. We must remark that these pages are just a proof-of-concept of the semantic enrichment, and they lack many of the fancy features and complex templates of the already-existent applications which generate plain HTML.

CONSUMING MAILING LIST METADATA

Buxon

Buxon is a multi-platform desktop application written in PyGTK. It allows end users to browse the archives of mailing lists as if they were using

their desktop mail application. Buxon takes the URI of a `sioc:Forum` instance (for example, a mailing list exported by SWAML, although any `sioc:Forum` instance is accepted) and fetches the data, retrieving additional files if necessary. Then, it rebuilds the conversation structure and displays the familiar message thread list (see Figure 7).

Buxon also gives users the ability to query the messages, searching for terms or filtering the messages in a date range. All these queries are internally translated to SPARQL (Prud'hommeaux & Seaborne, 2007) to be executed over the RDF graph. Newer versions of Buxon can send the sioc:Forum URI to PingTheSemanticWeb.com, a social web service that tracks semantic web documents. That way, Buxon contributes to establish an infrastructure that lets people easily create, find and publish RDF documents.

Other Browsers and Clients

The SIOC RDF data can be explored and queried using any generic RDF browser, such as Tabulator (Berners-Lee et al., 2006). The most interesting applications appear when instances of `sioc:User` are linked to FOAF descriptions of these

Figure 8. Plotting the geographical coordinates of the members of a mailing list using KML and Google Maps.

users. For instance, it is trivial to write a query to obtain the geographical coordinates of members of a mailing list and to codify them into a KML file (Ricket 2006), provided they describe their location in their FOAF file using the basic `geo` vocabulary (Brickley 2006). The KML file can be plotted using a map web service such as Google Maps (Figure 8).

It is also possible execute visualize the messages in a time line view using the Timeline DHTML widget by the MIT SIMILE project using a query like the one we propose in Figure 9.

EXPERIMENTATION

A corpus of RDF data with many `foaf:Person` instances was assembled by crawling and scrapping five online communities. There is a shared topic in these communities, namely open source development; hence we expect them to have a significant number of people in common. We continue the work started in Berrueta et al (2007) to mine online discussion communities, and we extend it to new information sources. More details are described in Berrueta et al We use the following sources:

- *GNOME Desktop mailings lists:* All the authors of messages in four mailing lists

(evolution-hackers, gnome-accessibility-devel, gtk-devel and xml) within the date range July 1998 to June 2008 were exported to RDF using SWAML.

- *Debian mailing lists:* All the authors of messages in four mailing lists (debian-devel, debian-gtk-gnome, debian-java and debian-user) during years 2005 and 2006 were scrapped from the HTML versions of the archives with a set of XSLT style sheets to produce RDF triples.
- *Advogato:* This community exports its data as FOAF files. We used an RDF crawler starting at Miguel de Icaza's profile. Although Advogato claims to have +13,000 registered users, only +4,000 were found by the crawler.
- *Ohloh:* The RDFohloh (S. Fernández, 2008) project exposes the information from this directory of open source projects and developers as Linked Data. Due to API usage restrictions, we could only get data about the +12,000 oldest user accounts.
- *Debian packages:* Descriptions of Debian packages maintainers were extracted from apt database of Debian packages in the main section of the unstable distribution.

Instances generated from these data sources were assigned a URI in a different namespace for

Figure 9. SPARQL query to extract the information required to visualize a time line of the messages posted to any sioc:Forum instance.

```
PREFIX sioc: <http://rdfs.org/sioc/ns#>
PREFIX rdf: <http://www.w3.org/1999/02/22-rdf-syntax-ns#>
PREFIX dcterms: <http://purl.org/dc/terms/>
PREFIX dc: <http://purl.org/dc/elements/1.1/>
SELECT ?start ?title ?description ?link
WHERE {
  ?post rdf:type sioc:Post .
  ?post dcterms:created ?start .
  ?post dc:title ?title .
  ?post sioc:link ?link .
  ?post sioc:content ?description
}
```

each source. Some of these data sources do not directly produce instances of `foaf:Person`, but just instances of `sioc:User`. An assumption is made that there is a `foaf:Person` instance for each `sioc:User`, with the same e-mail address and name. These instances were automatically created when missing. This assumption obviously leads to redundant instances of `foaf:Person` which will be later detected by the smusher.

The ultimate goal of our experiments is to exercise the smushing processes described previously against a realistic dataset. Two million RDF triples were extracted from the sources described above, and put into OpenLink Virtuoso server which provides not only an effective triple store, but also a SPARQL endpoint that was used to execute queries using scripts.

We evaluated two smushers: the first one smushed `foaf:Person` instances assuming that `foaf:mbox_shalsum` is an IFP; the second one smushed the same instances comparing their `foaf:name` labels for string strict equality, without any normalization. Both smushers were implemented using SPARQL CONSTRUCT rules. The newly created `owl:sameAs` triples were put in different named graphs. These links were analyzed to find co-occurrences of people in different communities.

Some communities use the e-mail address as their primary key to identify its users. However, other communities use a different primary key, thus allowing users to repeat their e-mail addresses. For instance, a small number of users have registered more than one account in Advogato with the same e-mail (these accounts have been manually reviewed, and they seem to be accounts created for testing purposes).

Our data acquisition process introduces a key difference between how user accounts are interpreted in Debian mailing lists and GNOME mailing lists. The former considers e-mail address as globally unique, i.e., the same e-mail address posting in different Debian mailing lists is assumed to belong to the same user.

On the other hand, a more strict interpretation of how Mailman works is made with respect to the GNOME mailing lists, where identical e-mail address posting in different mailing lists are assumed to belong to a priori different users. In the second case, we rely on the smushing process to merge the identities of these users.

Although they must be handled with extreme care due to the issues afore-mentioned, the combined results of the two smushing processes are consistent with the expected ones. For instance, there is a very high overlap between the Debian developers (maintainers of Debian packages) and the Debian mailing lists. Obviously, Debian developers are a relatively small group at the core of the Debian community, thus they are very active in its mailing lists. Another example is the overlap between Advogato and GNOME mailing lists. Advogato is a reputation-based social web site that blossomed at the same time that the GNOME project was gaining momentum. Advogato was passionately embraced by the GNOME developers, who used Advogato to rate each others' development abilities.

We also studied whether there are some people that are present in many of the communities at the same time. We chose communities which are closely related to each other, consequently, we expected a high number of cross-community subscribers. There are several people who are present in many communities. We can conclude that almost all the most active open source developers in our dataset are core members of the Debian community. Another interesting fact is that only a few people among the top members of the communities consistently use a single e-mail address and just one variant of their names. This fact proves the difficulty of the smushing process, but also its usefulness.

CONCLUSION AND FUTURE WORK

There are a lot of ongoing efforts to translate data already reachable on the web into formats which are semantic web-friendly. Most of that work focuses on relational databases, micro-formats and web services. However, at the time of this writing and to the best of our knowledge, e-mail was almost excluded from the Semantic Web. Our project, in combination with the generic SIOC framework, fills this gap, conveniently providing an ontology and a parser to publish machine-readable versions of the archives of the countless mailing lists that exist on the Internet.

Furthermore, the SWAML project fulfills a much-needed requirement for the Semantic Web: to be able to refer to semantic versions of e-mail messages and their properties using resource URIs. By re-using the SIOC vocabulary for describing online discussions, SWAML allows any semantic web document (in particular, SIOC documents) to refer to e-mail messages from other discussions taking place on forums, blogs, etc., so that distributed conversations can occur across these discussion media. Also, by providing e-mail messages in RDF format, SWAML is providing a rich source of data, namely mailing lists, for use in SIOC applications.

The availability of these data leads to some benefits. In the first place, data can be fetched by user applications to provide handy browsing through the archives of the mailing lists, providing features that exceed what is now offered by static HTML versions of the archives on the web.

Secondly, the crawlers of the web search engines can use the enhanced expressivity of the RDF data to refine search results. For instance, precise semantic descriptions of the messages permit to filter out repeated messages, advance in the fight against spam, or introduce additional filter criteria in the search forms.

Another consequence of no lesser importance is that each e-mail message is assigned a URI that can be resolved to a machine-readable description of the message. This actually makes possible to link a message like any other web resource, and therefore enriches the expressivity of the web.

Integration of the SWAML process with popular HTML-based mailing list archivers, such as Hypermail or Pipermail, would be a giant push to speed up the adoption of SWAML. It is well known that one of the most awkward problems of any new technology is to gain a critical mass of users. The semantic web is not an exception. A good recipe to tackle this problem is to integrate the new technology into old tools, making a smooth transition without requiring any extra effort from users. Merging the SWAML process into the batch flow of tools such as Hypermail would allow users to generate both RDF and production-quality, semantically enriched HTML versions of the archives.

So far, no semantic annotation relative to the meaning of the messages is considered. Obviously, such information can not be automatically derived from a RFC 4155-compliant mailbox. However, it is conceivable that it could be added by other means, such as social tagging using folksonomies, or parsing the metadata added by the authors of the messages using micro-formats or RDFa when posting in XHTML format. The inherent community-based nature of mailing lists can be exploited to build recommendation systems (Celma 2006).

We have also explored smushing techniques to spot redundant RDF instances in large datasets. We have tested these techniques with more than 36,000 instances of foaf:Person in a dataset automatically extracted from different online open source communities. We have used only public data sources, consequently, these instances lack detailed personal information.

We are aware of the extreme simplicity of our experimentation using label comparison. In our opinion, however, it contributes to show the potential of this smushing technique. We note that it is possible to have more usages for it, for instance, smushing not just by people's names, but also by their publications, their organizations, etc. Surprisingly, the named-based smushing finds a high number of redundant resources even if the comparison strategy for labels (names) is very simplistic (in this case, case-sensitive string equality comparison). More intelligent comparison functions should lead to a higher recall. In this direction, we are evaluating some normalization functions for names. We have also evaluated classical information retrieval comparison functions that take into account the similarity of the strings (e.g., Levenshtein); nevertheless, their applicability to compare people's names is open to discussion.

We believe that the ratio of smushing can be further improved if the dataset is enriched with more detailed descriptions about people. Experiments are being carried out to retrieve additional RDF data from semantic web search engines as a previous step to smushing.

We have implemented a smusher application for persons, and we intend to use it to further investigate the potential for the optimization of the smushing process. The way in which these techniques are translated into actual algorithms is critical to achieve a promising performance of the smushing process, especially for very large datasets. In parallel, increasing the precision of smushing will require to study how to enable different smushing strategies to interrelate and reciprocally collaborate.

ACKNOWLEDGMENT

The authors would like to express their gratitude to Dr. John Breslin and Uldis Bojārs from DERI Galway, whose support and contributions have been a great help to this work. Also thanks to Ignacio Barrientos for his contribution packaging SWAML for Debian GNU/Linux.

REFERENCES

Adida, B., & Birbeck, M. (2008). *RDFa Primer*. Technical Report, W3C Working Draft.

Berners-Lee, T. (2006). *Linked Data Design Issues*. Available at http://www.w3.org/DesignIssues/LinkedData.html

Berners-Lee, T. et al, (2006). Tabulator: Exploring and Analyzing linked data on the Semantic Web. *Proceedings of the 3rd International Semantic Web User Interaction Workshop (SWUI06) workshop*, Athens, Georgia.

Berrueta, D., Fernández, S., & Shi, L. (2007). Bootstrapping the Semantic Web of Social Online Communities. *In Proceedings of workshop on Social Web Search and Mining (SWSM2008), co-located with WWW2008*, Beijing, China.

Berrueta, D. et al, (2008). *Best practice recipes for publishing RDF vocabularies*. Technical Report, W3C Note.

Bojārs, U. & Breslin, J. (2007). *SIOC Core Ontology Specification*. Available at http://rdfs.org/sioc/spec/.

Breslin, J. et al (2006). *SIOC: an approach to connect web-based communities. International Journal of Web Based Communities*, 2(2), 133-142.

Breslin, J. et al (2005). Towards Semantically-Interlinked Online Communities. *Proceedings of the 2nd European Semantic Web Conference, ESWC 2005*, Heraklion, Crete, Greece.

Brickley, D. (2006). *Basic geo (WGS84 lat/long) vocabulary*. Technical report, W3C Informal Note.

Brickley, D., & Miller, L. (2005). *FOAF Vocabulary Specification*. Technical report.

Broekstra, J. et al (2002) Sesame: A generic architecture for storing and querying RDF and RDF

Schema. In *Springer Lecture Notes in Computer Science, 2342*, 54–68.

Celma, O. (2006). FOAFing the music: Bridging the semantic gap in music recommendation. *Proceedings of the 5th International Semantic Web Conference*, Athens, USA.

Clark, K. G. (2008). *SPARQL protocol for RDF*. Technical report, W3C Recommendation.

Connolly, D. (2007). *Gleaning Resource Descriptions from Dialects of Languages (GRDDL)*. Technical report, W3C Candidate Recommendation.

Fernández, S., Berrueta, D., & Labra, J. E. (2008). A Semantic Web Approach to Publish and Consume Mailing Lists. *IADIS International Journal on WWW/Internet, 6*, 90-102.

Fernándrez, S. (2008). *RDFohloh, a RDF Wrapper of Ohloh. Proceedings of 1st workshop on Social Data on the Web (SDoW2008), collocated with 7th International Semantic Web Conference*, Karlsruhe, Germany.

Hausenblas, M., & Rehatschek, H. (2007). mle: Enhancing the Exploration of Mailing List Archives Through Making Semantics Explicit. *Semantic Web Challenge 07*, Busan, South Korea.

Hall, E. (2005). *RFC 4155 - the application/mbox media type*. Technical report, The Internet Society.

Klyne, G., & Carroll, J. J. (2004). *Resource Description Framework (RDF): Concepts and abstract syntax*. Technical report, W3C Recommendation.

Pan, Z. et al (2006). *An investigation into the feasibility of the semantic web*. Technical Report LU-CSE-06-025, Dept. of Computer Science and Engineering, Lehigh University.

Patel-Schneider, P. F., Hayes, P., & Horrocks, I. (2004). *OWL Web Ontology Language: Semantics and Abstract Syntax*. Recommendation, W3C, February.

Prud'hommeaux, E., & Seaborne, A. (2008). *SPARQL Query Language for RDF*. Technical report, W3C recommendation.

Resnick, P. (2001). *RFC 2822 - internet message format*, Technical report, The Internet Society.

Ricket, D. (2006). Google Maps and Google Earth integration using KML. In *American Geophysical Union 2006 Fall Meeting*.

Shi, L., Berrueta, D., Fernández, S., Polo, L., & Fernández, S. (2008). Smushing RDF instances: Are Alice and Bob the same open source developer? *Proceedings of 3rd ExpertFinder workshop on Personal Identification and Collaborations: Knowledge Mediation and Extraction (PICKME 2008), collocated with 7th International Semantic Web Conference*, Karlsruhe, Germany.

Chapter V
Web 2.0 Social Networking Sites

D. Sandy Staples
Queens University, Canada

ABSTRACT

This chapter describes one of the Web 2.0 technologies, Social Networking Sites (SNS). A definition of SNS is offered, as is a short history of these sites. The existing research is reviewed and organized to summarize what we know about SNS usage (from the perspectives of student use, general population use and organizational use), and what we know about the antecedents and outcomes of SNS use. The chapter concludes with discussion of new developments, challenges and opportunities. There are many opportunities for future research and organizational applications of SNS as SNS adoption grows at incredible rates.

INTRODUCTION

Offline social networks have existed since the beginning of humankind and have been the study of anthropologists and others for many years (Clemons, Barnett, & Appadurai, 2007). Social networks can be groups of people who have interacted in the past for some common purpose or interest, and that have ongoing relationships with members of the group. Membership in networks can be relatively permanent (i.e., family relations) or flexible and short-term (i.e., members come and go as their interests and need for membership changes). The shared experiences and perceived shared values or needs can build trust among members and value, such that members tend to rely on each other and perceive shared information to be reliable and trustworthy (Clemons et al., 2007).

In the past decade or so, advances in technology have made it possible to use electronic communication tools to create social network applications and online social networks. The applications, sometimes called social networking tools, are web-based locations that lets a user create a self-profile and connect to others (who are using the same application) to build and maintain a personal network (Skiba, 2007). This type of application is part of the Web 2.0 evolution toward more collaboration via the web and examples include MySpace, Facebook, and LinkedIn, to name just a few of the largest. While the terminology used to describe these sites varies, recently the term Social Networking Sites (SNS) has become the common way to refer to them. The focus of this chapter is on these SNS and the chapter is organized as follows. The next section discusses what SNS are and presents a brief history. The third section describes what is known in the literature about the usage of SNS. This is followed by a discussion of potential business uses and anticipated developments, discussing both opportunities and challenges.

WHAT IS A SOCIAL NETWORKING SITE (SNS)?

In this section, we first define SNS and then describe typical characteristics. The history of SNS is briefly discussed. Two of the current leading SNS are profiled in this history: MySpace and Facebook.

Social Networking Sites Defined

Boyd & Ellison (2007) appropriately defined SNS as "web-based services that allow individuals to (1) construct a public or semi-public profile within a bounded system, (2) articulate a list of other users with whom they share a connection, and (3) view and traverse their list of connections and those made by others within the system." (p. 211). They prefer the word network over networking in SNS, although they acknowledge the terms are used interchangeably in the literature, because they

argue that networking emphasizes the initiation of relationship, often between strangers and that not all users are doing this. Many users use SNS's to communicate with people that they already know (i.e., the people are already part of their offline social network).

Others argue that "networking" is more appropriate since the term social "network" site would be too broad a term, approaching the same meaning as Web 2.0 (Beer, 2008). Supporting this view, networking is defined by Dictionary.com and MS Word's reference function, respectively, as:

a supportive system of sharing information and services among individuals and groups having a common interest.[1]

the process or practice of building up or maintaining informal relationships, especially with people whose friendship could bring advantages such as job or business opportunities.

Neither of these definitions suggest that networking would have to include creating new relationships (in addition to maintaining existing relationships). Therefore, while we adopt boyd and Ellison's three key characteristics of SNS, we suggest that Social Networking Sites is a more appropriate term for SNS and this terminology will be adopted for this paper. We next expand on SNS characteristics and typical functions provided to the user.

Characteristics of Social Networking Sites

Social networking sites are organized around people. Earlier online communities and their websites were organized around interests and topics. A unique characteristic of SNS is that users can specify their social networks and make them visible to others (boyd & Ellison, 2007). This is done by users developing profiles of themselves and identifying acquaintances (termed Friends[2] in most SNSs). The starting point for a new user is to develop their profile which typically contains a picture of the user, some demographic information such as age, location, school affiliation/history, and personal interests.

Users then identify other system users that they have a relationship with or wish to develop a relationship with. Most SNSs required bi-directional confirmation, where a user requests a Friend connection. The system sends the request to the potential Friend, and if he/she accepts the request, then each other's profile becomes linked. In this way, the social network of a user becomes visible to their Friends and Friends can see overlap in their social networks and invite Friends of Friends to join their social networks, if they choose to. Typically, a powerful database makes every entry field in profiles searchable, making it possible for a user to see who shares interests and backgrounds. Visibility of profiles can vary depending on the system design and user privacy settings.

SNS also typically provide a single point of access to multiple communication tools and support a person's ability to construct a digital identity. To do this, other possible features include things such as instant messaging within members of the network (synchronous communication), semi-public asynchronous messaging (e.g., in Facebook, Friends can post comments on an area in a Friend's profile called the Wall which is visible to all Friends), private asynchronous messaging (email), and blog-like features (called notes in Facebook). Most SNS allow the posting of pictures and videos. The capabilities of SNS can also be extended greatly by adding applications (discussed further below).

A Brief History of SNS, MySpace and Facebook

The first SNS was SixDegrees.com launched in 1997. Over the last decade or so, many SNSs have started and many have failed or declined in popularity (e.g., Friendster). MySpace is currently the largest SNS, with Facebook following and growing rapidly. LinkedIn is another large SNS that specifically targets professional networking. Some Social Networking Sites are very specific, targeted for specific communities of users (e.g., Dogster, a SNS for dogs aimed at dog owners), ethnic groups (e.g., BlackPlanet, iMatter for Arab women) or specific geographic regions (e.g., LifeAt for apartment buildings) or linguistic groups (e.g., Cyworld in Korea). There is even one site, Ning, that provides a platform to host user-created SNSs (boyd & Ellison, 2007; Rosenfeld, 2008). See boyd and Ellison (2008) for a more complete SNS history. Although currently the web has more than 100 popular SNS (Wang, 2008), two of the leaders are MySpace and Facebook and these two SNS are featured more fully below.

MySpace was started in August 2003 and grew rapidly with the 100 millionth account being created in August 2006.[3] By mid-2008, it had grown to a world-wide community, with dedicated communities in over 25 countries using multiple languages. It has a strong artist/band community, with artists being able to post songs on their sites so fans can listen to their music. The company generates revenue through advertising and has a significant agreement with Google for advertising. Anyone can join MySpace and use the various features. The user profiles are highly customizable by incorporating html code or CSS (style sheets). In early 2008, MySpace created a developer platform based on Google's Open Social API to allow developers to build their own applications for MySpace, resulting in expanded functionality for users. Currently, there are over one thousand applications available to choose from, covering a wide range of topics including games, travel, shopping, job hunting, and politics.

Facebook was started in February 2004 using a network model. Facebook was originally designed to help students on college/university campuses network so members had to have a valid educational-institution email address to register. It expanded to high schools and in 2006, opened registration up so anyone could join. Non-educational registrants could join job-related networks or networks based on their geographic area. The network membership determined access to information (depending on how users set privacy on profiles). By May, 2008, there were 55,000 regional, work-related, collegiate and high school networks, and over 60% of Facebook users were outside colleges. Currently Facebook has over 70 million active users, it is the second most-trafficked SNS in the world, and is the number one photo sharing application on the web, with 14 million photos being uploaded daily. In mid-2006, Facebook launched its development platform which enabled outside developers to build applications and offer them to users. Currently, there are over 20,000 applications available and growing at a rate of 140 per day.[4] A key decision that facilitated the development of applications and resulting increased functionality for users was letting developers keep all the advertising revenues they might earn (Anonymous, 2007a).

USAGE OF SOCIAL NETWORKING SITES

This section reviews current knowledge about the amount of usage and the various uses of SNS. Details are based on a review of the academic and practitioner literature conducted in early 2008. Specifically, searches were done in several electronic databases including ProQuest, PsychInfo, and Scholar's Portal. The electronic libraries of three associations were searched since these contain many conference proceedings (as well as journals): ACM, IEEE and AIS. Key words such as social networking, facebook and myspace were used. Other online sources were also used (e.g., CIO.com, Gartner) and targeted searches were done by examining the lists of references in relevant articles. Discussion below is organized

into trends with students, the general public and organizations.

Student Usage and Uses

Estimates of the number of US college students using Facebook are very high, varying between 80 and 92 percent (Cain, 2008; Eberhardt, 2007). US students at one college reported spending between 10 and 30 minutes each day on average on Facebook, and having between 150 and 200 Friends (Ellison, Steinfield, & Lampe, 2006).

Student uses in the USA include checking for comments, messages and updates from Friends, arranging events, parties and dates, keeping in touch with people they already know, and checking out people before meeting them (Raskin, 2006). Participants used the SNS to maintain relationships by doing things such as recognizing special events like birthdays and re-connecting with old friends. Developing new relationships was also a use, although users suggested the friendships were superficial (Dwyer, 2007). Generally students use Facebook more to keep in touch with people that they know offline than meeting new people. Consistent with this, survey results from 225 undergraduate US students indicated SNS was as useful for learning about classmates, friends, current or potential romantic partner as other media options, and that they were likely to use SNS for seeking information about these types of people. SNS were not considered useful for seeking information on family members (Westerman, 2008).

The majority of SNS communication appears not to be related to academic activities. For example, a study of 694 Facebook student users in the UK and the postings on their Wall found that only 4% (n=2496) of the Wall interactions were academically-related. This sub-set of Wall posting was analyzed and organized into five topic themes. These were: recounting and reflecting on the university experience (e.g., discussing a recently finished lecture), exchanging practical, logistical information (e.g., scheduling of lectures), exchanging academic information (e.g., course requirements), displays of supplication and/or disengagement (e.g., seeking moral rather than intellectual support), and banter (e.g., humorous, sarcastic and/or ironic exchanges) (Selwyn, 2007).

Not all SNS have the same structure, target audience or history. To examine this, a study of the potential differences between college student users of different SNS on the same US campus found several significant predictors (Hargittai, 2007). Eighty-eight percent of college students were users, and 74% reported using at least one SNS often. Women were more likely to use SNS, consistent with literature indicating women have higher propensity to communicate online person-to-person. Students who lived at home were less likely to use SNS than those living in residence or on their own. Ethnic group usage also varied for different SNS; specifically, Hispanic students were found to be more likely to use MySpace while Whites were more likely to use Facebook. Asians/Asian Americans were less likely to use Facebook and more likely to use Xanga and Friendster (possibly because these SNS are more popular in some of the Asian countries). Parental education was also found to predict some types of use, with MySpace users having parents with lower levels of schooling and Facebook users having parents with higher levels of education (Hargittai, 2007).

SNS Usage and Uses in the General Population

Research suggests that most SNSs are used to maintain relationships that existed previously offline (boyd & Ellison, 2007). While these relationships may not be very strong (i.e., weak ties), there is some offline connection (e.g., through a previous school or job). Also, part of the motivation for people to join online communities is that people want access to information that interests them (Wise, Hamman, & Thorson, 2006). For example, a study of 226 MySpace and Facebook users suggested that effectiveness and efficiency in developing and maintaining relationships were the main reasons for use. Convenience comes from having the information they want to share with friends in one place, also making the task quicker too (Dwyer, 2008). Significant positive correlations were found between the fit of the site functionality and self-presentation goals (i.e., resulting impression given by profile), the fit between the site and the use to meet people, and the effectiveness of the site to keep in touch with close friends. The results supported parts of the authors' suggested Fit Appropriation Model called the Social Software Performance Model (Dwyer, 2008).

SNS usage is fairly high in the US. More than 50% of US teens have a profile on at least one SNS and close to 25% of US adults use a SNS (Schafer, 2008). However, the US is not the most active country in SNS use. A 2006 international survey found South Korea ranked first in people visiting a social networking site, followed by Brazil, China and Mexico. USA was fifth, with 20% of active Internet users visiting a social networking site within the past 30 days. General uses vary across countries. For example, in China, 80% discuss hobbies and 78% used SNS to meet new people. SNS usage for these activities is lower in the USA (37% and 33%, respectively). In the USA, 36% use a SNS to chat with people they know or connect with people they have lost touch with, 18% discuss work-related topics online, and 23% discuss personal issues online (Russell, 2007).

A second study also explored cross-cultural SNS usage (Chapman & Lahav, 2008). Thirty-six SNS users in the US, France, South Korea and China were interviewed and observed. Results suggest that SNS in the US were used primarily to share personal information, whereas Chinese users were much less likely to post personal information. Chinese respondents used SNS to have personal discussions with people they did not know well, possibly because having these sort of discussions with close friends is difficult in their culture. In Korea, the most common use was sharing of photos. Users in France tended to discuss interests and hobbies and were somewhat less personal than US users. These results demonstrate the need to understand local cultures and preferences in order to successfully introduce a social networking site into a new country.

Several studies have examined SNS usage in specific countries and again found differences, reflective of the differences in national cultures and communication processes. For example, Cyworld is a very popular SNS in South Korea serving nearly 50% of the entire population and nearly 90% of people in the 24-29 age range. Cyworld users have dual motivations for use: maintaining existing social networks (those that pre-existed offline), and reflecting on themselves via a diary-like feature. Users suggested that they could be more uninhibited with their thoughts and self-reflections in Cyworld than they could offline. The Korean culture prefers indirect communication in face-to-face communications. Being able to express feelings more directly in Cyworld, and having the asynchronous benefit of being able to edit expression was seen as very valuable to Cyworld users (Kim & Yun, 2007).

A survey of 55 Orkut (a SNS owned by Google) users in India and Pakistan found that most of these users were IT professionals. Advertising among Friends was extremely unwelcome, reflective of the cultural and religious backgrounds of the countries. The ability to search Friends was a very valuable feature, and a significant percentage of users (45.7%) would find Facebook's feature of no publicly viewable profiles desirable (Wang, 2008).

Interviews with 33 15-24 year old Australian young adults (Arthur, Sherman, Appel, & Moore, 2006) suggest that this group used MySpace for the following five reasons, all of which they value: to express their identities, for social interaction which is fun, for immediacy and constant entertainment, to discover new things, and to be creative and be able to create a record of who they are.

Churn between sites has been high. For example, half of the users regularly visit more than one site and one in six actively use three or more sites. Friendster peaked at 20 million users a few years ago and in late 2006 was down to less than 1 million (Russell, 2007). Helping us understand why churn may be high, a 2007 study of 200 users from four Norwegian online communities investigated why users leave or reduce their participation in online communities. Approximately one-quarter to one-fifth of respondents indicated reasons for leaving or lower use were lack of interesting people/friends attending, low quality content, and low usability in terms of user interface. Other reasons for leaving given less frequently were harassment/bullying, time-consuming/isolating, low trust and over-commercialization. These results indicate that low satisfaction with the nature of the social interaction is the highest factor for reduced use; however, site designers should also be aware of the importance of usability, the danger of over-commercializing, and the need to have some mechanism to police harassment (Brandtzeg & Heim, 2007).

What people put in their profiles and who is in their social networks creates impressions with others. Friend connections helps define one's identity in SNS. People also infer meaning from not only what users post on their profiles, but also what is on their Friends' profiles and what Friends post on their walls (boyd, 2006). A study of the lists of interests in MySpace profiles also found that users were significantly different than their top friends, indicating that users develop their lists of interests to differentiate themselves and that users tend to list interests to assert their prestige (Liu, 2007).

Some SNS allow users to create fake profiles, whereas others require authentic information (to varying degrees). The ability to create false profiles, the inability to authenticate relationships in some SNS, and the tendency to accept almost anyone as Friends, devalues the value of Friend connections because trust can not be assumed (boyd, 2006). Facebook information has been found to be mostly genuine, which may be why users tend to trust Facebook more than some other SNS.

Differences in use based on age was investigated in one study. 240 MySpace profiles were randomly-selected and analyzed. Results indicate that older (60+ years of age) users have fewer Friends (average = 18) compared to teenagers (aged 13 – 19) who had 95 Friends on average. Teenager's Friends were also mostly in their own age range, whereas older users had a wide age distribution among their Friends, likely due to the higher number of life experiences and resulting higher complexity of existing offline social networks (Arjan, Pfeil, & Zaphiris, 2008).

Another use of SNS has been for customer advocacy and activism (Eberhardt, 2007). In one example, a Facebook user connected with several hundred similar investors who were concerned about the status of their investment in non-bank asset-backed commercial paper (since the ability to recover investments was in question). By sharing information, event updates, emotional support, and possible tactics, the group was able to recover their investment (Simon, 2008).

Organizational SNS Usage and Uses

While it is difficult to find conclusive evidence about organizational use of SNS, likely because it is evolving so fast, one study found 20% of employees at large companies said they contribute regularly to blogs, social networks, wikis and other web 2.0 services (Green, 2007). A 2007 global survey by McKinsey of executives (44% of responses were C-level) found that 37% of 2,173 respondents were using or planning to use social networking in their organizations, while 39% said this Web 2.0 technology was not under consider-

ation. Nineteen percent of respondents said their companies had invested in social networks. Of the respondents that used any Web 2.0 technologies, the various way the technologies were being used were: to interface with customers (70%), to interface with suppliers and partners (51%), and to manage collaboration internally (75%). Although respondents indicated calculating returns from the investments in SNS and other Web 2.0 technologies was very difficult, they suggested the benefits were clear in terms of better communication with customers, more efficient collaboration within the company, stronger sense of community, and improved abilities to manage online reputation (Martin, 2007).

The discussion above suggests rapid growth of SNS adoption in organizations. Three major current uses seem to be: recruiting, advertising, and internal collaboration. To assist corporate recruiting, employees can tell their contacts about job openings via their network. Companies can also create Facebook groups at no or little cost, which can help to promote their opening and opportunities (and enhance their brand image). Recruiting companies can also create applications (mini-programs) that users can add to their profiles at no charge. For example, Jobster has created an application that sends a message to a user whenever a job position is created that is potentially of interest to them (Rocha, 2007). Ernst & Young has a very active Facebook service page, and even the CIA recruits on Facebook. Recruiters tend to prefer Facebook over MySpace, even thought it has fewer users, because it is somewhat cleaner and more organized, and has a more mature member-body (Rocha, 2007). Employee-referred hires are more successful (80% versus 50% for non-referrals) (Anonymous, 2007b), suggesting that increasing the number of referrals via avenues like SNS will have significant value for companies.

A survey of executives found that 35% thought social networking sites would be most useful in the recruiting efforts over the next three years

(Anonymous, 2008h). A Manpower survey in the UK found that 17% of users use their SNS to research potential employers and 10% use it for networking and generating new business. This suggests that the practice of using SNS to aid recruiting is likely to grow. However, companies should be sensitive to the fact that some potential employees feel the information they put on the SNS profiles should not be used for making recruiting decisions. One study found that over half SNS users would consider it unethical if employers used SNS to learn about potential or existing employees' activities (Anonymous, 2008i). And another study found 60% of students felt that Facebook information should not be used in hiring decisions (versus 28% of employers) (Cain, 2008). Interestingly, recruiting of high school students by colleges and universities via Facebook and MySpace methods was acceptable to the majority of students (Roach, 2006).

Advertising is the main source of revenue for large SNS like Facebook. Emarketers suggest MySpace and Facebook got 72% of all ad revenues for social network sites in 2007 in the USA (Russell, 2007). Companies can potentially mine profile pages to identify potential customers. Users of SNS represent an important demographic for marketers (Raskin, 2006). There are few studies that have established the effectiveness of this advertising, as of yet.

Using SNS internally to mine in-house expertise, sharing information internally, and save time now spent in mailing documents and emailing comments all has significant potential (more efficient collaboration). Serena Software and Nissan are two other examples that are featured in the literature for their use of SNS.

Serena Software Inc. is a global company with 800 employees that is using Facebook to connect coworkers at various sites. They are making Facebook the company's intranet and encouraging use through Facebook Fridays where employees are encouraged to spend one hour of personal time on their profiles and connect with others. The aim is to let employees get to know each other as people, help them understand the business and products, and help to serve customers, on demand. The corporate culture is evolving to foster a sense of community and fun, which the CEO believes will help them get more done (Anonymous, 2007c).

Nissan launched a social networking site, called N-Square, to connect up to 50,000 of its 180,000 employees globally. Users are able to create online profiles, blogs, communities, discussion groups and share data files. A main reason for launching the site was to provide employees with a way to avoid bureaucratic channels and create new partnerships, hopefully reducing the inefficiency of traditional tools and channels. N-Square may also help employees feel more connected to their jobs, perhaps reducing turnover and facilitating retention of top people. Nissan's initiative was sparked by seeing what IBM was doing with their social networking applications (Anonymous, 2008g).

Companies are also trying various ways to take advantage of SNS potential to reach the users on SNS. For example, companies, such as MTV, Warner Bros and Woolworths, are developing applications for Facebook that push products to users, such as TV shows and album releases. However, the uptake of these applications by users has been very low, typically only a few active users per day, making the recovery of the cost to develop the branded application unlikely (Anonymous, 2008a). A health planner/reminder application to help people keep track of appointments, has been developed by Healthplan provide HAS in the UK (Anonymous, 2008d). And Amazon has developed Facebook applications that make it easy for users to see shopping wish lists and link them through to make a purchase at Amazon (facilitating online social shopping) (Birchall, 2008)

Only one study was found that examined corporate SNS use from the perspective of the user. A study of 68 Facebook users within IBM in 2007 found three different patterns of use. The first (and largest) group, called "Reliving the College Days" had a high number of school contacts and few connections in the corporate network. These were the youngest and appear to have started using Facebook during their college studies, and continued to use it to maintain contact with college friends. The second group, called Dress to Impress, had a mix of school and work Friends, had fewer Friends than the first group, and listed more information about their job. The third group, called Living in the Business World, appeared to have recently joined Facebook and only had Friends within the corporation. They appeared to join to be part of the online community of coworkers. The latter two groups appear to be managing their image recognizing that professional colleagues are viewing their profile, whereas users in the College Days group have profiles with much more personal information, with very little work-related information. The Dress to Impress group appear to manage their profile different than they did in college (more professional), whereas the College Days users appear to not have changed their use of the SNS. The Living in the Business World group appear to have used Facebook to enhance their existing relationships with coworkers by keeping in touch with both local and remote coworkers. It is expected this type of usage will grow in organizations and help people create common ground and mutual interest. This study illustrates the difficulty of using a single site for professional and non-professional use. While it is possible in Facebook to create limited access profiles, this takes extra time to both create and maintain (DiMicco & Millen, 2007).

Antecedents and Outcomes of SNS Use

While the research on what influences SNS use and the outcomes is limited, it is undoubtedly growing fast. Five topics related to SNS use were found in the research: the development of social capital, perceptions created by profile content, student perceptions of faculty due to faculty use, privacy concerns due to use, and productivity impacts of use.

One study examined the relationship between SNS use and social capital. Social capital refers to resources gathered through interpersonal relationships and is seen to generally have a positive impact on people in social networks (via increased trust, mutual support, goodwill, etc.) A study of 286 US undergraduate students found their use of Facebook was a significant positive predictor of social capital, suggesting that using Facebook helped students maintain and strengthen relationships, both weak and close ones. (Ellison, Steinfield, & Lampe, 2007; Ellison et al., 2006). This study supports the proposition that SNS use does strengthen social networks and is beneficial, especially in an undergraduate setting.

SNS users create an image for others via the personal information they choose to share on their profiles and whom they link to as Friends. Several studies have examined the impressions created from different angles, including the number of friends, profile content, and appearance. For example, experimental results with 153 U.S. undergraduate students found that the number of Friends on Facebook can provide a significant cue by which others make social judgements. Individuals who had too few Friends (approximately 100) or too many Friends (greater than 500) were perceived more negatively in terms of social attractiveness, indicating a curvilinear effect. A somewhat similar relationship was found with perceived extraversion, although the negative effect after the 500 Friend level was considerably more level (Tong, Van Der Heide, Langwell, & Walther, 2008). The respondents had an average number of Friends on their Facebook accounts of 395, suggesting that people judge other's social attractiveness on the number of Friends they have and use their own number of Friends possibly as a reference point.

The relationship between number of Friends and profile structure (i.e., which fields are completed) has also been investigated to determine if the completion of certain profile fields predicts Friendship, via creating common ground or signaling (Lampe, Ellison, & Steinfield, 2007). Over 30,000 profiles at a US university were examined. On average, users completed 50% of the fields available in Facebook. Positive associations were found between the number of fields completed and the number of Friends. Causality can not be inferred from this, as there are several plausible explanations including: a more complete profile generates more Friends, more active users could both complete more fields and seek out Friends, and people with more Friends could feel more pressure to add more information to their profiles.

Semi-structured interviews of 19 US students were conducted to examine how the participants used SNS to present themselves to others and manage the impressions created (Dwyer, 2007). Subjects suggested that creating a good impression was important. One subject said: "You can't just completely be yourself, you have to play the game, and have some sort of cool factor [so that] people are interested in speaking to you." (p. 5). Participants were concerned about privacy but suggested that it was up to them to control it by not posting any information they felt was private. Based on these results, the author suggested that key attitudes which influence the management of interpersonal relationships are concerns for information privacy and impression management. SNS technology features that can enable interpersonal relationship management included profile management, visibility management and identity management (Dwyer, 2007).

Impression formation was further studied by examining the impact of how what people write on Facebook walls and the physical attractiveness of Friends affected perceptions about the profile owner (Walther, Van Der Heide, Kim, Westerman, & Tong, 2008). 342 undergraduate US students participated in this experiment. Results suggest that having physically attractive Friends is positively associated with perceptions of the profile owner's physical attractiveness (and had no effect on task attractiveness – the ability to complete work reliably). Prosocial statements by Friends about profile owners was positively associated with social and task attractiveness, as well as credibility. Gender did moderate some of the effects, consistent with the sexual double standard (i.e., some remarks were seen as negative for women and positive for men – e.g., remarks about excessive drinking, promiscuous sexual behaviour).

Two studies have examined the impact of university faculty having Facebook accounts on student perceptions. A 2006 study of 166 US students on Facebook indicated that seeing their professors on Facebook (i.e., viewing their profile, etc.) had neither a positive or negative effect on student ratings (Hewitt & Forte, 2006). However, an effect was found when the content of the professor's profile was studied. An experimental study was conducted with 133 US college students where teacher self-disclosure on Facebook was manipulated via different photos, biographical profile information and Wall postings. High disclosure involved including information about social gatherings with comments, group membership and personal information (the amount of information provided was less in the low and medium disclosure conditions). Students viewing the high disclosure profiles believed the classroom climate would be more positive, anticipated higher levels of affective learning with those teachers, and had higher anticipated motivation levels. Most (84%) of the comments from students viewing the high disclosure profiles were positive, whereas a small number were negative, expressing concerns about loss of professional image (Mazer, Murphy, & Simonds, 2007).

Given the ability to make a considerable amount of personal information available to others (which many users do), privacy is a natural concern in SNS. Early work (Gross, Acquisti, & Heinz, 2005) found that US university students on Facebook disclosed a great deal of personal information on their profiles (e.g., pictures of themselves – 90.8%, birth dates 87.7%, residence addresses – 50.8%, and phone numbers – 39.9%). Analysis implies that almost all of this information is genuine. Only a few percent of people used available privacy settings to restrict the ability to view their profiles within their network, indicating that most users were either unaware or unconcerned about their personal privacy.

Another survey of US college students was conducted to make Facebook users aware of the privacy options available to them and alert them to possible privacy issues. The profiles of participants were then examined after they completed the study to see if they changed the amount of information on their profile (presumably from being made aware of privacy issues and being concerned about the potential privacy problems). Of the 84% of participants that knew they could change the privacy settings within Facebook, less than 48% had made any changes prior to the survey (indicating they left the privacy settings on default which provides visibility of the profile to anyone in their networks). Only a few percent of participants made changes to their profiles within 5 days after the survey was conducted inferring that most users were comfortable with the amount of information they were sharing (Govani & Pashley, 2005).

Another US study of privacy concerns surveyed 294 students found that privacy concerns were stronger in non-users than users of Facebook (although the differences were not statistically significant within undergraduate respondents). Therefore, privacy concerns appeared to be affecting Facebook use in non-undergraduates. For undergrads, even those students who had privacy concerns provided a significant amount of personal information in their profile. The strongest motiva-

tion in providing information was to have fun and provide enough information so that people benefit from Facebook (Acquisti & Gross, 2006)

Antecedents of information sharing and the development of new relationships were studied in 117 MySpace and Facebook users. Concerns about privacy, trust in the SNS, and trust in other members of the SNS were proposed as antecedents to sharing and relationship development. Facebook users had higher SNS trust and they disclosed more personal information such as real name and email address. MySpace members were more likely to disclose their relationship status. MySpace users also were more likely to agree that they could easily meet new people with their SNS and were more likely to extend new online relationships by contacting the person via other communication channels (e.g., telephone, F2F, instant messaging (IM), email). Results are consistent with previous research suggesting Facebook users use the SNS to extend existing offline relationship more frequently than initiating new online relationships. However, in MySpace, where trust is lower, there was a fair amount of activity establishing new online relationships. Few significant relationships were found with respect to privacy concerns, the exception being that people with high privacy concerns were less likely to share their IM screen name (Dwyer, Hiltz, & Passerini, 2007).

Time spent on SNS is a growing concern to many companies. With SNS usage growing, organizations see both threats and opportunities. Corporations are creating, and adopting SNSs to stimulate internal usage and are advertising on SNSs to reach target markets. However, companies also see threats in terms of wasted time and security concerns, to the degree that some companies have blocked access to SNSs during work time (e.g., the US Military, the Canadian government) (boyd & Ellison, 2007). Two-thirds of UK companies surveyed are banning the use of Facebook during office hours, although other companies feel this is too extreme since people's working and personal lives are blurring, making it difficult to leave personal life outside when they enter the work site (Brockett, 2007). Another survey, done in July 2007, suggests that approximately 50% of companies are blocking access to SNS at work (Green, 2007).

One poll in the UK estimated that Facebook and MySpace use was costing UK companies approximately 6.5 billion pounds annually in lost productivity, based on a finding that office workers are spending at least 30 minutes per day on social networking (Hathi, 2008). The assumption behind this claim is that the time spent on SNS is of no benefit to the organization. Counterarguments suggest that time spent on SNS can help with recruitment, can improve employee morale and corporate loyalty, and improve company transparency. While IT departments typically would like to ban SNS (for security), use of SNS in organizations is often driven by HR. HR is concerned with team building, recruitment and retention, and corporate culture (Hathi, 2008).

Concern about the time spent on SNS also exists outside the corporate setting. The number of Friends in SNS is typically two to three hundred. The ability to create any real relationships with this many people is the subject of debate, and there is a concern that very close relationships (which typically are just a few) may get weakened as people spend more time and energy maintaining distant relationships (MacLeod, 2008).

NEW DEVELOPMENTS, CHALLENGES AND OPPORTUNITIES

This section is organized into three parts. Challenges and opportunities for using SNS in companies is first discussed. The second part deals with the privacy challenge of SNS use, since this is a major concern in the literature. The last section summarizes some of the recent and foreseeable developments that may lead to new opportunities for SNS use.

Using SNS in Organizations

There are many opportunities for companies to use SNS. Departments that should benefit from SNS include sales (identifying and engaging customers) and operations (so employees can help each other and find more effective ways of working). Research and development could also use SNS to gather ideas and insights from customers (Bernoff & Li, 2008).

Companies could use existing SNS like MySpace and Facebook to reach current and potential customers. While SNS advertising is growing, companies need to interact with customers in meaningful ways, such as creating conversations and affinity-based networks. SNS can potentially be used to reach customers and get advice on new products, feedback on existing products, and ideas about brand building (Webb, 2007). Knowing whom to reach out to is important too. While it is relatively easy to mine existing profiles and the data in fields to segment targets, it would be valuable to also identify what people do on their sites (versus whom they say they are). In this way, marketers could identify the creators and key influencers and target these people based on how they act. So far, SNS operators have not been willing to provide marketers with this sort of data (Klaassen, 2008).

However, companies have to be sensitive to the culture of existing SNS and the receptiveness of members to advertising. Clemons et al. (2007) caution that SNS have risks for advertisers, as the effectiveness of the advertising is largely unproven and is in need of future research. While offline social networks are based on and create trust and credibility, it is unclear how much of an online SNS is built on trust. If SNS are built on trust, there are concerns that commercializing the network via push advertising may undermine that trust. And, as mentioned above, one of the reasons found for leaving a SNS is over-commercialization.

SNS can also help companies collaborate internally. Small companies could use an SNS like

Facebook as their collaborative platform and this is starting to happen (Anonymous, 2007b). The email and document management capabilities fit these needs well and could enhance the ability to work in teams and from remote locations. The research showing that students develop social capital through SNS use is encouraging for corporate use. Users could use SNS internally to maintain weak ties with colleagues and to learn about expertise within the organization (like a knowledge management system).

Using an externally hosted SNS can create security and privacy concerns for corporations. Depending on the nature of the business, there may be a need to build safeguards to ensure discussions and document sharing is tracked, to be certain employees meet government regulations and don't create legal problems (Green, 2007). There are SNS options from major software vendors so companies do not have to use externally hosted SNS like Facebook. For example, IBM has a product called Lotus Connections which provides a number of Web 2.0 tools, including profiles and social networking[5] (Everest, 2008). A company could use a product like this to create an internal SNS which would facilitate collaboration internally while controlling security (since the application would be within the corporate firewall and not open to people from outside the company).

Another opportunity for companies is to partner with existing SNS and develop applications that offer customers more value. For example, CIO magazine has partnered with LinkedIn to connect relevant events and articles. LinkedIn widgets and the CIO.com website allow users to see who at a company featured in a CIO article is part of the LinkedIn network. Users can also view want ads and see who is connected to the advertising company. CIO media events are enhanced by LinkedIn's Event service that shows a user who else in the network is planning on attending, as well as manage the networking potential at the event (Anonymous, 2008c).

The Privacy Challenge of SNS Use

SNS are mediated public sites where technology allows people to gather publicly. Unique properties of mediated publics include persistence, searchability, replicability and invisible audiences (Cain, 2008). As previously mentioned, all of these properties can create privacy issues, challenges and concerns. Information is in SNS that is typically not included in resumes or uncovered by general background checks (Cain, 2008). Professional and private lives can blur together, especially if prospective employers see photos of actions that might cause them to question the candidate's judgment.

Digital identities (i.e., profiles and reported activities) are increasingly viewed by third-parties that the profile owner is not aware of. The legality of this is still unclear and undoubtedly will vary across countries depending on privacy legislation (Hodge, 2006-2007). Companies routinely use search engines to do background checks on applicants and police and university authorities have used Facebook profiles to collect evidence and leads. Even if a user removes some potentially compromising information from his/her site, there is always the danger the information has been captured elsewhere, creating a digital record that is out the control of the creator. Users need to recognize that they are not operating in a protected environment (Rosenblum, 2007).

In response to user privacy concerns, SNS companies such as Facebook have developed various privacy settings, such that now it is possible to control what is viewable by whom to a much greater extent than it was several years ago. However, research has found that many users do not change the privacy settings and many users are very open to accepting Friend requests from total strangers, thereby giving the stranger access to the personal information on their profile (Gross et al., 2005). This can lead to data re-identification, where a third party connects information from different sources and has the potential for identity theft and/or fraud. Other risks include damage to reputation, receiving unsolicited message and offers, and being exploited by social predators. The latter is rare but there have been reported cases of sexual predators, stalkers, child molesters and pornographers using SNS to approach minors (Rosenblum, 2007).

Installing applications also causes privacy and security concerns. For example, users should also be aware that installing Facebook applications gives the application access to some of the profile (some information can be restricted). The application developers can then use the information to target ads. There is a fair bit of uncertainty about how the data is kept safe and the potential exists for it to be combined with information about individuals, which could lead to problems such as identity theft or spoofing and phishing (Irvine, 2008). Users should also be aware of the potential for downloading applications on SNS that are malware programs. Although users have become aware of this danger when using email, the same degree of caution is not currently prevalent in SNS use. And many of the young SNS users are fairly inexperienced and naïve about the risks of using electronic media (Douglis, 2008).

Given all these risks, organizational users (as well as individual users) need guidelines to protect the users and the company. For example, guidelines about what information can and can not be posted should be specified. Privacy protection recommendations include assuming anything you post is public so you have to exercise good judgment in what personal information is shared in a SNS, do not have an open profile (i.e., use the available privacy setting to control who has access to information), do not accept Friend requests from strangers, and avoid installing applications (Munro, 2008).

Developments in SNS

While most users stick with a single site (Watson, 2008), they may move from one to another

as popularity declines and builds. Maintaining multiple sites takes time and effort since currently sites are independent applications using their own architectures. However, companies are trying to create integration mechanisms that would allow information from different SNSs to be shared via one platform. Developments are coming that will allow users to pull information about friends and colleagues from numerous SNS and other websites. FriendFeed is one of the first of these (Green, 2008). Google is developing an open source framework, OpenSocial and SocialStream, that would allow many of the popular SNS to be connected into a unified social network (Russell, 2007; Weaver, 2008).

Mobile access, via mobile phones, to SNS such as MySpace and Facebook is growing (Anonymous, 2008b; 2008f). Mobile social networking will help put users' content into context since their social interactions will be able to occur in real time (DeJean, 2008). Mobile social networking systems are also developing that, among other things, allow users to be aware in real time of social activities. Slam is one of these systems, and while not a full SNS (given the lack of profile and social network visibility), some of the features and functionality are similar (Counts, 2008).

SNS are also evolving to attempt to offer more value to users. For example, MySpace is developing a music service with Universal, Song BMG and Warner and is working with Merlin on future licencing arrangements (Cardew & Emanuel, 2008). SNS are spreading to new countries and cultures (e.g., MySpace recently launched a dedicated community for Indian users (Anonymous, 2008e)). And given the high level of Facebook use in university settings, it is natural that educators are considering if and how to use Facebook as a learning tool. One developer recently received funding to work on a learning management system based on Facebook (Goth, 2008). Potential other applications include health care (Watson, 2008) where users can get personal health information from SNS like Facebook (Sinnema, 2008).

CONCLUSION

What SNS are and what we currently know about them has been presented. SNS usage is fairly new and growing incredibly fast. There are many possible benefits of use and some significant areas of concern. Research opportunities are also numerous. For example, the focus of research so far has largely been on the SNS user. While the user is obviously very important to the story, and current data is needed as usage and concerns evolve, there are other stakeholders that warrant research attention. This would include designers and operators of SNS and the underlying infrastructures, developers of algorithms, conduct of third parties using SNS, and marketers and advertisers who are trying to strengthen their brands (Beer, 2008). The majority of research has been with students in the US, leaving many opportunities for studies of corporate use (especially as this use grows), and use in other countries. The future of SNS appears to be bright, and the future for SNS researchers should be exciting!

REFERENCES

Acquisti, A., & Gross, R. (2006). *Imagined communities: Awareness, information sharing, and privacy on the facebook.* In G. Danezis, & P. Golle (Eds.), (pp. 36-58). Berlin Heidelberg: Springer-Verlag.

Anonymous. (2007a). Business: Social graph-iti; internet companies. *The Economist, 385*(8551), 90.

Anonymous. (2007b, Nov 21). Facebook time with recruits. *National Post,* (pp. WK.1).

Anonymous. (2007c). Serena software adopts facebook as corporate intranet. *Canada News-Wire,, 1.*

Anonymous. (2008a). Branded apps on facebook fail to attract users. *New Media Age, 2.*

Anonymous. (2008b). CellSpin launches the first MySpace and facebook instant mobile posting application for audio, video, photos and text on 300+ phones worldwide. *Canada NewsWire.*

Anonymous. (2008c). CIO and LinkedIn share common goals. *MIN's B 2 B, 11*(16).

Anonymous. (2008d). Healthplan provider HSA launches unique facebook personal planner. *PR Newswire Europe Including UK Disclose.*

Anonymous. (2008e). MySpace india launches. *Wireless News.*

Anonymous. (2008f). Myspace mobile launches on verizon wireless. *Telephone IP News, 19*(5).

Anonymous. (2008g). Nissan launches "N-square" for staff. *Strategic Communication Management, 12*(1), 9.

Anonymous. (2008h). Quick study: Moms drive word of mouth; getting hired through social networks; greenbacks versus green initiatives. *PR News, 64*(17).

Anonymous. (2008i). Workers naive over online presence. *Strategic Communication Management, 12*(1), 9.

Anonymous. (2008j). How to...use LinkedIn as an effective business tool.(2008). *PR News, 64*(16)

Arjan, R., Pfeil, U., & Zaphiris, P. (2008). Age differences in online social networking. *CHI '08: CHI '08 Extended Abstracts on Human Factors in Computing Systems,* Florence, Italy. (pp. 2739-2744).

Arthur, D., Sherman, C., Appel, D., & Moore, L. (2006). Why young consumers adopt interactive technologies. *Young Consumers, 7*(3), 33.

Beer, D. (2008). Social network(ing) sites... revisiting the story so far: A response to danah boyd & nicole ellison. *Journal of Computer-Mediated Communication, 13*(2), 516-529.

Bernoff, J., & Li, C. (2008). Harnessing the power of the oh-so-social web. *MIT Sloan Management Review, 49*(3), 36.

Birchall, J. (2008, Mar 14). Amazon taps facebook potential. *Financial Times,* (p. 18).

boyd, d. m., & Ellison, N. B. (2007). Social network sites: Definition, history, and scholarship. *Journal of Computer-Mediated Communication, 13*(1), 210-230.

Boyd, D. (2006). In Heer J. (Ed.), *Profiles as conversation: Networked identity performance on friendster.*

Brandtzeg, P. B., & Heim, J. (2007). User loyalty and online communities: Why members of online communities are not faithful. *INTETAIN '08: Proceedings of the 2nd International Conference on INtelligent TEchnologies for Interactive enterTAINment,* Cancun, Mexico. (pp. 1-10).

Brockett, J. (2007). Face to face with social networking. *People Management, 13*(16), 15.

Cain, J. (2008). Online social networking issues within academia and pharmacy education. *American Journal of Pharmaceutical Education, 72*(1), 1.

Cardew, B., & Emanuel, H. (2008). Merlin enters MySpace talks. *Music Week, 1.*

Chapman, C. N., & Lahav, M. (2008). International ethnographic observation of social networking sites. *CHI '08: CHI '08 Extended Abstracts on Human Factors in Computing Systems,* Florence, Italy. (pp. 3123-3128).

Clemons, E. K., Barnett, S., & Appadurai, A. (2007). The future of advertising and the value of social network websites: Some preliminary examinations. *ICEC '07: Proceedings of the Ninth International Conference on Electronic Commerce,* Minneapolis, MN, USA. (pp. 267-276).

Counts, S. (2008). In K. E.Fisher (Ed.), *Mobile social networking: An information grounds perspective.*

DeJean, D. (2008). Social networking gets moving. *Computerworld, 42*(15), 30.

DiMicco, J. M., & Millen, D. R. (2007). Identity management: Multiple presentations of self in facebook. *GROUP '07: Proceedings of the 2007 International ACM Conference on Supporting Group Work,* Sanibel Island, Florida, USA. (pp. 383-386).

Douglis, F. (2008). *On social networking and communication paradigms.*

Dwyer, C. (2007). *Digital relationships in the "MySpace" generation: Results from a qualitative study.*

Dwyer, C. (2008). In S. R.Hiltz (Ed.), *Understanding development and usage of social networking sites: The social software performance model.*

Dwyer, C., Hiltz, S. R., & Passerini, K. (2007). Trust and privacy concern within social networking sites: A comparison of facebook and MySpace. *Proceedings of the Thirteenth Americas Conference on Information Systems,* Keystone, Colorado.

Eberhardt, D. M. (2007). Facing up to facebook. *About Campus, 12*(4), 18-26.

Ellison, N. B., Steinfield, C., & Lampe, C. (2007). The benefits of facebook "Friends:" social capital and college students' use of online social network sites. *Journal of Computer-Mediated Communication, 12*(4), 1143-1168.

Ellison, N., Steinfield, C., & Lampe, C. A. C. (2006). Spatially bounded online social networks and social capital: The role of facebook. *Annual Conference of the International Communication Association (ICA),* Dresden, Germany.

Everest, K. (2008) *Business drivers for social networking* (Presentation May 2, 2008. Queen's University.

Goth, G. (2008). *Are social networking sites growing up?*

Govani, T., & Pashley, H. (2005). Student awareness of the privacy implications when using facebook. *Student Poster,* Pittsburgh, PA: Carnegie Mellon University.

Green, H. (2007). The water cooler is now on the web. *Business Week,* (4052), 78.

Green, H. (2008). One place for your many online lives. *Business Week,* (4080), 54.

Gross, R., Acquisti, A., & Heinz, H. J.,III. (2005). Information revelation and privacy in online social networks. *WPES '05: Proceedings of the 2005 ACM Workshop on Privacy in the Electronic Society,* Alexandria, VA, USA. (pp. 71-80).

Hargittai, E. (2007). Whose space? differences among users and non-users of social network sites. *Journal of Computer-Mediated Communication, 13*(1), 276-297.

Hathi, S. (2008). Billions lost from social networking. *Strategic Communication Management, 12*(2), 9.

Hesseldahl, A. (2008). In browsers, flock may lead the flock. *Business Week (Online).*

Hewitt, A., & Forte, A. (2006). Crossing boundaries: Identity management and Student/Faculty relationships on the facebook. Paper presented at the *CSCW'06 Poster,* Banff, Alberta, Canada.

Hodge, M. J. (2006-2007). Fourth amendment and privacy issues on the new internet: Facebook.com and myspace.com, the. *Southern Illinois University Law Journal, 31*, 95-123.

Irvine, M. (2008, Apr 28). Social networking applications can pose security risks. *Telegraph-Journal,* (p. B.5).

Kim, K., & Yun, H. (2007). *Cying* for me, *cying* for us: Relational dialectics in a korean social network site. *Journal of Computer-Mediated Communication, 13*(1), 298-318.

Klaassen, A. (2008). Actions louder than words on social nets. *Advertising Age, 79*(14), 3.

Lampe, C. A. C., Ellison, N., & Steinfield, C. (2007). A familiar face(book): Profile elements as signals in an online social network. *CHI '07: Proceedings of the SIGCHI Conference on Human Factors in Computing Systems,* San Jose, California, USA. (pp. 435-444).

Latham, R. P., Butzer, C. C., & Brown, J. T. (2008). Legal implications of user-generated content: YouTube, MySpace, facebook. *Intellectual Property & Technology Law Journal, 20*(5), 1.

Liu, H. (2007). Social network profiles as taste performances. *Journal of Computer-Mediated Communication, 13*(1), 252-275.

MacLeod, E. (2008, Apr 17). Facing our past on facebook; when long-lost 'friends' reach out it's best just to slam the electronic door, experts advise. *Toronto Star,* (p. L.4).

Martin, J. (2007). How businesses are using web 2.0: A McKinsey global survey. *The McKinsey Quarterly,* (March), May 8, 2008. Retrieved from http://www.mckinseyquarterly.com/home.aspx.

Mazer, J. P., Murphy, R. E., & Simonds, C. J. (2007). I'll see you on "Facebook": The effects of computer-mediated teacher self-disclosure on student motivation, affective learning, and classroom climate. *Communication Education, 56*(1), 1.

Munro, K. (2008, Apr 30). Simple rules that make social networking safer. *Financial Times,* (p. 4).

Raskin, R. (2006). Facebook faces its future. *Young Consumers, 7*(2), 56.

Roach, R. (2006). Prospective college students receptive to electronic social networking recruitment methods, survey finds. *Diverse Issues in Higher Education, 23*(23), 40.

Rocha, R. (2007, Sep 1). Even the CIA is recruiting using facebook. *Calgary Herald,* (p. D.6).

Rosenblum, D. (2007). *What anyone can know: The privacy risks of social networking sites.*

Rosenfeld, E. (2008). Expanding your professional network with nings. *Teacher Librarian, 35*(3), 60.

Russell, J. (2007). Social networking: Applications for health care recruitment. *Nursing Economics, 25*(5), 299.

Schafer, I. (2008). An open letter to CEOs of social-network sites: Get a relationship point person. *Advertising Age, 79*(15), 38.

Selwyn, N. (2007). *Screw blackboard... do it on facebook!': An investigation of students' educational use of facebook'.* Unpublished manuscript.

Simon, B. (2008, Apr 14). Campaigning investors turn to facebook the networking site helped activists get a hearing, says bernard simon. *Financial Times,* (p. 14).

Sinnema, J. (2008). Facebook could help save health care: Expert. *CanWest News.*

Skiba, D. J. (2007). Nursing education 2.0: Poke me. where's your face in space? *Nursing Education Perspectives, 28*(4), 214.

Tong, S. T., Van Der Heide, B., Langwell, L., & Walther, J. B. (2008). Too much of a good thing? the relationship between number of friends and interpersonal impressions on facebook. *Journal of Computer-Mediated Communication, 13*(3), 531-549.

Walther, J. B., Van Der Heide, B., Kim, S., Westerman, D., & Tong, S. T. (2008). The role of friends' appearance and behavior on evaluations of individuals on facebook: Are we known by the company we keep? *Human Communication Research, 34*(1), 28-49.

Wang, Y. (2008). In Kumar V. (Ed.), *Will the overseas expansion of facebook succeed?*

Watson, M. (2008). Social networking: An opportunity for health and social care? *Journal of Integrated Care, 16*(1), 41.

Weaver, A. C. (2008). In Morrison B. B. (Ed.), *Social networking.*

Webb, G. (2007). A new future for brand marketing. *The British Journal of Administrative Management,* 13.

Westerman, D. (2008). How do people really seek information about others? Information seeking across internet and traditional communication channels. *Journal of Computer-Mediated Communication, 13*(3), 751-767.

Wise, K., Hamman, B., & Thorson, K. (2006). Moderation, response rate, and message interactivity: Features of online communities and their effects on intent to participate. *Journal of Computer-Mediated Communication, 12*(1), 24-41.

ENDNOTES

[1] Networking. (n.d.). *Dictionary.com Unabridged (v 1.1).* Retrieved May 19, 2008, from Dictionary.com website: http://dictionary.reference.com/browse/networking

[2] Friends is capitalized to designate meaning a person linked to another's profile and distinguish the term from the common meaning of "friend" since not all Friends in SNSs are necessarily close friends.

3   http://en.wikipedia.org/wiki/Myspace (accessed May, 2008)

4   From Facebook's online Press Room - http://www.facebook.com/press.php (accessed May, 2008).

5   http://www-142.ibm.com/software/dre/ecatalog/Detail.wss?locale=en_CA&synkey=O035990J93692T45

Chapter VI
Teachers' Personal Knowledge Management in China Based Web 2.0 Technologies

Jingyuan Zhao
Harbin Institute of Technology, China

ABSTRACT

Knowledge is taken as core competitive power in the current society. The teacher as an educational operator often touch much knowledge, if they could manage knowledge efficiently, the work efficiency will be increased greatly. To mine knowledge and make tacit knowledge explicit, teachers should manage personal knowledge. By the survey of teachers' personal knowledge management in China, the study finds some problems in terms of Chinese teachers' personal knowledge management, especially many Chinese teachers are not good at making use of Web technologies to assist them on managing knowledge and communicating with other teachers. One studying focus of Web 2.0 technologies is personal knowledge management, and Web 2.0 provides a series of effective tools and platforms for personal knowledge management. The chapter discusses on the concept of teachers' personal knowledge management, and presents the strategies of teachers' personal knowledge management based Web 2.0 technologies, using for reference for teachers' personal knowledge management practice.

INTRODUCTION

Drucker (1993) claimed that the capital was no longer the dominant force of economic development in the knowledge society after capitalism, the application and production of knowledge was the driving force for economic growth. OECD (1996) put forward the concept of knowledge-based economy claiming that knowledge-based economy was the new economy focusing on R&D

and innovation, and knowledge-based economy was a kind of economic efficiency and economic values generated by knowledge innovation, knowledge transmit and knowledge transfer. Knowledge-based economy emphasize on knowledge acquisition, accumulation, sharing, application and innovation, namely the spirit of knowledge-based economy is initiative innovation, moreover the driving force of knowledge-based economy is to foster talents. Knowledge-based economy is driven mainly by talent training, and the school is not only the main venue to train talents, but also the place of knowledge transmit and creation, teachers should recognize the important role played by themselves, pursuing professional growth to meet the need of knowledge-based economy. In the face of the impact of knowledge-based economy era, knowledge management has become the current important issue, teachers certainly should be in capability of personal knowledge management, and foster teachers' professional capability and enhance the efficiency of teaching and learning by means of teachers' personal knowledge management (TPKM).

Knowledge can be categorized into explicit knowledge and tacit Knowledge (Nonaka and Takeuchi, 1995). Edvinsson and Malone (1997) divides knowledge into individual knowledge, organizational and structural knowledge: individual knowledge exists only in individual mind; organizational knowledge is the kind of knowledge occurring in groups or departments; structural knowledge roots in organizations through the procedures, manual, and ethics and tenets. The three kinds of knowledge above can be explicit knowledge or tacit knowledge (O'Dell and Grayson, 1998). In teachers' personal knowledge systems, part of knowledge is explicit knowledge, and part of knowledge is tacit knowledge. The explicit knowledge of teachers is obtained through reading and lectures, including the subject content knowledge, curriculum knowledge, subject pedagogical knowledge and part of general cultural

principles. Teachers' tacit knowledge is continually growing knowledge in the course of professional practice, which makes teachers become more mature on teaching along with experience accumulated and adapt to situations with higher ability, influencing and dominating teachers' education conduct. From this point of view, most knowledge of teachers is tacit knowledge, however the tacit knowledge is with high-situations and implicit, and is difficult to express by using simple words. Teachers mainly impart existing knowledge to students rather than help students with constructing knowledge initiatively in the course of traditional education, which results in the issue that teachers their own practical knowledge can not be exchanged and shared in a large scale. To mine teachers' knowledge and make their tacit knowledge explicit, teachers should carry out personal knowledge management.

By analyzing the questionnaires on the survey of Chinese teachers' personal knowledge management, this study finds that, at present, 30 percent of teachers in the survey usually focus on personal knowledge management, 50 percent of teachers in the survey pays normal or even less attention on colleagues' experience. With respect to professional and teaching knowledge, 75 percent of teachers in the survey claim that they achieve little or none professional knowledge since they teach. Some problems exist in terms of Chinese teachers' personal knowledge management according to the survey results.

Knowledge is taken as core competitive power in the current society. The teacher, as an educational operator, often touches much knowledge, if they could manage knowledge efficiently according to knowledge characteristics, their work efficiency will be increased greatly. One of research hotspots of Web 2.0 is personal knowledge management, and Web 2.0 provides a series of effective technologies and platforms for personal knowledge management. Regarding personal knowledge management of

Chinese teachers, this study brings forward the framework and strategies of teachers' personal knowledge management under the condition of Web 2.0 technologies.

TEACHERS' PERSONAL KNOWLEDGE MANAGEMENT

Conception of Personal Knowledge Management

Throughout the examination of some knowledge management literature, it appears that the minority of the literature emphasizes so-called personal knowledge management, which is classified into the perspectives of individualism and socialism. Alley (1999) indicates that personal knowledge management is needed to help knowledge workers to obtain and maintain lifelong preparation for the global knowledge economy. Cope (2000) claims that personal knowledge can be regarded as personal capital which has its value dependent on the demand for certain capabilities in the market. Therefore, to maximize the worth of an individual, he or she needs to take ownership for the development and maintenance of his/her knowledge, which infers the significance of individual commitment. Frand and Hixon (1999) defined personal knowledge management as a conceptual framework that individuals organized and collected important information for a part of individual knowledge. David Skyrme Associates(1999) and Skyrme(1999) described the strategies of personal knowledge management at great length from the point of experiential view. On the contrary, other personal knowledge management practitioners consider not only individuals' endeavours but also the importance of human interaction and collaboration. Galbreath (2000) found that knowledge management should start by means of individuals, then individual units of organizations, then cross-units or cross-fields,

then the global, the last was extended to cooperate with other agencies, and the regular work for knowledge managers was to search, use, create and share. Zuber-Skerritt (2005) advocates a soft methodological model of action learning and action research (ALAR) consisting of a system of seven values and principles and seven matching actions with applications and examples, indicated through the ACTIONS and REFLECT acronym respectively. It is highlighted that the value and practice of ALAR not only carry out the access, communication and management of personal knowledge but also develop individuals' innovative and creative capabilities individually and collectively.

Cope's (2000) assertion of personal knowledge management infers that the notion of individuals' value and competitiveness. Whereas, Zuber-Skerritt (2005) denotes that the focus of personal knowledge management is on individuals' capabilities to access, communicate, create and manage tacit forms of knowledge through the activities of reflection and collaboration under open and non-positivist attitudes and leadership commitment, which brings about individual and group learning and therefore enhances individuals' knowledge and capabilities. The above discussion implies that the promotion of personal knowledge management may result in personal effectiveness and competitiveness in the market.

Connotation of Teachers' Personal Knowledge Management

Some scholars study on the connotation of personal knowledge management. Chin (2002), Chen(2003), Yang(2004) and Lin(2007) find teachers' knowledge management involves the process of knowledge acquisition, storage, sharing, application and creation which are carried out under diverse strategies. Some scholars demonstrate the role and significance of teachers' personal knowledge management, and find that there is a mutual influence relationship between knowledge management and teacher professional growth; teachers who realize their personal knowledge management and professional performance are positively correlated have better knowledge management. And thus, their professional performance will be improved accordingly. (Handal and Lauvas, 1987; Chen, 2002; Zahner, 2002; Kao,2002; Yang,2004; Huang, 2005; Huang,2008).

Through analyzing and generalizing the content of teachers' personal knowledge management based on scholars' studies, this study reaches the conclusion that the core of teachers' personal knowledge management is teachers' professional self-examination and practice by means of the circle of knowledge management processes- knowledge acquisition, knowledge storage, knowledge sharing and communication, knowledge application, knowledge assessment and knowledge creation.

Knowledge acquisition is that teachers achieve knowledge relevant with teachers' business through learning methods, approaches and systems at any time, and information technologies can assist teachers to obtain knowledge. Knowledge classification, integration and storage mean that teachers store knowledge by using Internet or database, process a variety of teaching activities or operation and record them in data files, manage schools or classes' routine data files through digital information classification management, set up teachers' their own teaching files in electronic or written forms, manage schools' old files in digital information to facilitate inquiry, and record colleagues' excellent ideas in written records. Teachers classify and store acquired knowledge, so that the personal knowledge base of teachers can be established. Knowledge sharing and communication mean that teachers should share knowledge by using Internet or database, share knowledge and information through the relationship networks, impart knowledge to colleagues or students through website or e-mail, and develop

group learning and community discussion among teachers. Knowledge application, assessment and creation mean that teachers use personal knowledge in course of teaching, evaluate teachers' individual knowledge in order to examine their own teaching and learning practice so as to amend knowledge, design curriculum materials etc by themselves or with their colleague, which makes tacit knowledge explicit during the course of communication and discussion so as to create new knowledge. The application of knowledge management technologies, tools and platforms can support and assist teachers with their personal knowledge management. By means of personal knowledge management, teachers can ultimately foster their own professional growth, and improve the effectiveness of teaching and learning. See Figure 1.

SURVEY OF CHINESE TEACHERS' PERSONAL KNOWLEDGE MANAGEMENT

The questionnaire is designed for this study, and some teachers are selected from colleges, secondary and primary schools in different provinces of China, the e-mail addresses of teachers are found by teachers' home pages via school websites. 200 questionnaires are distributed via e-mail in order to acquire information and data about Chinese teachers' personal knowledge management, and 93 questionnaires are turned, valid questionnaires are 71. By analyzing the questionnaires and referring to the literatures on Chinese teachers' personal knowledge management, the study finds that, at present, there are some problems in terms of Chinese teachers' personal knowledge management.

Lack of awareness of personal knowledge management. Hargreaves (2000) proposed that teachers' often ignoring their professional knowledge could result in teachers' no sharing and ap-

Figure 1. Connotation of teachers' personal knowledge management

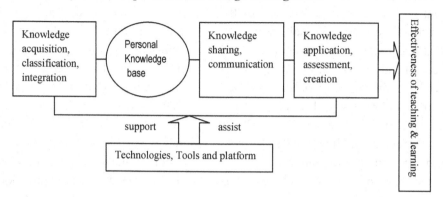

plying these knowledge, in the same way, teachers would not be able to find the new knowledge that teachers need to create when they didn't know which knowledge they lacked. In China, teachers lack the awareness of knowledge management, and are not good at managing the knowledge they already obtained. The survey shows that only 16.7 percent of teachers in the survey write down postscript after teaching, other teachers in the survey never or occasionally reflect on their own day-to-day teaching through this way. 75.3 percent of teachers in the survey believe that they have achieved little or even nothing in terms of professional knowledge since they worked.

Lack of awareness of knowledge sharing. Most of Chinese teachers focus on teaching in accordance with teaching materials, teachers' work turn into the process of operation, so that creative work turn into simple and duplicate work. The main focus of teachers' work is not to find new knowledge, but rather heritage the established, authoritative knowledge. Chinese teachers lack the desire of knowledge sharing. As many as 45.6 percent of teachers in survey have no contact with other teachers in schools, and 32.8 percent of teachers in survey have only occasional contact. For the sake of interest, teachers often reserve individual knowledge, and would not like to impart individual knowledge and experience

to others, refuse to share with others, or do not want to provide the time and resources to support the transmit of knowledge.

Lack of tools and platforms of personal knowledge management. From the point of view of knowledge characteristic, explicit knowledge can be made to public through the written words, or by means of modern technologies to disseminate or communicate directly face-to-face, however sharing explicit knowledge needs a sharing platform and approach. Many teachers lack the knowledge-sharing platform, and don't set up teachers' personal knowledge base, or even can not use computers or surf online. All mentioned above will hold up teachers' knowledge communication and sharing. The communication and discussion via Internet can benefit for making teachers' tacit knowledge explicit, and benefit for teachers' knowledge sharing and creation. Only 64.1 percent of surveyed teachers master and use one or more Web tools to communicate and share knowledge, carry out E-learning and personal knowledge management, the other 35.9 percent of teachers reply that they don't skill in Web tools and platforms of personal knowledge management, even some of teachers don't know Web tools and platforms at all.

Lack of efficiency of utilizing knowledge management tools. At schools, teachers should not only complete their teaching tasks, but also prepare for the title selection, leader inspection, as well as the education department assessment, many teachers do not want to spend time to gather information from the Internet, write postscript and rethink. Blog will not be updated any more after several months since blog opened. Among teachers surveyed, only 25.7 percent of teachers' blog lasts for more than one year.

According to survey result, Chinese teachers should strengthen the awareness of personal knowledge management importance, pay attention to the implementation of personal knowledge management, and actively participate in knowledge sharing and communicating activities so as to enhance the professional growth and increase the efficiency of utilizing knowledge. Meanwhile, it is an important task for Chinese teachers to learn and grasp the effective tools and platforms of personal knowledge management

SUPPORTING FUNCTIONS OF WEB 2.0 ON TEACHERS' PERSONAL KNOWLEDGE MANAGEMENT

At present, the typical technological applications of Web2.0 for personal knowledge management are as following:

- **Blog:** It is Web log, which is chronological record made by individuals or groups. The communication is achieved mainly through track back, message and comment.
- **Wiki:** It is an open network encyclopedia spontaneously self-supported and maintained by netizen.
- **RSS:** It is a simple way by which one Web site can share resource with other Web sites on the basis of XML. RSS users can subscribe Web resources relevant with their interests and researches by client-side tools

supporting RSS or by network subscription service.

- **Tag:** By using Tag, Internet users can collaborate to classify by means of defining key words freely. According to the needs, users make personalized labels and definition on articles or Blog, which is more useful for searching, finding the online articles or making Blog correlation and aggregation.
- **SNS:** It is social network software, which can enlarge the network of personal relationships by means of knowing friends' friends according to the theory of Six Degrees of Separation.
- **Social Bookmark:** It is a kind service preserving the link on the Web page, which allows users to add favorite sites to their network bookmarks at any time, tag and organize bookmarks by more than key words, and share the favorites with others.
- **Diigo.:** By Diiggo, learners can add endorsement directly on Web pages while reading, but not modify the page itself, that is, obtain information and knowledge of multimedia synthesis including text by using of computer and network technologies, and achieve Hypertext reading.
- **Podcasting:** It is composed by iPod and broadcasting. Users can leave video messages or discuss by Podcasting.

How to integrate Web 2.0 with teachers' personal knowledge management, bring the advantages of Web 2.0 into full play so as to make teachers' personal knowledge management to its maximum efficiency by Web 2.0 tools and platforms is the focus of teachers' personal knowledge management under Web 2.0 environment. Teachers can acquire personal knowledge via information push services of RSS, information recommendation services of Bookmark, customizing of Tag, professional search engine; organize knowledge by mutual Tag; create and exchange knowledge by Blog and Wiki; and share knowledge by the technologies and platforms of RSS, social network software and Social Bookmark. Everyone' learning process is completed by cooperation with others, no one in the learning process does not have an impact on other people (Gerald and Rob, 2002). Web 2.0 technologies not only provide a good platform for sharing knowledge, and create a harmonious information environment of social network, but also make individual learning grouping. The establishment of sharing atmosphere is the primary objective of knowledge management. Communication and sharing are useful for making teachers' tacit knowledge explicit. Web 2.0 technologies especially support teachers' communication, sharing, intercourse and discussion by means of Blog, Tag, IM, Wiki, SNS, Podcasting.

TEACHERS' PERSONAL KNOWLEDGE MANAGEMENT FRAMEWORK AND STRATEGIES BASED ON WEB 2.0 TECHNOLOGIES

Teachers' Personal Knowledge Management Framework Based on Web 2.0 Technologies

Some scholars focus on personal knowledge management strategies to promote teacher professional development (Chen, 2003, 2005, 2006; Li, 2005), and find that the effective implementation of personal knowledge management is an important way to promote the professional growth of teachers, and suggest some measures of knowledge management, such as personal knowledge base, e-learning, and e-diary of narrative. Chen(2003)claims that those strategies comprise participating in professional seminars and communities, reading up-to-date educational issues,

making the most of ICT, talking and exchanging teaching portfolios with other teachers, engaging in the activities of peer observation, problem-solving, brainstorming, benchmarking, experimental teaching and educational research and being flexible. Wu and Huang (2006) discuss on knowledge management implementation strategies of four dimensions: human resources, an information or technological infrastructure, a mechanism for knowledge sharing, and an institutional regulatory system. Hu and Chen (2008) focus on the study of knowledge management toolkit, and suggest carry out personal knowledge management with high effectiveness by means of Web-based distributed toolkit.

On the basis of studies of scholars, according to the process of teachers' personal knowledge management including knowledge search, acquirement, classification, integration, storage, application, assessment, sharing, creation, this study presents teachers' personal knowledge management framework based Web 2.0 social software. See Figure 2. The framework of teachers' personal knowledge management is to take knowledge mining, knowledge coding and knowledge transfer as core functionality, and to achieve knowledge production, utilization and sharing by means of Web 2.0 tools and platforms.

In Web 2.0 era, teachers' personal knowledge management based Web 2.0 technologies is to mine knowledge as the basis, transfer knowledge as the key, share knowledge as the essence, apply and create knowledge as the fundamental purpose. By means of Web 2.0 technologies, the model and mentality of teachers' personal knowledge management is developed from simple reading, request and management to writing, contribution and aggregation, and teachers' personal knowledge management advances from passive acceptance, information management forward to active knowledge mining, aggregation and radiation.

Figure 2. Teachers' personal knowledge management framework based Web 2.0 social software

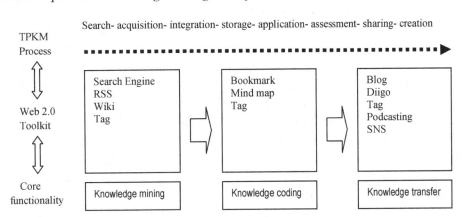

Teachers' Personal Knowledge Management Strategies Based on Web 2.0 Technologies

Search and Acquisition of Teacher Knowledge

Learning is a kind of mechanism through knowledge acquisition, processing, storage, then finally application, in which the most important part is knowledge acquisition (Helleloid and Simonin, 1994). Only when with a lot of knowledge, personal knowledge management is meaningful, the learning, also known as knowledge acquisition, is the first step of knowledge management. The starting point of teachers personal knowledge management is knowledge acquisition, collection and collation, first of all is to determine knowledge resources based on individual needs, then to obtain knowledge by reading periodicals and books, participating in teaching seminars, listening lectures of experts, visiting actual teaching, and searching by Web, and so on. In everyday life and routine, teachers should has own knowledge learning methods and systems, including several types of channels: the accumulation of their own practice;

traditional media; visits and discussions between teachers; training organized by schools or regions; personal networks of teachers; Internet.

One of ways of knowledge acquisition is Internet, searching knowledge by Search Engine, mining data by RSS, sharing collective wisdom by Wiki. Different from traditional search engines, Search Engine as a search tool used in knowledge management can have the following features. Scholar search: access to knowledge unit with high-efficiencies; distribution node search: extract distribution node Web site; trend search: search the trends of study. Search Engine is extremely effective for capturing distribution node and search trends so as to identify source of knowledge, and lay the foundation for knowledge subscription and classification. The primary function of RSS is information push of distribution node and information subscription in the academic circle, on this basis, achieve effective resource mining and subscription of polymer resource. RSS can accelerate the update speed of information resources, send independently booked resources by learner at the first time directly to the destination, RSS is micro-content-based, and easy to constitute a micro-unit knowledge, composed with Tag, it is easy to form knowledge chain taking questions or theme as the center, and lay the foundation for effective organization and integration.

Teacher personal networks is also a way to obtain knowledge. The teacher should make full use of tools at hand such as Outlook, mobile phone, PDA, and other tools. There is another important way is to make full use of existing information systems in schools, such as OA, CRM, and so on. SNS can be a tool to expand individual teacher's networks, under Web 2.0 environment, each user has own Blog, Wiki, or Social Bookmark. Users can connect together by Tag, RSS, or IM, e-mail and so on. According the theory of Six Degrees of Separation, in the networks, it is possible to get to know any strange friends, and can be able to achieve the goal as long as through a maximum of 6 friends in the course. Each individual's social circles have been enlarged and finally into a large-scale networks.

Integration and Storage of Teacher Knowledge

The first step of knowledge management is knowledge acquisition, however it is also important to manage those material and information. Therefore, the second step of teacher personal knowledge management is to establish their own knowledge system frame which will assist teachers to store knowledge systemically to facilitate fetching quickly in future. Due to the lack of systematic classification structure, it will waste a lot of time in terms of integrating knowledge and creating knowledge in the near future. Teachers can set up personal knowledge base, and put all knowledge resources owned into the personal knowledge management system according to classification, in order to facilitate application in practice and learning.

The personal knowledge management based on personal network learning system is a process to manage, integrate and make use of the objective information resources obtained in learning process and knowledge resources arising from knowledge production process, and makes personal knowledge systematized so as to build personal knowledge base (Schreiber and Harbo, 2004). The storage of teacher personal knowledge includes non-electronic data storage and electronic data storage. Non-electronic data is stored in individual study or studio space, as well as admission device files of data. Electronic data is stored in the hard disk space and the planning directory. Teachers also can store knowledge in the Internet and Web database.

Web 2.0 provides the technologies of knowledge coding and storage for teacher knowledge management, teachers can take Social Bookmark as knowledge warehouse to make discrete resources connected, and centrally manage resources of distribution node. In fact, every social software has a variety of functions. Bookmark, for example, is a sharing tool of collecting Web pages, can become a knowledge warehouse when sorting and storing Web pages. Bookmark can be used for the storage of knowledge, and also be able to effectively make discrete resources aggregated and management distribution node. Learners can access to their favorite pages at any time, and share other people's Bookmark, also can recommend content among teachers based on the similarity of knowledge. Constructing Mind Map can form knowledge chain which center is the theme, which makes resources clustered so that heterogeneous resources orderly integrated through sorting. Mind Map also can be shared, by interactive Mind Map knowledge can be effectively integrated and organized, learners can build their own personalized knowledge storage that is consistent with personal custom of cognition. Based on Mind Map, teachers can communicate and share with the others to create new dynamic resources.

Application, Sharing and Innovation of Teacher Knowledge

The essence of knowledge management is knowledge sharing and innovation. Personal knowledge management should not only focus on knowledge accumulation but not pay attention to the use of existing knowledge. The intent of knowledge learning and accumulation is to apply knowledge and create new knowledge in the course of knowledge application and communication. The application of teacher knowledge is a cycle process, after learning new knowledge, teachers apply new knowledge to teaching and research so as to solve the problems existing in terms of teaching, and then form new knowledge through rethink, and then practice again. In this way, the knowledge innovation can be achieved through repeat way. Using existing knowledge to achieve knowledge innovation is the purpose of teacher personal knowledge management.

Social engines refer to establishing frameworks so that information can flow through appropriate channels inside entire organizations, that is, emphasizing social interaction and communication with other teachers, cooperating closely with each other to accelerate personal growth. Social engines and dialogue platforms are suggested to establish for individual teacher. This point is identified according to the characteristic of teacher knowledge, since tacit knowledge accounts for a large proportion of teacher personal knowledge, however the acquisition of tacit knowledge can only transfer unobtrusively and imperceptibly in the course of communication of groups. Therefore, teachers should be actively and positively to contact with other teachers in order to communicate with respect to teaching experience and expertise knowledge. The knowledge transmit in teacher community not only enhances the value of knowledge, but also stimulate the capability of personal knowledge creation.

Web 2.0 technologies provide tools to enhance the communication and sharing of study and research, promoting the rethink capability. Teachers use Blog to record and express their feelings about teaching and learning, making ideas and intellectual sparks preserved. After a period of knowledge management, teachers can further realize their own mental models so as to do self-evaluation and rethink to achieve self transcend. Web 2.0 provides teachers a self-learning platform through which teachers can fully display their own learning and cognitive capability crossing the boundaries of time and space to carry out communication, discussion, exploration, cooperation to solve problems of teaching and learning, thereby to achieve the sharing of experience and wisdom. Teachers can comprehend other people's knowledge so that practical problems can be solved smoothly, making teachers generate the actuation of learning and creating new knowledge during the course of community communication, which can foster the innovation capacity of individual teacher. Hereon, Web 2.0 technologies provide teachers with the sharing and communication tools and platforms. Teachers share knowledge and rethink via Blog, exchange knowledge through Tag, expand social connections by SNS, communicate with each other by IM, such MSN, OICQ, leave video message or discussion by Podcasting, evaluate knowledge by Diigo, namely real-time mark and social comments.

CONCLUSION

Web 2.0 provides a series of effective technologies and platforms for teachers' personal knowledge management. Regarding personal knowledge management of Chinese teachers, this study presents the framework and strategies of teachers' personal knowledge management under the condition of Web 2.0 environment:

- At present, the typical technological applications of Web2.0 for personal knowledge management are Blog, Wiki, RSS, Tag, SNS, Social Bookmark, Diigo, Podcasting, and so on, which can facilitate teachers' personal knowledge management during the process of knowledge acquisition, integration, storage, application, assessment, sharing and creation. Communication and sharing are useful for making teachers' tacit knowledge explicit. Web 2.0 technologies especially support teachers' communication, sharing and discussion by means of Blog, Tag, IM, Wiki, SNS, Podcasting.

- The framework of teachers' personal knowledge management is to take knowledge mining, knowledge coding and knowledge transfer as core functionality, teachers can carry out personal knowledge management by means of Web 2.0 toolkit during the entire process of knowledge management. By means of Web 2.0 technologies, the model and mentality of teachers' personal knowledge management is developed from simple reading, request and management to writing, contribution and aggregation.

- Chinese teachers should strengthen the awareness of personal knowledge management, and actively participate in knowledge sharing and communicating activities so as to increase the efficiency of knowledge application and create new knowledge. Chinese teachers should utilize the effective tools and platforms of personal knowledge management. Some strategies of teachers' personal knowledge management in terms of knowledge acquisition, storage, integration, application, sharing and innovation are presented in this study, teachers can efficiently carry out knowledge management by means of Web 2.0 tools and platforms.

REFERENCES

Alley, L. R. (1999). Diverting a crisis in global human and economic development: A new transnational model for lifelong continuous learning and personal knowledge management. *Higher Education in Europe, 24*(2), 187-195.

Chen, J. T. (2003). *A study on feasible strategies and impeditive factors for elementary teachers' application of knowledge management in Tainan County.* Master dissertation, National Kaohsiung Teachers University.

Chen, M. Y. (2002). The future development of personal knowledge management on teacher professional. *Secondary Education, 53*(3), 84-93.

Chen, M. Y. (2005). Teachers college students' personal knowledge management and it's impact on professional learning and development. *Journal of National Taiwan Normal University, 50*(2), 181-202.

Chen, M. Y. (2006). Application research of teacher personal knowledge management in the professional development: Nine-year curriculum as an example. *Curriculum and Teaching, 9*(1), 99-122.

Chin, Y. J. (2002). *Teachers' knowledge management in elementary schools: Analyses at individual and organisational levels.* Master dissertation, National Taipei Teachers' College.

Cope, M. (2000). *Know your value? Value what you know.* Essex: Financial Times Prentice Hall Prentice Hall.

David Skyrme Associates (1999). *Knowledge management assessment: A practical tool from David Skyrme Associates,* December 15, 2000, http://www.skyme.com/tools/index.htm

Edvinsson, L., & Malone, M. S. (1997). *Intellectual capital: Realizing your company's true value by finding its hidden brainpower.* New York: Harper Collins.

Frand, J., & Hixon, C. (1999). *Personal knowledge management: Who, what, why, when, where, how.* Retrieved June 25, 2007. http://www.anderson. ucla.edu/faculty/jason.frand/researcher/speeches/ PKM.htm.

Galbreath, J. (2000). Knowledge management technology in education: An overview. *Educational Technology, 40*(5), 28-33.

Gerald, S. E., & Rob, P. (2002). Creating shared knowledge: Instructional knowledge management systems. *Educational Technology & Society, 5*(1), 100-104.

Handal, G., & Lauvas, P. (1987). *Promoting reflective teaching: Supervision in practice.* London: Open University Press.

Hargreaves, D. H. (2000). The knowledge creating school. *British Journal of Education Studies, 47*(2), 122-144.

Helleloid, D., & Simonin, B. (1994). Organizational learning and a firm's core competence. In G. Hamel & A. Heene (Eds.), *Competence-Based Competitive,* Wiley, New York (pp. 213-239).

Hu, Y-W., & Chen, M-F. (2008). A knowledge management method which based on Web 2.0 distributed toolkit. *Modern Educational Technology, 16*(6), 98-101.

Huang, S. Y. (2005). The Relationships among Professional Growth, Organizational Enablers, and Knowledge Management for Primary School Teachers. *MCU Thesys,* http://ethesys.lib.mcu.edu. tw/ETD-db/ETD-search/view_etd?URN=etd-0822105-041457, pp. 27-57.

Huang, N. S. (2008). A study on elementary school teachers' knowledge management and teachers' professionalism in Kaohsiung city. *NPUE. Thesys,* http://etd.npue.edu.tw/ETD-db/ETD-search-c/view_etd?URN=etd-0118108-084133

Kao, Y. J. (2002). A study of the Relation of Teachers' Knowledge Management, Learning Style, Professional Growth and Professional Performance in the Elementary Schools. *Electronic Theses and Dissertations System,* http://etds.ncl. edu.tw/theabs/site/sh/detail_result.jsp?id=090N KNU0332047, pp. 122-136.

Li, Q. (2005). Teacher professional growth and knowledge management in the age of information. *Zhejiang Education Science, 5,* 23-24.

Lin, Y-H-K. (2007). *Teachers' Personal Knowledge Management: Theoretical Foundations and Building Blocks,* May 18, 2008, http://www. atee2007.org.uk/docs/LinYHK.doc

Nonaka, I., & Takeuchi, H. (1995). *The Knowledge-Creating Company.* Oxford: Oxford University Press.

O'Dell, C., & Grayson, C. J. (1998). If only we knew what we know: Identification and transfer of internal best practice. *California Management Review, 40*(3), 154-174.

OECD (1996). *The knowledge-based economy report.* Paris.

Schreiber, T., & Harbo, K. (2004). Information literacy and personal knowledge management. Paper presented at the *Nord I&D, Knowledge and Change, 12th Nordic Conference on Information and Documentation,* Aalborg, Denmark, (pp. 106-114).

Skyrme, D. J. (1999). *Knowledge Networking: Creating the Collaborative Enterprise.* Oxford: Oxford University Press.

Wu, C-S., & Huang, H-C. (2006) A Study of Knowledge Management in Elementary Schools: Advantageous Situations, Difficulties, and Strategies. *Bulletin of Educational Research, 52*(2), 33-65.

Yang, S. P. (2005). *A Study on the Relationship between Elementary School Teachers' Personal Knowledge Management and Their Professional Performance.* Institute of Education Management and Administration, National University of Tainan, unpublished Master thesis, http://lib.nutn.edu.tw, (pp. 69-74).

Zahner, J. (2002). Teachers explore knowledge management and e-learning as models for professional development. *TechTrends, 46*(3), 11-16.

Zuber-Skerritt, O. (2005). A model of values and actions for personal knowledge management. *The Journal of Workplace Learning, 17*(1/2), 49-64.

Chapter VII
CUSENT:
Social Sentiment Analysis Using Semantics for Customer Feedback

Ángel García-Crespo
Universidad Carlos III de Madrid, Spain

Ricardo Colomo-Palacios
Universidad Carlos III de Madrid, Spain

Myriam Mencke
Universidad Carlos III de Madrid, Spain

Juan M. Gómez-Berbís
Universidad Carlos III de Madrid, Spain

ABSTRACT

The current chapter introduces CUSENT, a tool for semantics-enhanced sentiment analysis of customer opinions expressed in corporate blogs. The research work presents the examination of emotions and sentiments from the perspective of information systems, and, in particular, provides a review of the principal efforts for the conceptualization of emotions and sentiments in texts. Subsequently, a description of the proposed architecture of the platform is outlined. The authors aim to contribute a solution which automates the analysis of customer opinions in company blogs that relies on existing techniques, but further exploits these methods to store and reuse customer feedback. The novel combination of opinion mining with an ontology of emotions can thus be used in organizational creation and innovation processes, which characterize the new forms of communication derived from the institutional and commercial use of Web 2.0.

INTRODUCTION

The Internet is changing the forms in which people relate among each other. Many of the tools which are unique to the Internet, such as blogs, wikis or virtual worlds, are used by people as the fundamental tools to construct relationships. According to O'Reilly (2005) a fundamental principle of Web 2.0 is that users add value by generating content through these applications, resulting in network effects among the community of users. This circumstance is instigating more and more organizations to attempt to exploit the gains of Web 2.0. In this new scenario, collaboration and co-creation with customers has emerged through habitual use of Web 2.0, by both companies and clients alike (Vargo & Lusch, 2004). According to Manyika, Roberts & Sprague (2007), in the environment of Information Technology related technology trends, co-creation, alongside the use of customers as innovators and making businesses from information, has been termed as one of the trends to watch. It is precisely these three trends which comprise the key motivation for the current research.

In the first place, in relation to distributed co-creation, today many companies involve customers and other players in the creation of new products. Current technology enables companies to benefit from partial externalization of the co-creation process. In the current research, the aim is to extend the process of co-creation, delegating the control to customers, as illustrated in the work by Prahalad & Krishnan (2008). The work aims to benefit from one of the most important assets held by these fundamental stakeholders: their opinion oriented towards co-creation.

In the second place, it is aimed to exploit the innovation capacities of customers. Involving customers in design, testing and the after-sales process can be used as an element to gain better insights into customer needs and behavior, and may be able to cut the cost of acquiring custom-ers, engender greater loyalty, and speed up development cycles (Manyika, Roberts & Sprague, 2007). By means of the application of technologies characteristic of the Web 2.0, a further objective of the research is to benefit from the metadata generated by such a platform of interaction and communication, dealing with some of its weaknesses, but at the same time benefiting from its undeniable advantages.

A final objective can be defined as the following: Making businesses from information. More concretely, the task is to exploit the interactions produced in Web 2.0 in order to generate business, using the capacities for processing and analysis of information provided by the technology. According to a study by McKinsey consultants (McKinsey, 2007) where 2,847 executives were interviewed, respondents inform that Web 2.0 technologies are strategic and that they plan to increase these investments, moreover, they say they are using Web 2.0 technologies to communicate with customers and business partners and to encourage collaboration inside the company. More precisely, executives inform blogs are also frequently mentioned as a channel to communicate with customers and, in some cases, critics.

This is the acting environment of CUSENT. Applying text analysis methods, an analysis has been carried out of the responses which clients post on a determined organizational blog. The use of semantics enables the categorization of sentiments in an ontology which is populated with emotions, which CUSENT detects from the results of a text classification algorithm constructed to perform sentiment analysis. The subsequent use of the information extracted aids innovation processes by means of the active support of customers.

The remainder of the chapter has been structured as follows. Initially, the basic concepts of sentiments, emotions and semantics are outlined. Secondly, the principal initiatives for sentiment analysis are discussed. The next section sketches how the CUSENT architecture and implementation fits in the picture. Lastly, the principal conclusions of the paper are presented, and some suggestions for resolving the problems encountered are outlined, as well as proposals for future research.

SENTIMENTS, EMOTIONS AND SEMANTICS

The study of human emotions and passions is a classical theme in the history of thought. Disciplines such as psychology, among others, have widely adopted the legacy of the study of sentiments and emotions initiated by philosophers. The first work in which the concept was introduced is The Phileb by Plato. The Greek author compares pain and pleasure in the dialogue between Socrates and Protarcus, in order to illustrate his theory of emotions. Subsequent to Plato, there were many significant and important philosophers who studied the theme of emotions: Aristotle, Descartes, Hobbes, Spinoza, Kant, Schopenhauer, Heidegger, to cite some of the principal ones.

In previous research on emotion, a debate exists regarding its nature. Some theories focus on the aspects shared by distinct cultures, that is, they stress the universal characteristics of emotion, (e.g. Plutchik, 1980; Ekman, 1984; Tomkins, 1984), while other schools of thought maintain that it is cultural factors which principally determine emotional experiences (e.g. Solomon, 1976; Levy, 1984; Harré, 1986). Taking into account that the current work does not have as objective to re-debate previous theories, the first focus mentioned above will be adopted. This supports the aim of being able to carry out a universal semantic categorization by means of the use of ontologies. This assumption of the universality of emotions, following Russell (1991) has been adopted by diverse streams. One tradition stems from Darwin's argument that the communication of emotion is part of our biological heritage. Others, stemming

from rationalist philosophy, claim that most of our concepts and emotions are innate. Finally, there are other authors, like Johnson-Laird and Oatley (1989), that assert that emotions such as fear or anger are indefinable semantic primitives. In plain words, a semantic primitive is a term used to explain other terms or concepts, but which cannot itself be explained by other terms. Concepts on emotion and semantic primitives can be found in the work of Wierzbicka (1992). In sum, according to Russell (1991), it is assumed that what varies with culture are events that surround the emotion. Emotion itself is universal.

Determining a unique definition of the term "emotion" represents a complicated task. In research work at the beginning of the 1980s, Kleinginna & Kleinginna (1981) found 92 definitions and classified them into 11 categories. Other authors pointed out that "almost everyone except the psychologist knows what an emotion is…". Leaving aside the discussion concerning the concreteness and universality of the definition of the concept of emotion, for the purpose of the current work, the definition proposed by Izard (1977) will be adopted. This theory was considered the theory which most accurately combined the set of elements that constitute emotion for this research. Izard (1977) claimed that emotion is composed of three aspects: a) the experience or conscious feeling of emotion, b) the processes that occur in the brain and nervous system, and c) the observable extensible patterns of emotion. In the case of this research, we will use written patterns.

As we are dealing with written text, it must be assumed that languages differ in the number of words they provide to categorize emotions. In the English language, Wallace and Carson (1973) found over 2,000 words for categories of emotion, but as definitions may differ from study to study, Storm & Storm (1987), found only 577 English words concerning emotion. The enormous quantity of words thus requires the categorization of terms. In response to this situation, Storm &

Storm (1987) constructed a hierarchical taxonomy (positive, neutral and negative) of semantically homogeneous terms that are associated with specific emotions. Wallace & Carson (1973) ordered their classification over 2,000 words in 29 groups. Other authors consider that basic emotions exist. Ekman (1972) lists 6 basic emotions: sadness, happiness, anger, fear, disgust, surprise. Stemming from this research, other authors have attempted to identify basic emotions, using various criteria for the task (E.g. Plutchik, 1980; Tomkins, 1984; Ortony & Turner, 1990; Parrott, 2001)

For the purpose of the current research work, it was an obvious selection that the Hierarchy of consumer emotions would be used, proposed by Laros & Steenkamp (2005). This taxonomy classifies emotions into three levels. The first level represents the valance of emotions, that is, positive and negative effect. The next level is considered as the basic emotion level, and the lowest, subordinate, level consists of groups of individual emotions that form a category named after the most typical emotion of that category. Figure 1 shows the hierarchy of consumer emotions.

Given that research into emotions in the customer domain is not a new field, (see for example, Bagozzi, Gopinath & Nyer, 1999; Huang, 2001; Zeelenberg & Pieters, 2004; van Dolen, de Ruyter & Lemmink, 2004; Gountas & Gountas,

2007; Schoefer & Diamantopoulos, 2008), the current work is situated along these research lines, but it has been substantially enhanced by the advent of the Web 2.0. This new web offers limitless opportunities for companies to engage their customers (Eikelmann, Hajj & Peterson, 2008), for example, Southwest airlines' s blog has received more than 6,300 comments since it started in April 2006, in response to little more than 250 posts. Rather than ignoring or fearing criticism or opinion generated in Web 2.0 forums, companies should seize Web 2.0 tools to respond and gain competitive advantage (Eikelmann, Hajj & Peterson, 2008). It is in this environment where the objective of the research is focused, responding to stimuli initiated by the customer in an adequate and organized manner.

In order to be able to categorize the opinions of clients in a definitive and standard way, the use of ontologies and the Semantic Web is fundamental for fulfilling the aims of this work. In recent years, several research works have focused on emotion recognition. Some authors have analyzed the recognition of emotions from speech, facial expressions, text and mixed scenarios. In the domain of the detection of emotions in text, many initiatives have emerged (E.g. Subasic & Huettner, 2001; Boucouvalas, 2002). The use of ontologies in this domain is a natural progression

Figure 1. Hierarchy of consumer emotions

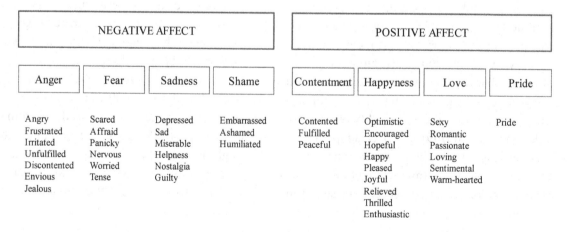

and constitutes an advancement of this type of research.

Ontologies (Fensel, 2001) are the technological cornerstones of the Semantic Web, a term coined by (Berners-Lee, Hendler & Lassila, 2001). Ontologies provide structured vocabularies that describe a formal specification of a shared conceptualization. The fundamental aim of the Semantic Web is to answer the ever-growing need for data integration on the Web. Ontologies based on Description Logics paradigm include definitions of concepts –OWL classes–, roles –OWL properties– and individuals. In this scenario, the use of ontologies for modeling emotions in a broad sense has many examples, such as those proposed by López, Gil, García, Cearreta & Garay (2008). Additionally, there is a W3C Emotion Markup Language Incubator Group (http://www.w3.org/2005/Incubator/emotion/), working on the definition of valid representations of those aspects of emotional states that appear to be relevant for a number of use cases in emotion scenarios.

In the field of speech recognition, work has been performed by Francisco, Gervás & Peinado (2007), and in the concrete environment of analysis of emotion in text, work was carried out by Mathieu (2005). An amplification of the ontology developed by the latter author has been proposed, with the objective of containing the Hierarchy of consumer emotions proposed by Laros & Steenkamp (2005).

SENTIMENT & EMOTION ANALYSIS

Although the research field referring to the extraction of information which represents sentiments in text has been termed "sentiment analysis", it fundamentally refers to extraction of the entities which indicate emotion in text. The prevailing approaches to the task of sentiment analysis are based on machine learning methods, used in the research area of Natural Language Processing (NLP) defined as Information Extraction. Ap-

plied in NLP, the principal objective of machine learning is the classification of electronic documents based on defined linguistic features, in the current application, words or phrases which indicate the sentiment of a text. A machine learning technique constructs a text classifier by an automated process where the classifier 'learns' pre-defined categories, by extracting features from texts in pre-defined categories, and associating the features with these classes (Lee, 2003). In this research framework, the text classes into which each customer opinion is classified are thus automatically aligned with the equivalent classes in the ontology, and input according to polarity strength; polarity strength will be detailed further in Section 3.1. A machine learning framework can comprise various approaches. For example, probabilistic classifiers, support vector machines, neural networks, and latent semantic indexing. The following section details machine learning techniques, and discusses the application of machine learning approaches to different problems in sentiment analysis, also referred to as opinion mining, or sentiment tracking.

Sentiment Analysis: Techniques

A number of machine learning approaches have been applied to sentiment tracking problems in diverse disciplines such as marketing, political science, and economics. Sentiment analysis determines the sentiment of an author towards products, companies, specific political ideologies, or any other objects, by extracting the semantic features which define the relationship between the author and the object. It is precisely these semantic features which are required for the ontology used in the system. For the current work, the objective was to apply sentiment analysis for customer product opinion mining. As sentiment analysis is an application of machine learning, any machine learning technique, such as probabilistic methods based on Naive Bayes, support vector machines, and Latent Semantic Indexing may be applied to determine the sentiment category of texts in a corpus. For example, the sentiment category of a corpus may be positive or negative. The sections which follow describe some of the most widely used methods for sentiment analysis.

Naïve Bayes

The Naive Bayes probabilistic framework applies Bayes theorem to calculate the probability of a class given the document in question. For example, given document X whose class is not known, and a particular class C, the probability of a class C given document X is calculated by Bayes' theorem:

$$P(C|X) = P(X|C)P(C) / P(X)$$

In the above equation, P(C|X) is referred to as the posterior probability of the class C based on the data, document X. P(X|C) is the posterior probability of a document given a class. P(C) is the probability of a class. This probability is estimated and known as the class prior parameters, where the parameters are estimates of a particular probability. P(X) is the probability, or likelihood, of a document. The key characteristic of a Naïve Bayes classifier is the assumption that the probabilities of the features are independent of the class. In the case of text classification, the features refer to the words in the documents, and the class refers to the category, for example, as mentioned above, positive or negative.

Latent Semantic Indexing

In the SVM model, which will be explained in further detail in the subsequent section, frequency vectors are normalized for text length and may be allocated importance weights. When a feature selection process is performed as part of any text categorization technique, Zipf's law is the factor that underlies normalization and the assignment

of weights to features in the SVM calculations[1]. However, even when weights are assigned to features, the construction of vectors is based on the assumption that the features are independently distributed. The existence of semantic relations in text such as synonymous and polysemous words breaches this assumption. Latent Semantic Indexing (LSI) is a model of text categorization which attempts to overcome the presence of ambiguous lexical relations in texts. Sebastiani (2002) describes LSI as a method of dimensionality reduction by term extraction which exploits the inter-relationships between synonymous, near-synonymous and polysemous lexical relations. It is viewed as a dimension reduction technique because it is a similar term extraction model to SVMs, but the vectors have a lower-dimensional space, as their dimensions are generated from the patterns of co-occurrence in the dimensions of the original vectors. The terms extracted represent the 'latent' semantic relations in the texts. Given that support vector machines are the method used in the current architecture, they will now be reviewed in more detail.

Support Vector Machines

The SVM algorithm exploits the use of vectors which model the distributions of features in texts. WordNet was used to populate the feature vectors for the categories (WordNet, 2008). Each vector is a point in a n-dimensional space (n is the number of features), which can hold either a Boolean value signifying whether or not the feature exists in the document, or the frequency of occurrence of the feature (Lee, 2003). The objective of SVM modeling is to define the optimal line (hyperplane) which divides groups of vectors into separate categories. In its simplest form, SVMs can be used to differentiate two categories. The support vectors are the vectors in closest proximity to the line. The task is to determine which of these vectors best describe the division between the two categories. Diederich & Kindermann (2003) refer to the distance of the hyperplane which separates the two categories as the maximum interclass distance, the margin. They present the model below as an outline of the algorithm of all statistical techniques for text classification, which is also applicable to SVMs.

- **Feature Selection:** Identification of Features
- **Model Selection:** Selection of suitable distributions describing feature values
- **Learning:** Estimation of free parameters for different categories from available data
- **Classification:** Selection of a potential category for a new text

The Model selection phase corresponds to the defining of the vectors. The division of clusters of vectors into categories just described above can be expressed mathematically, where each class (of a linear SVM) is defined as:

$$u = w * x + b$$

w is the normal vector to the hyperplane, and x is the input vector. The optimal margin is expressed as:

$$\text{minimize } \frac{1}{2} \| w \|^2 \text{ subject to } y_i(w * x_i + b) \geq 1, \forall i$$

x_i is the i-th training example and $y_i \in \{-1, 1\}$ is the correct output of the SVM for the i-th training example.

Sentiment Analysis: Overall View

Viewing sentiment analysis as an application of text categorization, the texts to be categorized are usually represented as a "bag of words". The "bag of words" is a set of features predefined by the user of the method which denote positive or negative sentiment. The features are word n-grams; for example, the word unigram 'great' to denote positive sentiment, or the word bigram "awfully boring" to indicate negative sentiment. The type of n-grams (or units) which are selected to represent a text usually are usually contingent upon which n-grams the user of the machine learning technique chooses to test their accuracy in classifying the sentiment of a corpus of texts. One type of unit proposed by Hiroshi & Tetsuya (2004) is the sentiment unit, which when culled from a sentence represents a single sentiment towards an object. In the example below, the word [favorable] in the parse 1(a) embodies one sentiment; favorable.

It has excellent lens, but the price is too high. I don't think the quality of the recharger has any problem. (1)

[favorable] excellent (lens) (1a)
[unfavorable] high (price) (1b)
[favorable] problematic+neg (recharger) (1c)

Once the units have been extracted from each corpus text (this may be done using a concordancing algorithm, for further explanation regarding concordancing, see Mencke (2007)), the concordanced texts are input to a machine learning method.

All of the techniques prevalent in sentiment classification or opinion mining (OM) can be summarized as attempting to effectuate three essential tasks, postulated by Esuli and Sebastiani (2006). These are listed below.

Determining Text SO (Subjective/Objective)-Polarity

In the sentence above, SO stands for the binary categories Subjective and Objective.

The goal is to verify whether the text is a statement of fact or opinion; whether it expresses, for example, a product opinion, or contains exclusively factual information. Ideally, the corpus texts collected as input to the method should be subjective, for example, film reviews, customer feedback on a particular product, or political opinions.

Determining Text PN (Positive/ Negative)-Polarity

Having established the text as Subjective, the method of analysis determines whether the opinion expressed is Positive or Negative. This step corresponds to the actual implementation of the machine learning method, for example, a Naive Bayes classifier, to classify the texts as positive or negative.

Determining the Strength of the PN-Polarity

The final step is to gauge the extent of positive or negative opinion based on, for example, benchmarks such as Strongly Agree, Agree, Mildly Agree, Agree, Mildly Disagree, Disagree or Strongly Disagree (When the text is in response to a particular opinion).

In the section which follows, some of the problems in sentiment analysis are discussed.

Sentiment Analysis: Problems

Given the idiosyncratic nature of human language, it has emerged that algorithms which classify sentiment are frequently confronted by numerous problems due to the variation exhibited in human expression, and must be tailored to cope with such "fuzzy" instances in the most accurate form possible.

In fact, even though a success rate comparable to success rates in other text classification tasks is achievable using traditional methods, such as Naïve Bayes, maximum enthropy, and support vector machines, applied by Pang et al. (2002),

more sophisticated techniques are required for performance improvement. Pang et al. (2002) point out some of the reasons which provoke inaccuracies, introducing the "thwarted expectations" phenomenon. This occurs where an author states the positive aspects of a film, which could equally arise regarding product opinions. However, the author proceeds to state that these "positive" or good aspects did not live up to expectations. In particular, Pang et. al. (2002) provide the example below, which successfully highlights linguistic quirks not detectable by traditional computational algorithms.

This film should be brilliant. It sounds like a great plot, the actors are first grade, and the supporting cast is good as well, and Stallone is attempting to deliver a good performance. However, it can't hold up.

In the current system, performance is tested without considering this characteristic of customer jargon, which decreases performance. However, it should be mentioned that until now there are few text classification algorithms which are able to perform such detection, if any. Therefore, precision and recall rates should be considered relative to the performance of other sentiment analysis systems. Pang et. al. (2002) suggest the application of deeper discourse analysis, a linguistic technique which could be explored for future versions of the current application.

In spite of the difficulty in achieving precision when performing sentiment analysis due to noisy data, previous research has demonstrated that it is still possible to achieve a scientifically acceptable level of accuracy in sentiment analysis when compared with similar studies in text classification evaluation. In particular, in the noisy domain of customer feedback, Gamon (2004) used support vector machines to build large feature vectors combined with reduced feature sets, and concluded that the highest classification success rate achievable was 85.47%, as indicated by the F-measure. The corpus used was comprised of 11399 customer feedback texts from a Global Support Services Survey, and 29485 documents from a Knowledge Base survey.

CUSENT: ARCHITECTURE

In this section, we will present the CUSENT architecture by introducing a number of software components that use the technologies described in previous sections. Then we discuss a use case scenario where the advantages of CUSENT are outlined.

Fundamentally, an architecture is the set of significant decisions about the organization of a software system, the selection of the structural elements and their interfaces of which the system is composed, together with the behavior as specified in the collaboration among those elements, the composition of these structural and behavioral elements into progressively larger subsystems and the architectural style that guides this organization: these elements, their interfaces, their collaborations and their composition.

In CUSENT, the architecture is composed of a number of software components with interfaces and collaborations that we will detail in what follows:

- *Sentiment Crawler:* A web crawler (also known as a web spider) is an application or automated script which browses the Web in a methodical, automated manner. In this case, our Sentiment Crawler spiders the structured data in blogs or Web 2.0 sites, by hoarding semi-structured information and processing it.
- *Sentiment Analyzer:* This component uses the techniques described in Section 3 to perform Sentiment Analysis over the crawled data. The approach is systematically performed with various strategies in order

to find out which one is the optimal. The first outcome of this software component is a dataset of structured data, referred to one particular product on a one-to-one basis. Assuming that there is a lot of information about a Blackberry Bold on the set of resources where the Sentiment Crawler has been pooling out data, this harvested data will go through the Sentiment Analyzer to ensure all the information is related with the specific product, the Blackberry Bold. The second and final outcome is the actual relationship between those sets and the hierarchy of costumer emotions described in Section 2. The Sentiment Analyzer populates instances of the ontology associating the concepts of the hierarchy with the sets of structured data.
- *Product Feedback Manager:* Once the ontology is populated, we have a knowledge-base where to use inference based on the underlying logical formalism of the ontology.
- *Ontology Repository:* This component deals with the ontology storage.

In Figure 2 the logical layer diagram in which CUSENT is divided can be observed. A 4-layered architecture was selected because of its adaptability, flexibility and reusability. The system was

Figure 2. CUSENT architecture

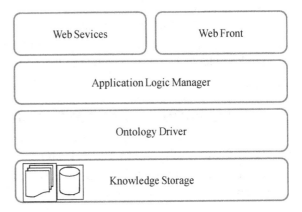

97

developed in an incremental and evolutionary manner that needed those main characteristics to grant a successful fulfillment. A four-layered architecture also offers the advantage of easing the localization of errors, since it avoids the transfer of errors between layers.

In the upper layer, the presentation, a component for web services was included. Logically it is an element that does not belong to this layer, but was included for simplicity. It also shows the possibility of communication with external systems, using programmatic interfaces.

The Application Layer is the responsible for managing all the application logic. In fact, we separated the application logic from business logic, allowing a better decoupling of responsibilities in the final system. The layer will be composed of interfaces that will offer a complete coverage of all the functionality defined for the system. In this application layer, the Sentiment Crawler and the Sentiment Analyzer are located.

The Business Layer will handle all CUSENT business logic, which, in this case, means the ontology handling and its managing. In order to ease the handling, the system uses existing reasoners that are in charge of implementing all operations over ontologies allowed. Initially, the framework chosen for CUSENT was Jena, although due to its lack in inference capacities, Pellet was also included. The system was specifically defined to allow a flexible inclusion of new frameworks that could give a better performance in required processes. In this layer, the Product Feedback Manager is located.

Finally, the Data layer is in charge of handling ontologies in a low level, which means, it manages the knowledge storage contained in the system.

CONCLUSION AND FUTURE WORK

In this paper we present CUSENT, an environment for the analysis of the opinions revealed by customers in corporate blogs. The categorization

of emotions was carried out by means of an ontology in which relevant indicators of emotions and context were integrated. The results of the research will be used as support for improved analysis of the behavior and reactions of customers, and additionally, to achieve a better integration of clients in the co-creation and innovation process. This is realized by improved processing and use of the capacities of information in blogs, and the interactive aspects which Web 2.0 has brought to corporate environments.

From the experience gained from the research, it is proposed that empirical studies are carried out to automatically measure the emotions of customers. Such studies could be used to reveal the weights of different emotions in customer commentary, and additionally, carry out a factorial analysis to elucidate whether any of the factors which occur in the opinion forming process hold significant qualities with respect to others. For example, with regard to gender analysis, the time of the commentary, relative to sector, product typologies, product success, among other factors. Another future task which the current work calls for is to carry out an analysis of opinion profiles which enables the construction of a taxonomy of users and opinions.

One of the final objectives of future work is to integrate a more complex linguistic analysis to the system in order to improve precision. This objective will also be contingent upon other research developments in this field. A further task which will aid in implementing performance measures is to test the performance of the other sentiment analysis techniques described in this paper on the output and consequent success rate of the system.

REFERENCES

Bagozzi, R. P., Gopinath, M., & Nyer, P. U. (1999). The role of emotions in marketing. *Journal of the Academy of Marketing Science, 27*(2), 184-206.

Berners-Lee T., Hendler J., & Lassila O. (2001). The Semantic Web. *Scientific American, 284*(5), 34-44.

Boucouvalas, A. C. (2002). Real time text-to-emotion engine for expressive internet communications. In G. Riva & F. Davide (Eds.), *Emerging Communication: Studies on New Technologies and Practices in Communication.* IOS Press.

Bussler, C. (2008). Is Semantic Web Technology Taking the Wrong Turn? *IEEE Internet Computing, 12*(1), 75-79.

Diederich, J., & Kindermann, J. (2003). Authorship Attribution with Support Vector Machines. *Applied Intelligence, 19*(1/2), 109–123.

Eikelmann, S., Hajj, J., & Peterson, M. (2008). Opinion piece: Web 2.0: Profiting from the threat. *Journal of Direct, Data and Digital Marketing Practice, 9*(3), 293–295.

Ekman, P. (1972). Universals and Cultural Differences in Facial Expressions of Emotion, In, J. Cole (Ed.), *Nebraska Symposium on motivation,* (pp. 207-283).

Ekman, P. (1984). Expression and the nature of emotion. In K. Scherer & P. Ekman (Eds.), *Approaches to emotion.* Hillsdale, NJ: Erlbaum.

Esuli, A., & Sebastiani, F. (2006). SentiWordNet: A Publicly Available Lexical Resource for Opinion Mining. *Proceedings of LREC 2006 - 5th Conference on Language Resources and Evaluation,* 22-28/5/2006, Genova (IT).

Francisco, V., Gervás, P., & Peinado. F. (2007). Ontological reasoning to configure emotional voice synthesis. In M. Marchiori, J. Z. Pan, & C. de Sainte Marie (Eds.), *Web Reasoning and Rule Systems, 1st Int. Conf., RR 2007,* (pp. 88–102).

Gamon, M. (2004). Sentiment Classification on Customer Feedback Data: noisy data, large feature vectors, and the role of linguistic analysis. *Proceedings of the 20th international conference on Computational Linguistics,* Geneva, Switzerland. Article No. 841.

Gountas, J., & Gountas, S. (2007), Personality orientations, emotional states, customer satisfaction, and intention to repurchase. *Journal of Business Research, 60*(1), 72-75.

Harré, R. (1986). *The social construction of emotions.* Oxford: Blackwell.

Hiroshi, K., & Tetsuya, N. (2004). Deeper Sentiment Analysis Using Machine Translation Technology. *Proceedings of International Conference on Computational Linguistics (COLING2004),* August 23 - 27, University of Geneva, Switzerland.

Huang, M. H. (2001). The Theory of Emotions in Marketing. *Journal of Business and Psychology, 16*(2), 239-247.

Izard, C. E. (1977). *Human Emotions.* New York: Plenum Press.

Jonhson-Laird, P. N., & Oatley, K. (1989). The language of emotions: an analysis of a semantic field. *Cognition and Emotion, 3,* 81-123.

Kleinginna, P. R., & Kleinginna, A. M. (1981). A categorized list of emotion definitions, with suggestions for a consensual definition. *Motivation and Emotion, 5*(4), 263-291.

Laros, F. J. M., & Steenkamp, J. B. E. M. (2005). Emotions in consumer behavior: A hierarchical approach. *Journal of Business Research, 58*(10), 1437-1445.

Lee, K. H. (2003). *Text Categorization with a Small Number of Labeled Training Examples.* Ph.D. thesis, School of Information Technologies, University of Sydney.

Levy, R. I. (1984). The emotions in comparative perspective. In K. Scherer & P. Ekman (Eds.), *Approaches to emotion.* Hillsdale, NJ: Erlbaum.

López, J. M, Gil, R., García, R., Cearreta I., & Garay, N. (2008). Towards an Ontology for Describing Emotions. *In Proceedings of the 1st World Summit on the Knowledge Society. LNCS/LNAI, 5288*, 96-104. Springer.

Manyika, J. M., Roberts, R. P., & Sprague, K. L. (2007). Eight business technology trends to watch. *The McKinsey Quarterly*. December 2007. Available http://www.mckinseyquarterly.com/PDFDownload.aspx?L2=13&L3=0&ar=2080 (last verified: 29 December, 2008)

Mathieu, Y. (2005) Annotation of emotions and Feelings in texts. In J. Tao, T. Tan, & R.W. Picard (Eds). ASCII 2005, *LNCS 3784*, 350-357.

McKinsey (2007). How businesses are using Web 2.0: A McKinsey Global Survey. *The McKinsey Quarterly*, March 2007. Available http://www.mckinseyquarterly.com/PDFDownload.aspx?L2=16&L3=16&ar=1913&gp=0 (last verified: 29 December, 2008)

Mencke, M. (2007). *Benchmarking a Text Classification Technique*. M.Sc. Thesis, School of Computer Science and Statistics, Trinity College Dublin, Ireland.

Mullen, T., & Malouf, R. (2006). A preliminary investigation into sentiment analysis of informal political discourse. *Proceedings of the AAAI-2006 Spring Symposium on Computational Approaches to Analyzing Weblogs.*

O'Reilly, T. (2005). *What Is Web 2.0. Design Patterns And Business Models For The Next Generation Of Software*. 30 September 2005. http://www.oreillynet.com/pub/a/oreilly/tim/news/2005/09/30/what-is-web-20.html (last verified: 29 December, 2008)

Ortony, A., & Turner, T. J. (1990). What's basic about basic emotions? *Psychological Review, 97*, 315-331.

Pang, B., Lee, L., & Vaithyanathan, S. (2002). Thumbs Up? Sentiment Classification Using Machine Learning Techniques. *Proceedings of EMNLP 2002*, (pp. 79–86).

Parrott, W. (2001). *Emotions in Social Psychology.* Philadelphia: Psychology Press.

Plutchik, R. (1962). *The emotions: Facts, theories and a new model.* Nueva York: Random House.

Prahalad C. K., & Krishnan, M. S. (2008) *The New Age of Innovation: Driving Co-created Value through Global Networks*. McGraw-Hill.

Russell, J. A. (1991). Culture and the categorization of emotions. *Psychological Bulletin, 110*(3), 426-450.

Schoefer, K., & Diamantopoulos, A. (2008). Measuring experienced emotions during service recovery encounters: construction and assessment of the ESRE scale. *Service Business, 2*(1), 65-81.

Sebastiani, F. (2002). Machine Learning in Automated Text Categorization. *ACM Computing Surveys, 34*(1), 1–47.

Solomon, R. C. (1976). *The passions*. Garden City, NJ: Anchor Press.

Storm, C., & Storm, T. (1987). A taxonomic study of the vocabulary of emotions. *Journal of Personality and Social Psychology, 53*, 805-816.

Subasic, P., & Huettner, A. (2001). Affect Analysis of Text Using Fuzzy Semantic Typing. *IEEE Transactions on Fuzzy Systems, 9*(4), 483–496.

Tomkins, S. S. (1984). Affect theory. In K. R. Scherer & P. Ekman (Eds.), *Approaches to emotion*. Hillsdale, NJ: Lawrence Erlbaum Associates.

van Dolen, W., de Ruyter, K., & Lemmink, J. (2004). An empirical assessment of the influence of customer emotions and contact employee performance on encounter and relationship satisfaction. *Journal of Business Research, 57*(4), 437-444.

Vargo, S. L., & Lusch, R. F. (2004). Evolving To A New Dominant Logic For Marketing. *Journal of Marketing, 68*(1), 1-17.

Wallace, A. E. C., & Carson, M. T. (1973). *Sharing and diversity in emotion terminology. Ethos, 1*, 1-29.

Wierzbicka, A. (1992). Defining emotion concepts. *Cognitive Science, 16*(4), 539 – 581.

WordNet. http://wordnet.princeton.edu/. Last verified: 02 October, 2008.

Zeelenberg, M., & Pieters, R. (2004). Beyond valence in customer dissatisfaction A review and new findings on behavioral responses to regret and disappointment in failed services. *Journal of Business Research, 57*(4), 445-455.

Zipf, G. K. (1949). *Human Behavior and the Principle of Least-Effort.* Addison-Wesley.

ENDNOTE

[1] Zipf's law is a principle of mathematical statistics which when applied to natural language, states that language is characterized by very high frequencies of common words, and very low frequencies of uncommon words, scientifically formulated as "*the nth most common word in a language occurs with a frequency of 1/n*".

Chapter VIII
Can Knowledge Management Assist Firms to Move from Traditional to E-Commerce:
The Case of Greek Firms

Irene Samanta
Technological Education Institute of Piraeus, Greece

ABSTRACT

This chapter is to define the firm's innovative core and create frameworks to integrate innovation throughout the management of knowledge by generating implementing ideas, strategies and plans applied that cultivate a thinking organization aims to associate innovation with business targets. It argues that companies which manage and transform the knowledge effectively reap the rewards of scientific and technological achievement in order to adopt innovation concept in their operation. Furthermore, the author hopes that firms understanding the information received from the current global business world and transmit it to reap the rewards of scientific achievement will increase their competitiveness competition not only for sales, but also for technical know – how and skills. At the company level depends on the speed with which new products can be brought to the market place and on the importance of achieving new cost – saving improvements.

INTRODUCTION

The first question arisen is what the cause of emphasis in knowledge management is. The most important reason leading to the need of focusing on business knowledge is the successive changes in the business context. Today firms are exposed to a constantly changing environment and are frequently affected by technological and scientific changes. Markets keep changing and the international competition is increasing. Customers are becoming more demanding as far as quality, flexibility and speed are concerned. Competitive threats are a daily phenomenon while recognition and utilization of business opportunities remain a crucial factor of success. The firm requirement of the 21st century is more demanding. It should, first of all, adapt the inside environment of the company in order to confront such rising conditions and also t reform new relationships based on mutual trust along with the employees, the customers partners and the suppliers as well. The future and success of the business are now defined by the ability of the company to be able to take advantage of the most valuable resource: knowledge management. In addition the employees should be more activated in the creation of innovative ideas. A second question is how the knowledge management (KM) is defined. KM includes abilities and skills of its members, the prospectives of innovation and creativity, as well as the best business practices and patterns. KM exists not only in the abilities of its members but also in the procedures and systems within the company and the relationships between the firs and the stakeholders. Summarizing the challenge for the company is not only to broaden the knowledge of its employees but also to secure the procedures of mechanisms that will turn the individual into a more corporate knowledge asset. Recently know-net universities and European Consortium gave the following definition for KM: "KM is a new sector of management science concerning the systematic and corporate creation, diffusion and use of knowledge with the purpose the radical improvement of efficient organizing and business competition as well as the development of innovation. The vital factors of success for KM can be included in the following: support from the leadership, development of business strategy and definition of organizing roles, business culture and system of estimating efficiency and the use of appropriate technology. The present

research is to examine the strategies applied by firms to associate innovation with business targets moving to e-world of business. Specifically, the study investigates the leadership skills of 99 Greek firms that guide knowledge management concepts and applies and spread it into the firm's internal environment in order to reap the benefits of new economy.

IS KNOWLEDGE MANAGEMENT NEW?

KM considers that sharing knowledge in power. Technology offers the ability of access to any distant knowledge sharing. K however on order to encourage or promote new ideas is not something new. The basic principles of KM have to do with the culture of people and technology. Most specialist believe that 80% of KM contains cultural elements and only 20% concern the technology of KM. Peoples' ideas and culture are deeply rooted on organizational behavior. Technology is founded on technical intellectuality, knowledge engineering and information systems. What make KM rather difficult in the change from an individual competitive behavior called "knowledge is power" into a corporate behavior called "sharing knowledge is power".

The dissemination and use of knowledge throughout the organization, in order to create innovation and sustain competitive advantage, is indisputably a core process that needs to be cared for. Hence, companies are seeking to implement special knowledge management projects, which aim to install a working environment administrative to more efficient knowledge production, conveyance, and use. Therefore organizations should attempt to improve the knowledge management process focus on KM projects trying to build up to date and cultural acceptance to knowledge and create motives to alter the traditional behavior relating to knowledge to a new one in order to reap the benefits of new e-ra.

According to Hansen (1999), the knowledge management strategy focuses on technology. This strategy is mainly concentrated on codification and storage, so that knowledge can be easily accessed and used by anyone in the organization. They call this 'codification strategy', which uses the 'people-to-documents' approach. On the other hand the main management efforts of the so-called 'personalization strategy', focus on dialogue between individuals. This approach transferred throughout the organisation in one-to-one brainstorming meetings and conversations (Hansen et al 1999) and not codified. Webber (1993) points out that "in the new economy, conversations are the most important form of work"; and as Davenport and al (1998) illustratively say "in the knowledge-driven economy, talk is the real work". These two strategies are used either jointly or separately. Further investigation, however, has revealed firms that manage knowledge efficiently aim one strategy as a mainstream and use the second strategy to support the first. However, the succeed of these strategies organizations should be focused in creating value for their customers and it depends on which stage of life cycle is found the product. Therefore, the codification strategy is identified to be more applicable for firms that sell mature products, which profit from knowledge experience. In reverse, firms that offer their customers innovative products use the personalization strategy, pursuing innovative ideas.

The barriers to disseminate effectively knowledge initiatives are exceptionally hard to achieve dispersed organizations. Orlikowski (2002) indicates that the existence of technology infrastructure or technological equipment or any strategy does not guarantee the use of knowledge in firms to operate in the global environment. It is apparent that companies should develop both collective and distributed competence in everyday practices among the organizational members. The steps that empower the firm to gain a collective efficiency are the knowledge of the organization

and the employees developing their skills , as well as, the coordination of firm's recourses to participate effectively in order to create an innovation culture

Therefore, this new way ensures knowledge sharing, learning and change by communities of practice bound together add value to the firm by shared expertise, skills and abilities - instead of titles and hierarchical status - for a learning organization Davenport, T.H. and L. Prusak (1998)

BUILDING KNOWLEDGE SHARING CULTURE

In the process of implementing a knowledge-management system have raised a number of issues include: why firms do not receive information and knowledge to share with organizational members? What causes a firm to retain in its traditional situation and not respond to the needs of new economy? What are the main impedes an organization may confront when trying to raise knowledge sharing among its employees? And finally, how firms overcome those barriers? (Cabrera and al, 2002).

Hansen, (2002) identified that factors that restrain knowledge transfer are the cultural. Among the others the most important factors are lack of trust; different cultures,; lack of time and meeting places; narrow idea of productive work; status and rewards to knowledge owners; while (Nonaka and Takeuchi,1995) emphasize the lack of top management to support knowledge transfer as well their inability to manage it enable so as lead the organization in new economy. According to Choo, (1998) the above factors results lack of innovation culture and resistant to allow the knowledge to be shared. Choo, (1998) indicates that commitment among individuals to shared success on the basis of trust and relationships facilitate to better manage the knowledge received, and successfully collaborate with internal and external environment. Great emphasis in the existing literature review is being placed on the building of an organisational knowledge-sharing culture. Galbraith and Lawler (1993) determine culture as the shared values, beliefs and practices of individuals in the organization considering the cultural impedes to be overcome, a knowledge management effort should be designed and implemented so as the culture to be changed. Thus, Choo, (1998)suggests that management should have as a priority to pay more attention in a face-to-face interaction and establish the norms of cooperation among members though team structure, workflow issues and collaboration.

FROM BUSINESS PROCESS REDESIGN TO E-BUSINESS MODEL INNOVATION

In this new world of business, most enterprises success or failure would be depend upon their ability to incessantly question and adapt their programmed logic underpinning their business

models and business processes to the sustained dynamic and radical changes in the business environment. The 'old world' of pre-determined and pre-defined forms of success still exist side-by-side with the world of re-everything in most business enterprises. However, companies' competitive survival and ongoing sustenance would primarily depend on their ability to continuously receive information and convert it to knowledge. Consequently, as the e-business is moving so quickly that can't predict it the firm's ability to quick responds to challenges raised from intense competition is the effective knowledge received and shared and its adoption with the organizational goals and purposes. Figure 1 provides a synopsis of the transition from the 'old' world of business to the e-world of business.

The new world of business puts less premium on playing by pre-defined rules and more on understanding and adapting as the rules of the game-as well as the game itself-keep changing. The new world imposes a greater need for ongoing questioning of the programmed logic, very high level of adaptability to incorporate dynamic

Figure 1. The transition from the 'old' world of business to the e-world of business

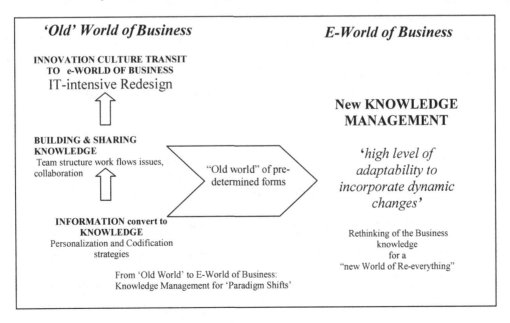

changes into the business knowledge and information architecture and ability to develop and grow systems that can be readily adapted for the dynamically changing business environment. Organizations operating in the new business environment therefore need to be adept at creation and application of new knowledge as well as ongoing renewal of existing knowledge archived in company databases.

THE EMPIRICAL STUDY

Research Methodology

Realizing the importance of individual compliance for the success of knowledge management initiatives, an attempt to examine the factors influencing knowledge management in the organizational context was made. The purpose of the study was to develop an understanding of the factors influencing KM of an individual professional group, using widely accepted theories. In more detail, the KM behavior of firm's employees' was examined based on the theoretical framework of Ajzen's (1991) and past research models on the field. Knowledge management is a well-established discipline in many large organizations. But what is its status and role in medium-sized enterprises and what are the policy implications?

The sample which participates consists of medium sized firms. The criteria used for the selection of the participant firms were the sector categorization with a satisfactory representation of different kinds of companies commercial, industrial and services. The population of the MSFs comprises of 1525 business firms according to the ICAP (2004) research study. The firms chosen for the sample should have an R & D department or invest to that direction. The number of firms that composed the sample was 425 of which 99 responded from the greater area of Greece. Regarding the structure of the sample, firms come from the most of the main regions of Greece representing the half of the sample (South Greece 15.6%, North and Central Greece 25%) . However the rest of them which is the majority establishes in the area of Athens (see Table 1). Out of the firms selected 99 responded to our research. There is a satisfactory representation of different kinds of companies according to the sector of business sercices (66.3%), industrial (15.1%) and commercial (18.8%) which B2B companies belong. A total of 425 questionnaires were administered using mainly the 'in-person drop-off method, whereas, for geographically dispersed companies, questionnaires were sent either through e-mail or post. The survey questionnaires were distributed and collected between October 2007 and January 2008. A total of 99 usable questionnaires were collected (response rate of …%). Respondents were employees of various designations - deputy head of departments (73.2%), head of departments (9.4%), deputy managers (5.1%), managers (9.4%) and other designations (2.9%),whereas the age of the respondents ranged from 22 to 60 years old. The majority of the respondents were university

Table 1. Medium sized firms in Greece ICAP 2004

Total MSF's in Greece	Commercial	Industrial	Services	A/O (Others)
2.342	534	984	742	82
MSF's in greater area of Athens (Attica)				
1.525	414	483	579	49

graduates (50.7%) and their work experience ranged from 0.5 to 35 years.

Defining the Firms' Behaviors Toward New e-Ra

From the research analysis, two groups of firms emerged which include different characteristics towards knowledge management. In the first group, the internal and external environment, which directly influences the companies through the use of new technical equipment and quality systems, affects the companies. In the present research, it is noticed that top management has a tendency to deal with the knowledge in order to innovate, which has as a result a reference to a specific innovation strategy with specific procedures towards innovation with fast ways of innovation transmission to new e-Ra, so that networks that promote innovation are developed. Organizations belong to the first group spends most of its innovation effort envisioning the change to new e-Ra and shape their strategies to that direction (Table 2).

In the second group, the companies are placed in a human-centric system with a future prospect to move from the traditional business to new-e-Ra. There is a conjugation and a balance between the human-centric and the technocratic systems, because this is an in-between situation and provides balance between humans and machines. The company's development for creating scale

economies is accomplished through an occasional partnership or stable long-term partnership. This shows the psychological tendency of managers to maintain their independence, given that a great percentage of medium – sized businesses, in Greece, are referred to as family businesses.

Knowledge Management Cycle in Medium–Sized Firms in Greece

The research results were verified that the dissemination and utilization of the knowledge management in order to adopt innovation culture processes by Greek firms it is in a satisfactory level. The high management has focused to the importance of an innovation culture and has inspired innovation values, to a certain extent, in the business environment.

The most important factor that assists a firm to be the leader is the extent to which the knowledge efficiently and effectively managed, influence action on transforming, transferring, predicting outcomes in order to make better decisions. The majority of Greek firms have developed knowledge management processes to contribute effectively creating an innovative cycle, where new ideas are generated from different perspectives. The codification of the received information will assist to embody the ideas into a more transferable form. The next stage encapsulated on the associated knowledge in manufacturing processes and organizational procedures. The diffusion of the

Table 2. Firms' behavior towards new e-Ra

Final Cluster Centers	"New world" of e-Business	"Old world" of business
Responding/Reacting to Change to new e-Ra	16	19
Experimenting with Change to new e-Ra	7	1
Anticipating the need to Change to new e-Ra	8	8
Envisioning Change to new e-Ra	36	4
Cluster number of cases	**67**	**32**

knowledge is transmitted through the products which are distributed in the marketplace or processes are implemented throughout the organization. Their application then generates ideas for improvements, and so the cycle repeats.

Knowledge Management Benefits

Firms consistently tracks the benefits realized from innovative activity by measuring some important factors. As far as innovation benefits are concerned, managers of Cluster 1 pay attention firstly to the satisfaction of the customers. This shows the orientation with which corporations innovate, wanting to top their customer's preferences.

Improvement of the product's value is of equal importance by loyalty to the firm's brand. By measuring the benefits pay less attention to their employees' performance as managers don't consider it as a semantic indicator. This is due to the fact that medium-sized firms are customer-oriented in order to acquire profit in the short-term and they don't invest to their employees for long-term benefits as result of the high level of their performance (Table 3).

'Old World' to E-World of Business through Knowledge Management

The majority of the respondents in Cluster 1, in order to create a product or to improve their processes, prefer mainly to research the procedures

their competitors/customers apply in the market. Regarding the technology acquisition, firms prefer to develop technology into their R&D department, considering research as the most reliable way of technological and competitive advantage.

The basic characteristic of the innovative first group of firms is the introduction of the new processes to be adapted in the new e-Ra, while the second group of firms aims to improve the processes. Therefore the cluster 1 of firms has adapted radical business processes and changes to face the dynamic business environment. The 'old world' of businesses still exist side-by-side with the world of re-everything in firms of cluster 2. Firms of Cluster 1 continuously redefine and adapt organizational goals, purposes, and manage the knowledge as a «way of doing things». The (Figure 1) provides a synopsis of the current situation in Greek business environment from the 'old' world of business to the new e-Ra of business.

Collaboration with external organizations is considered to be an important innovation source. The sample indicates that most of the sample's companies cooperate occasionally with an external organization, such as a university, research institute etc., aiming at gaining useful information for potential market and technological changes.

An important finding is that a significant 28.1% does not accept the concept of partnerships. Regarding technology acquisition, firms prefer to develop technology in their R & D department, considering research as the most reliable way of achieving technological and competitive advan-

Table 3. Knowledge Management benefits

Final Cluster Centers	"New world" of e-Business		"Old world" of business	
	Yes	No	Yes	No
Value creation in products/services	31	35	12	20
Brand loyalty	31	36	12	20
Customer satisfaction	53	14	24	8
Employee performance	19	48	5	27

Figure 2. Current business situation for future direction to new economy

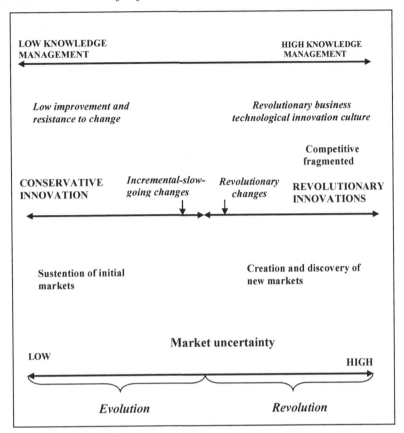

tage. Access to innovation is created by the vast majority (53.1%) through the development of an R & D department, which is also verified by the previous result concerning independence maintenance, while a small percentage (18.8%) develops innovative technology through a partnership. The managers' leadership skills are sufficiently developed, providing the personnel with the right directions for innovative results (Table 4).

Regarding technology acquisition, Table 5 demonstrates that firms prefer to develop technology in their R&D department, considering research as the most reliable way of technological and competitive advantage. Access to innovation is created by the majority of the sample in Cluster 1 (53,1%) through the development of the R/D department investing to buy equipment, while

a small percentage (18,8%) develops innovative technology through a partnership.

Organizations' Leadership Competencies that Manage Knowledge Driving to the Innovation Culture

This section is designed to specify organizations manage of knowledge management to approach to innovation culture due to the new e-Ra. Thus, a set of variables identifies the leadership's competencies in the area of knowledge management and innovation culture. On a scale from one to five ("not at all" to "consistently and effectively") the two groups of firms demonstrate the following behaviours.

Table 4. Collaboration with external organization

Collaboration with external organization * Cluster Number of Case Cross tabulation			
	Cluster Number of Case		
	"New world" of e-Business	"Old world" of business	Total
No collaboration	16	17	33
Occasional collaboration	32	9	41
Constant and long-term collaboration	19	6	25
Total	67	32	99

Table 5. Technology acquisition organizations

Technology acquisition * Cluster Number of Case Cross tabulation			
	Cluster Number of Case		
	"New world" of e-Business	**"Old world" of business**	**Total**
Developed in the R&D department	24	10	34
Buying royalties	3	1	4
Buying equipment	24	12	36
Collaboration with another firm	16	9	25
Total	67	32	99

Managers' leadership skills in cluster I are sufficiently developed the knowledge management, providing the personnel with the right directions for innovative results. Managers' leadership skills appear sufficiently developed, providing the personnel with the right directions for innovative goals. As a result the benefits derived from these leadership competencies are innovation culture, and the encouragement of active communication between co-workers and among other divisions. Cooperation, team spirit and lastly emphasis on idea-generation are the main priorities for managers to create an innovative model that ties business strategy into the day-to-day innovative process in order to adapt in e-world of business.

The results from cluster 2 show that top management neither hasn't adopted a step-by step process that facilitates idea collection, nor has built networks, pathways and platforms that promote the flow of innovation both internally and externally through alliances and partnerships. Leadership appears to have a lack of a clear definition of innovation based on the organizational culture as they don't manage effectively the information received to spread in business's internal environment..

Table 6. Operational strategies affecting the innovation management

Final Cluster Centers	"New world" of e-Business	"Old world" of business
Specific innovation strategy	4,24	3,41
Development of innovation culture	4,27	2,91
Development of networks promoting innovation	3,99	2,78
Specific innovation procedure	4,04	2,53
Innovation spread	3,97	2,63
The devekopment of a clear definition of innovation based on our organizational culture and internal/external parameters.	3,96	2,66
(Positioning the innovation within business unitas an integrated aspect of organization's overall success	4,01	2,88
(Strategic Decision Making) Targeting important challenges that require innovative solutions.	3,82	2,97
Encouragement for active communication facilitating the discussion across the organization through teamwork anf team thing, but also among divisions.	4,40	3,50

Resource Allocation and its Impact on Innovation Success

The results below recognize how the Greek firms is allocating resources in relation to their innovation strategies. The first cluster of Greek firms (41 firms) is allocating resources in relation to their innovation strategies. They have mandated a certain percent of an individual's work time to be dedicated to informal idea generation, exploratory thinking, and experimentation. Specifying the time they allocate is among 6-10% and 11-15% of staff's time. In addition firms to build the capabilities of leaders, teams and individuals allocated funds for performance improvement programs and tools to utilize their innovative potential and perform to their fullest 58/17. Also, funds have been allocated by the first group of firms to create a dynamic, knowledge-based e-learning system for communicating across the organization. Finally organization rewards and recognizes innovative outcomes on the part of individuals and teams.

CONCLUSION

Based on the results each company that wants to deal with the knowledge in order to innovate and transmit its activities to new e-Ra, should primarily introduce the innovation concept within the company itself by developing at the same time methods of communication among the employees who will adopt that knowledge. Organizations should create ways of producing and collecting ideas, aiming at the differentiation of the certain product that finally will be offered to the customer, along with providing privileges that will not be easy to be copied by competitive companies. The next step concerns the intentions of tools and methods that will help the easy flow of innovation in every department or level of the business so as to create the image of a company that can pioneer and has the potential to advance and progress. The concept of innovation should be linked with the company targets with the purpose different attitude to prevail that would characterize an idea useful only if it offers innovative results. Liebowitz and Beckman (1998) refer to a procedure of 8 steps concerning KM. The stages are:

- **Stage 1. Recognition:** Definition of main assignments, strategies and the field of knowledge.
- **Stage 2. Conception:** Reformation of the existing knowledge.
- **Stage 3. Selection:** Definition of the meaning, value and accuracy of knowledge. Analysis of contradictors knowledge (K).
- **Stage 4. Storing:** Representation of corporate memories in knowledge stores with the assistance K shapes.
- **Stage 5. Sharing:** Distribution K automatically to users according to their interests and work and cooperating with them.
- **Stage 6. Applying:** The K and use it in decision making, problem solving, supporting and work automation and education.
- **Stage 7. Creating:** Discovering new knowledge through research, experimenting and creative knowledge.
- **Stage 8. Selling:** Developing and selling product and services based on K.

In the present study Greek firms procedures to take advantage from knowledge follow four steps:

- **Stage 1. Creating:** Discovering new knowledge through research, experimenting and creative K.
- **Stage 2. Sharing:** Distribution K automatically to users according to their interests and work and cooperating with them.
- **Stage 3. Selection:** Definition of the meaning, value and accuracy of knowledge. Analysis of contradictors knowledge (K).
- **Stage 4. Applying:** The K and use it in decision making, problem solving, supporting and work automation and education.

The dimension of firms' knowledge is strongly determined by two economic variables, three organizational variables and one infrastructure variable. Specifically, the companies that demonstrate innovative leadership are: characterized by a relative high contribution of machinery and equipment cost to their operations; devote relatively more company resources to R&D; consider innovative ideas promptly; have a strategic plan in operation that lead their team through a process to define what innovation really means inside their organization/business unit. They've developed a clear, concise definition of innovation based on their organizational culture and internal/external parameters and co-operate with research institutions and universities.

The variables associated with this dimension of organizational innovativeness have been documented by many researchers in the past. Specifically, Szeto, (2000) has found that innovative firms spend more on R&D than the less innovative firms. Other authors, Tidd et al (2001), Kyriazopoulos, (2000), Kim et al,(1998) documented that firms possessing internal technical expertise are more innovative than firms without such expertise.

Finally, Cabrera *et al (2002)* and Kyriazopoulos (2000), among others, have shown that innovative firms co-operate with outside scientific and technical establishments and make deliberate efforts to survey externally generated ideas. Our results stipulate the benefits to be gained from the co-operation of a firm with research institutes and universities and from the prompt consideration of innovative ideas.

Therefore, it has been observed that companies which develop new technologies or purchase royalties make an effort to spend time and power in order to create an ideal environment for the implementation of innovative ideas.

Another conclusion derived from this survey is the definition of the benefits which corporations that "push" innovation into their interior acquire. Firstly, it has been briefly showed that

Figure 3. The adoption of innovation culture through knowledge

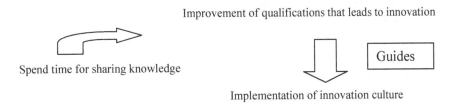

corporations that invest in innovation seem to have more modifications in production on account of import of automation, than these ones that do not invest in innovation. The more innovative policy a company has, the more modification in production will be appeared.

This research investigates if there is some kind of benefit when a manager managing the knowledge orders the employees to spend as much time as they can so as to adopt an innovation culture. The deduction is that corporations which make this kind of order bring the following benefits: connection of innovation with the goals of corporation, purifying defiance, and communication, all parameters of the qualifications that guide to the innovation (Figure 3).

Finally, one important benefit that corporations using innovative policy have, is the increase of turnover from new products. It is showed clearly the differentiation that this variable has between the two types of clusters of companies (adopt innovation-not adopt innovation). It is logical one innovative company to increase its turnover from new products. If a company that does not adopt innovation increases its turnover from new products, then this company could be characterized as an innovative one! These two variables (innovation-increase of turnover from new products) seem to have a linear relationship.

MANAGERIAL IMPLICATIONS

Knowledge management (KM) has been gaining ground in the management agenda, since it has been realized that caring for organizational knowledge is perhaps the only way to enhance innovation and achieve sustainable competitive advantage in the contemporary business environment. From the research work firms to succeed in new e-Ra need a better and continuous absorption of external knowledge – that encompass many sorts of knowledge such as knowledge of the competition, knowledge of customers needs , technology and product trends, knowledge of core science, technologies and processes from other networks.

Greek managers admit that in order to be innovative they should deal with the knowledge effectively and have a tendency to manage it. Top management should try to activate the indoor resourcing of the firm while others use outsourcings in order for the indoor resourcing to be activated. The leadership skills have to be focused mainly with the internal effective communication development in order to be created the conditions for diffusion of knowledge and the generation of ideas by the low management. As a result should have a reference to a specific innovation strategy with specific procedures and ways of innovation transmission, so that networks that promote innovation are developed.

As a result innovation culture should harmonize with targets of the firm so as to meet the needs of globalization.

ACKNOWLEDGMENT

The author would like to express her gratitude to Prof. Kyriazopoulos Panagiotis from Business School of Graduate Technological Educational Institute of Piraeus in Greece, whose support and contributions have been a great help to this work.

REFERENCES

Ahanotu N. D. (1998). Empowerment and production workers: a knowledge-based perspective. *Empowerment in Organizations, 6*(7), 177-18.

Cabrera, A., & Cabrera, E. F. (2002). Knowledge-sharing dilemmas. *Organization Studies, 23*(5), 687-710.

Carneiro, A. (2000). How does knowledge management influence innovation and competitiveness? *Journal of Knowledge Management, 4*, 87-98.

Choo, C. (1998). *The Knowing Organization: How Organizations Use Information to Create Meaning, Create Knowledge, and Make Decisions,* Oxford University Press, Oxford, UK.

Davenport, T. H., De Long, D. W., & Beers, M. C. (1998). Successful knowledge management projects. *Sloan Management Review, 39*(2), 43-57.

Davenport, T. H., & Prusak, L. (1998). *Working Knowledge: How Organizations Manage: What They Know Best.* Boston, MA: Harvard Business School Press.

Davenport, T. H., & Prusak, L. (2000). *Working knowledge: How organizations manage what they know.* Boston, MA: Harvard Business School Press.

Galbraith, J. R., & Lawler, E. E. (1993). *Organizing for the Future.* San Francisco, CA Jossey-Bass Publishers.

Hansen, M. T. (1999). The Search- Transfer Problem: The Role of Weak Ties in Sharing Knowledge Across Organization Subunits. *Administrative Science Quarterly, 44*(1), 82-111.

Hansen, M. T. (2002). Knowledge networks: Explaining effective knowledge sharing in multiunit companies. *Organization Science, 13*(3), 232-48.

Ingram H. (1997). Performance management: processes, quality and team working. *International Journal of Contemporary Hospitality Management, 9*(7), 295-303.

Johnson, G. N. Y., & Scholes, K. (1997). *An Integrated Approach.* Boston: Houghton Mifflin Company. *Exploring Corporate Strategy,* London: Prentice Hall.

Kim, D., Cameron, S., & Quinn, R. E. (1998). *Diagnosing and Changing Organizational Culture: Based on the Competing Values Framework.* (Addison-Wesley Series on Organization Development) by Addison-Wesley Pub Co.

Kyriazopoulos, P. (2000). The Modern firm in the starting of the 21st century. In S. Ekdotiki (Ed.), *E-Commerce* (pp. 284-323) Athens.

Nonaka, I. (1994). The dynamic theory of organizational knowledge creation. *Organization Science, 5*(1), 14-37.

Nonaka, I., & Takeuchi, H. (1995). *The Knowledge Creating Company: How Japanese Companies Create the Dynamics of Innovation.* New York: Oxford University Press.

Orlikowski, W. J. (2002). Knowing in practice: enacting a collective capability in distributed organizing. *Organization Science, 13*(3), 249-273.

Szeto, E. (2000). Innovation capacity: working towards a mechanism for improving innovation within an inter-organizational network. *The TQM Magazine, 12*(2), 149-158.

Thomond P., & Lettice F. (2002). Disruptive Innovation Explored. *9th IPSE International Conference on Concurrent Engineering: Research and Applications* (CE2002).

Tidd, J., & Bessant, J., & Pavitt, K. (2001). *Managing Innovation, Integrating Technological, Market and Organizational Change.* John Wiley.

Chapter IX
Knowledge Management and Lifelong Learning in Archival Heritage:
Digital Collections on a Semantic Scope for Educational Potential

Triantafillia Kourtoumi
General State Archives of Greece, Greece

ABSTRACT

Archives have a key role to play in underpinning learning in its broadest sense, both as a formal activity within an institution and informally within the community. This is becoming especially important in an increasingly KM-based environment. This chapter provides an overview of technologies that can be applied to archival knowledge management. Furthermore, it assesses their actual or potential contribution to the basic processes of knowledge sharing within archival organizations, with a focus on lifelong learning. The scope of the first section (the screens) is to identify new developments that seem to be significant and to relate them to technology research in the archival field. The second section (the frames) discusses the concepts supporting digital collections by integrating collections of digitised archival resources to create new services and infrastructures. The third section (the agendas) analyses -from the educational perspective of lifelong learning- important social benefits, both quantitavely and qualitatively, of developing new infrastructures for accessing and using archival resources.

INTRODUCTION

Structured information of historical nature traditionally represents the vast majority of data collected and accessible to archival organizations. Acquisition records, exhibition catalogues and use data are all examples of these, even though they are still largely created in paper form. Exploiting this information in the information age requires systems for managing and extracting tacit knowledge from large collections of structured archival data and applications for discovering patterns and relationships (=Knowledge Management Technology, KMT).

The so-called Semantic Web revolution has exposed users of archival collections to the experiences of searching and taxonomy browsing and has reshaped their expectations of the knowledge retrieval process from archives, not only while browsing the Web, but more importantly, while at office, performing their research. In order to achieve this semantic integration, KMT proposes the usage of metadata and ontologies as the conceptual backbones of digital archival description; more, of the inclusive conceptualization of data needed to reflect the content, the context and the structure of the archival information in the digital world.

Several benefits are estimated of using such an approach in the archival sector. First, in the area of domain modeling ontologies facilitate interoperability between IT systems (=correlation engines) by providing shared understanding of the specific thematic domain. Second, ontologies provide the formalization of shared understanding necessary to make such understanding machine-process able. Such machine process ability is the basis for the next generation of the World Wide Web, allowing archivists and users to achieve compliance with existing Web standards. Finally, the explicit representation of the semantics of data, in combination with ontologies, enables IT systems to provide a qualitatively new level of archival services in a global environment (Stojanovic, 2004). The vision is to construct digital libraries for archival collections within the semantic scope; thus, to provide knowledge-based electronic access to collection level descriptions of the archival material.

THE SEARCH SCREEN: MAPPING SEMANTIC CHALLENGE IN THE ARCHIVAL INFRASTRUCTURE

Participation in the web of archival institutions requires a common language, a common technological structure and development of content that is relevant and captivating. In this context, archiving different historical collections in the digital age presents for the archival sector at least two semantic challenges:

- Incorporating established prime sources *content vocabularies (=metadata)* for built-thesaurus that are sensible to all communities of different users, scholars, students, life-long learners ("language for humans").
- Implementing a technological structure that classifies these terms and defines their relationships in a *scheme (=ontologies)* that can be processed by users-friendly electronic applications ("language for machines").

The archival domain --along with the other two major cultural sectors, libraries and museums-- is one that has long experience of developing and implementing metadata systems, appropriate for archival finding aids. Traditionally, the archives have taken the lead in the development of descriptive metatada standards for historical information; they have also developed controlled vocabularies for subjects and the names of people, organizations and geographical entities.

A large component of archival activities have been focussed on context. Elucidating and preserving context is what assists with identifying and preserving the evidential value of records in and over time; it is what facilitates the authentication of those objects, and it is what assists researchers with their analysis and interpretation. While archival metadata has primarily existed in print form until recently (=accession records, finding aids and catalogues records), it is increasingly distributed on line. Meeting the new challenges in the knowledge age, the archival sector is facing a main issue: digital collection creation and management of its material in a common language, readable by both humans and machines.

In the beginning of this evolution, often one of the biggest issues for archivists in describing and cataloguing was that of professional culture. Because the initial impetus behind digital cataloging was to reduce original cataloging by copy cataloging, and because archival materials are primarily unique, archivists and manuscripts curators operated until recently as independent agents (Chandler, 2002). The concept of describing for the purposes of digital sharing outside of the institution is a relatively new one for archives and manuscript repositories. Subsequently, concessions to controlled vocabulary use as well as other standards initiatives have to be readjusted.

For this purpose, however, of late there has been a considerable increase in co-operation among the archival institutions worldwide. A significant trigger for increased collaboration and co-operation --especially over metadata-- is a common involvement in things like digital content creation and the delivery of services through networks. This concept has been reflected especially by the system developed the International Council of Archives (ICA) and called ISAD (G), "General International Standard Archival Description". Another system, the Encoded Archival Description (EAD) is quite frequently used to generate metadata based on the EAD-DTD. Special Professional Associations (e.g. the International Association of Sound and Audiovisual Archives, IASA) have developed "site specific'" "cataloguing rules" on different levels (fonds, collections, etc). Taking in consideration the need for co-operation within and outside the archival domain for cross-sector and cross-domain cultural information retrieval, a more radical approach is provided by the Dublin

Core. The approach maps domain specific elements into 15 "core" elements, applied to all three cultural sectors (archives, libraries and museums) (Mischo, 2005).

A more sophistic approach might be to look "behind the scenes". Taking the term "creator" of a collection/ of a file and/or of a document, it can be assumed that this is a person, an organization or a robot fulfilling a function ("role") in relation to an object ("thing"). An (information) object here is defined as a digital item or group of items, regardless of type or format that can be addressed or manipulated as a single object by a computer. This concept can be confusing in that it can be used to refer both to actual content (such as digitized images) and to content surrogates (such as catalogue records or finding aids) (Howarth, 2001).

Incorporating some common data elements, such as the Encoded Archival Description and the Dublin Code, are making it easier for users to negotiate between descriptive surrogates of information objects and digital versions of the objects themselves, and to search at both the item and collection level within and across information systems. Thus, the term "ontology" is introduced, which is defined in different ways. Artificial intelligence and Web researchers have adopted this term for their own purposes. For them, ontologies provide a way of capturing a shared understanding of a domain that can be used both by humans and systems to aid in information exchange and integration (Gilliland-Swetland, 2000).

An ontology is, then, a representation of a shared conceptualization of a particular domain. Such a common conceptualization is necessary for every communication process. An ontology allows people (in our case, archivists and users) to reason and react about sameness as well as differentness of concepts and to derive mappings for establishing semantically correct communication channels. Furthermore, ontologies serve help an organization (in this case, an archival organization) to keep track of all concepts and notions used in its documents/collections and to clarify the importance of transactions and description processes.

From a technology point of view, ontologies can be seen within archival institutions as databases of concepts. Concepts are conceived as complex structures, tightly interconnected one another. There are several proposals on how to define, to organize and to structure domain concepts in the cultural heritage domain. The Knowledge System Laboratory, Stanford, defines ontology as "specification of concepts to be used for expressing knowledge". Basic elements of this framework are: Types of entities, Attributes and properties, Relations and functions, constraints. The consortium of interchange of e.g. museum information (CIMI) has introduced the metadata elements: who, what, when, where ("4w") which can be considered as a domain independent conceptualization of four entities (person, thing, time, place) (IDEF, 2001).

Looking into the integrated definition of the Ontology Description Capture (IDEF5) that distinguishes different levels of ontologies and applying it to the archival sector we can consider the "4w" or Dublin Core elements belonging to a *"domain ontology"*; metadata used in a document's and/or a file's description as part of a *"practice ontology"*; and metadata used within e.g. a photographic collection as part of a *"site ontology"* (Berolazzi, 2001).

THE EDUCATIONAL SCREEN: ADOPTING A SOCIAL POLICY FOR LIFELONG LEARNING

New information technologies are catalysts of change, both social and political; and perhaps nowhere more so than in the area of culture. The stuff of culture—the production of ideas, meanings, identities, and narratives, as concepts of common memory—has always been inseparable from the possibilities and constraints of the dominant technological media. New information technologies, from the printing press to the Internet to the semantic web, have always been engines of cultural innovation—keys to reshaping creative possibilities, notions of self and community, cultural institutions, and the roles of cultural actors.

The array of technological, social and political conditions is transforming the way scientific and societal knowledge is produced and also disseminated in archival institutions. The emergence of collaborative technologies, the shifting influence of non-academic versus academic organizations and private versus public investments are challenging archives, as traditional cultural agents of education and research. To understand this new knowledge ecology, archives coordinate research on new models of organizational collaboration, emerging fields of research and changing forms of scholarship, transformations of education, transitions to institutions, and innovative programs in interdisciplinary and integrative learning. A range of broad issues, reflecting on the constantly changing political and societal expectations of education can be addressed. The question arises as to how archival institutions apply and manage knowledge that is created by education institutions and other knowledge generators. It is in this context that the concept of learning is introduced, defined as knowledge and the capacity to make due use of it (Hepburn, 2004).

For the archival sector, where users are the most important assets, is critical to adopt a social policy in managing knowledge for lifelong learning purposes; thus, to evolve users' skills, capabilities, interests and experience. "Knowledge" here means how technologies change the ways users think about their archives, their collective memory and identity. Knowledge also refers to how archivists, as professionals, organize, access and use information--indeed, how they transform primitive historical information into knowledge within the digital framework. "Social policy" refers to what archivists, should do about these both as individuals- information management expertises, and as governments- public sectors representing national heritage within the global environment. "Lifelong learning" is a core element of this strategy, central not only to competitiveness and employability but also to social inclusion and cohesion, active citizenship and personal development. It enables all persons to acquire the necessary knowledge to take part as active citizens in the knowledge society and the labour market (Lisbon European Council, 2000).

Archival institutions benefit from digital applications in a number of ways. They use computer technologies to secure accessibility of their resources for the future, i.e. long-term preservation of complex digital collections; to reach out to special target groups, i.e. youngsters, people living in disadvantaged areas, people with access disabilities; to enhance their educational services, i.e. by developing on-line material for formal and informal educational purposes; and, to improve access to their holdings, both quantitavely, i.e. by making their resources more widely accessible, that is *information*, and qualitatively, i.e. by providing meaningful, conceptualized resources that relate to people's lives, by encouraging users' interaction, that is *knowledge.*

Undoubtedly, in recent years the shift in the scope of Information Technology Systems (ITS) from the information-based focus toward the knowledge-based focus highlighted the importance of the archival domain and the need to manage archival sources including competencies. Knowledge management, as a concept with people taking the centre stage, has prompted archivists, as information professionals, to rethink information management and focus from trying to improve intelligent systems to developing tools for intelligent people (McKay, 2003).

THE DEFINITION FRAME: CONSTRUCTING DIGITAL LIBRARIES FOR ARCHIVAL COLLECTIONS

Knowledge Management Systems/Services (KMS), such as classifications, gazetteers, lexical databases, ontologies, taxonomies and thesauri, model the underlying semantic structure of a domain. Applied to the archival domain, they act as semantic road maps in constructing digital libraries for archival collections and make possible a common orientation by indexers and future users (whether human or machine). It is crucial at this point to deal with the difficulties about defining digital libraries. It helps to clarify goals in creating collections in digital form.

The concept of digital library has been certainly an important phrase in archivists- and not only- lexicon since at least the mid 1990s. It is worth noting, though, that there is still not a clear consensus about exactly what constitutes a digital library within this community. The concept, however, has several differing perspectives and interpretations, derived from different cultural heritage actors involved in digital library research, practice, organization, and distribution (Lynch, 2002).

For economy reasons, examined from the methological prospective, the focus here is on two communities within the cultural heritage domain: the research and the practice ones. While they work and proceed independently of each other, they can be considered on two ends of a spectrum, which as yet have not met in the middle. On one of the spectrum lies the research community. It is grounded mostly in computer science and asks research questions directed toward future vision or visions of digital libraries for applications in the cultural information, or rather of their various technology oriented aspects and components, unrestricted by practice. On the other end of the spectrum, lies the practice community. It is grounded mostly in information science (librarianship, archival studies and museology) and, asks developmental, operational, and use questions in real-life institutional contexts, restrictions, and possibilities, concentrating on applications on the use end of the spectrum (Lynch, 2003).

A rather complex definition of digital libraries is chosen here, a definition that may be considered as a bridge between the research community definitions and practical community definitions. Borgman (1999) states that "digital libraries are a set of electronic resources and associated technical capabilities for creating, searching, and using information. They are an extension and enhancement of information storage and retrieval systems that manipulate digital data in any medium …The *content* of digital libraries includes data, [and] metadata … Digital libraries are constructed, collected, and organized, by (and for) a community of users, and their functional capabilities support the information needs and uses of that community".

Following these perspectives, the *content* choices fall into categories that are based on: systems, networks, and technology; collection and resources in various media; representation, organization, and operability; storage and searching; functionality, access and use; institutions and services; and user communities and related applications (Dalbello, 2004).

In the archival environment digitization includes taking a physical object or analog item, such as a tape recording, a map, or correspondence, from a collection that is rare or unique, often extremely fragile, and taking photographs of the item, and transferring the photographs to a digital medium. The negatives or prints are scanned into digital format (Library of Congress, 2000). Digital files are imported into, and managed with the use of software programs (=digital libraries). Digital files may be read, compressed, transferred and retrieved over computer networks then made accessible and viewed on computer monitors.

All of these efforts are producing numerous large collections of material, databases that are open to exploration and presentation in dozens of different directions. These are collections- raw material. The focus so far is on creating large amounts of digital content and providing some fairly simple access tools, rather than upon sophisticated systems for ongoing use or apparatus providing interpretation (McKay, 2003). However, the end product is determined by how well these functions are performed. Here, the concept of digital collection comes. It is needed to make a "conceptual leap" in order to preserve information in the digital age. It is the informational content that must be preserved. The problem lies in the fact that the content may now be completely removed from the physical artifact (Besser, 2002). It will take a conscious effort to make sure that the digital content information survives.

THE RESEARCH FRAME: VALUING THE ARCHIVAL PERSPECTIVE IN THE KNOWLEDGE MANAGEMENT ERA

In the conceptual leap of constructing digital libraries for archival collections metadata is the first line of defense to protect digital information and content. By providing detailed metadata, archival institutions may minimize the risks of digital resources becoming inaccessible in the future. Important unique technical information may be captured including: scanning specifications, operating systems, software versions, and decompression schemes. In addition to the institutional administrative data, it is important to maintain the digital integrity of the files (Beamsley, 1999).

For example, the significance of an archival collection is heavily based on its provenance or the context in which it was created. Consequently, the nature of archival description in the digital form must incorporate this focus. The ramifications for digital cataloging under the "conceptual scope" (=metadata and ontologies) are the overwhelming need for notes that provide the context such as biographical or historical notes concerning the creating person or body, as well as extensive content and scope notes. However, the *authorship* concept can at times be somewhat difficult to discern due to the principle of provenance, that is, the person or body who actually physically produced an item may not be as significant as the body within which it has context. Also it is often a matter of some debate in constructing digital as to how to categorize the writer of a letter for instance, either as an *author* (who) or if they write about themselves within that letter as a *subject* (what). How an entity is digital cataloged can have ramifications on how it will be found, that is, what kind of electronic search will retrieve that entry.

The depth and manner in which a collection/a file and/or a document are catalogued have consequences for its ability to be retrieved by a potential user. Given the problems of addressing the needs of a diverse audience, it might seem that comprehensive cataloguing is the answer, however this is a very time- intensive and ultimately costly process. It becomes clear then that there is a huge problem in describing the full possible subject content of a collection/ a file and/or a document and the many meanings and potential uses it might have to various users. A digital index that captures this full range of possibilities would be impossibly costly and labour-intensive to build internally. One approach to developing such an index might be to permit the actual users of the images to add their own keywords, annotations, or notes on the ways they have used it (Gilliland-Swetland, 2000).

Archival institutions are starting to invest in digital projects within the semantic scope by carefully designing metadata results for several reasons, including:

- Reducing over-handling of material in order to preserve it.
- Assisting in promoting the collections and the institution in a global environment.
- Providing intellectually access to value-added information through tracing tacit knowledge derived from raw sources.
- Achieving the best information and knowledge management of their material in the short and long-term.

The move toward the knowledge-based economy highlighted the importance of tacit knowledge and the need to manage knowledge resources including skills and competencies. Knowledge management as a concept with people taking the centre stage has prompted archival institutions to rethink information management and shift focus on archival heritage from trying to develop intelligent systems to that of developing tools for intelligent people. It is this realization that makes knowledge management attractive to archival organizations. While the focus in information management is mostly on explicit knowledge, knowledge management brings a new dimension in research and learning, the need to manage tacit knowledge by focusing on people and enhance their capability by improving communication, information transfer and collaboration in a global environment.

By creating digital surrogates of their collections on a semantic scope, archival institutions continue to support the notion that there is value in the materials they house in a global environment. However, research in scale-up is very difficult to perform except by building and deploying a large-scale digital --knowledge-based-- library system. Establishing infrastructure and tools to facilitate experimentation with large-scale systems is essential, as is funding to study use and behavior of large-scale systems once deployed through this infrastructure.

THE SOCIAL AGENDA: CAPTURING KNOWLEDGE FOR LIFELONG LEARNING APPROACHES

Archives play a vital role in enabling communities to access lifelong learning opportunities through offering access, professional guidance and training to global resources in a local setting (Eduards and Usher, 2000). They provide a wide range of services to millions of students, researchers and members of the public, as well as access to a huge range of high quality raw content. The conventional functions of an archival organization are to collect, process, disseminate, store and utilize document information to provide service for the society. Archival institutions provide access to collections of unpublished materials -in the form of a "document"- about the past and a wide framework of topics related to the past. These collections include manuscripts, letters, diaries, organization records, state and local government records, photographs, films, oral histories and many other kinds of unique materials documenting the concept of collective memory (Buckland, 1997).

The rapid changes and applications of Semantic Web in the means of archival access have spawned an upheaval in describing and managing archival resources. They have added valuably to the arsenal of tools used for educating the public but also for interpretation and research by experts in the fields of education and cultural heritage. In parallel, these advanced technologies have potentially contributed to an increasing awareness that knowledge can be extracted by the users via the developments of "user-friendly" metaphors in human-computer interaction; they have facilitated the acceptance of "interactivity" as one of the key elements of digital media in the archival domain (Gilliland-Swetland, 2000).

It is this realization that makes knowledge management attractive to archival organizations. While the focus in information management is mostly on explicit knowledge, knowledge management brings a new dimension: the need to manage semantic knowledge by focusing on people and enhance their capability by improving communication, information transfer and collaboration. Facilitating interactivity and conceptualizing it in the lifelong learning framework requires (Kourtoumi, 2004):

- Discovery of existing knowledge (*archival description*)
- Acquisition of knowledge (*indexes and inventories*)
- Creation of new knowledge (*schemas, ontologies*)
- Storage and organization of knowledge (*metadata*)
- Sharing of knowledge (*public access, user-friendly systems*)
- Use and application of knowledge (*learning environment*)
- Feedback (*educational programs, course packs*)

The identification of knowledge needs of the users are based on the principles of lifelong learning, the basic stages of which are:

- Information (*discovery of existing knowledge*)
- Tacit knowledge (*acquisition of knowledge*)
- Understanding (*creation of new knowledge*)
- Application (*storage and organization of knowledge*)
- Analysis (*sharing of knowledge*)
- Synthesis (*use and application of knowledge*)
- Evaluation (*feedback and digital libraries*)

The core philosophy of the lifelong learning process is the discovery of knowledge, not the passive reception of information. It is a condition of constant apprenticeship- mobile, flexible and adaptable (Ainley and Rainbird, 1999). In all stages archives are used as a dictionary, a databank, a thesaurus or a quilt index. In all dimensions they work as a comprehensive, trans- institutional online collection tool built upon an open source digital repository: the user opens it every time he or she needs to find out something and comes back to it when he or she needs it again.

In the archival domain investing on knowledge management by providing a user-friendly e-learning conceptual environment, can be viewed as a process. In this process the target is to optimise the effective application of intellectual capital to achieve organizational objectives: to maximize effectiveness and efficiency of archival institutions in the global environment (Bouthillier & Shearer, 2002). The challenge in lifelong learning is to discover and capture the tacit intellectual capital -that contained in the primary sources- in order for archives to enable the general public to "construct" its learning:

- By sharing their capital through world-wide connectivity and interoperability, to leverage corporate capital.
- By encompassing learning for personal, civic and social purposes as well as for employment-related purposes.

THE PEDAGOGIC AGENDA: CONSTRUCTING DIGITAL COLLECTIONS AS SOCIALLY INTELLIGENT AGENTS

As Smith (1998) noted in the American Historical Association's newsletter, many web sites "seduce the senses without engaging the mind". In the digital era the archival sector sees a spectrum of e-learning user types emerging, ranging from the inexperienced, novice user, to the highly proficient and advanced user of digital resources. In the archival environment digitisation includes

taking a physical object or analogue item, such as a tape recording, a map, or correspondence, from a collection that is rare or unique, often extremely fragile, and taking photographs of the item, and transferring the photographs to a digital medium. The negatives or prints are scanned into digital format (Library of Congress, 2000). Digital files are imported into, and managed with the use of software programs. Digital files may be read, compressed, transferred and retrieved over computer networks then made accessible and viewed on computer monitors.

The focus lately is moving from creating large amounts of digital content and providing some fairly simple access tools, upon constructing sophisticated systems for ongoing use or apparatus providing interpretation. All of these efforts are producing numerous large collections of material, databases that are open to exploration and presentation in dozens of different directions (Oluic-Vukovic, 2001). While digitising and making available collections through the Internet has been a laudatory goal for archives, there is still a evolving need to push this accessibility further to more deeply engage users with the rich historical sources that the database would highlight, exploiting the pedagogical and interactive possibilities of the medium. Although many archival institutions have embraced digital archives to make their collections more accessible to support learning as a social experience, few have joined in multi–state efforts to combine resources concerning a specific topic to explore the medium's pedagogic potential (Mercier and Wykoff, 2005).

Digital archival collections need to be considered from the vantage point of the content and functionality they are providing as well as the context of the activities they are intended to support. As complex resources are designed and developed for education in particular, careful research on how archival users learn using such resources should inform the construction of these digital collections. If such pedagogically structured resources are made available, users will learn how to decipher, judge, apply, and learn from these digital collections. In terms of significant lifelong learning, such knowledge will serve the users well.

Meanwhile, archival institutions invest in digital projects within the semantic scope by carefully designing metadata results for lifelong purposes, including:

- Reducing over-handling of material in order to preserve it (*diagnosing learning needs*)
- Assisting in promoting the collections and the institution in a global environment (*formulating learning needs*)
- Providing intellectually access to value-added information (*identifying human material resources for learning*)
- Achieving the best information and knowledge management of their material in the short and long-term (*choosing and implementing appropriate learning strategies and evaluating learning outcomes*)

On pedagogic grounds, then, the issue for archival institutions is not a choice between conventional and e-learning delivery methods, but a choice of the most appropriate balance between the uses of these different methods in different contexts. This is a process, which involves the professional judgment of educators, taking into account the changing needs, demands, interests and capabilities of students (O'Brien, 2005). However, there is a significant scope to enhance the quality and reach of education by appropriate and well-planned developments of e-learning in archival institutions: to embrace the idea that the most useful forms of representation of archival information and knowledge, the most powerful analogies, illustrations, examples, explanations, and demonstrations; in a word, the most powerful the ways of representing and formulating the subject that make it comprehensible to students (Bothman, 2002).

On pedagogical content knowledge embedding digital libraries of archival material also includes an understanding of what makes the learning of specific topics easy or difficult: the conceptions and preconceptions that students of different ages and backgrounds bring with them to the learning of those most frequently taught topics and lessons focused on databases from archival sources (Shulman, 1987). This "conceptual infrastructure" databases for archival sources need to be linked with new tools whereby both verbal and visual quoting is an integral part of the software. Access to it is combined with spaces for collaborative and personal creation and co-creation. There are challenges to find new ways of visual and verbal quotation, of reference, of building on the richness of the past to arrive at a more creative future. Combining the universal approaches of art and sciences through the particular approaches of historical evidences, as presented in the archival heritage from the past to the present, offers a valuable key to future creativity (Hedstrom, 2002).

On the semantic web educators and their students can locate archival sources, put the collected ones in their historical context, classify and present them by time, geography, theme, or subject, in addition to keyword searches. Thus, they construct their own digital libraries, within the archival digital collections. This feedback works as powerful tool to help activate the background knowledge of students on a particular topic or issue and spark an interest to find out more (Stiles, 2002). It can even supplements their narratives with virtually unbounded collections of sources, notes, graphs, charts, images, and links that even a profligate publisher could not hope to fit into a book. In addition, given the open access of the web, it seems appropriate to cast the widest possible net, highlighting materials that can be tied into classroom curriculum. This is preferable more than just focusing on figures such as official data and national policies which will likely dominate coverage in print of relative textbooks (Bloom & Stout, 2005).

The marginal cost of reaching different open access archives is almost zero. With the semantic web interested colleagues can access an online subject-based archival source (in a form of a photo, a diary, a catalogue, an oral history interview or a document) as cheaply and simply as a dozen. Moreover, the structure of the semantic web allows interested parties to access the primary source material from any internet-connected computer, at any time, and even to search the evidence for phrases or keywords. Educators and students alike may link this piece of evidence to others on the web, catalogue and copy it, and even print it if so desired (Cohen, 2004).

The massive knowledge capacity of the semantic web means that educators and students (=users) can push beyond the selectivity of paper collections to create more comprehensive archives with multiple viewpoints and multiple formats (including audio and video as well as text). These archives, hopefully partially making up for their lack of the curator's touch with their size, scope and immediacy, will in turn require more sophisticated tools for future research (for example, see the two Harvard's Open Collections Programs, "Women Working, 1800-1930" (http://ocp.hul. harvard.edu/ww/) and "Immigration to the United States, 1789-1930 (http://ocp.hul.harvard.edu/ei). If carefully developed, such collections- ideally interoperable with others of their ilk- provide history engaged and history aware students, with the means to understand the past in a more direct and coherent way and, hopefully, more deeply (Mercier & Wykoff, 2005).

Educators and students will be able, then, to express the inimitable regional and local dimensions of history. They will entail simultaneously realities at local, regional and national levels internationally, illustrating the importance of the cultural context in how educational ideas are interpreted, reshaped and realized to improve classroom learning (Barnes, 1992). Providing

"conceptual infrastructure" in the web for archival sources, new knowledge-based approaches can be achieved in the domain for formal education programs, leading in (Kourtoumi, 2005):

- Providing frameworks for information exchange and resource interoperability in high quality primitive resources
- Assisting users in understanding historical content
- Assisting information providers with conceptualising a topic
- Mapping out the conceptual structure and providing a common language for research/ curriculum fields in social studies
- Providing classification/typology and concept definitions
- Clarifying concepts by putting them into context
- Providing orientation and serving as a reference tool for educators and students
- Assisting with the exploration of the conceptual context of a research problem and in structuring the problem
- Providing the conceptual basis for the design of good research, for the consistent definition of variables
- Providing the accumulation of research results within the curriculum and/or for lifelong learning purposes
- Providing the conceptual basis for the exploration of the various aspects of a program in program planning, in the identification of approaches and strategies, and in the development of evaluation criteria
- Supporting (both technical and human) for consistent communication between educational communities and archival institutions

THE INNOVATION AGENDA: APPLYING ARCHIVAL KNOWLEDGE PRODUCTION FOR LEARNING SCENARIOS

Knowledge based e-learning has already become central to the creation of the intellectual capacity on which archival knowledge production and utilisation depend. Archival institutions have to promote lifelong-learning practices and update knowledge and skills if they are to retain competitive advantage. As traditional institutions of primitive historical information, they have an important role to play in this regard, by underpinning learning in its broadest sense, both as a formal activity within an institution and informally within the community. They have to take advantage of the opportunities offered by the new information and communications technologies. Failure to do so will mean the widening of the digital divide that is facing most of the developing countries, particularly the low-income countries (EBLIDA, 2001).

By creating digital surrogates of their collections on a semantic scope, archival institutions continue to support the notion that there is value in the materials they house in a global environment. However, research in scale-up is very difficult to perform except by building and deploying a large-scale digital knowledge-based collection system. Establishing infrastructure and tools to facilitate experimentation with large-scale systems is essential, as is funding to study use and behaviour of large-scale systems once deployed through this infrastructure.

Applying such infrastructure and tools in archival sources is valuable for creating learning materials and learning scenarios. Archival knowledge is then directly introducing into the lifelong learning processes at all level in arts, humanities, science and vocational courses. These learning environment focus primarily on older and historic manmade structures and environments, promoting their use in curriculum as visual resources for teaching knowledge and skills; as resources for the study of a continuum of cultures; and as real and actual places that users of all ages can experience, study and evaluate first hand (Coleman, 1988).

The essence of the digital collections approach is to enable access to web-accessible material through interoperable repositories for metadata sharing, publishing and archiving (Hepburn, 2004). It arise out the archival community, where a growing need for low-barrier interoperability solution to access fairly heterogeneous repositories of raw historical information lead to the establishment and promotion of interoperability standards that aim to facilitate the efficient dissemination of archival content.

Once a workable schema is in place, the next task is to enable users to provide input in the system. It is seen vital that the capture of knowledge has to happen within the domain that the users are focusing on (highly contextual), and represent that context correctly to others. As a consequence, specific forms of users' innovation are evolving (Houle, 1961):

- **Goal-orientated innovations:** For those users who use education as a means of accomplishing fairly clear cut objectives.
- **Activity-orientated innovations:** For those users who take part in such activities because of an attraction in the circumstances of learning rather than in the content or announced purpose.
- **Learning-orientated innovations:** For those users who seem to seek knowledge for their own sake.

Principally, two types of knowledge need to be captured. The first is as an annotation to existing content. The techniques of annotation have been found useful to retain context while avoiding unnecessary changes in the original knowledge object. On-line news bulletins, allow discussion treads, user feedback and user ratings directly attached to the "document". Secondly, new content needs to be added to the knowledge base. To maintain the integrity of the knowledge base, only users with suitable access rights should be able to add this level of content, or additions need to be moderated and accepted prior to addition in the knowledge base (Verhaart, 2003). The final part of the content management system is the ability to reorganize the domain content for use in different lifelong learning situations. At this level it will be important that the annotations and any new or additional content are flagged so that any anomalies or updated content can be added to this reorganized taxonomy.

CONCLUSION

In the knowledge era archives attempt to share their collections by digitizing and indexing them on the web. Since knowledge is recognized as an essential asset for archives to survive on increasingly competitive and global environment, knowledge management has become an important effort in many archival organizations. The Semantic Web as a context for deploying digital library systems for archival collections offers an unprecedented opportunity -- not only technically by providing connectivity to an enormous potential user base but also culturally, given the Internet community's models and traditions of technology diffusion through the distribution of publicly available prototype software -- to move ahead large-scale experiments. Research efforts within the archival community should exploit these opportunities in humanizing information technology.

It seems clear that the inevitable presence of large amounts of valuable, proprietary archival information -- which can be viewed as another form of scale-up in digital libraries for archival

collections -- also shapes the research agenda in new ways. The near-term focus is on overcoming the infrastructural barriers to supporting proprietary content information. The development of an increasingly global marketplace for archival resources in the Semantic Web may:

- Create new opportunities in all areas of the research agenda presented above that archivists can not overlook.
- Allow professionals to explore vital new questions in the development of archival description, navigation, access, and resource discovery and retrieval technologies and systems that can function in this broader environment of the semantic web.

As archivists -and other information professionals in the cultural heritage domain- are using digital information systems and objects, they are called to resolve some key questions:

- Indentify which metadata and ontologies schemas are best applied in their case to best meet the needs of the information creator, repository and users.
- Ensure that they have chosen the most current versions of the metadata and ontologies schemas being applied in the market.

Undoubtedly, there are research issues and outstanding questions in the design of such an infrastructure. There are also operational and policy problems impeding deployment. While some of the research issues are complex and will require ongoing exploration, putting at least the first steps towards the necessary infrastructure in place to accommodate such valuable content information is a high priority in advancing the research agenda and addressing scale-up issues.

Within the education paradigm of lifelong learning and by encouraging the general public to share their discoveries and engage in more sophisticated use and analysis of archives, the application of semantic web change the way that "documents" as educational materials are designed, developed and distributed. It also changes the roles that the "student" - the user- and the "educational provider" - the archival institution - play and the interaction between these "players" in the educational setting.

REFERENCES

Ainley, P., & Rainbird, H. (Eds) (1999). *Apprenticeship: towards a new paradigm for learning* (p. 58). London: Kogan Page.

Barnes, D. (1992). The significance of teachers' frames for teaching. In T. Russell & H. Munby (Eds.), *Teachers and teaching: from classroom to reflection* (pp. 9-32). London: The Falmer Press.

Beamsley, T. (1999). Securing digital image assets in museums and libraries: A risk management approach. *Library Trends, 48*(2), 358-378.

Berolazzi, P., Krusich, C., & Missikoff, M. (2001). *An Approach to the Definition of a Core Enterprise Ontology: CEO*, http://cersi.luiss.it/oesseo2001/papers/9.pdf

Besser, H. (2002). The Next Stage: Moving from Isolated Digital Collections to Interoperable Digital Libraries. *First Monday, 7*(6), http://firstmonday.org/issues/issue7_6/besser

Bloom, N., & Stout, C. (2005). Using digitised primary source materials in the classroom: A Colorado case study. *First Monday, 10*(6), http://firstmonday.org/issues/issue10_6/bloom/index.html.

Borgman, C. L. (1999). What are digital libraries? Competing visions. *Information Processing and Management, 35*(3), 227-243. http://portal.acm.org/citation.cfm?id=779042.779051&dl=GUIDE&dl=ACM

Bothman, B. (2002). The past that archives keep: Memory, history, and the preservation of archival records, *Archivaria, 51,* 48–80.

Buckland, M. K. (1997). What is a "document"? *Journal of the American Society of Information Science, 48*(9), 804-809, http://www.interscience.wiley.com/

Bouthillier, F., & Shearer, K. (2002). Understanding knowledge management and information management: The need for an empirical perspective. *Information Research, 8*(1), No. 141, http://InformationR.net/ir/8-1/paper141.html

Chandler, R. L. (2002). Museums in the Online Archive of California (MOAC): Building Digital Collections Across Libraries and Museums. *First Monday, 7*(5), http://firstmonday.org/issues/issue7_5/chandler/index.html

Cohen, D. (2004). History and the second decade of the web. *Rethinking History, 8*(2), 293-301. http://chnm.gmu.edu/resources/essays/essay.php?id=34.

Coleman, J. (1988). Social Capital in the Creation of Human Capital. *American Journal of Sociology, 94*, Supplement, 95-120.

Dalbello, M. (2004). Institutional Shaping of Cultural Memory: Digital Library as Environment for Textual Transmission. *Library Quarterly, 74*(3), 265-29. http://64.233.183.104/search?q=cache:qIBn7-HYNMgJ:www.scils.rutgers.edu/~dalbello/research/Dalbello%2520(LQ74_2004).pdf+Tefko+Saracevic,+Marija+Dalbello-+article&hl=el&ie=UTF-8&inlang=el

EBLIDA (2001). Why is lifelong learning important for archives and libraries? *EBLIDA statements in response to European Commission memorandum on lifelong learning.* www.eblida.org/topics/lifelong/lifelonglearning.htm

Eduards, R., & Usher, R. (2000). *Globalization and pedagogy: Space, place, identity* (p. 83). London: Routeldge.

Harvard's Open Collections Programs, *Women Working, 1800-1930.* http://ocp.hul.harvard.edu/ww

Harvard's Open Collections Programs, *Immigration to the United States, 1789-1930.* http://ocp.hul.harvard.edu/ei

Hedstrom M. (2002). Archives, memory, and interfaces with the past. *Archival Science, 2,* 21–43.

Hepburn, G. A. (2004). Seeking an educational commons: The promise of open source development models. *First Monday, 9*(8), http://www.firstmonday.org/issues/issue9_8/hepburn/

Howarth, L. C. (2001). Designing a Metadata-Enabled Namespace for Enhancing Resource Discovery in Knowledge Bases [Version presented at the International Conference]. In M. Guerrini & S. Gambari, & L. Sardo (Eds.), *Proceedings International Conference Electronic Resources: Definition, Selection and Cataloguing*, Rome, 2001, http://66.249.93.104/search?q=cache:a8QFjPNp_p0J:eprints.rclis.org/archive/00000174/ ca,+Murtha+what:+Introduction+to+Metadata:+Pathways+to+Digital+Information+&hl=el&ie=UTF-8&inlang=el

Houle, C. O. (1961). *The Inquiring Mind. A study of the adult who continues to learn* (pp. 34-36), Madison, Wisconsin: University of Wisconsin Press.

Gilliland-Swetland, A. J. (2000). Setting the stage: Defining metadata. In M. Baca (Ed.), *Introduction to Metadata: Pathways to Digital Information.* 2nd ed. Los Angeles: Getty Information Institute, http://www.getty.edu/research/institute/standards/intrometadata/index.html

Gruber, T. R. (1993). A Translation Approach to Portable Ontology Specifications. *Knowledge Acquisition, 5*(2), 199–220.

IDEF- (2001). *A What is.com definitions.* http://64.233.183.04/search?q=cache:syss-28wuqsoJ:cersi.luiss.it/oesseo2001/papers/9.pdf+IDEF5+(integrated+definition)+&hl=el&ie=UTF-8&inlang=el

Kourtoumi, Tr. (2004). 'Intelligent' Cultural Heritage & Archival Applications: A Case Study of Usefulness of Semantic Indexing in a Collection Level Description. In J. Hemsley (Ed.), *Conference Proceedings, EVA 2004.* London: The London Institute of Archaeology, University College London, July 26-30, 29.1-29.11.

Kourtoumi, Tr. (2005). Knowledge management technology: Facing the challenge of managing archives. *International Journal of Knowledge, Culture and Change Management, 5*(4), 25-30, http://ijm.cgpublisher.com/product/pub.28/prod.259

Library of Congress (2000). *Digitizing the collection: American Memory.* http://lcweb2.loc.gov/ammem/daghtml/dagtech.html

Lisbon European Council (2000). *Resolution on lifelong learning.* http://europa.eu.int/eurlex/pri/en/oj/dat/2002/c_163/c_16320020709en00010003.pdf

Lynch, C. A. (2002). Digital Collections, Digital Libraries and the Digitization of Culture Heritage Information. *First Monday, 7*(5). http://www.firstmonday.org/issues/issue7_5/lynch/author

McKay, S. (2003). Research Library, Getty Research Institute, "Digitization in an Archival Environment. *Electronic Journal of Academic and Special Librarianship, 4*(1). http://64.233.183.104/search?q=cache:C80VfMVXulcJ:southernlibrarianship.icaap.org/content/v04n01/Mckay_s01.htm+content-+archival+collection-+digital&hl=el&ie=UTF-8&inlang=el

Mercier, L., & Wykoff, L. (2005). Engaging the public with digital primary sources: A tri–state online history database and learning center. *First Monday, 10*(6), http://firstmonday.org/issues/issue10_6/mercier/index.html

Mischo, W. H. (2005). Digital Libraries: Challenges and Influential Work. *D-Lib Magazine, 11*(7/8), http://66.249.93.104/search?q=cache:37 XAKs6S7JAJ:www.dlib.org/ William+H.+Mischo,+%26%238220%3BDigital+Libraries:+Ch allenges+and+Influential+Work%26%238221% 3B,+D-Lib+Magazine,+Vol+11,+No+7/8,+July/ August+2005&hl=el&ie=UTF-8&inlang=el

n.a. (2003). *Institutional Repositories: Essential Infrastructure for Scholarship in the Digital Age, ARL, 226,* 1-7. http://www.arl.org/newsltr/226/ir.html

O'Brien L. (2005). E-Research: An Imperative for Strengthening Institutional Partnerships. EDUCAUSE, 40(6), http://www.educause.edu/apps/er/erm05/erm0563.asp

Oluic-Vukovic, V. (2001). From information to knowledge: some reflections on the origin of the current shifting towards knowledge processing and further perspective. *Journal of the American Society for Information Science and Technology, 52,* 54-61.

Shulman, S. (1987). Knowledge and teaching: Foundations of the new reform. *Harvard Educational Review, 57*(1), 1-22.

Smith, Carl (1998). Can you do serious history on the Web? *AHA Perspectives, 36*(5), http://chnm.gmu.edu/resources/essays/serioushistory.php

Stojanovic, L., Schneider, J., Maedche, A., Libischer, S., Studer, R., Lumpp, Th. Abecker, A., Breiter, G., & Dinger, J. (2004). *The role of ontologies in autonomic computing systems, IBM Systems Journal, 43*(3). http://www.research.ibm.com/journal/sj/433/stojanovic.html

Verhaart, M. (2003). Developing a system to capture knowledge based on sharable and self documenting learning objects. *International Forum of Educational Technology & Society.* http://www.ymlp.com/pubarchive_show_message.php?eLearning+138

Chapter X
Application of Web 2.0 Technology for Clinical Training

Adela Lau
The Hong Kong Polytechnic University, China

Eric Tsui
The Hong Kong Polytechnic University, China

ABSTRACT

In clinical training, students plan, implement and evaluate their learning activities by themselves. They apply theories and concepts in a real clinical environment and learn through social interaction and reflective thinking to experience, conceptualize, apply and create new knowledge to solve clinical problems. Since students are sent to different clinical locations for training and are mentored on a one-to-one basis, it is difficult for students to share their knowledge, make enquiries or interact with their peers and mentors for social and reflective learning. Web 2.0 provides a collaborative and social interactive platform that allows learners to exchange, share, acquire, codify, distribute, and disseminate knowledge. Its functions and features are able to construct a virtual and distributed environment for learners to gather, filter and update the knowledge over different Internet sources. This chapter thus aims to discuss the functions and features of Web 2.0 technology and its applications to clinical training.

CLINICAL TRAINING IN NURSE EDUCATION

Clinical training and hospital attachment are the areas of thematic learning in nursing education. It is normal practice for nursing institutes to send their final year students to placements for clinical training. Each student is attached to one clinician to learn and practice their clinical skills in a real environment. Students are required to plan, implement, and evaluate their own learning activities by themselves (Dornan et al., 2005).

Students are asked to take notes and share their clinical experience (Iyamu et al., 2007) with mentors and peers in the placement. Through such social and reflective learning, knowledge on clinical operations can be shared, exchanged and collaborated (Meskó et al., 2007), stimulating students' to think and create new knowledge (Dornan et al., 2005; O'Neill et al., 2002). More importantly, students are trained in the ability to integrate their knowledge and skills in their workplaces thereby approaching clinical operations with increased confidence.

Web 2.0 is a people-based knowledge management tool that supports knowledge collaboration, exchange, sharing, and creation. It provides the platform and tools, such as blogs, wikis, podcasts, social bookmarks, really simple syndication (RSS), tags and social network software, for learners to interact and communicate in a virtual and distributed environment (Santoro, 2007; Lee, Tsui and Garner, 2008; Gooding, 2008). Following the rapid growth of the usage of Web 2.0 in e-learning (Santoro, 2007), this paper investigates how Web 2.0 can be applied for clinical training in nurse education and what issues to be considered in developing a Web 2.0 platform for clinical knowledge sharing.

WEB 2.0 TECHOLOGY DEVELOPMENT

Web 2.0 technologies include blog, wiki, podcast, social bookmark, tags, really simple syndication and social network software and has the features of social interaction and collaboration to facilitate knowledge sharing and exchange over internet platform (Lau et al., 2009). It allows community to publish and share content by themselves and to edit content collaboratively and interactively. Through such social interaction and collective intelligence, knowledge is created, exchanged, shared and created.

Blog

A blog is a user-friendly content management tool that allows users (bloggers) to publish their own content on the web (Santoro, 2007; Gooding, 2008; Kamel et al., 2007; Boulos et al., 2006; McGee et al., 2008; McLean et al., 2007). A blogger shares his writings (blog) with other bloggers who are in the community or the general public. Other bloggers write comments or share their feelings and opinions about the posted blog, or link it to other blogs. Through such blogs' linking and sharing, communities with the same interest and discussion topics are formed. Bloggers share, exchange, distribute and disseminate their knowledge and experience through such social interaction and communication. In clinical placements, students are allocated to different clinics for placement. They take notes and share their clinical experiences with their mentor and peers. Blogs overcome the geographical problems and help students to post and share their clinical experience with peers or mentors in other locations, connecting them in a virtual social environment that results in clinical knowledge sharing, exchange, distribution and dissemination, and facilitates learning through social interaction and reflective thinking. By analyzing blogs' linking, students with similar study topics are linked and clustered together to form an expert locator, topic directory or community. This helps learners to navigate the required clinical knowledge more easily, and to locate experts or peers with similar clinical experience for knowledge acquisition. Thus, blogs can be used as discussion forum, expert locator, topic directory or case repository for social and reflective learning in clinical training.

Wiki

A wiki is a collaborative editing tool that allows authors to co-edit a document (O'Neill et al., 2002; Gooding, 2008; Kamel et al., 2007; Boulos et al., 2006; McLean et al., 2007). It provides the functions/features of content management, versioning control, right management, etc. Authors collaboratively edit a single document. They review, add comments and revise the content. Through such collective intelligence and collaboration, knowledge is created. Each student is attached to one clinician for training. Students are sent to different clinics and supervised by different mentors, but they may handle similar clinical cases in their placements. Wikis allow students to share their clinical experience and work collaboratively to edit, among other, similar clinical cases. Through such collaboration and collective intelligence, students can create knowledge for problem solving. Most importantly, all the similar clinical cases can be grouped into certain topics for sharing. Thus, a wiki can be used as a collaborative platform for groupwork and to build a knowledge repository for social learning.

Podcast

A podcast is a series of audio or video digital-media files for playback on portable media players and computers (Santoro, 2007; Kamel et al., 2007; Sandars et al., 2007). It can be syndicated, subscribed to and downloaded automatically when the content is updated. Podcasters distribute and disseminate the digital-media files over the internet and subscribers obtain the podcasts via a simple syndication feed reader in real time. Thus, students can capture clinical skills and techniques in image, audio or video files during clinical training, and distribute and disseminate these podcasts via RSS feed reader to their peers or mentors. Their peers and mentors can view the podcasts through their ipods or computers at anytime and anywhere. Thus, podcasts can be used as digital-media teaching material and facilitating knowledge distribution, dissemination and acquisition for clinical training.

Social Bookmark

A social bookmark is a method for internet users to store, organize, search and manage webpage bookmarks (Gooding, 2008; Yang et al., 2008). Social bookmark software allows users to input tags (i.e. keywords or terms) informally and personally to describe the webpages, and share the tagged bookmarks with others. By relating the tags of the bookmarked pages, bookmarks can be linked and clustered into different topics. Students in clinical placements already share their blogs, podcasts and clinical websites with their peers or mentors, and social bookmarks further allow them to add bookmarks and tags to these internet sources. By classifying and relating the bookmarks into different categories collaboratively, students can more easily search for the required knowledge on a certain topic from the social bookmark websites. Thus, the social bookmark is a knowledge collaboration and sharing method for bookmarking. It is used as a community-based bookmarking tool for learning resources indexing, which shortens students' searching time.

Tags

Tags are the keywords or terms for describing digital media content such as social bookmarks, audio clips, video clips, blogs, wikis, websites, etc. Tags are built by a community and are used to describe its content. The tag cloud function collects and counts the number of tags used by a community, and groups and classifies them into different topics that enable a search engine to search more accurately (Connor, 2008). Students can add tags to their podcast, blog, wiki or social bookmarks content and share the tags with their peers or mentors for tagging or content searching. The more accurate search results from such tagging of knowledge collaboration and sharing help students acquire the required knowledge more effectively and efficiently. Tags can therefore be used as community-based taxonomy to describe the learning content of podcasts, blogs, wikis, social bookmarks or clinical websites.

Really Simple Syndication

Really Simple Syndication (RSS) is a feed reader for content distribution, dissemination and acquisition (McLean et al., 2007) over internet sources such as blogs, wikis, podcasts, social bookmarks or websites. When the source content is updated, the RSS feed reader authomatically sends an alert signal and pushes the updated content to RSS subscribers so that RSS subscribers gather the most updated information in real time. By adding the RSS to clinical internet sources, knowledge can be distributed and disseminated to students efficiently. Students can subscribe to an RSS feed reader and gain clinical experience from clinical cases and discussions via blogs, wikis, social bookmarks or other websites automatically. In other words, an RSS feed reader can be used as a learning content updater in clinical training, speeding up the knowledge dissemination and distribution processes and students' knowledge acquistion processes.

Social Network Software

Lastly, social network software provides social networking functions such as audio/video conferencing, IP telephony, desktop sharing, chat rooms, whiteboards, etc., for a community to communicate and interact in a virtual environment (Bonniface et al., 2007). It provides community-building functions such as an electronic portfolio, resume builder, and social networking, so that people can be connected together to form online communities to exchange and share knowledge (Rapoza, 2008). In clinical training, social network software allows students to create communities, connect with people, spread ideas, and share knowledge in a virtual community environment that facilitates social learning among students and overcomes geographical barriers for knowledge sharing and exchange. Thus, social network software can be used as a platform to build a community for social learning. Students can exchange, share and create knowledge through such social interaction and communication.

In summary, Web 2.0 provides the features of collaborative work, social networking, community, and self-management. By using Web 2.0 tools, students can build communities and learn through knowledge collaboration, exchange and sharing. Web 2.0 provides a networked environment for learners to interact with each other in a single place and to create new knowledge through social interaction and reflective thinking. Web 2.0 links up internet learning sources in a virtual and distributed environment that facilitates knowledge dissemination and distribution over the Internet. Learners can plan and implement their own learning activities with Web 2.0 applications and evaluate their learning outcomes by themselves. In other words, Web 2.0 technology links people and internet learning sources and builds communities. It overcomes some of the geographical and one-to-one mentoring problems for social and reflective learning.

ISSUES CONCERNING THE USE OF A WEB 2.0 PLATFORM FOR CLINICAL KNOWLEDGE SHARING

In summary, Web 2.0 provides the functions and features for knowledge collaboration, exchange, sharing and creation. It can be applied to clinical training for improving clinical knowledge through social and reflective learning. Thus, in order to implement a usable clinical training Web 2.0 platform, other issues such as interface design, learning content, patient privacy, perceptions of knowledge-sharing behavior of nurse, factors for increasing the likelihood of nurse on using web-based platform, and organizational culture are required to be studied.

ACKNOWLEDGMENT

The authors like to thank The Hong Kong Polytechnic University for its funding of this research under project code 8CBX.

REFERENCES

Bonniface, L., & Green, L. (2007). Finding a new kind of knowledge on the HeartNET website. *Health Information and Libraries Journal, 24*(1), 67-76.

Boulos, M., Kame, N., Maramba, I., & Wheeler, S. (2006). Wikis, blogs and podcasts: a new generation of *Web*-based tools for virtual collaborative clinical practice and education. *BMC Medical Education, 6*, 41.

Connor, E. (2007) Medical librarian 2.0. *Medical Reference Services Quarterly, 26*(1), 1-15.

Dornan, T., Hadfield, J., Brown, M., Boshuizen, H., & Scherpbier, A. (2005). How can medical students learn in a self-directed way in the clinical environment? Design-based research. *Medical Education, 39*, 356–64.

Dornan, T., Scherpbier, A., King, N., & Boshuizen, H. (2005). Clinical teachers and problem-based learning: A phenomenological study. *Medical Education, 39*, 163–70.

Gooding, J. (2008). Web 2.0: A Vehicle for Transforming Education. *International Journal of Information and Communication Technology Education, 4*(2), 44-53.

Iyamu, E. O. S., & Ukadike, J. O. (2007). Perception of Self-Directed Cooperative Learning Among Undergraduate Students in Selected Nigerian Universities. *International Journal of Information and Communication Technology Education, 3*(4), 13-20.

Kamel, B., Maged, N., & Wheeler, S. (2007). The emerging Web 2.0 social software: an enabling suite of sociable technologies in health and health care education. *Health Information and Libraries Journal, 24*(1), 2-23.

Lau, A., & Tsui, E. (2009). Knowledge Management Perspective on E-learning Effectiveness. *Knowledge-based Systems* (in print).

Lee, H., Tsui, E., & Garner, B. J. (2008). Leveraging Web 2.0 concepts to create an open and adaptive approach to Corporate Learning. *Cutter IT Journal, 21*(1), January, 2008, 14-20.

McGee, J. B., & Begg, M. (2008). What medical educators need to know about "Web 2.0". *Medical Teacher*, (2), 164-9.

McLean, R., Brian, H. R., & Janet, I. W. (2007). The effect of Web 2.0 on the future of medical practice and education: Darwikinian evolution or folksonomic revolution? *The Medical Journal of Australia, 187*(3), 174-7.

Meskó, B., & Dubecz, A. (2007). New possibilities provided by the internet in medicine. *Orvosi hetilap, 148*(44), 2095-9.

O'Neill, P.A., Willis, S. C., & Jones, A. (2002). A model of how students link problem-based learning with clinical experience through 'elaboration'. *Academy of Medicine, 77*, 552–61.

Rapoza, J. (2008). Social Engineering. *eWeek, 25*(3), 39-45.

Sandars, J., & Schroter, S. (2007). Web 2.0 technologies for undergraduate and postgraduate medical education: an online survey. *Postgraduate Medical Journal, 83*(986), 759-62.

Santoro, E. (2007). Podcasts, wikis and blogs: the web 2.0 tools for medical and health education. *Recenti progressi in medicina, 98*(10), 484-94.

Yang, I. S., Ryu, S. S., Cho, K.,J., Kim, J. K., Ong, S. H., Mitchell, W. P., Kim, B. S., Oh, H. B., & Kim, K. H. (2008). IDBD: Infectious Disease Biomarker Database. *Nucleic Acids Research, 36*(1), 455-460.

Chapter XI
Pattern Matching Techniques to Identify Syntactic Variations of Tags in Folksonomies

F. Echarte
Universidad Pública de Navarra, Spain

J. J. Astrain
Universidad Pública de Navarra, Spain

A. Córdoba
Universidad Pública de Navarra, Spain

J. Villadangos
Universidad Pública de Navarra, Spain

ABSTRACT

Folksonomies offer an easy method to organize information in the current Web. This fact and their collaborative features have derived in an extensive involvement in many Social Web projects. However they present important drawbacks regarding their limited exploring and searching capabilities, in contrast with other methods as taxonomies, thesauruses and ontologies. One of these drawbacks is an effect of its flexibility for tagging, frequently producing multiple syntactic variations of a same tag. In this chapter the authors study the application of two classical pattern matching techniques, Levenshtein distance for the imperfect string matching and Hamming distance for the perfect string matching, to identify syntactic variations of tags. This chapter explores the use of pattern techniques to identify syntactic variations of tags in order to reduce the existing noise in certain folksonomies. This chapter focuses on two classical distances used to perform perfect string matching as the Hamming's Distance, and imperfect string matching as the Levenshtein's Distance.

INTRODUCTION

Folksonomies (Vander Wal, 2008) are based in the assignation of text tags to different resources, such as photos, web pages, documents, etc., in order to classify these resources in Web 2.0. Users use these tags to annotate resources defining collaboratively the meaning of the annotated resources, and the used tags.

New search and exploration approaches are possible with Folksnomies, based on the use of the tags (Millen, 2006; Golder, 2005). Users can search for tags, or use navigation systems such as clouds of words, to locate resources tagged by other users and to find information.

Though folksonomies have a great success in current web, mainly due to their simplicity of use, they have also important disadvantages. The fact of users creating tags and assigning them freely to resources produces the inexistence of any structure among these tags. As folksonomies become larger, more problems appear regarding the use of synonyms, syntactic tag variations and different granularity levels (Gruber, 1993). All these problems make more and more difficult the exploration and retrieval of information (Mathes, 2004; Guy, 2006) decreasing the quality of folksonomies Thus, the reduction of syntactic tag variations aids to improve the quality of folksonomies.

There exist different types of syntactic variations of tags: typographical misspellings in the annotation process (*semanticweb/semnticwev/ zemantcweb*); grammatical number (singular or plural) of the same word (*semanticweb/ semanticwebs*); separators (*semantic-web/semanticweb*); or a combination of them (*semntic-web/smanticweb, semntic-webs*, etc.). The existence of these variations causes the classification of the resources under different tags, when they should be classified under just one. This fact makes more confusing the clouds of words, the location of information and the navigation on the folksonomy. However, by identifying all of them as variations of the same label *"semantic web"* and grouping them under the same tag, a user can access this tag obtaining all the information concerning the resources associated with it and its syntactic variations.

This chapter focuses on the application of pattern matching techniques to identify syntactic tag variations. We propose the utilization of pattern matching techniques to identify syntactic variations of tags. We study two classical pattern matching techniques as Levenshtein (Levenshtein, 1966) and Hamming (Hamming, 1950) distances on a large real dataset, evaluating how these techniques perform the identification of both variations of known tags and new (non-existing) tags.

We show the percentages of correct identification achieved with each distance considering different types of variations, as typographic errors, transpositions of adjacent characters, singulars and plurals, and substitution/deletion of separators.

To our knowledge, there is not any study about the application of pattern matching techniques to the identification of syntactic variations of tags. Only in (Specia, 2007) a pre-filtering of the tags is performed before applying an algorithm for tag clustering. This is used to minimize the effects of syntactic variations and to increase the quality of tag clustering. Authors group similar tags using the Levenshtein similarity metric to determine morphological variations, although over a reduced experimental data set and following a non in detail described process. Another way to represent these variations is presented in (Gruber, 1993) where a ontology with three properties associated to tags (*prefLabel*, *altLabel* and *hiddenLabel*) is used.

The use of pattern matching techniques designed to automatically recognize syntactic variations of tags provides mechanisms to improve the quality of folksonomies.

Approximate string matching techniques allow dealing with the problem introduced by syntactic variations on folksonomies. The problem consists on the comparison of a candidate input string called α, maybe containing errors, and a pattern string ω in order to transform α in ω (Navarro, 2001).

Edit operations (insertion, deletion and change of a symbol) allow recovering those errors transforming α in ω. The number of edit operations needed to recover an input string provides a distance measure between the input string and the pattern string. This distance, known as edit distance, can be expressed in terms of similarity and distance (dissimilarity) measures between strings. Classical techniques (Gonzalez, 1978) consider the error correction on input strings introducing new rules in the grammar modelling the considered errors (Schneider, 1992).

The Hamming distance between two strings of equal length indicates the number of positions for which the corresponding symbols are different. It measures the minimum number of substitutions required to transform the candidate string into the pattern string. The Hamming distance can be shown as the number of errors that transform one string into the other. The Hamming distance is commonly used to perform perfect matching between pairs of strings but in our case we deal with pairs of strings with different length strings by padding white spaces at the end of the shortest string. However, for these situations and for those cases where not just substitutions but also insertions or deletions have to be expected, a more sophisticated metric like the Levenshtein distance is more appropriate.

Probably, the most relevant contribution in the field of imperfect string matching is the Generalized Levenshtein Distance. The main drawback of these techniques is the limited number of errors that can be considered due to the finite number of rules introduced in the grammar to model edit operations.

We present an easy method to organize information, due to its simplicity comparing with other alternatives like taxonomies, thesauruses or ontologies. Users collaborates assigning tags to different resources: web pages, pictures, videos, tourist places, etc.

The rest of the chapter is organized as follows: section 2 introduces the addressed problem, section 3 describes the experimental scenario, section 4 presents and analyzes the experimental results obtained; and finally, conclusions and references end the chapter.

PROBLEM DESCRIPTION

Uncontrolled vocabulary, the inexistence of any a priori structure among tags, synonyms, syntactic variations, granularity levels... all of these problems make more and more difficult the exploration and retrieval of information decreasing the quality of folksonomies.

This chapter focuses on reducing the problems derived from the existence of syntactic variations. This existence causes the classification of the resources under different tags, when they can be classified under just one. Browsing and finding of information procedures become more difficult due to this classification. A reduction of the tag entropy provides a handy browsing without a lack of information. Figure 1 shows a tag cloud where we can appreciate some syntactic variations like "flower/flowers", "girl/girls", "mountain/mountains"... It is important to minimize the number of tag variations in a tag cloud, since a given tag can be split in different tag variations reducing its relevance on the cloud. In this sense, a great number of syntactic variations cannot appear in the tag cloud due since the cloud contains the more frequently used tags. Furthermore, the existence of several syntactic variations of a given tag often implies the absence of this tag in the tag cloud, since the total amount of references is distributed among the tag and all its syntactic variations. These variations have a very low relevance themselves, but their contribution can grant the presence of the given tag in the tag cloud.

In order to illustrate the problem to solve, we present a search over Flickr. Flickr[1] is an image and video hosting website, considered one of the

Figure 1. Example of tag cloud

animals architecture art august australia autumn baby band barcelona beach berlin bird birthday black blackandwhite blue boston bw california cameraphone camping canada canon car cat chicago china christmas church city clouds color concert cute dance day de dog england europe fall family festival film florida flower flowers food football france friends fun garden geotagged germany girl girls graffiti green halloween hawaii hiking holiday home house india ireland island italia italy japan july june kids la lake landscape light live london macro may me mexico mountain mountains museum music nature new newyork newyorkcity night nikon nyc ocean paris park party people photo photography photos portrait red river rock rome san sanfrancisco scotland sea seattle show sky snow spain spring street summer sun sunset taiwan texas thailand tokyo toronto tour travel tree trees trip uk urban usa vacation vancouver washington water wedding white winter yellow york zoo

earliest Web 2.0 online community platforms. Flickr is a photo repository where users share personal photographs. These photos can be tagged and browsed by folksonomic means. Note that a given user wants to retrieve photos concerning the Guggenheim Museum sited in Bilbao. Figure 2 illustrates the results of this search. We can appreciate that 557 photos are tagged with a misspelled word (Gugenheim). Near a 2% of the images are not properly tagged due to this undesired variation of the word Guggenheim, so the resources incorrectly tagged are not accessible by users who search correctly.

We propose the utilization of pattern matching techniques to identify syntactic variations of tags and group them. These techniques are based in the comparison of a pattern string and a candidate string. We focus our job in analyzing and comparing two classical techniques as Hamming and Levenshtein distances.

WORKBENCH

This section describes the experimental scenario we have used to evaluate Levenshtein and Ham-

ming distances, paying special attention to the datasets and the methodology followed. This workbench is available on the web[2].

Datasets

We have collected data from the social web CiteULike (which contains bibliographic cites) in order to evaluate our proposal, collecting a total number of 2,290,740 annotations. Each annotation consists on a tag assigned by a user to a resource, at a given date. In this way, one annotation with several tags would be represented by one registry for each tag assigned to the resource.

After a first analysis of the resulting data set, we can appreciate the existence of two tags with a significantly larger number of annotations than the rest. This could be interpreted as it would be generated by any automatic procedure. These tags were "bibtex-import", with 178,813 annotations and "no-tag", with 73,755 annotations. Once deleted the annotations associated to these tags, the resulting data set has the following characteristics: (1) 2,038,172 annotations (one record per user-tag-resource), (2) 494,206 resources, (3) 21,480 users, and (4) 151,522 tags.

Figure 2. Searching for the Guggenheim Museum in Bilbao

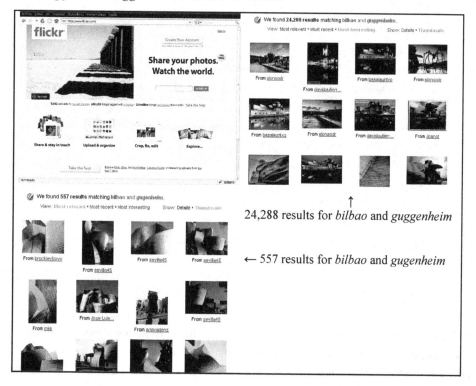

24,288 results for *bilbao* and *guggenheim*

← 557 results for *bilbao* and *gugenheim*

In order to evaluate Levenshtein and Hamming distances, we have created two data sets: one with the aim of checking the correct identification of variations (DS1) and another (DS2) to check the recognition of new tags.

DS1 is obtained from the 10,000 most often used tags. These tags are used in 1,557,198 annotations, representing the 76.4 % of the total amount of annotations. DS1 consists of a set of tuples <*pattern tag-candidate tag*>: *pattern* is one of the 10,000 related tags, and *candidate* is a syntactic variation of the *pattern*. These variations are created automatically. These syntactic variations consider different cases: (i) the singular or plural, (ii) simulation of a typographical error, (iii) simulation of transposition of adjacent symbols, (iv) removal and replacement of separators, and (v) the own pattern tag in order to verify that the used distances recognize the correct pattern when both tags fit. In the creation process, if a syntactic variation of a pattern tag *t* fits another pattern tag *t'*, the candidate tags obtained from *t'* are addressed to *t* and *t'* is deleted. After the whole process, DS1 contains 8,806 different pattern tags and 39,255 tuples (*pattern, candidate*) to check.

DS2 contains 5,000 tags not included as pattern tags in DS1. These tags are used in 122,394 annotations representing the 6% of the total amount of annotations.

We create a dictionary with the 8,806 pattern tags contained in DS1. This dictionary is used to perform the Levenshtein and Hamming distances over DS1 and DS2 datasets. We use a trie structure to store the dictionary when computing the distances.

Methodology

The identification of syntactic variations of tags becomes useful whenever: (1) the pattern matching techniques used ensure a high recognition rate of tags, which are variations of an existing one; and (2) identify, with a high degree of success, new tags that do not fit any existing one. The goal is to maximize the number of syntactic tag variations identified without conditioning the recognition of new tags. In our experimental scenario, the goal is to maximize the number of correctly identified tuples *<pattern, candidate>* on DS1; and to maximize the number of tags identified as new tags on DS2.

To perform this evaluations a discriminator is used. This discriminator consists of the dictionary created from DS1 and a distance (Hamming or Levenshtein). The discriminator accepts as input one tag and checks it with the tags defined in the dictionary. As output the discriminator provides two values, (1) the most similar tag in the dictionary to the provided one, and (2) the distance value. We denote in the following by *candidate* the input at the discriminator, and by *pattern'* its output as depicted in Figure 3.

We take the *candidate* tag from each tuple in DS1 and we apply Levenshtein and Hamming distances over the dictionary at the discriminator.

Then, we get for each *candidate* a corresponding *pattern'*. Note that the algorithm could select a pattern tag (*pattern'*) different to the correct pattern (the associated to the *candidate* tag in DS1). In addition, the discriminator provides the distance values between *candidate* and *pattern'*. In order to interpret the results of the experiment, we denote by *OK* the case when the tag selected by the algorithm (*pattern'*) is the *pattern* associated to *candidate* tag in DS1. That is, the algorithm selects the expected pattern tag. We use *NOK* to describe the case when *pattern'* and *pattern* do not fit.

A threshold level, called *Th*, determines the accuracy of the discriminator. The *candidate* tag is classified as a syntactic variation of the *pattern'* tag if the discriminator provides a distance less than or equal to this threshold (see Figure 3). Thus, for example *NOK & ≤TH* indicates that *candidate* and *pattern'* tags match with a low distance between them, but *candidate* derives from *pattern* tag (in DS1) which is different to *pattern'*.

Dealing with the problem of new tags identification, when the distance values obtained for the tags contained in DS2 (*candidates*) are greater than *Th*, tags are considered as new pattern tags (*New*). In other case tags will be considered as syntactic variations (*Not New*) of the *pattern'* provided by the discriminator.

Figure 3. Methodology schema for DS1 data set evaluation

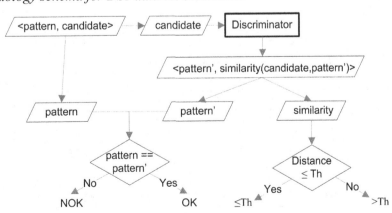

EXPERIMENTAL RESULTS

Table 1 shows the results of processing data sets DS1 and DS2 with the Levenshtein and Hamming distances, using the dictionary with the 8,806 different tags of DS1. Results on DS1 are shown in four different columns, representing if the correct pattern has been identified for each candidate string (*OK*) or not (*NOK*), and if the distance is less than or equal to a determined threshold ($\leq Th$). Threshold values for each distance have been set to 1.0 experimentally, so only one edit operation by string is considered.

Table 1 shows that Hamming distance is more restrictive at the recognition of pattern variations in DS1 (*OK & $\leq Th$*) and that it does not overcome distance threshold in more cases than the Levenshtein distance. This shows that Hamming distance trends to identify less variations and therefore to identify them as new tags.

It corresponds with the results on DS2, where we can appreciate a greater identification ratio than the obtained for the Levenshtein distance.

A breakdown of these results based on the different variation types is presented in Table 2. The variation labelled as *Self*, represents that both pattern and candidate are the same strings, so the distance is null and both Hamming and Levenshtein distances should identify them always correctly. Table 2 shows that both distances identify correctly the pattern and candidate strings when they match (Self / OK & $\leq$TH).

Regarding the failures, both distances provide similar results for Plural/Singular, Typo Error and Transposition variations. However, Levenshtein distance identifies correctly a greater number of variations associated to substitution/deletion of separators.

Transposition variations imply the existence of two edit operations, so a threshold value of

Table 1. Process results on datasets DS1 and DS2

	DS1				DS2	
	NOK & >Th	NOK & $\leq$Th	OK & >Th	OK & $\leq$Th	> TH (New)	$\leq$TH (Not New)
Hamming	3,095	2,152	8,127	25,881	4,162	838
Levenshtein	1,641	2,516	7,767	27,331	4,016	984

Table 2. Breakdown of the results of Hamming and Levenshtein distances by variation type

	NOK & >Th		NOK & $\leq$ Th		OK & >Th		OK & $\leq$ Th	
	Ham.	Lev.	Ham.	Lev.	Ham.	Lev.	Ham.	Lev.
Self	0	0	0	0	0	0	8,788	8,788
Plural/Singular	233	253	523	617	928	896	7,291	7,209
Typo error	65	21	669	762	24	60	8,195	8,110
Transposition	1,022	1,358	934	1,108	6,807	6,280	6	23
Separators	1,775	9	26	29	368	531	1,601	3,201
Total (#)	3,095	1,641	2,152	2,516	8,127	7,767	25,881	27,331
Total (%)	7.88%	4.18%	5.48%	6.41%	20.70%	19.79%	65.93%	69.62%

1.0 avoids the identification of this kind of variation. The greater number of results corresponds to *OK&>Th*, representing that they are able to identify correctly the original pattern, but with a high distance.

One way to deal with this situation is increasing the threshold, however this implies the acceptance of a higher number of edit operations, and this would produce an increase in the incorrect identification of variations among short tags. For example, a threshold value of 2.0, would allow identifying as variations many of the transposition cases, but would affect negatively in the identification of new tags on DS2 for both distances. In the case of Hamming distances, identifications as new tags (*>Th*) decreases from 4,162 to 3,281 and in the case of Levenshtein, from 4,016 to 2,957. Another way is to consider transposition operations as a unique and atomic edit operation, assigning a unitary cost as occurs in (Oommen, 1997).

Both distances provide good results identifying variations originated by typographic errors in which one letter has been replaced by another, providing a distance lower or equal than the threshold value.

Performance changes when dealing with separators. Both distances perform well when separators are changed by other characters, but results differ when the separator is deleted. Hamming distance is negatively affected when separators are deleted in the middle of the patterns. This fact produces that the rest of characters in *candidate* and *pattern* are considered as different. This shows that Levenshtein distance provides better results for character insertion or deletion when there are more characters after the inserted or deleted one.

Moreover, both distances perform well when dealing with plural/singular syntactic variations. In many cases the variation associated to a plural or singular is just only the deletion or insertion of an 's' at the end of the tag, so this allows the distance between patterns to be lower or equal than the threshold value. Both distances also provide similar results for more complex plurals, as (*library* and *libraries*). In these cases the distance values are greater than the threshold value.

Regarding the lengths of candidate strings, Figure 4 shows the identification errors between *candidate* and *pattern* strings (*pattern'* ≠ *pattern*),

Figure 4. Failures of Hamming and Levenshtein distances on DS1 per candidate string length

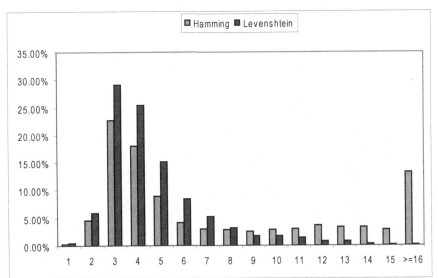

attending to the candidates string length. It shows that in both cases (Hamming and Levenshtein) the greater number of errors happens for tags with lengths of 3 and 4 characters. It can be also seen that Hamming distance has lightly less identification errors for lengths in the range between 4 and 7, and worse results from this point.

Most of the identification errors are associated to lengths 3 and 4. The reason is that any variation in short length strings can produce the resultant strings will be more similar to other patterns distinct to the original. For instance, comparing the candidate string *mul* and *wark*, created from *uml* and *work* patterns, the resultant strings from both distances have been *mdl* and *dark*, instead of the original patterns *uml* and *work*.

Regarding identification errors for string lengths between 4 and 7, Levenshtein distance get lightly worse results because it is not so much affected by the deletion or insertion of new characters as Hamming distance, so an insertion or deletion can make the candidate have less distance with other known patterns different from the original. For instance, the candidate string *vace*, generated from pattern *face* with a typographic

error changing the first character. Hamming distance gets the correct original pattern *face*, but Levenshtein distance gets *ace* as the nearest pattern.

However, Hamming distances starts to increase the number of incorrect identifications in comparison with Levenshtein distance, from the pattern length 8. The reason is due to the fact that from these length is more frequent the use of separators in tags, and Hamming is more affected by the elimination of characters in the middle of patterns. So for instance, for the candidate string *websearch*, generated from the pattern *web_search*, Levenshtein identifies correctly the original pattern, but Hamming distance gets as results the pattern *substance*.

With the objective of ignoring strings with lengths less than or equal to 3, information about the amount of tags in the initial dataset of CiteULike have been obtained. Figure 5 shows the number of tags per length and Figure 6 shows the number of annotations involved per tag length.

Based on these data, trying to identify variations only for lengths greater than 3, the distances would be used for a 95.37% of the tags in the initial

Figure 5. Number of tags of each length in the original folksonomy

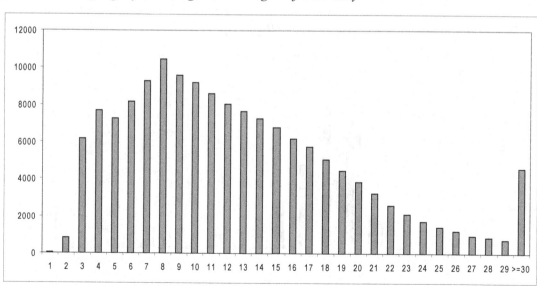

Figure 6. Number of annotations involved per tag length in the original folksonomy

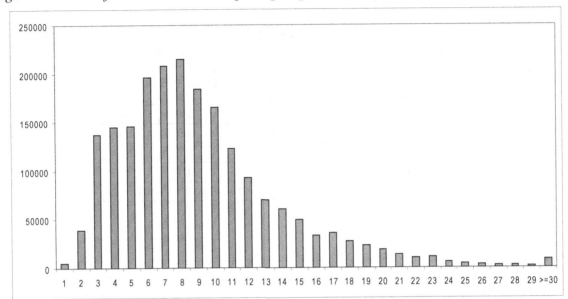

Table 3. Process results on DS1 and DS2 ignoring lenghts <=3

	DS1			DS2		
	NOK & >Th	NOK & ≤Th	OK & >Th	OK & ≤Th	>Th (New)	≤ Th (Not New)
Hamming	2,966	587	8,111	24,431	4,171	418
Levenshtein	1,539	871	7,751	25,934	4,076	513

CiteULike data set, corresponding to a 91.07% of the total number of annotations.

Table 3 summarizes the results obtained applying Hamming and Levenshtein distances on DS1 and DS2 data sets, ignoring tags with length less than or equal to 3. It shows that the number of incorrectly identified patterns with distance less than or equal to the threshold (*NOK&≤Th*) has been reduced: from 2,152 to 587 (72.73%) in the case of Hamming distance, and from 2,516 to 871 (65.38%) in the case of Levenshtein. Regarding results on DS2, it shows that both distances keep the number of correctly tags identified as new, while they reduce the number of tags identified as known tags (*Not New*): from 838 to 418 in the

case of Hamming distance and from 984 to 513 in the case of Levenshtein. This shows that both distances were detecting tags with lengths less than or equal to 3 as variations of some known tag.

Table 4 shows a breakdown of the results on DS1 based on the different variations. It can be seen that the number of identification errors has been reduced in the three types of variations where we get more errors previously: plurals/singulars, typographic errors and transpositions. The greater reduction in associated to transposition variations: from 934 errors to 216 in the case of Hamming distance and from 1,108 to 281 in the case of Levenshtein. The reason is that any transposition

Table 4. Breakdown of the results of Hamming and Levenshtein distances by variation type ignoring lengths <=3

	NOK & >Th		NOK & ≤ Th		OK & >Th		OK & ≤ Th	
	Ham.	Lev.	Ham.	Lev.	Ham.	Lev.	Ham.	Lev.
Self	0	0	0	0	0	0	8,088	8,088
Plural/Singular	172	201	180	220	916	884	6,827	6,790
Typo error	54	13	175	248	24	59	7,918	7,851
Transposition	970	1,318	216	381	6,805	6,279	1	14
Separators	1,770	7	16	22	366	529	1,597	3,191
Total (#)	2,966	1,539	587	871	8,111	7,751	24,431	25,934
Total (%)	8.22%	4.26%	1.63%	2.41%	22.47%	21.47%	67.69%	71.85%

in short patterns has high probability to generate another different pattern with less distance.

CONCLUSION

In this work we have analyzed the performance of two pattern matching techniques to identify syntactic variations in folksonomies: Levenshtein distance for the imperfect string matching, and Hamming distance for the perfect string matching. We have performed the analysis over a large dataset in two different ways: (i) identifying pattern-candidate combinations and (ii) identifying new tags. Experiments show that both techniques provide similar results for some syntactic variation types as typographic errors and simple plurals/singulars, but Levenshtein gets significantly better results than Hamming identifying variations based in the insertion/deletion of characters. However both techniques do not perform as well as desired when identifying variations based in the transposition of adjacent characters or some kind of singulars/plurals (*library/libraries*). Moreover, both techniques improve their results ignoring candidate tags with lengths less than four.

These results show that this techniques can be used to identify syntactic variations of tags, though they should be adapted to perform better with some variation types as plurals/singulars and transpositions of adjacent characters.

ACKNOWLEDGMENT

Research supported by the Spanish Research Council TIN2006-14738-C02-02.

REFERENCES

Echarte, F., Astrain, J. J., Córdoba, A., & Villadangos, J. (2007). Ontology of Folksonomy: A New Modeling Method. In S. Handschuh, N. Collier, T. Groza, R. Dieng-Kuntz, M. Sintek, & A. de Waard, (Ed.), *Semantic Authoring, Annotation and Knowledge Markup -SAAKM 2007-* (pp. 63-70), Sun SITE Central Europe: RWTH Aachen University.

Golder, S. A., & Huberman, B. A. (2005). The Structure of Collaborative Tagging Systems. *Journal of Information Science, 32*(2), 198-208.

Gonzalez, R. C., & Thomason, M. G. (1978). *Syntactic Pattern Recognition. An Introduction.* Reading: Addison-Wesley.

Gruber, T. (1993). A Translation Approach to Portable Ontology Specifications. *Knowledge Acquisition, 5*(2), 199-220.

Guy, M., & Tonkin, E. (2006). Folksonomies - Tidying up Tags? *DLib Magazine, 12*(1).

Hamming, R. W. (1950). Error Detecting and Error Correcting Codes. *Bell System Technical Journal, 26*(2), 147-160.

Levenshtein, V. I. (1966). Binary codes capable of correcting deletions, insertions, and reversals. *Soviet Physics Doklady, 10*(8), 707-710.

Mathes, A. (2004). Folksonomies - Cooperative Classification and Communication Through Shared Metadata. *Computer Mediated Communication – LIS590CMC*, University of Illinois Urbana-Champaign. Retrieved Jan. 30th, 2007, from http://www.adammathes.com/academic/computer-mediated-communication/folksonomies.html

Millen, D. R., & Feinberg, J. (2006). Using Social Tagging to Improve Social Navigation. In: *Workshop on the Social Navigation and Community based* Adaptation Technologies. In Conjunction with *Adaptive Hypermedia and Adaptive Web-Based Systems.*

Navarro, G. (2001). A Guided Tour to Approximate String Matching, *ACM Computing Surveys, 33*(1), 31-88.

Oommen, B. J., & Loke, R. K. S. (1997). Pattern recognition of strings with substitutions, insertions, deletions, and generalized transpositions. *Pattern Recognition, 30*(5), 789-800.

Schneider, M., Lim, H., & Shoaff, W. (1992). The utilization of fuzzy sets in the recognition of imperfect strings. *Fuzzy Sets and Systems, 49*(5), 331-337.

Specia, L., & Motta, E. (2007). Integrating Folksonomies with the Semantic Web. In: *European Semantic Web Conference -ESWC 2007-. LNCS Vol. 4519. The Semantic Web: Research and Applications.* (pp. 503-517), Springer. Heidelberg.

Vander Wal, T. (2008). *Folksonomy.* Retrieved October 27, 2008, from http://vanderwal.net/folksonomy.html

ENDNOTES

[1] Flickr: *http://www.flickr.com/* and *http://en.wikipedia.org/wiki/Flickr* for more information.

[2] http://www.eslomas.com/index.php/publicaciones/tagspatternmatching

Chapter XII
Insights into the Impact of Social Networks on Evolutionary Games

Katia Sycara
Carnegie Mellon University, USA

Paul Scerri
Carnegie Mellon University, USA

Anton Chechetka
Carnegie Mellon University, USA

ABSTRACT

In this chapter, we explore the use of evolutionary game theory (EGT) (Nowak & May, 1993; Taylor & Jonker, 1978; Weibull, 1995) to model the dynamics of adaptive opponent strategies for a large population of players. In particular, we explore effects of information propagation through social networks in evolutionary games. The key underlying phenomenon that the information diffusion aims to capture is that reasoning about the experiences of acquaintances can dramatically impact the dynamics of a society. We present experimental results from agent-based simulations that show the impact of diffusion through social networks on the player strategies of an evolutionary game and the sensitivity of the dynamics to features of the social network.

INTRODUCTION

We use EGT (Cabrales, 2000; Hofbauer & Sigmund, 2003; Weibull, 1995) to model the dynamics of adaptive opponent strategies for a large population of players. Previous EGT work has produced interesting, and sometimes counter-intuitive results about how populations of self-interested agents will evolve over time (d'Artigues & Vignolo, 2003; Frey & Luechinger, 2002).

In our model, at each stage of the game, boundedly rational players observe the strategies and payoffs of a subset of others and use this information to choose their strategies for the next stage of the interaction. Building on EGT, we introduce a model of interaction where, unlike the standard EGT setting, the basic stage game changes over time depending on the global state of the population (state here means the strategies chosen by the players). More precisely, each player has three strategies available (cooperate C, defect D, and do-nothing N), and the payoffs of the basic stage game are re-sampled when the proportion of the players playing D crosses a certain threshold from above. This feature requires long-term reasoning by the players that is not needed in the standard EGT setting. A possible example of a similar real-world situation is a power struggle between different groups. When cooperation drops sufficiently and there are many defections—the situation turns to chaos. When order is restored, that is, when cooperation resumes, the power structure and thus, the payoffs, will likely be different than before the chaos. The payoffs are kept constant while most of the players Cooperate (support the status quo) or do-Nothing, but when enough players are unhappy and choose to Defect, the power balance breaks and a radically different one may emerge afterwards.

The available strategies were chosen to abstractly capture and model violent uprisings in a society. Players playing C cooperate with the current regime and receive reward when interacting with others playing C. If a player has a good position in a regime, it has a large incentive to continue playing C. D is a strategy played to change the payoffs over a long term, but at an unavoidable immediate cost. Intuitively, it resembles resorting to insurgency or other violent tactics to overthrow a regime. When many players play D, playing C can lead to very low payoffs. For example, one can imagine a person trying to run a small business during a violent uprising. If these costs are too high, but the player has no

incentive to change the regime, playing N can limit payoffs—both negative and positive, until the situation stabilizes. Intuitively, this might correspond to going into hiding or temporarily leaving the conflicted area.

Similar to Nowak and May (1993) and Killingback and Doebeli (1996), we investigate the spatial aspect of the interaction. Previous work has shown that spatial interaction can change which strategies are most effective, for example, in Brauchli, Killingback, and Doebeli (1999) an interaction lattice changed which strategies were most effective in an iterative prisoner's dilemma game. In our model, the players are connected into a *social network*, through which the rewards are propagated (Travers & Milgram, 1969; D. J. Watts, Dodds, & Newman, 2002). Thus the players can benefit (or suffer) indirectly depending on how well off their friends in the network are. We show empirically that the connectivity pattern of the network, as well as the amount of information available to the players, have significant influence on the outcome of the interaction. In particular, the presence of a dense scale-free network or small-world network led to far higher proportions of players playing C than other social network types.

GAME DETAILS

We consider a finite population X of players. At each stage all the players are randomly matched in triples to play the basic stage game. Each player thus participates in every stage. Each player has three strategies available: cooperate (C), defect (D), and do-nothing (N) (one can interpret these choices as participating in democratic process, resorting to insurgency, and minimizing interactions with the outer world correspondingly). The payoff $p_i(k)$ of the stage k game to player x_i is shown in Table 1 ($\#_i(N)$ means the number of agents playing N), where $cc_i - 2 > n > dc > dd > cd$. Here is a simple rule for distinguishing between

Table 1.

		0 opponents play D	1 or 2 opponents play D
x_i's strategy	C	$cc_i - \#_i(N)$	cd
	D	dc	dd
	N	n	

these four variables: the first letter corresponds to x_i's strategy, the second letter is c if both of the x_i's opponents play C and d otherwise. For example, cd is the payoff of playing C given that at least one of the opponents plays D. Note that the payoff matrices for different players can only differ in the value of cc_i. All the other payoffs are constant across the population.

Denote $SD(k)$ the proportion of the population that defected during stage k:

$$SD(k) = \frac{\text{number of players that played } D \text{ during stage } k}{|X|},$$

Before the start of the first stage, c_i are sampled uniformly from an interval $[CC_{min}, CC_{max}]$. If during stage k^* the series $SD(k)$ crosses a fixed threshold (see the end of this section for the interpretation of the threshold) $T \in (0,1)$ from above, that is,

$$SD(k^* - 1) > T \text{ and } SD(k^*) < T,$$

then all cc_i are re-sampled. Otherwise they stay the same as for previous stage. For example, in an individual run plotted in Figure 1, the values of cc_i would be re-sampled only at point B.

One can interpret the previous interaction as a power struggle: If the proportion of players supporting status quo (i.e., cooperating or doing nothing) is high enough, the payoffs for each individual players do not change. When enough players defect, the system "falls into chaos" and after it emerges back from this state, a new power balance is formed and the payoffs change correspondingly. Threshold T in this interpretation

is the minimum number of defectors that brings the system into chaos.

Impact of Social Networks

A social network for finite population X is an undirected graph $<X,E>$. Two players i and j are neighbors in the network if and only if $(x_i, x_j) \in E$. We investigate the effect of reward sharing in social networks. After each stage k every player x_i obtains in addition to its own payoff p_i a shared payoff ps_i:

$$ps_i(k) = a \sum_{x_j \in \text{neighbors}(x_i)} p_j(k),$$

where $\alpha \in [0,1]$ is a parameter of the system.

Notice that this does not incur payoff redistribution: The shared payoff is not subtracted from payoffs of the players that cause it. One can interpret this phenomenon as players being more happy when their friends are happy.

Social Network Type

The *small-world property* of the network means that the average distance between two nodes in the network is small. It has been shown (D. Watts & Strogatz, 1998) that regular non-small-world networks, such as grids, may be transformed to small-world ones by changing only a small fractions of edges. We followed the algorithm from D. Watts and Strogatz to generate the networks with probability 0.1 of rewiring any edge of the regular structure.

Figure 1. An example trace of an individual run of the system. x-axis is the stage number ("time step"), y-axis is the proportion SD of the population playing D. The level of threshold T is also plotted for a reference.

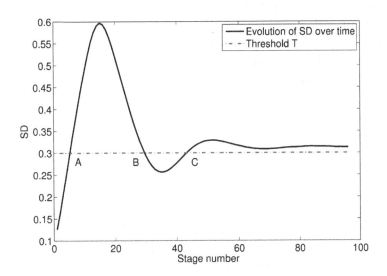

In scale-free networks (Barabási & Albert, 1999) the number of neighbors of a vertex is distributed according to a scale-free power law, therefore few highly connected vertices dominate the connectivity. Many real-world networks possess the small-world and/or scale-free properties (Barabási & Albert, 1999; D. Watts & Strogatz, 1998).

The impact of both small-world and scale-free networks are explored next.

PLAYER REASONING

Information Available to Players

Before describing the player reasoning algorithm one has to define what information is available to the player, that is, define an observation model. We assume that the players are aware of the overall behavior of the game, but may not be aware of the true values of parameters, such as the pro-portion $SD(k)$ of the population that played D at stage k. The players only observe the actions of their opponents for the given stage, as opposed to observing the whole population. Therefore, the observations available to i after stage k are its payoff $p_i(k)$, shared payoff $ps_i(k)$, and proportion $SC_i^{obs}(k), SD_i^{obs}(k), SN_i^{obs}(k) \in \{0, 0.5, 1\}$ of its direct opponents playing C, D and N during the kth stage.

Note that the information about the global properties of social network connectivity, such as density or whether the network is small worlds or scale free, is not available to players. Therefore, this global information is not used in the reasoning algorithm.

The Reasoning Algorithm

It is easy to see that for any triple of players, a single-stage game has 2 Nash equilibria in pure strategies: everybody cooperating and everybody defecting. The cooperative equilibrium

Pareto-dominates the "all-defect" equilibrium. Therefore, if the "all-cooperate" payoffs cc_i were always held constant across the stages, one would expect a population of rational players to always play C. However, the payoffs are re-sampled once the proportion of players playing C drops below T and then grows above T again. This provides an incentive for the players that happened to receive relatively low values of cc_i, to play D for some period of time in order to try and cause the re-sampling of payoffs. On the other hand, if a significant share of the players play D, some of the players may decide to play N, which guarantees a fixed payoff and provides an opportunity to "wait until the violence ends."

A natural way for a player to choose a strategy for the next stage is to compare the (approximate) cumulative future expected payoffs resulting from different strategies. Denote $EP_i(X)$ the approximate cumulative future expected payoff for player i and strategy X. Let $SX_i(k)$ be i's estimate of the share of population playing X on time step k. Then the action selection for step $k+1$ is as follows. If $SD_i(k) > T$, player i chooses action $\arg\max_{X=C,N} EP_i(X)$. Otherwise it chooses $\arg\max_{X=C,D,N} EP_i(X)$. The reason for treating situation $SD_i(k) > T$ specially is that once the share of defectors reaches the threshold, reducing the share of players below T is in common interest of all the players, and the approximate computations of expected utilities do not always capture this feature.

The previous paragraph assumed $EP_i(X)$ to be known. We now turn to their approximate computation.

First consider $EP_i(D)$. The only incentive for a player i to play D is to try to bring the system into chaos in hopes that, when the system emerges from chaos, the re-sampled all-cooperate payoff cc_i for that player will be higher than it is now. Denote TTC_i the i's estimate of the number of stages that it will need to play D before the share of those playing D is higher than T, TC_i—estimate

of the number of stages that the system will spend above the threshold and finally, TS_i the length of the following "stability period." Then

$$EP_i(D) \approx (TTC_i + TC_i)E[p_i(D)] + TS_i E[cc_i^{new}]$$
$$= TTR_i E[p_i(D)] + TS_i \frac{CC_{min} + CC_{max}}{2}, \quad (1)$$

where $TTR_i \equiv TTC_i + TC_i$ is "time to re-sampling" and

$$E[p_i(D)] = P(\#_i(D) = 0)dc + P(\#_i(D) > 0)dd.$$

Expected payoff for action C over the time period is approximated as

$$EP(C) \approx TS_i(p_i(C) + ps_i) + TTC_i E[p_i(c)]$$
$$+ TC_i \left(P(\#_i(D) > 0)cd + P(\#_i(D) = 0)(p_i(C) + ps_i) \right) \quad (2)$$

where $P(\#_i(D) > 0) = 1 - (1 - T)^2$ and

$$E[p_i(C)] = P(\#_i(C) = 2)cc_i + P(\#_i(C) = 1, \#_i(N) = 1)(cc_i - 1)$$
$$+ P(\#_i(N) = 2)(cc_i - 2) + P(\#_i(D) > 0)cd$$

(note that the probabilities here sum to one).

Finally, expected payoff for N over the same time interval is

$$EP(H) = (TTC_i + TC_i + TS_i)n.$$

One can see that a player only expects to get the shared payoff in case of all-cooperative outcomes.

In our model, time of stability TS_i and time in chaos TC_i are system constants that do not differ across the population.

The belief $SX_i(k)$ about the proportion of players playing X at stage k is maintained by each player individually. After each stage each player learns about the strategies of its opponents for that stage. SX_i is then updated according to

$$SX_i(k+1) = \gamma \, SX_i^{obs}(k+1) + (1-\gamma)SX_i(k) \quad (3)$$

where $\gamma \in (0,1]$ is learning rate. Each player also maintains $\delta SX_i(k)$, an estimate of

$$\delta SX(k) \equiv SX(k) - SX(k-1),$$

using an expression analogous to Equation 3 to update it. In the expressions (1-2) $P(\#_i(X))$ are approximated straightforwardly using SX_i, for example

$$P(\#_i(C) = 2) \approx SC_i^2(k)$$

Having SX_i and dSX_i, each player can estimate TTC_i using a linear approximation. For $SD_i < T$, we have (TTC is a system-wide constant)

$$TTC_i = \begin{cases} TTC, & \delta SD_i \leq 0 \\ \dfrac{T - SD_i}{\delta SD_i}, & \delta SD_i > 0 \end{cases}$$

for $SD_i^3 T$, $TTC_i = 0$.

EXPERIMENTAL RESULTS

In our experiments the population size was fixed to 1,000 players. The numerical values of payoff constants were

$$dc = -1, dd = -3, cd = -5, CC_{min} = 3, CC_{max} = 10$$

Estimated time of stability was fixed to $TS_i = TS = 50$ stages, "chaos threshold" $T=0.3$. Initial player-specific values were $SC_i(0) = 1$, $\delta SC_i = -0.02$. For each set of specific parameter values the results were averaged over 500 runs. Unless otherwise noted, the players were connected via a scale-free network with average density of 8.

We were primarily interested in how different parameters of the model affect the evolution of proportion of players playing C over time. On all graphs x-axis denotes the stage of the interaction, y-axis denotes SC, SD, and SN. In a previous work (Sycara, Scerri, & Chechetka, 2006), we presented results for the case where action N was not available to the players. In each of the following figures we contrast the results when N is and is not available to the players.

Note that because the plotted results are averages over 100 runs, averages provide more meaningful information about the influence of the parameters values on the system, than do individual runs which can vary distinctly from run to run. Most parameter values allow the SC to fall below T on some occasions, but what varies is how often this occurs, how rapidly changes happen, and how quickly cooperation resumes. These effects are more clearly seen on graphs of averages than many individual runs superimposed on a single graph. Notice that the fact that the value of SD on the plots rarely rises above T does not mean that payoffs are almost never re-sampled—individual runs have much more variance and re-sampling happens quite often. It simply means that on average SD is below T.

Figure 2 shows the baseline configuration, with 2(a) showing the case where N is available and 2(b) showing the case where it is not. In both cases, early in the game many players choose D to either try to change the payoffs or protect against losses. When N is available to the players, many choose this action in response to others playing D. Eventually this discourages the use of D and an equilibrium settles in. While the initial dynamics in both cases are similar, notice that over time the proportion of C is far higher in the case where N is available than when it is not. This may indicate that if players are able to avoid spasms of violence without getting hurt, the outcome for all will be better.

Figure 3 shows the impact of setting the network density to 2, 4, 8, and 16. In general, the higher the average network degree, the more players played C and the more quickly players stopped playing D. For the less dense networks, players often chose D early on, but in the most

Figure 2. Baseline configuration (scale-free network with density 8) with available action N (a) and with N not available (b)

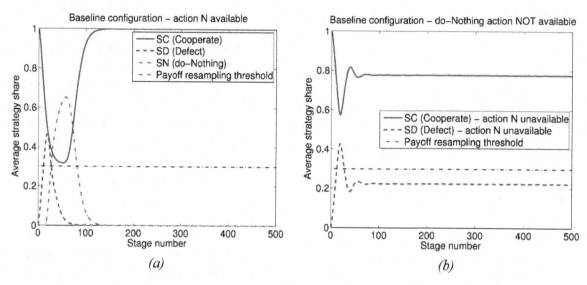

(a) *(b)*

Figure 3. Impact of network density on the players' strategies. In the top row, the share of players playing cooperate, in the bottom—defect. On the left, the action N is available to the players, on the right—not available.

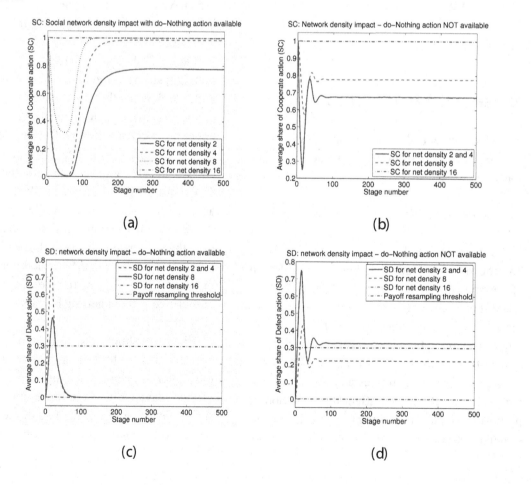

(a) (b)

(c) (d)

dense network, the lure of shared rewards was too high for players to have incentive to try to move the system towards chaos. In the less dense networks, the availability of the *N* action allowed the system to move toward all playing *C*, but as in the baseline case, without the *N* action, some level of *SD* persisted. When the average network density was 4, the system moved back towards *SC*=1 faster than when the network density was 2. This result may indicate that dense social networks are critical to stable societies.

Figure 4 shows what happens when there is no sharing across the social network. The sharp early peak in *SD* is similar to the sparse network shown above. This is one of the few cases where the availability of the *N* action leads to a lower *SC* over the course of the game. However, the option to play *N* is extensively used and *SD* is reduced to 0. Over an extended period of time, *SC* does rise to 1, but *N* dominates for a long time.

If the type of the network is set to small-world instead of scale-free (with the average of four neighbors), *SC* stays very close to 1 regardless of the availability of *N* to the players (there is no plot for this case, because the results are so trivial). This remarkable relative stability is likely due to the very even sharing of reward across all members of the team, reducing the possibility of a cascade towards chaos. This result may suggest that human societies that have a more scale-free nature will be more likely to descend into chaos.

Figure 5 shows the result as the learning rate is set to 0.05, 0.1, 0.4, and 0.8. Smaller learning rate means that the players are reluctant to change their estimates of the parameters; the closer the learning rate to 1, the more importance is attributed to the most recent observations.

Several interesting effects occur due to the learning rate. Firstly, an intermediate learning rate induces an oscillation in behavior with increasing and decreasing *SD*. Higher or lower learning rates induce different behavior. A high learning rate quickly settles the population down to playing *C*, because the players are better able to estimate future rewards which are maximized by a stable society. A low learning rate eventually allows a stable society but not before a large *SD* has occurred. Interestingly, none of these effects were observed when the *N* action was not available to the players. With learning eventual behavior (except for the intermediate learning rate) *SC* was higher when *N* was available.

Figure 4. Results with reward sharing disabled with available action N (a) and with N not available (b)

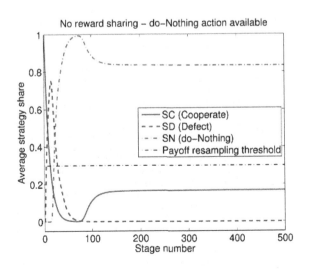
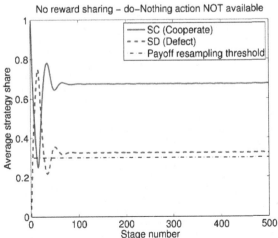

CONCLUSIONS AND FUTURE WORK

This chapter presented an evolutionary game with players connected into a social network, sharing payoffs with their neighbors in that network. If individual players reason that increased long-term payoffs might be higher if the whole society can be forced into chaos, they will accept significant short-term costs and risk, to bring that situation about. The key conclusion from this game is that a society of *rational* agents who will all gain if they all play cooperative strategies can easily be

induced to play strategies that are guaranteed to lead to a negative payoff.

Our experiments show that the existence and nature of a social network makes a dramatic difference to the evolution and conclusion of the game. Very dense networks or small-world networks had far higher proportions of players playing cooperative strategies than when there is a sparse scale-free network. This result has implications for all EGT where interaction occurs between players, but only simple social networks are used. It is possible that such results will change if different interaction networks are used.

Figure 5. Impact of learning rate on the players' strategies. In the top row, the share of players playing cooperate, in the bottom—defect. On the left, the action N is available to the players, on the right—not available

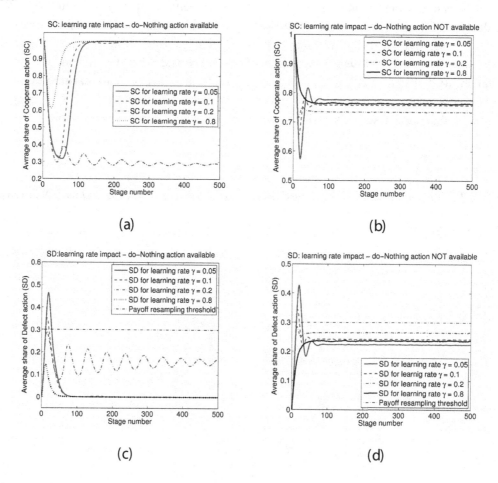

REFERENCES

Barabási, A.-L., & Albert, R. (1999). Emergence of scaling in random networks. *Science, 286*.

Brauchli, K., Killingback, T., & Doebeli, M. (1999). Evolution of cooperation in spatially structured populations. *Journal of Theoretical Biology*.

Cabrales, A. (2000). Stochastic replicator dynamics. *International Economic Review, 41*(2).

d'Artigues, A., & Vignolo, T. (2003). Why global integration may lead to terrorism: An evolutionary theory of mimetic rivalry. *Economics Bulletin, 6*(11).

Frey, B. S., & Luechinger, S. (2002). Terrorism: Deterrence may backfire. *European Journal of Political Economy, 20*(2).

Hofbauer, J., & Sigmund, K. (2003). Evolutionary game dynamics. *Bulletin of the American Mathematical Society, 40*(4).

Killingback, T., & Doebeli, M. (1996). Spatial evolutionary game theory: Hawks and doves revisited. In *Proceedings of The Royal Society (Biological Sciences)*.

Nowak, M., & May, R. (1993). The spatial dilemmas of evolution. *International Journal of Bifurcation and Chaos, 3*.

Sycara, K., Scerri, P., & Chechetka, A. (2006). Evolutionary games and social networks in adversary reasoning. In *Proceedings of the international conference on complex systems*. Boston.

Taylor, P., & Jonker, L. (1978). Evolutionary stable strategies and game dynamics. *Mathematical Biosciences, 40*.

Travers, J., & Milgram, S. (1969). An experimental study of the small world problem. *Sociometry, 32*, 425-443.

Watts, D., & Strogatz, S. (1998). Collective dynamics of small-world networks. *Nature, 393*.

Watts, D. J., Dodds, P. S., & Newman, M. E. J. (2002). Identity and search in social networks. *Science, 296*(5571), 1302-1305.

Weibull, J. (1995). *Evolutionary game theory*. Cambridge, MA: MIT Press.

This work was previously published in Applications of Complex Adaptive Systems, edited by Y. Shan and A. Yang, pp. 306-323, copyright 2008 by IGI Publishing, formerly known as Idea Group Publishing (an imprint of IGI Global).

Chapter XIII
Application of Semantic Web Based on the Domain-Specific Ontology for Global KM

Jaehun Joo
Dongguk University, Korea

Sang M. Lee
University of Nebraska – Lincoln, USA

Yongil Jeong
Saltlux, Inc., Korea

ABSTRACT

This chapter introduces an application of the Semantic Web based on ontology to the tourism business. Tourism business is one promising area for Semantic Web applications. To realize the potential of the Semantic Web, we need to find a killer application of the Semantic Web in the knowledge management (KM) area. The ontology as a key enabler is deigned and implemented under a framework of the Semantic-Web-driven KM system in a tourism domain. Finally, we discussed the relationship between the Semantic Web and KM processes.

INTRODUCTION

There are two important limitations in exploiting the Web as the space for global KM. These limitations are:

- lack of the mechanism for providing information and knowledge that computers or software agents can understand and process
- information overload owing to keyword-based search modes.

One limitation results from Web documents represented in Hyper Text Markup Language (HTML). In most cases, computers including software agents neither understand or process data or information automatically on the Web, nor integrate them, in particular, in heterogeneous environments. The other occurs in lack of semantics in information retrieval. The more information resources exist on the Web, the more information overload arises out of search results.

The Semantic Web provides the opportunity for global KM by integrating the resources dispersed across the Internet Web as well as other resources including the existing knowledge base. There are many opportunities to apply the Semantic Web to a variety of areas. One very promising area of the Semantic Web is KM. However, there are still no successful application areas of the Semantic Web because it is in its infancy. Ontology is seen as a key enabler for the Semantic Web. Also, ontologies are useful for improving the accuracy of Web searches (Antoniou & Harmelen, 2004). Thus, ontology development in a variety of domains will enable us to realize the potential of the Semantic Web. In addition, there is a need to develop ontology based on widely accepted or de facto standards such as Resource Description Framework (RDF)/RDF Schema (RDFS) and Web Ontology Language (OWL) in order to ensure the easiness of integration among ontologies.

The purpose of this paper is to present a domain-specific ontology, to propose a conceptual model of a Semantic-Web-driven KM system with such components as resource, metadata, ontology, and user and query layers. Finally, we discuss how the Semantic-Web-driven KM systems can support KM process by overcoming the limitations existing in current KM.

This chapter is organized as follows: after this introductory section, "Relevant Liturature and Scenarios" reviews related literatures and presents two scenarios in the tourism business domain. "Ontology Design for Tourism Business" designs the ontology providing answers to queries of the

scenarios. The fourth section, "Implementation," discusses the result of the implemented system. The fifth section, "Global Knowledge Management Based on the Semantic Web," presents a conceptual model of the Semantic-Web-driven KM systems, and discusses the relationship between the Semantic Web technology, KM systems, and the KM process. The final section presents "Conclusion and Future Trends."

RELEVANT LITERATURE AND SCENARIOS

Capabilities of the Semantic Web come from semantics and machine-processable ability. It resolves information overload problem and offers opportunities to semantic integration across heterogeneous and distributed systems as well as business process automation. There are a number of areas to which the Semantic Web technology can be applied (Antoniou & Harmelen, 2004). One very promising application area of the Semantic Web is KM. Figure 1 shows research areas on the Semantic Web for KM. The studies are classified into four areas: (1) developing infrastructure and architecture, (2) killer applications, (3) business management issues, and (4) other social issues.

The most surprising research area is technical issues related to architecture design and building of infrastructure for KM based on the Semantic Web. According to Berners-Lee, Hendler, and Lassila (2001), the Semantic Web, as an extension of the current Web, enables knowledge representation by using extensible markup language (XML), RDF, and ontologies including rules to make inferences. They also insist that the real power of the Semantic Web will be realized by agents collecting Web content as knowledge, processing it and exchanging the results with others. D'Aquin, Bouthier, Brachais, Lieber, and Napoli (2005) presented an architecture of the systems for knowledge representation, reasoning and visual editing relying on Semantic Web

Figure 1. Research areas of the Semantic Web in KM

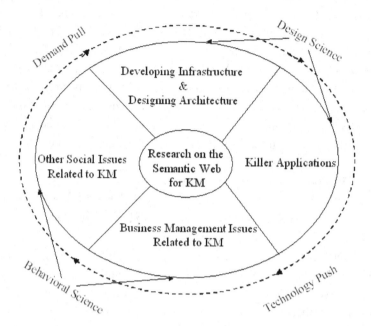

principles, in the domain of oncology, providing support for the medical treatment of people with cancer. Ontology itself facilitates knowledge sharing in organization or inter-organizational context. Edgington, Choi, Henson, Raghu, and Vinze (2004) discussed how to adopt ontology to facilitate knowledge sharing. Maedche, Motik, Stojanovic, Studer, and Voltz (2003) suggested an architecture of ontology management systems enabling ontology mapping and its evolution. The architecture shows how to support multiple ontologies and manage ontology evolution, not in global context such as the Internet Web, but in enterprise wide. The studies on extension of organizational KM systems to the Internet Web have been conducted. Tiwana and Ramesh (2001) discussed how to integrate knowledge on the Web. The Internet Web has been recognized as a medium of access and connection to integrate distributed applications and information before the advent of the Semantic Web. The Semantic Web enables knowledge representation and allows organizations to manage Web contents as knowledge resources with inference abilities.

Recently, a few projects for killer applications as well as building infrastructure have been conducted. On-To-Knowledge project as a typical example aimed at developing an ontology-based tool suit that efficiently processes the large numbers of heterogeneous, distributed, and semistructured documents. The following tools from this project were developed:

- OntoBuilder extracts machine-processable metadata from documents in RDF formats. It consists of two modules, OntoExtract and OntoWraper. OntoExtract extracts information from unstructured free text while OntoWraper does information from structured sources.
- Sesame stores RDF and RDFS data extracted by OntoBuilder and provides query facilities.
- OntoShare facilitates and encourages the sharing of information between communities of practice.
- OntoEdit is a graphical editing tool enabling knowledge engineers to codify and manage an ontology.

- QuizRDF (or RDFferret) is a search engine that combines full-text search with an ability to exploit RDF data in searching.
- Spectable personalizes information as a content presentation platform featuring custom-made information presentations.

Although the project contributed to build an infrastructure for applications of the Semantic Web to KM as well as development of tools, it did not deal with business issues associated with being considered as strategic relationships between information technology (IT) and management. Also, it is at an early stage to claim that such tools can become killer applications. The realization of the Semantic Web capabilities requires a killer application. According to Chen (2004), developers need to build applications available to the public because there is no killer application. KM is a very promising area of killer applications for the Semantic Web. Developing research agendas on killer applications is necessary for the realization of the potential for the Semantic Web through its application to KM. The view that widespread adoption of IT is dependent on the development of a killer application has widely been recognized (Meyer, 1998). According to Middleton (2003), in particular, it is important to develop the killer applications in user-centric view rather than provider-centric view.

As Orlikowski and Iacono (2001) pointed out, it is necessary to study the complex ensemble of people, culture, and technology embedded in social contexts as well as a specific organizational level. However, there are no such studies in the area of KM applying the Semantic Web because the Semantic Web itself is in its infancy.

According to Hevner, March, Park, and Ram's (2004) dichotomy of the research on management information systems, studies on the infrastructure and architecture and the killer applications refer to design science while two other issues in Figure 1 do behavioral science. The former has more char-

acteristics of technology push than the latter. The dotted circle with arrows in Figure 1 shows the interactive relationship between technology push and demand pull. Research in aspect of demand pull in the stage of introduction of the Semantic Web can contribute to improve the performance of IT investment like prototyping improves productivity of waterfall model in system development methodology. Such research is important under the environment of a rapid advance of IT.

This study focuses on tourism area as a killer application of the Semantic Web for KM and deals with two research areas together: killer application and business management issues.

The tourism industry is one of the more successful application areas of the Semantic Web as well as e-commerce because it is a consumer-oriented industry where services and information play a large part in transaction processes (Cardoso, 2004; Dell'Erba, 2004; Fodor & Werthner, 2004; Joo, 2002; Joo & Jeong, 2004). Figure 2 shows an overview of the business model for an electronic tourism market. The electronic tourism market is a marketplace allowing the players to electronically interact and mutually coordinate their benefits. It also provides an infrastructure of e-commerce with its applications to players and becomes a single interface for customers. According to Cardoso (2004), the development of a suitable ontology for the tourism industry serves as a common language for travel-related terminology and a mechanism for promoting the seamless exchange of information across all players such as service producers; intermediaries and tourism associations; facilitators; and travelers, as shown in Figure 2. Thus, the tourism market is one of the most promising areas enabling automation of business and transaction processes by applying the Semantic Web.

Consider the situation where tourists are planning to visit Gyeongju (an old imperial city of Shilla Dynasty in Korea). The tourists need information based on their tour schedule, indi-

Figure 2. Overview of the business model for an electronic tourism market

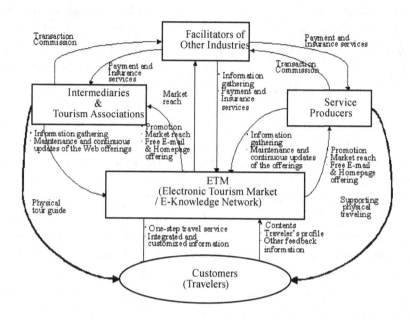

vidual preferences, and budget. Let us consider the following two scenarios:

Scenario 1. Accommodation recommendation for tourists

"Recommend an appropriate accommodation for the knapsack tourist who plans to visit Gyeongju city"

Scenario 2. Search for sightseeing spots in nearby regions

"Find attractive sightseeing sites near Kolon Hotel in Gyeongju for the tourist who has about four hours of tour time"

Consider the case as we use Web search services such as Google or Yahoo. In each of the previous scenarios, appropriate keywords are critical to extract good search results. Although desired keywords may be selected, limitations of a keyword-based search cannot be overcome.

ONTOLOGY DESIGN FOR TOURISM BUSINESS

It is necessary to build ontologies to get answers for the tourist in the two scenarios. Figure 3 shows some of the major classes and properties representing the relations among them in the tourism domain. For example, both GroupTour and IndividualTour are subclasses of the class Tour and the class SchoolJourney is that of the class Grouptour. There are classes of concepts which constitute a hierarchy with multiple inheritances such as the class BusinessTour and the class KnapsackTour as depicted in Figure 3.

The property hasTour relates the class Person to the class Tour. In other words, resources have properties associated with them. For example, Person has Tour. In the relationship between the class Person and the class Tour, the reverse is true. Thus we can say "the Tour is provided to the Person."

Figure 4 presents the extended ontology to that of Figure 3 by adding the class Region and the class Distance. The relation between the class

Figure 3. Tour package ontology for tourism business

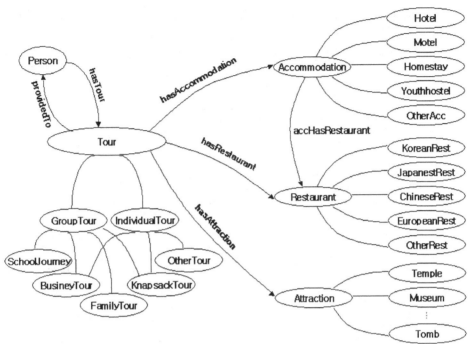

Figure 4. Region-distance ontology

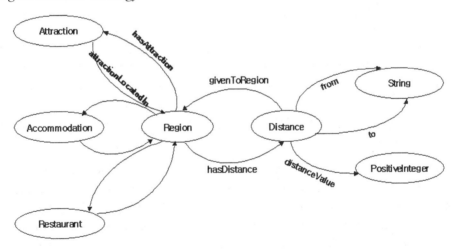

Attraction and the class Region makes it infer that a region may have some tourism attraction sites. Inversely, we can infer that an attraction site is located in a region. For example, the relation allows software agents to infer that TombOfKingMunmu is located in only one place. To get the answer for

query of scenario 2, we need an ontology enabling the system to identify the terminology, "nearby." The region-distance ontology shown in Figure 4 is used to represent knowledge about distance between two regions.

Figure 5 describes the ontology of Figure 4 as a semantic graph form. RDFS defines a property's

Figure 5. A semantic network representing region-distance ontology

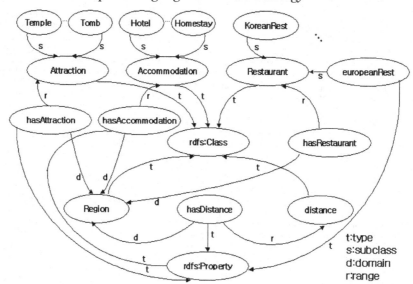

Table 1. Types of property elements in region-distance ontology

Object Property	HasDistance	FunctionalProperty	inverseOf
	GivenToRegion	InverseFunctional Property	
	has Attraction hasReataurant ...		inverseOf
	LocatedIn	TransitiveProperty	
DatatypeProperty	From	String type	
	To		
	DistanceValue	Integer Type	

domain—resources that can be subjects of the property, and a property's ranges—resources that can be objects of a property. For example, the property hasDistance may have a class Region as its domain and a class Distance as its range.

In OWL, there are two types of properties: object property and datatype property. The former relates objects to other objects. The latter relates objects to datatype values. OWL provides a powerful mechanism for enhanced reasoning about a property (World Wide Web Consortium, 2004a). Table 1 summarizes property characteristics for those depicted in Figure 4. For example, hasDistance and givenToRegion are ObjectProperty and there is an inverse relation between them. A region have distance, the distance is given to the region. The relation in either direction is true. The hasDistance property is functional, that is, a region can have at most one distance. The givenToRegion property is inverse functional, that is, a distance must be given to a region. Properties, from, to, and distanceValue are datatype. The property distanceValue takes a positive integer.

We can define tourist as the person who has at least one tour package. In the RDF syntax, for example, Tourist represented in PersonÇTour would be written as:

```
<owl:Class rdf:ID="Tourist">
 <rdfs:subClassOf>
  <owl:Class>
   <owl:intersectionOf rdf:parseType="Collection">
    <owl:Class rdf:about="#Person"/>
    <owl:Class rdf:ID="Tour"/>
   </owl:intersectionOf>
  </owl:Class>
 </rdfs:subClassOf>
</owl:Class>
```

The example defines the class Tourist to be the intersection of Person and Tour. OWL allows us to express the intersection of classes by using owl:intersectionOf.

In general, knapsack tourists do not want to stay in expensive hotels. Following ontology represented in OWL requires only accommodations except hotels to be recommended to them.

```
<owl:Class rdf:about="#KnapsackTour">
 <rdfs:subClassOf>
<owl:Restriction>
<owl:onProperty rdf:ID="#hasAccommodation"/>
<owl:allValuesFrom>
     <owl:Class>
      <owl:oneOf rdf:parseType="Collection">
      <owl:Class rdf:about="#Homestay"/>
      <owl:Class rdf:about="#Motel"/>
      <owl:Class rdf:about="#OtherAcc"/>
      <owl:Class rdf:about="#YouthHostel"/>
      </owl:oneOf>
     </owl:Class>
    </owl:allValuesFrom>
   </owl:Restriction>
  </rdfs:subClassOf>
</owl:Class>
```

As shown in Figure 3, the class KnapsackTour is a subclass of IndividualTour or GroupTour. Both classes, IndividualTour and Grouptour, are subclasses of Tour. The classes Hotel, Motel, Homestay, Youthhostel, and OtherAcc are all subclasses of Accommodation. The hasAccommodation property only has values of a class whose members are the individuals Homestay, Motel, YouthHostel, and OtherAcc. The property hasAccommodation has the domain of Tour and the range of Accommodation. That is, it relates to instances of subclasses of Tour to instances of subclasses of Accommodation.

The example states that the class Knapsack-Tour is a subclass of an anonymous OWL class that has as its extension a set of all individuals for whom the property hasAccommodation has values in only one class among Homestay, Model, OtherAcc, and Youthhostel. The example defines that Knapsack is subclass of an anonymous class with a property restriction. The element, owl:allValuesFrom is used to specify the class of possible values the property specified by owl:onProperty can take. In other words, the class KnapsackTour has a property called hasAccommodation restricted to have allValuesFrom only in one class among the collection of Homestay, Model, OtherAcc, and Youthhostel. Therefore, the class KnapsackTour never has a value from the instance of the class Hotel.

```
<owl:InverseFunctionalProperty rdf:about="#attraction
LocatedIn">
   <rdfs:domain rdf:resource="#Attraction"/>
   <rdf:type rdf:resource="http: //www.w3.org/ 2002/07/
owl#ObjectProperty"/>
   <rdfs:range rdf:resource="#Region"/>
</owl:InverseFunctionalProperty>
```

The owl:InverseFunctionalProperty defines a property for which two different objects cannot have the same value. If two instances of the class Attraction are respectively defined as TombOfKingMunmu and DaewanamUnderwaterTomb, we can infer that these two resources must refer to the same thing in the example.

```
<owl:FunctionalProperty rdf:ID="hasDistance">
   <rdfs:range rdf:resource="#Distance"/>
   <owl:inverseOf>
       <owl:InverseFunctionalProperty rdf:
ID="givenToRegion"/>
   </owl:inverseOf>
   <rdfs:domain rdf:resource="#Region"/>
   <rdf:type rdf:resource="http://www.w3.org/2002/07/
owl#ObjectProperty"/>
 </owl:FunctionalProperty>
```

The property hasDistance relates the class Region to the class Distance. The hasDistance defined as owl:FunctionalProperty has at most one unique value for each instance of the class Region.

As shown in Figure 4, the properties from and to defined as Datatype properties have string values and the property distanceValue has a positive integer. We can infer the instances of the class Region having distance values less than a particular value for a given region.

IMPLEMENTATION

We use Jena (n.d.) toolkit to implement the ontology design for the tourism business. Jena is an open-source Semantic Web developer's kit as a set of Java application program interfaces (APIs) for manipulating RDF models. It comprises a number of modules including RDF API, ARP RDF/XML parser, ontology API, RDQL,(World Wide Consortium, 2004b) and storage modules (Jena, n.d.). We used J2SDK 1.4.2 to develop applications of the system.

Figure 6 presents a sequence diagram that displays object interactions arranged in a time sequence. The actor who is user or knowledge engineer may set up environment variables by invoking the object Configurator. The object SearchOwl activates the inference engine to create a new inference model with the query data sets and returns search results of RDF triples by exploiting RDQL (World Wide Consortium, 2004b). The

Figure 6. A sequence diagram of the search system in tourism ontology

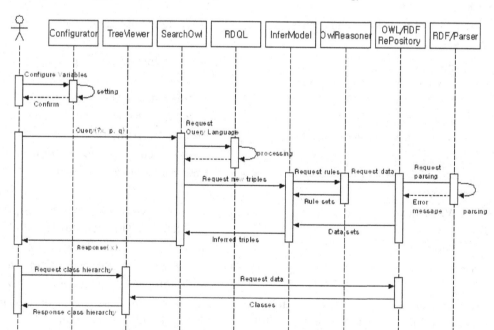

InferModel invokes the OwlReasoner to create a new inference model that is built in triple types (subject, predicate, object) as an extension of the Jena RDF triple. The Reasoner of Jena supports OWL Lite and OWL-DL reasoning (Jena, n.d.). The OwlReasoner provides inference rules based on Description Logics. The OWL/RDF repository stores ontologies represented as OWL language and RDF/RDFS, and allows access and reuse of ontologies.

Figure 7 shows the hierarchy of classes created in the ontology buildings in the tourism business area. Figure 8 shows search results for the query of scenario 2.

GLOBAL KNOWLEDGE MANAGEMENT BASED ON THE SEMANTIC WEB

Conceptual Model of the Semantic-Web-Driven KM Systems

Figure 9 shows a conceptual model for the global KM systems exploiting the Semantic Web technol-ogy. The model is composed of four layers. The resource layer refers to a variety of knowledge resources including contents of the Internet Web. The Semantic Web enables us to manage Web contents as organizational knowledge as well as the existing internal knowledge such as database and knowledge base. Also, it allows us to define a part of a document or a sentence as a knowledge piece corresponding to a resource. Thus, system users can find more focused and personalized knowledge and seamlessly integrate knowledge extracted from various resources. The metadata layer includes RDFs as the foundation for process-ing metadata extracted from the resource layer. The system requires middleware modules or tools to support automatic knowledge extraction from unstructured and semi-structured data in heterogeneous resources. In this layer, we need RDF (World Wide Consortium, 1999) manage-ment subsystems including RDF repositories, XML/RDF parser, and RDF APIs which enable the interaction with ontology and resources lay-ers. The ontology layer including RDFS (World Wide Consortium, 2004) and inference engine plays a critical role in the system. Ontology APIs

Figure 7. Treeview for the tourism ontology

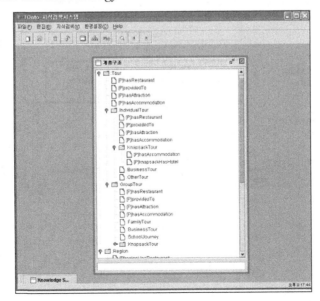

Figure 8. Query result for the scenario 2

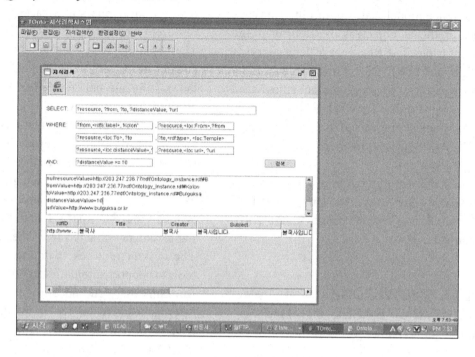

Figure 9. Conceptual model for KM based on the Semantic Web

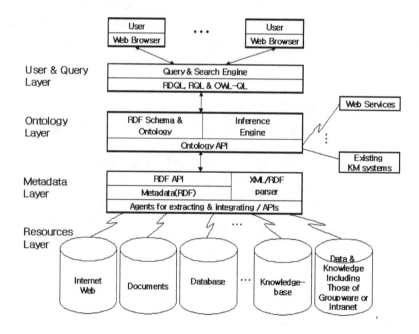

enable Web services or existing KM systems to be integrated into the system. Finally, users can find necessary knowledge through query and semantic search.

Innovation of KM Process

Recently, many organizations design and use KM systems as specialized information systems into which various technologies such as the Internet Web, groupware, intranet, artificial intelligence, virtual community, and data warehousing are integrated. Although KM systems are helpful for KM and increase organizational effectiveness and competitiveness, they have technical limitations in maximizing objectives of KM due to the following:

- limitations of keyword-based search as well as limited knowledge categorization;
- limitations to integration of heterogeneous systems as knowledge resources and to integration of existing KM systems with Web resources;
- inconvenience of KM systems use resulting from slow response and instability of KM systems; and
- time and space limitation in KM systems use and limitation of access methods in KM systems.

In this section, we focus on how to overcome the technical limitations through the Semantic-Web-driven KM systems. Figure 10 shows the relationship between Semantic Web technology,

Table 2. Supporting technologies, components, and issues for each layer

Layers	Supporting technologies, components, and issues
User & Query Layer	- There are RDQL, RQL (ICS-FORM, 2005), and OWL-QL (Fikes et al., 2004)as query languages for RDF, RDFS, and ontology. - Users can query knowledge on the Web as well as internal knowledge resources as if they use an integrated database system. - It is necessary to develop tools by which the queries with natural language from users are automatically transformed into the formats of the query language exploited
Ontology Layer	- Ontology editors refer to the system for loading, editing, and storing ontologies. Protégé-2000 (Noy et al., 2001) and OntoEdit are typical GUI-based ontology editors. - Inference engine is a core component of the ontology layer and is used for several tasks like semantic validation and deduction of implicit information. Description Logics (DL) is exploited in reasoning support in OWL. - Ontology layer needs several sets of interfaces such as ontology API ensuring independence between usage and storage of ontologies and APIs for integrating with Web Services or existing KM systems. - It is important to develop the tools for mapping or merging ontologies (Noy & Musen, 2004).
Metadata Layer	- Metadata layer needs components to edit, store, and manage RDFs as metadata. The component should have the ability to test validation of RDF models. RDF/XML parser plays a role as a core component in the metadata layer. Many parsers such as Redland and SiRPAC are available. - One of the important issues in this layer is to develop tools that automatically extract metadata from various resources on the Web. Such tools are necessary to incorporate Dublin Core (dublincore.com) and RSS (RDF Site Summary, web.resource.org/rss/1.0/spec) in order to efficiently build RDF.
Resource Layer	- Resource layer needs the component offering APIs which enable document files, database, knowledge base, or groupware to be integrated into the metadata layer.

KM systems, and KM process. The capabilities such as semantics and machine-processable, enabled by the Semantic Web technology, allows the Semantic-Web-driven KM systems to have the opportunity to or possibility of semantic integration and thus resolving information overload. Ultimately, the Semantic-Web-driven KM systems support KM process by overcoming the limitations of systems integration and knowledge search embedded in existing KM systems.

All resources in the Semantic Web are represented in RDF as metadata and this representation method makes possible for users to query and get answers as if they use database management systems. The Semantic Web also supports RDFS and ontology which enables semantic analysis on vocabularies contained in query and domains as well as syntactic analysis. Thus, the Semantic Web can provide accurate knowledge suitable to users. Any documents and data being either inside or outside the organization as well as Web resources can be represented as a resource in RDF. This means that a resource of RDF that we

call a knowledge object can be searched with an independent knowledge unit as if a user searches a document in document management systems. A specific part or sentence of a Web page or a part of a document may be represented as a knowledge object. This capability allows the Semantic Web-driven KM systems to search for a knowledge object unit rather than a document unit. Therefore, the Semantic Web allows the current KM systems to resolve the problem of knowledge/information overload and duplication.

There are three types of integration: (1) data integration, (2) application integration, and (3) process integration (Giachetti, 2004). The goal of data integration is data sharing where different systems exchange data with each other. The goal of application level is to achieve interoperability between systems. The obstacles of integration arise at syntactic and semantic heterogeneity between different information systems or applications (Giachetti, 2004; Noy, Doan, & Halevy, 2005). Until recently, the approaches to provide interoperability include standardization and middleware or mediators as well as enterprise application integration (EAI). The enterprise knowledge portal (EKP) is a system integrating various tools for KM in the perspective of users. Although the traditional integration approaches such as middleware and standardization easily integrate the structured data extracted from heterogeneous databases, they have limitations when integrating the unstructured data or knowledge from the various knowledge sources such as HTML, word processor files, and spreadsheet files. EKP does not play the role of a content integrator that automatically extracts related knowledge from different knowledge sources and aggregates them, but as an interconnected integrator which integrates different applications and offers one access point for users.

Figure 11 shows the comparison of the traditional integration and semantic integration based on the Semantic Web. Although the traditional approach enables syntactic and structural integration

Figure 10. Relationship between Semantic Web technology, KM systems, and KM process

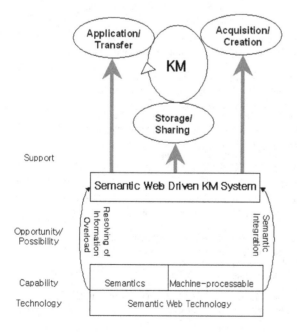

Figure 11. Semantic integration

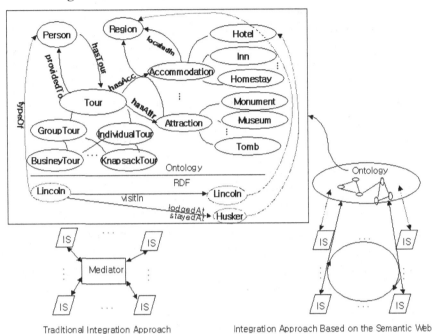

at the application level as well as the data level, it cannot provide the semantic integration. In other words, the traditional approach allows users to share data between different systems and provides them with the interoperability between systems by exploiting the mediator as shown in Figure 11. The traditional approach needs n*(n-1) mediators for mapping and translating between systems in the worst case. However, software agents cannot understand the meanings of the terms differently represented in different systems and also process them without human intervention.

In the integration approach based on the Semantic Web, the software agents understand the meanings of the terms and automatically process them by exploiting the RDF and ontologies as illustrated in the upper and right part of Figure 11. Assume that two different systems have same term, *Lincoln* that actually means different things while the two systems have different terms, *stayed* and *lodged* that mean the same thing. For example, consider the sentence, "President *Lincoln* visited *Lincoln* and *stayed* (or *lodged*) at *Husker*." The sentence is written in the RDF in the manner as shown in Figure 11. The software agents capture the instance of the RDF and understand the meanings of the terms by referring to ontologies. President *Lincoln* is a type of Person while the other is a type of Region which means the name of a city. *Husker* is a type of Hotel as a subclass of Accommodation and also both stayed and lodged mean the same thing.

In the Semantic-Web-driven KM systems, a software agent can access heterogeneous systems and provide knowledge and information suitable to users. The Semantic Web enables software agents to extract some parts of the related knowledge from different resources including those of resources layer shown in Figure 9 and to automatically aggregate them without the user's intervention.

When the Semantic Web is combined with ubiquitous computing (Chen & Finin, 2004), users can conveniently access KM systems anytime and anywhere. The Semantic-Web-driven KM systems with the support of peer-to peer (P2P) technology (Davies, Fensel, & Harmelen, 2003) can improve personalized KM services. Therefore, the Semantic Web enables the current KM systems to overcome the limitations such as time/space and inconvenience through a combination of ubiquitous networks and P2P technology.

Many researchers define KM process differently. In this chapter, we follow the classification of Alavi and Leidner (2001) with minor modifications as knowledge acquisition/creation, storage/sharing, and application/transfer depicted in Figure 10.

As shown in the resources layer of Figure 9, the Semantic-Web-driven KM systems extends the scope of KM to Internet Web resources beyond those of intra-organization. The Semantic Web-driven KM systems not only broaden the scope of knowledge acquisition but also enhance the quality level of knowledge acquisition through semantics. The Semantic-Web-driven KM systems support knowledge creation through enhancement of connectivity and e-learning. For example, semantic blogging which is a powerful tool for establishing and maintaining an online community by embedding the Semantic Web technology within a blogging framework provides a new way of knowledge creation as well as knowledge sharing and transfer (Cayzer, 2004). The Semantic Web-driven KM systems enable knowledge to be represented as a knowledge object (or granularity of knowledge) rather than a document unit. It facilitates knowledge application by supporting automatic aggregation and integration from the various knowledge resources. Software agents disseminate and transfer knowledge more efficiently so that users can select suitable knowledge according to their preference because of machine-processable representation and semantic search.

CONCLUSION AND FUTURE TRENDS

Ontologies were designed to support semantic search and solve problems of two scenarios derived

from the tourism domain. The ontology will be widely used as a fundamental tool in building a global KM system in the tourism domain. To develop a prototype of the ontology including RDF and RDFS, we used OWL and Jena (n.d.) toolkits. The results of the systems implementation indicated satisfactory search routines.

We developed a conceptual model of the Semantic-Web-driven KM systems with four layers classified into user and query, ontology, metadata, and resource. The Semantic-Web-driven KM systems support KM process by enabling the current KM systems to overcome their search and integration limitations in several ways.

First, the Semantic-Web-driven KM systems enable global knowledge acquisition and creation by extending the scope of KM to the Internet Web beyond intra-organization. The Semantic-Web-driven KM systems also promote knowledge creation with the extended CoP (Communities of Practice) to the Internet space and support of e-learning. Second, the Semantic-Web-driven KM systems enable us to share global knowledge without making a change in given storage modes whether they are files, documents, or databases, because all knowledge resources are represented as metadata based on RDF. Finally, software agents disseminate and transfer knowledge more efficiently so that users can use knowledge suitable to their preferences because of machine-processable representation and semantic search. This paper sheds new insights on the application of the Semantic Web to KM as an IT innovation and provides a framework of the Semantic Web-based KM systems.

In perspective of the technology push, the Semantic Web will be converged with other IT. For example, the Semantic-Web-driven KMS can be incorporated into ubiquitous computing and P2P technology. The technologies will support context-aware capabilities and personalization of the KM systems. To realize the potential of the Semantic Web, we need to find a killer application of the Semantic Web in the KM area as if the

Semantic Web is a killer application of the Internet Web and KM is also a killer application of the Semantic Web. In ensemble view of technology as Orlikowski and Iacono (2001) pointed out, technology should be studied as an evolving system in a complex and dynamic context. Minimization of the gap between technology and the realization of its potential requires research on strategies triggering organizational change through application of the Semantic Web to KM.

REFERENCES

Alavi, M., & Leidner, D. E. (2001). Review: Knowledge management and knowledge management systems: Conceptual foundations and research issues. *MIS Quarterly, 25*(1), 107-136.

Antoniou, G., & Harmelen, F. (2004). *A Semantic Web prime.* Cambridge, MA: MIT Press.

Berners-Lee, T., Hendler, J., & Lassila, O. (2001). The Semantic Web. *Scientific American, 284*(5), 34-43.

Cardoso, J. (2004). Semantic Web processes and ontologies for the travel industry. *AIS SIGSEMIS Bulletin, 1*(3), 25-28.

Cayzer, S. (2004). Semantic blogging and decentralized KM. *Communications of the ACM, 47*(12), 47-52.

Chen, A. (2004, July 5). Semantic Web is 2 steps closer. *eWeek,* p. 46.

Chen, H., & Finin, T. (2004). An ontology for context aware pervasive computing environments. *Knowledge Engineering, 18*(3), 197-207.

D'Aquin, M., Bouthier, C., Brachais, S., Lieber, J., & Napoli, A. (2005). Knowledge editing and maintenance tools for a semantic portal in oncology. *International Journal of Human-Computer Studies, 62*(5), 619-638.

Davies, N. J., Fensel, D., & Harmelen, F. V. (Eds.). (2003). *Toward the Semantic Web: Ontology-based knowledge management.* Hoboken, NJ: John Wiley & Sons.

Dell'Erba, M. (2004). Exploiting Semantic Web technologies for data interoperability. *AIS SIGSEMIS Bulletin, 1*(3), 48-52.

Edgington, T., Choi, B., Henson, K., Raghu, T. S., & Vinze, A. (2004). Adopting ontology to facilitate knowledge sharing. *Communications of the ACM, 47*(11), 85-90.

Fikes, R., Hayes, P., & Horrocks, I. (2004). OWL-QL: A language for deductive query answering on the Semantic Web. *Web Semantics: Science, Service and Agents on the World Wide Web, 2*(1), 19-29.

Fodor, O., & Werthner, H. (2004). Harmonise: A step toward an interoperable e-tourism marketplace. *International Journal of Electronic Commerce, 9*(2), 11-39.

Giachetti, R. E. (2004). A framework to review the information integration of the enterprise. *International Journal of Production Research, 42*(6), 1147-1166.

Hevner, A. R., March, S. T., Park, J., & Ram, S. (2004). Design science in information systems research. *MIS Quarterly, 28*(1), 75-105.

ICS-FORTH. (2005). *The RDF query language (RQL).* Retrieved January 24, 2006, from http://139.91.183.30:9090/RDF/RQL/

J2SDK. (2006). *Sun developer network.* Retrieved February 24, 2006, from http://java.sun.com/j2se/1.4.2/download.html

Jena. (n.d.). A Semantic Web framework (Version 2.4) [Computer software]. Retrieved January 24, 2006, from http://jena.sourceforge.net/

Joo, J. (2002). A business model and its development strategies for electronic tourism markets. *Information Systems Management, 19*(3), 58-69.

Joo, J., & Jeong, Y. (2004). *An implementation of the semantic search system based on the ontology for global knowledge management in tourism business domain.* Paper presented KMIS Conference, Seoul, 448-454.

Maedche, A., Motik, B. Stojanovic, L., Studer, R., & Voltz, R. (2003). Ontologies for enterprise knowledge management. *IEEE Intelligent Systems, 18*(2), 26-33.

Meyer, P. (1998, January-March). Killer applications. *Business & Economic Review, 44* (2)13-17.

Middleton, C. A. (2003). What if there is no killer application? An exploration of a user-centric perspective on broadband. *Journal of Information Technology, 18,* 231-245.

Noy, N. F., Doan, A., & Halevy, A. Y. (2005). Semantic integration. *AI Magazine, 26*(1), 7-9.

Noy, N. F., & Musen, M. A. (2004). Ontology versioning in an ontology management framework. *IEEE Intelligent Systems, 19*(4), 6-13.

Noy, N. F., Sintek, M., Decker, S., Crubezy, M., Ferferson, R. W., & Musen, M. A. (2001). Creating Semantic Web contents with Protégé-2000. *IEEE Intelligent Systems, 16* (2) 60-71.

Oberle, D., Staab, S., Studer, R., & Volz, R. (2005). Supporting application development in the Semantic Web. *ACM Transactions on Internet Technology, 5*(2), 328-358.

OntoEdit. (n.d.). (Version 0.6) [Computer Software]. AIFB, University of Karlsruhe. Retrieved 2005, from http://www.ontoknowledge.org/tools/ontoedit.shtml

Orlikowski, W. J., & Iacono, C. S. (2001). Research commentary: Desperately seeking the "IT" in IT research. A call to theorizing the IT artifact. *Information Systems Research, 12*(2), 121-134.

Protégé. (n.d.). (Version 3.1.1) [Computer software]. Stanford Medical Informatics. Retrieved 2005, from http://protege.stanford.edu/

Tiwana, A., & Ramesh, B. (2001). Integrating knowledge on the Web. *IEEE Internet Computing, 5*(3), 32-39.

World Wide Consortium (W3C). (1999). *Resource description framework (RDF) model and syntax specification.* Retrieved January 24, 2006, from http://www.w3.org/TR19991/REC-rdf-syntax-19990222/

World Wide Consortium (W3C). (2000, March 21). *Resource description framework (RDF) schema specification 1.0.* Retrieved January 24, 2006, from http://www.w3.org/TR/2000/CR-rdf-schema-20000327/

World Wide Consortium (W3C). (2004a, February 10). *OWL Web ontology language overview.* Retrieved January 24, 2006, from http://www.w3.org/TR/2004/REC-owl-features-20040210/

World Wide Consortium (W3C). (2004b, January 9). *RDQL: A query language for RDF.* Retrieved January 24, 2006, from http://www.w3.org/Submission/2004/SUBM-RDQL-20040109/

This work was previously published in Semantic Web Technologies and E-Business: Toward the Integrated Virtual Organization and Business Process Automation, edited by A. Salam and J. Stevens, pp. 287-309, copyright 2007 by IGI Publishing, formerly known as Idea Group Publishing (an imprint of IGI Global).

Chapter XIV
Designing Online Learning Communities to Encourage Cooperation

Miranda Mowbray
HP Laboratories Bristol, UK

ABSTRACT

This chapter is concerned with how to design an online learning community in such a way as to encourage cooperation, and to discourage uncooperative or antisocial behavior. Rather than restricting design to visual and interface issues, I take a wide view, touching on aspects of the governance, social structure, moderation practices, and technical architecture of online learning communities. The first half of the chapter discusses why people behave antisocially in online learning communities, and ways to discourage this through design. The second half discusses why on the other hand people behave cooperatively in online learning communities, and ways to encourage this through user-centered design, applying some results of experiments in social psychology. The chapter is intended to be of practical use to designers of online learning communities.

INTRODUCTION

Human beings being what they are, any social venue is likely to experience some antisocial behavior. The kind of antisocial behavior that appears in a particular venue will depend on the characteristics and opportunities of the venue, and of the tenor of the social interaction that takes place; this applies to online venues as well as to off-line ones. In this section, I will give some examples of antisocial behavior in online learning communities. As will be seen, there are some differences in what is possible (and in what is common) online from off-line.

Flaming is disruptive emotional speech. It has been noted for a long time as a problem with online conversations. For instance, in an early experiment by Sproull and Kiesler (1991), a group solving a problem online threw more flames than a control group solving the same problem off-line (p.119). A flame by one annoyed, angry, or frustrated person can often bring another flame in response, leading to an escalation that disrupts the possibility of calm conversation.

Obscene or violent speech can be a problem in that it destabilizes the tone of communications in the learning community. Some online learning communities for teenagers, for example, have experienced students testing the boundaries of language permitted.

Harassment and bullying do occur in online learning environments, just as harassment and bullying by mobile text message, off-line written message, and the spoken word occur in off-line learning environments. In a survey of 770 UK youngsters aged 11 to 19 (NCH, 2005), 14% said they had been bullied by text message, 5% in Internet chat rooms, and 4% via e-mail. For the youngsters in formal education, half of the bullying messages happened at school or college, and 11% said that they had sent a bullying or threatening message using a digital medium.

Identity theft is easier to carry out online than off-line. I have been successfully impersonated in an online learning community, on several occasions, by a man; I doubt that he would have been successful face-to-face.

Malware can be spread via online communication and shows no signs of becoming less common. According to measurements by MessageLabs® (2005), about 1 in 28 e-mails sent in June 2005 contained computer viruses.

MessageLabs® also estimates that 2 out of every 3 e-mails sent in June 2005 were *spam*. Spam occurs not only via e-mail, but via other online media too. For example, open wikis and the comment pages of blogs have been invaded by spammers in the last few years. In addition to advertisers and fraudsters who try to reach as many people as possible over the public Internet, members of online learning communities can cause a problem if they decide to send many messages to a very large number of community members.

Privacy intrusion can be a problem in online learning communities, particularly if the norms of how information in the online environment may be used are not clear.

Online learning offers enhanced opportunities for *cheating* (Foster, 2003; Jones, 2003). The ease of cutting and pasting from Web pages, and the very wide variety of information available online, makes plagiarism easier than it was pre-Web. Ready-made essays on commonly set topics and illicitly obtained exam questions may be obtained from specialist Web sites or from other students. The ease of online impersonation may allow students to let a substitute sit their exam for them. Students have been known to change their marks by gaining entry to online databases containing their results.

Finally, online learning communities can suffer from a *low signal-to-noise ratio*. For instance one online learning community based at the University of Virginia, originally designed for serious discussions on postmodern literary theory, turned out to be very popular with members of the public who logged in from all over the world just to tell silly jokes. In general, the ease and convenience of online communication can lead to the practice of near-immediate responses in asynchronous media, allowing members little time to think about or edit their messages before sending them. Synchronous online media such as chat rooms allow little time for editing by their very nature.

Why do People Behave Badly in Online Learning Communities?

Possibly the main factor contributing to bad behavior in online learning is *disinhibition*. Contrary to early findings on computer-assisted communication by the RAND Corporation, modern online communication technology tends to have a disinhibiting effect. The Internet sage Esther

Dyson has likened the Internet to a beer party. This disinhibition can lead to greater feelings of involvement and social warmth than might be expected, but also weakens internal censorship of antisocial behavior.

The disinhibition arises from several factors. Online communication offers some protection from adverse consequences of antisocial behavior. Speaking aggressively to someone face-to-face may lead to a punch in the nose. If you do so online, your nose is safe. Some members of online learning communities regard the online environment as not the "real" world, but as some sort of theater or playpen, where normal courtesies and rules need not apply. Weak feedback may limit the effectiveness of social restraints; if I say something to your face that you take the wrong way, I have the opportunity of noticing that I have upset you and explaining that I did not intend to do so, and apologizing. If I say it online, I may not even notice that I have upset you. Finally, online learning environments have different social rules (for technical reasons, among others) from that of face-to-face environments—and indeed from other online environments that members are used to. Since the rules are different, it may not be clear to members what they are, or even if there are any rules at all, resulting in a loosening of inhibitions.

In addition to disinhibition, there are other factors contributing to bad behavior in online learning communities.

Disinhibition not only weakens self-censorship which otherwise would prevent a user from engaging in antisocial behavior, but it can also lead to *weakened defenses to emotional hurt* by the victims of such behavior. A student in a disinhibited state will be less shy about expressing her ideas and more open to positive social interaction, but will also be, for example, more vulnerable to harassment.

Several of the examples of antisocial behavior described previously would be more difficult or actually impossible off-line, because they are facilitated by *technical opportunities* for antisocial behavior. For instance, spam and computer viruses do not have precise off-line equivalents, because they are enabled by technical properties of the software and protocols used for online communication; and learning online may make it easier to cheat.

Some learning communities deliberately—and laudably—attempt to engage as diverse a studentship as possible, using the wide reach of the Internet as an enabler. Although the resulting *cultural diversity* can have strikingly positive outcomes, cultural differences can also compound the problem of unclear rules.

Some antisocial online behavior is partially motivated by the *opportunity to demonstrate technical and creative prowess*. An ingenious program that exploits a previously unknown flaw in the system to cause social disruption may be a source of pride to the programmer.

A final factor contributing to bad behavior is the extent to which online communication affects the environment, which Kollock (1999, p. 228) calls its *efficacy*. If you are in a very bad mood and are rude to everyone you meet for 10 minutes off-line, you may ruin the day of 20 or 30 people. If you broadcast an offensive message in an online learning community, you may be able to upset many more people than that. Online learning communities offer an efficient way of distributing communication, whether that communication is pleasant or unpleasant.

It is important to notice that most of these factors contributing to antisocial behavior have a positive side too. Eliminating these factors would reduce the capabilities of the community for socially positive behavior. We need ways to discourage antisocial behavior online without reducing the learning community's potential for good. Although many social, environmental, and technical factors influence the quality of interaction between the members of an online learning community, the design of the online community can have a significant effect. In the following sections I will discuss ways to design the online learning community to discourage antisocial or uncooperative behavior without reducing its positive capabilities.

DISCOURAGING ANTISOCIAL BEHAVIOR

Lessig (1999) makes a useful classification of methods for discouraging antisocial behavior into *law, norms,* and *architecture. Law* consists of sets of rule systems and punishments for transgressions. It does not refer exclusively to national or international laws—for instance, the "law" that aims to limit where cars can be parked includes national and local laws, but also includes notices saying PARKING FOR CUSTOMERS ONLY, and the car park attendants who enforce them. Lessig points out that laws are a relatively expensive way of controlling behavior, and should be regarded as a backup for when other methods fail. *Norms* consist of social pressure and socialization. Social norms can be the most effective approach to controlling behavior. Most car owners do not park on their neighbors' lawns, not principally because they are afraid of punishments for doing so, but because they have been socialized into believing that it would not be a good thing to do. Finally, by *architecture* Lessig refers to aspects of the design of the environment that make unwanted behavior difficult to carry out. For instance, putting a fence around a lawn makes it more difficult for neighbors to park there. I will discuss each of these approaches in turn in the context of online learning communities.

Law

Many online learning communities do have the equivalent of laws: they are the terms of service documents, which specify behavior that is forbidden in the community and sometimes the sanctions for such behavior. Unfortunately, the terms

of service for most online communities (with a few pleasant exceptions, such as those for the investment community The Motley Fool®) tend to be written in legal language and are heavy-going to read. The clearer your terms of service document is, the easier it will be to keep order. One student who admitted repeated online plagiarism threatened to sue his UK university for negligence, for allegedly not warning him that it was against their regulations (BBC, 2004). There are well-designed resources for teachers of pre-teens on the specific issue of cheating (online and off-line) at CastleWorks (2005).

Laws are of little use unless there are also means to enforce them, along with a procedure for resolving disputes about whether the laws have been infringed.

Reid (1994) has noted that online multi-player games have "mediaeval" punishment systems, with punishment as a public spectacle (Chapter II, p. i). More modern components of justice systems, including mediation, restoration, and rehabilitation, are worth incorporating in online learning communities. My own experience in the online community Little Italy was that some of the members who contributed most to the community had initially been problem members displaying antisocial behavior; the process of rehabilitation had succeeded in redirecting their energy from disruptive activities to positive ones.

Norms

In addition to the terms of service page, which specifies behavior that is forbidden, it can be helpful to have a netiquette page for your community to describe norms of polite behavior.

If new members join the community over time, more experienced members can play a role in socializing them and clarifying the community norms to them. Several online communities have official helpers, who are experienced members who volunteer to assist novice users of the community (and not-so-novice users), solving their technical problems, helping them to navigate community information sources, and advising them on etiquette.

A related idea, although one that is only applicable to some limited types of online learning communities, is to require new members to have a sponsor. A sponsor is an existing member who vouches for the new member's good behavior. It is the sponsor's responsibility to communicate the community's norms to the new member. If the member misbehaves, the sponsor may be penalized, and the sponsor is expected to take part in rehabilitating the offender.

Since novice users may make mistakes while they are learning the norms, one technique used in some online learning communities is for there to be a learner-driver period for new members, during which their communications are marked with some sign indicating to other members that they are new and should therefore be treated with patience if they infringe social norms.

Online mediation can be a useful technique for managing conflict between online learning community members. A disagreement or argument can be taken out of the public forum into a semi-private space until it is resolved by the disagreeing parties working with the mediator, and can be pursued again in the public space without causing disruption. It can be useful to have a mediator who is neither the administrator, nor immediately involved in the dispute, but a volunteer from the community.

The commonest and most effective tools for socialization in learning communities are social ridicule of disruptive members and reinforcement of pleasant behavior, carried out by other members as part of online conversations. Administrators of learning communities can set an example by the tone of their online interactions. As a consequence of the weakened feedback in online communications, explicit acknowledgment of positive online behavior is especially important. For good advice on hosting online conversations, see Rheingold (1998).

An entertaining way of countering bad language through social ridicule, invented by Lawrence Ladomery, is for a community administrator to edit nastier messages, substituting offensive words by flower names. The effect of this can be an outburst of "flowers" from the author before he or she works out what is going on.

The economic success of the auction site eBay®, which has a reputation system for its buyers and sellers based on ratings of their behavior by other members, has led to reputation systems becoming *de rigueur* for some categories of commercial Web sites. Resnick, Zeckhauser, Swanson, and Lockwood (1992) found in a controlled experiment that an established seller with high reputation could sell items on eBay® at prices 7.6% higher than a newcomer could. Reputation systems may also provide an incentive for good behavior in learning communities where it does not confer any economic advantage, by decreasing the likelihood of reciprocation for members with low reputation (and increasing it for those with high reputation), and by validating the positive self-image of cooperative members.

Reputation systems may award positive points for good behavior, negative points for bad behavior, or both. However, systems that award negative points may be fooled by miscreants who leave the community and return as apparent newcomers, thus wiping out their negative points. This can be prevented in some cases by identity checks on newcomers; for instance, if the online community is associated with an off-line course, it may be straightforward to tie members' online identities to their off-line ones. However, if such access control is not feasible in your online community, then you should use reputation systems that award positive points. Experiments by Yamagishi and Matsuda (2002) demonstrate that introducing positive reputation to an auction market without access control can increase the quality of the goods offered for sale, and the honesty of the sellers about their goods.

Reputation can be calculated not only for members, but also (or alternatively) for individual messages, and this information can be used to decide the prominence with which messages will be displayed.

Architecture

A few antisocial behaviors can be completely prevented by architecture—that is, by the code of the online site. For example, censorware can automatically prevent certain words from being published on the site (although it may not be able to suppress variations of the words that are still comprehensible to members). In some cases an architectural component does not completely prevent a particular behavior, but limits the damage that it can cause; for instance, a filter that allows a member to choose not to see any more messages originated by another particular member will not prevent harassment, but may prevent repeated harassment by the same person. (Good practice in the implementation of such a filter is that both the member that is filtered and a mediator are automatically informed when it is applied.)

More commonly, architecture does not provide a solution in itself, but can support other solutions. Disputes about whether prohibited behavior took place can be more easily resolved if conversations are automatically logged. It is helpful to have a separate channel for mediation, so as to isolate mediation from public conversations. Collaborative technologies such as collaborative filtering software and reputation software can harness community input to increase the signal-to-noise ratio, by making posts more prominent if community members judge them to be good, and by deleting posts judged to be worthless.

Some antisocial behavior in online communities, especially by teenagers and pre-teens, is attention seeking. A problem member who is very active and who likes to provoke arguments is known as an "energy beast," after a Star Trek® episode about an alien that feeds on intense emo-

tions. Paying attention to an energy beast just gives it more energy; the solution is to ignore it. One architectural approach to help achieve this is to give energy beasts their own space where they can post as many messages as they like, but where other members can choose not to go. Administrators should take care to avoid being provoked into disputes with energy beasts, and should answer any long messages from them with short but courteous replies.

COOPERATIVE BEHAVIOR IN ONLINE LEARNING COMMUNITIES

The problems described in the first half of this chapter tend to be minority phenomena. In general, online learning communities tend to have positive social atmospheres with remarkable amounts of cooperation. In this second half of the chapter, I will outline different types of cooperative behavior, reasons for such behavior, and ways of designing online learning communities to encourage it, applying some findings from social psychology.

Types of Cooperative Behavior

Perhaps the most obvious category of cooperative behavior in a learning community is the provision of useful information or interesting ideas related to the learning topic. There are however other kinds of cooperation and interpersonal support. One is to provide meta-level assistance, for instance helping other members to use the interface or underlying technology or to navigate the online space, or giving them information about social norms, or introducing them to others who might have interests in common, or giving input into the design of the learning community itself. Another is to stimulate and shape the online discussion, for instance asking fruitful questions, seeking clarifications, summarizing previous discussions, or bringing back a conversation to the main topic after a digression. Another kind of cooperation that is sometimes ignored by the designers of learning communities, but which can be extremely important to members, is emotional support. This can be as minor an activity as thanking someone for a contribution, or as major as supporting another member through bereavement. Yet another form of cooperation is to take real-world action implementing online suggestions and discussions, and to report back on this to the online community.

Internet technology also can enable some types of cooperation that are difficult or impossible off-line. A striking example of this is the story of LEGO® MINDSTORMS™ and BrickOS™. LEGO® MINDSTORMS™ products, which were developed for educational purposes, are kits for building programmable robots that can interact with their environment. Several school projects use them to teach students math, science, computing, and design technology, by getting students to program the robots to carry out particular actions. Schools can (and do) share their ideas for projects involving these via a community Web site (LEGO® Group, 2005). The "brain" of the robot is a special programmable LEGO® brick. When it was first sold, this brick could only be programmed using a special-purpose programming language. Markus Noga and others reverse-engineered the programmable brick's operating system to create the open source operating system BrickOS™, available for free on the Web, which allows the robots to be programmed in C and C++, and has much more power and flexibility than the original. The free availability of this operating system contributed to a remarkable creative proliferation of ideas for these robots. Enthusiasts published descriptions and photos of many new robots, together with the code to run them, on public Web sites. Although the reverse engineering had been carried out without permission, the LEGO® Group decided not to sue, perhaps because they saw the potential of the new operating system for increasing sales; the download site for BrickOS™

is now linked from the official LEGO® MIND-STORMS™ site. The Hall of Fame page (LEGO® Group, 1999-2001) on the official site, which contains programs voted for by the site's online community, includes code for—among many other things—a pinball machine, 3D scanner, and stair climber all constructed using LEGO® MINDSTORMS™, and a robot for painting stripes on Easter eggs. Neither the open-source creation and wide distribution of BrickOS™, nor the wide publication of code for interesting robots and the resulting mutual inspiration and learning by their creators, would have been possible without Internet technology.

Why do People Cooperate in Online Learning Communities?

Although people certainly do cooperate in online learning communities, it is not immediately obvious why. According to Volund (1993) and other sociobiologists, cooperation between non-kin should only happen in very long-lived groups with very stable membership. Online learning communities rarely have these characteristics. Indeed, one advantage of online learning is precisely that its flexibility allows for cooperation among learning groups that are short-lived or have rapidly changing membership. Short-lived groups can easily interact online without having to arrange to be in the same location, and standard software for online archiving and retrieval can make it easy for messages from members of rapidly changing groups to continue to be used after the member has left the group.

Similarly, Tarlow (2003) asked about Markus Noga: "What's in it for him? He didn't get *anything* for doing this. Why would he spend a huge amount of talent and knowledge developing something for LEGO®? I'm not sure I would."

Kollock (1999) discusses several motivations for cooperation in online communities (pp. 227-229). These are anticipated reciprocation (that is, the expectation of later help or information in return) increased personal reputation, a sense of efficacy, benefit to oneself as a member of a group, and attachment to a group.

Two more reasons that people cooperate in online learning communities are disinhibition—which can make members more emotionally supportive, for instance—and a desire to display creative or technical prowess. As remarked earlier, these can also motivate antisocial behavior. Finally, although it is possible to explain much of the cooperation that can be seen in online learning communities without assuming that members are motivated by altruism, there is general agreement among people with long experience of such communities that altruism does play a role.

ENCOURAGING COOPERATIVE BEHAVIOR

Now that I have outlined reasons why people cooperate in online learning communities, I will discuss ways to encourage and enhance such cooperation through user-centered design, applying some results of experiments in social psychology.

Are Tangible Rewards Effective?

It appears to be common sense that people are more likely to contribute to a community if they are rewarded for doing so, and this has led to a variety of tangible rewards being offered for contribution to online communities, ranging from additional course credits to personalized ballpoint pens.

In their study of online forums used in universities in Hong Kong, McNaught, Cheng, and Lam (Chapter VIII, this volume) found that structured forums with course credits offered for particular levels of activity were generally more successful than "free" forums, and that to make a free forum successful, it was necessary for the teacher to be particularly skilled at motivating students

to participate. However, it is not clear how much of the success of the structured forums was due to the extrinsic rewards and how much to, for example, the specific goals and integration with classroom activity, which were features of these forums but not of the free forums. McNaught et al. remark that it is not easy to maintain a forum of consistently high quality, and if students have only extrinsic motivation.

Moreover, research by Fahey (2005, pp. 81-90) reveals that tangible rewards can have a deleterious effect. Members of a large multinational knowledge-sharing community were offered points for contributions in the community, which they could save up and exchange for rewards such as key rings, mugs, or laptop bags. Fahey discovered that when these rewards were introduced, the quantity of messages rose, but their quality significantly deteriorated. There was conflict among members concerning abuses of the reward system, and a loss of collective trust. Fahey attributes these phenomena to the change in members' motivation for contribution. Before the introduction of rewards, members were motivated to contribute by collective interest and moral obligation; afterward, many members were motivated primarily by economic self-interest.

Although additional points were given for messages rated as useful by other members of the knowledge-sharing community, it was possible to gain some points merely by posting a message. It is possible that a more carefully constructed reward scheme, in which only high-quality messages were rewarded, might have led to an increase rather than a decrease in quality. Fahey however discusses the possibility that introducing *any* reward scheme into a successful online community may lead to a deterioration of quality, one reason being that members may lose interest in doing more than the bare minimum necessary to gain the reward. If rewards are given at the discretion of an administrator rather than at the achievement of some published minimum criteria, then members may devote energy to buttering up the administrator rather than contributing to the community. Certainly, if you plan to offer tangible rewards for contributions in your learning community, you should design your reward system with care, bearing in mind that it will encourage members to seek the easiest way of earning the rewards.

ENHANCERS OF COOPERATIVE BEHAVIOR

Several social psychologists have run (off-line) experiments using social dilemmas to discover the factors in group interaction that encourage cooperation (Brewer & Kramer, 1986; Kerr, 1996). They found that the presence of norms of cooperation, communication to other members of cooperative actions, awareness by members of the efficacy of their contribution, a strong group identity, and non-anonymity of group members all increase the amount of group cooperation. For each of these factors, I will now outline some ways that design of the online learning community can introduce or enhance the factor.

Cooperative Norms

In the first part of the chapter I described several ways to support norms that discourage antisocial behavior. These can also be used to support norms that encourage cooperative behavior. In addition there are a few design features that assist specifically with the development of norms of cooperation. A community structure that includes small teams of members who are expected to communicate more intensively with each other can allow for more repeat interactions among the same set of members, and hence increase opportunities both for more sophisticated cooperation and for the upholding of cooperation as a norm. Teams may be groups of members with particular interests, or groups of members who invite each other join their team, or failing that, teams may

be arbitrarily assigned. "Buddy list" technology can be used so that members know when another member of their team is online. Interfaces can include prominent design features for responses to contributions from other members, and for meta-level suggestions. However, it is good design practice to have a separate communication channel for meta-level discussions, to avoid them from interrupting the conversational flow.

Following the principles of user-centered design, members should be encouraged to participate in decisions affecting the design of the community (where design is understood in its widest sense). This not only encourages one form of cooperation, but also can strengthen cooperative norms by giving members a sense of ownership and a desire to support the smooth running of the community.

Communication of Cooperation

As mentioned earlier, making reputations visible to other members is one way of communicating that a member has behaved in a cooperative fashion.

Information about ways in which a member has contributed may be added (automatically or manually) to their personal profiles. For instance, a profile might contain the number of messages posted by that member that were highly rated by other members, with links to them, a reputation rating for the member, and a star awarded to a group of members for an act of particularly impressive cooperation, linked to a featured members Web page describing this cooperative act. Some of this information might be visible in icon form on messages sent by that member.

A personal profile displays information about a single member. If the number of community members is not too large, then a visualization tool such as i-Bee (Mochizuki et al., Chapter XVI, this volume) could be used to display some information about all the members at once, thus giving a picture of the overall level of cooperation in the community as a whole, or of how cooperation varies between different parts of the community.

Some architectural features can be effective in encouraging the basic cooperative act, that of engaging in discussion with other community members. One of these is *answer notify*; when another member responds online to a message, the author of the original message is automatically notified by e-mail. The introduction of this simple mechanism can lead to a noticeable increase in the frequency of messages and the level of conversational engagement. A similar effect is achieved by the *trackback* functionality of blogs, which can be used to link a blog back to other blogs that comment on its content, thus encouraging cross-blog conversations.

Efficacy

In order for members to know the efficacy of their contributions, it is useful to have specific goals for users or groups of users, and information on current progress toward those goals. The goals should, of course, be related to user needs and user requirements—that is, to the members' own tasks and goals, which user-centered design methodology will aim to discover.

One aspect of a system with high efficacy is that the effort required for cooperation and collaboration is small. Designers of online learning environments should therefore aim to reduce the steps required, both in terms of physical activity (the number of mouse clicks, for instance) and in terms of conceptual difficulty. When possible, steps to cooperation should be automated. For example, for some types of goals, information on progress toward the goals can be obtained automatically. Reputation systems may incorporate measurements that can be carried out by software instrumentation of the online learning environment in addition to feedback by other members.

Instrumentation may also automatically identify features of the online environment that are being rarely used, or rarely used by particular types

of members, and this information can be used to improve the environmental design. Software that identifies pairs of members with potentially matching interests can be a useful addition to personal recommendations.

Some experiments on ways to encourage contribution through increasing members' awareness of the efficacy of their contributions were carried out by the CommunityLab project (Ling et al., 2005) studying an online movie-rating community. They found that reminding individual members who rated rarely-rated types of movies of their uniqueness had the effect of increasing contributions by these members, and that groups of members who were set challenging, specific goals (to rate a specific number of movies) produced more ratings than those given the vague goal to rate "as many as you can." Collective goals for groups of 10 members produced higher contributions than individual goals; this is contrary to predictions from off-line research that individual goals are more effective than goals for groups of more than five or six members. Interestingly, reminding members of either the individual or the collective benefits (but not both) of the act of rating movies had the effect of decreasing the number of movies rated. The researchers suggest that this last effect may be because the reminder of a benefit of contribution may undermine other motivations; if this is the case, it suggests a common mechanism underlying both this effect and the deleterious effects of introducing tangible rewards observed by Fahey (2005).

The efficacy of past messages depends on the ease of finding them again. Good search technology is essential for large communities, and processes for categorization and editing of material can greatly improve the signal-to-noise ratio.

The environment of an online learning community includes the online environment itself, as well as the off-line environment in which it is embedded. Effects of actions on the online environment may be more immediately noticeable for members than off-line effects. Therefore following user-centered design principles in which users' preferences, goals, and actions feed back into the design of the online environment can enhance users' awareness of the efficacy of their contributions.

Group Identity

A unified on-screen look for the online community, with consistent colors, fonts, icons, buttons, and screen layouts, can help to support a group identity, as well as contributing to usability. A logo for the community can provide a handy visual identifier that can be used to link to the community site from other Web pages, or on publications and t-shirts.

Induction courses for new members can serve to foster a group identity as well as to introduce social norms.

A simple tool for assisting group identity that was first developed on Usenet newsgroups is the FAQ, a public list of frequently asked questions and answers to those questions. The FAQ can greatly reduce time spent answering common queries, but also can enhance group identity by recording the most useful community knowledge, or community decisions, in a quickly accessible form. A vocabulary list that records and explains technical terms that are commonly used by the community, or words that are used by the community with specialized meanings, can also be helpful. There needs, of course, to be a process by which the community can update the FAQ and the vocabulary list. Usenet FAQs typically had one volunteer editor who accepted suggestions from the community; wiki technology now allows the production of documents that any member can update at any time.

Online communities have one advantage over purely off-line ones when it comes to maintaining a group identity, in that online community software makes archiving very easy, and so it is relatively easy to have a group history available to current members. Techniques of editing, summarizing, and storytelling can help to produce a group history that is more conducive to the formation of a group identity than mere raw transcripts of past activity would be.

Non-Anonymity

In order to achieve non-anonymity, it is not necessary for members to be fully identified; it is enough for members to have persistent pseudonyms, which allow a history to be built up of a member's interactions with the community, and also allow the development of social reputation and nontrivial social relationships within the community. Personal profile pages can play a useful role in making individual members less anonymous. Some elements of the profile (for instance, numbers of postings and links to recent ones) may be automatically produced by the community software, while others (for instance, a list of interests) may be written or edited by the member herself. One effective way of reducing anonymity is to integrate online learning with activities where members meet each other face-to-face.

Integration with Off-Line Activities

My experience of several online learning communities suggests that cooperation is increased by integration of the online learning with face-to-face activities. Off-line activities may allow opportunities for extra communication of cooperation and for strengthening of group identity, enable additional forms of contribution, and decrease anonymity, so the apparent positive effect of this may be entirely explained by the factors discovered in the off-line social psychology experiments; however, it is also possible that such integration provides an extra boost to cooperation independent from these other factors.

Many online learning communities begin as extensions of off-line educational courses or have some other off-line interaction between their members right from the beginning. Although not all start this way, successful online learning communities develop new or strengthened off-line links: it is natural for people who have learned together online to wish to meet each other off-line as well.

Off-line interaction can significantly improve not only the amount of cooperation by community members, but also the quality of the online learning in general. This is understood, for instance, by the Open University, a UK university dedicated to distance education with around 150,000 undergraduates and 30,000 postgraduates, which has a policy of including residential or day schools as part of many of its courses. An assessment of teaching records in 2004 (Times Newspapers, 2004) put the Open University in the top five UK universities. In contrast, the educational model of several e-education companies that were started during the dot.com boom emphasized access to written course material over interaction (either on- or off-line) between teachers and students or between students, downplaying the social aspects of learning. The result was a reduction in learning quality.

If your community is associated with an off-line course, then it clearly makes sense to integrate the off-line and online learning, making the most of the different capabilities of off-line and online communication. For instance, threaded discussion boards, wikis, and Web sites can be used for students and teachers to hold non-real-time discussions and share information on course topics, set and deliver course assignments, suggest and discuss related reading, and communicate course logistics, without requiring the learning community members to be simultaneously present in the same physical space, and with easy archiving for later reference. Meanwhile, the greater capabilities of the off-line world for interaction with physical objects, for creating a sense of occasion, and for reaching group consensus on contentious issues can be exploited in the off-line meetings.

Online communities can also be used by students while they are actually present in an off-line class or meeting. For instance, law students can quickly find legal precedents online that are relevant to a legal question that comes up during an off-line discussion. One particularly interesting use of real-time online community support during lectures was initially tried out by a project at the University of California at San Diego (Ratto, Shapiro, Truong, & Griswold, 2003). The technology is now used by other universities as well. In this project, students used handheld wireless devices during lectures to suggest questions to be answered by the lecturer, to answer questions suggested by others if they had a good answer themselves, and to vote for which questions on the list of current suggested questions should be given priority by the lecturer. The identity of the student suggesting a question was not revealed to other students, although the lecturer could discover it later. Students' ability to ask questions without revealing their identity reduced their embarrassment about asking questions in class, and this produced questions of a high quality and broad range. The voting system allowed lecturers to know that a question was of interest to many students, rather than only to the questioner. A professor who used the system said (p. 7) that students asked questions that had not ever been asked in prior versions of the course, some of them especially insightful, with the result that all students were able to benefit.

If your community does not have an obvious off-line component, it makes sense to plan off-line meetings for community members. These should include both meetings for serious learning, and social meetings—or alternatively it is possible to combine the two, allotting time for socializing when planning the timetable for a study meeting. The technical and informational resources of the online learning community can be used to support off-line meetings. For instance, the agenda can be discussed in advance online, background material and introductions by speakers and delegates can be provided in advance, logistical and travel information can be circulated online, the venue and questions to put to speakers can be decided by online vote, and members unable to attend can use the online community to appoint delegates who will find out about a particular topic or make particular points on their behalf, reporting back to them. It can be possible for community members who are not physically present to take part in dialogs and question sessions during the meeting itself by, for instance, responding to live blogs written by members who are present.

After the meeting, edited write-ups of the meeting and summaries of any outcomes can be posted online, and follow-up discussions can take place there, taking advantage of the archiving capabilities of online communication as well as its capabilities for non-real-time, geographically distributed discussions. Write-ups and photos of social events can also be valuable for increasing social capital within the community.

Finally, it is a mistake to think of any online learning community as a completely self-contained entity. Its members will have links and affiliations with other organizations, both online and off-line, and these links can be exploited to enhance the community.

FUTURE TRENDS AND CONCLUSION

In the early days of online learning communities, students were likely to have Internet access only from a computer owned by their educational organization; now some have Internet access from their own mobile phone. Future technology trends are for personal Internet access to become increasingly available, mobile, and affordable. Simultaneously, there is a social trend (in Europe at least) toward lifelong learning, with learning taking place throughout a person's life, rather than being limited to formal education during a particular age span. The effect of this trend is that future learning management systems will need to be flexible, to allow remote personal access, and

to be easily integrated into the everyday lives of learners, who will not necessarily be in formal education. Online learning communities will be a crucial part of this. Many of the mechanisms for social control and promotion of cooperation that are used in traditional education are difficult to apply in a distributed community of learners outside formal education. Therefore it will be particularly important to design such online learning communities to encourage cooperation.

In this chapter I have given reasons for uncooperative and cooperative behavior in online learning, and suggested some ways to design online learning communities in order to encourage cooperation. However, the design of your community should be based on its specific purpose and the particular set of users that it is designed for. You will therefore need to adapt the recommendations to your particular circumstances, involving your users in the design from the beginning, and continuously feeding back users' tasks, goals, experiences, and ideas into potential design changes. For instance, if your community is designed for lifelong learning, and shared off-line activity is impractical, then you may find that users draw particular benefit from design features that foster a group identity and help to build cooperative social norms.

Finally, do not be afraid to experiment. Almost all the design suggestions that I have mentioned were developed through experimentation with the assistance and participation of users, and this is the best way to discover further design improvements that will be useful for your community's purpose. As Howard Rheingold's e-mail signature says, "What it is—is—up to us."

ACKNOWLEDGMENT

Thanks to the many people who contributed to the ideas in this chapter, including members of Little Italy, e-mint, the online communities seminar group at HP Labs, *Online Social Networks,* and the Interaction Design Institute, Ivrea.

REFERENCES

BBC (British Broadcasting Corporation). (2004). "Plagiarist" to sue university. *BBC News World Edition,* (May 27). Retrieved December 5, 2005, from http://news.bbc.co.uk/2/hi/uk_news/education/3753065.stm

Brewer, M., & Kramer, R. (1986). Choice behavior in social dilemmas. *Journal of Personality and Social Psychology, 50,* 543-549.

CastleWorks. (2005). *Resources by topic: Cheating.* Retrieved December 5, 2005, from http://pbskids.org/itsmylife/parents/resources/cheating.html

Fahey, R. (2005). *Knowledge management. The impact of rewards within communities of practice. A case study.* Unpublished master's thesis, Sheffield Hallam University, UK.

Foster, D. (2003). Test piracy: The darker side of certification. *Certification Magazine,* (January). Retrieved December 5, 2005, from http://www.certmag.com/articles/templates/cmag_feature.asp?articleid=2

Jones, K. (a.k.a. "handy vandal"). (2003). Student logs teacher's keystrokes. *Slashdot,* (February 5). Retrieved December 5, 2005, from http://yro.slashdot.org/article.pl?sid=05/02/03/0156243

Kerr, N. L. (1996). Does my contribution really matter? *European Review of Social Psychology, 7,* 209-240.

Kollock, P. (1999). The economies of online cooperation: Gifts and public goods in cyberspace. In M.A. Smith & P. Kollock (Eds.), *Communities in cyberspace* (pp. 220-239). London/New York: Routledge.

LEGO Group. (1999-2001). *LEGO.com MINDSTORMS Hall of Fame.* Retrieved December 5, 2005, from http://mindstorms.lego.com/eng/community/halloffame/default.asp

LEGO Group. (2005). *LEGO.com Educational Division—MINDSTORMS for schools.* Retrieved December 5, 2005, from http://www.lego.com/eng/education/mindstorms/home.asp?menu=community&pagename=community

Lessig, L. (1999). *Code: And other laws of cyberspace.* New York: Basic Books.

Ling, K., Beenen, G., Ludford, P., Wang, X., Chang, K., Li, X., et al. (2005). Using social psychology to motivate contributions to online communities. *Journal of Computer-Mediated Communication, 10*(4).

MessageLabs. (2005). *Monthly report: June 2005.* Retrieved December 5, 2005, from http://www.messagelabs.com/publishedcontent/publish/threat_watch_dotcom_en/intelligence_reports/june_2005/DA_118149.chp.html

NCH. (2005). *Putting U in the picture—Mobile bullying survey 2005.* Retrieved December 5, 2005, from http://www.nch.org.uk/uploads/documents/Mobile_bullying_%20report.pdf

Ratto, M., Shapiro, R. B., Truong, T. M., & Griswold, W. G. (2003). The ActiveClass project: Experiments in encouraging classroom participation. In B. Wasson, S. Ludvigsen, & U. Hopper (Eds.), *Computer support for collaborative learning 2003* (pp. 477-486). Dordect: Kluwer.

Reid, E. (1994). *Cultural formations in text-based virtual realities.* Unpublished master's thesis, University of Melbourne, Australia.

Resnick, P., Zeckhauser, R., Swanson, J., & Lockwood, K. (2002). *The value of reputation on eBay: A controlled experiment.* Working Paper Series No. RWP03-007, John F. Kennedy School of Government, Harvard University, USA.

Rheingold, H. (1998). *The art of hosting good conversations online.* Retrieved December 5, 2005, from http://www.rheingold.com/texts/artonlinehost.html

Sproull, L., & Kiesler, S. (1991). Computers, networks and work. *Scientific American, 265,* 116-123.

Tarlow, M. (2003, January 30). Paper presented at HP Laboratories, Palo Alto, CA.

Times Newspapers. (2004). The Sunday Times university guide 2004. *Sunday Times* (London), (September 12), supplement.

Volund, E. (1993). *Grundriss der soziobiologie.* Stuttgart/Jena: G. Fischer Verlag.

Yamagishi, T., & Matsuda, M. (2002). *Improving the lemons market with a reputation system: An experimental study of Internet auctioning.* Retrieved December 5, 2005, from http://joi.ito. com/archives/papers/Yamagishi_ASQl.pdf

This work was previously published in User-Centered Design of Online Learning Communities, edited by N. Lambropoulos and P. Zaphiris, pp. 102-121, copyright 2007 by Information Science Publishing (an imprint of IGI Global).

Chapter XV
Building Virtual
Learning Communities

Naomi Augar
Deakin University, Australia

Ruth Raitman
Deakin University, Australia

Elicia Lanham
Deakin University, Australia

Wanlei Zhou
Deakin University, Australia

ABSTRACT

This chapter introduces the concept of virtual learning communities and discusses and further enhances the theory and definitions presented in related literature. A model comprising four criteria essential to virtual learning communities is presented and discussed in detail. Theory and case studies relating to the impact of virtual learning communities on distance education and students from diverse cultural groups are also examined. In addition, this chapter investigates the enabling technologies and facilitation that is required to build virtual learning communities. Other case studies are used to illustrate the process of building virtual learning communities. Emerging technologies such as wikis and video lectures are also analysed to determine the effects they have on building and sustaining effective virtual learning communities.

INTRODUCTION

Virtual communities are created when people form groups online to share a common interest and create a social bond that is nourished with continued interaction over time (Powazek, 2002). Social virtual communities, also known as discourse communities, have existed on the Internet for many years. Communities supported by Internet discussion boards and the like are dedicated to interests as diverse as pop stars and football. All involve the sharing of knowledge, support, and common interests through ongoing social interaction online (Jonassen, Howland, Moore, & Marra, 2003; Rheingold, 1994; Wood & Smith, 2001).

Computer-supported collaborative work has been the subject of research since the 1970s when communications technology evolved to support virtual communities in the workplace (Lewis, 2002). Work-related virtual communities are also known as communities of practice (Wenger, 1998). These communities allowed their workers to share business knowledge and learn from and support one another (Jonassen et al., 2003). Employees at different offices and those working from home can also share a mutual sense of presence provided by such communities (Dourish & Bly, 1992; Schraefel, Ho, Chignell, & Milton, 2000).

The advent of the Internet has had a huge impact on teaching and learning around the world. The Internet and its associated communication media have the potential to revolutionise learning (Lewis, 2002). It is not only a powerful tool for content provision, but it also lends itself to the creation of groups of learners who can support each other in the learning process (Bruckman, 2002).

Traditionally, universities have used classroom-situated tutorials as a means of facilitating discourse among learners so they can construct a solid understanding of course materials through social interaction with their peers and instructors. Virtual learning communities can now provide a classroom online, in which students may interact with each other and their instructors. The virtual nature of the classroom means that students can join in regardless of their location. Consequently, participation in a learning community can be particularly beneficial to those who study entirely online, such as distance learners. It can help learners to overcome their feelings of isolation and enhance their learning experience through interaction with their peers (Blunt, 2001; Haythornthwaite, Kazmer, Robins, & Shoemaker, 2000; Lanham & Zhou, 2002).

The work of Haythornthwaite et al. (2000) describes a virtual learning community that used multiple technologies to connect distance learners. The distance program included some classroom-situated seminars. However, the bulk of the learning experience was conducted online. E-mail and Internet discussion boards were the prime means for communication among students and staff. Internet Relay Chat (IRC), a text-based synchronous discussion program, allowed students to partake in informal social communication known as "whispering" during real-time virtual lectures. IRC was also used by students to ask the instructor questions during the live lectures. The lectures were delivered online using PowerPoint slides accompanied by narration. Interviews conducted throughout the duration of the course showed that students who communicated actively identified themselves as members of a learning community and felt less isolated and less stressed than those who did not participate.

Palaver Tree Online is a virtual learning community that connects students with mentors who help the students build a database of oral history. Students interview elders online using specially developed discussion software that integrates individual profiles of the elders. Students can also create stories that summarise what they have learned in their interviews and publish them within the integrated online environment (Ellis & Bruckman, 2001).

Jonassen et al. (2003) describe several virtual learning community projects such as Knowledge Forum, CaMILE, SWiki, and Shadow netWorkspace. All share discourse as the common method for building communities of learners. The projects use various tailor-made software solutions to create flexible discussion forums and platforms for collaboration on documents and the construction of knowledge by students. Some of these communities also involve mentors interacting with students to share knowledge and achieve learning goals in a manner similar to the Palaver Tree Online project.

These examples illustrate some of the possibilities of virtual learning communities. Subsequently, this chapter defines virtual learning communities and discusses the technologies and facilitation required to build them. It explores the pedagogy of virtual learning communities and presents case studies to illustrate the community building process.

VIRTUAL LEARNING COMMUNITIES

The evolution of modern day virtual learning communities can be traced back to the industrial revolution and beyond. People have formed learning communities to share knowledge throughout history. Virtual learning communities facilitated by the Internet are an extension of this trend (Lewis, 2002).

There are varied notions of what constitutes a virtual community (Daniel, McCalla, & Schwier, 2002; Jones, 1997). A learning community is made up of individuals who work together in a shared space to increase their knowledge and understanding of a subject through study and experience (Saragina, 1999). In a virtual learning community, the shared space that the community inhabits is the Internet.

A virtual learning environment is created on the Internet using study materials, discussion boards, and instructors (Augar, Raitman, & Zhou,

2004a; Augar, Raitman, & Zhou, 2005; Oren, Nachmias, Mioduser, & Lahav, 1998).

However, the provision of content in a virtual environment accompanied by a discussion board is not sufficient in and of itself. For virtual communities to exist, they must have a minimum level of interactivity among a variety of communicators in a common public space, with a minimum level of membership sustained over time (Augar et al., 2004a; Jones, 1997; Wood & Smith, 2001).

A virtual learning community is a group of learners that interact in a common online environment to gain understanding of subject matter. Learners build on their knowledge by interacting with each other, their instructors, and learning materials. By sharing a common learning goal and interacting socially over a period of time, learners develop and share a sense of belonging and shared purpose (Augar et al., 2004a; Augar et al., 2005).

E-Learning Environment or Virtual Learning Community?

"Community" is a common word in current e-learning literature. This section compares and contrasts e-learning environments and virtual learning communities to clarify their similarities and differences.

An e-learning environment comprises the tools and content required to facilitate an online learning experience for students. It may comprise threaded discussions, synchronous chat, whiteboard tools, and content such as HTML, PDF files, or even multimedia presentations. Note that this definition implies that providing learning tools and content to students online does not automatically result in the creation of a virtual learning community. Such a view is technologically deterministic (Augar & Zhou, 2003; Jones, 1997). Rather, the provision of learning tools and content online creates an e-learning environment.

In most cases, e-learning environments require facilitation from teaching staff, as is the case for virtual learning communities. Facilitation may take the form of tutors moderating online discussion forums for students. E-learning environments and virtual learning communities are similar because students have a shared learning goal in both settings. However, the outcome of the shared learning goal in an e-learning environment is the successful completion of the subject. As later sections will discuss, virtual learning communities can encourage students to become more active in defining their shared learning goal. Moreover, virtual learning communities allow students to work together as a group to achieve shared learning goals.

Similarities aside, the key point that differentiates a virtual learning community from an e-learning environment is social context. Students develop social presence as a sense of community emerges in an e-learning environment. In developing social context, students feel a shared sense of community with their fellow learners and they identify with the community as a whole.

E-learning environments and virtual learning communities share the following common aspects: tools, content, facilitation, and shared learning goal. However, it is the development of social context among learners that turns an e-learning environment into a virtual learning community. Hence, careful consideration should be given to labelling an e-learning environment a "community." A host can provide the tools and facilitation that lay the foundations, but a community will only emerge if and when the participants choose to identify themselves as members of a community (Haythornthwaite et al., 2000; Powazek, 2002).

While this chapter will outline what the developer can do to increase the chances of building a virtual learning community, it is the users who will determine whether the developer's efforts are a success. As Jonassen et al. (2003) point out, virtual learning communities are an ideal that may not ever be completely attainable. Therefore, the important aspect to note is whether the learning

group is moving towards or away from the ideal of a community.

ESSENTIAL CRITERIA FOR VIRTUAL LEARNING COMMUNITIES

To further refine the discussion presented in the previous sections, four interrelated criteria are presented that are building blocks for the development of a virtual learning community. These criteria are: social context, facilitation, technology, and a shared learning goal. They are presented in the model depicted in Figure 1 (Augar et al., 2004a).

These four interrelated essential criteria are critical to the process of fostering a sense of community amongst learners. They are themes that will be reiterated throughout this chapter, as they are central to the process of building effective virtual learning communities. The following sections explore these criteria in greater depth.

Technology

For a sense of community to emerge in a virtual setting where people interact with one another in an online environment, there must be a shared space where communication can occur (Augar & Zhou, 2003; Blunt, 2001; Jones, 1997; Wood

Figure 1. Critical building blocks for a virtual learning community

Virtual Learning Community	
Social Context	Technology
Shared Learning Goal	Facilitation

& Smith, 2001). Technology allows learners to transmit, save, organise and extend the knowledge shared by the community members (Jonassen et al., 2003).

Consequently, technology is fundamental to the development of any virtual learning community. Reliability and ease of use are fundamental requirements for technology that supports e-learning. Students learning online can become alienated when they experience technical difficulties, which can diminish their motivation to participate (Augar et al., 2004a; Hara & Kling, 1999).

One of the most widely used technologies for enabling virtual learning communities is the asynchronous discussion forum. Asynchronous discussion tools and e-mail are used to create lively discourse relating to learning materials. Real-time collaboration tools may also be used, but they may disadvantage distance learners where time differences are a factor. Learning materials are provided as supplements to the interactive tools that facilitate the virtual learning community. Text-based and multimedia refer-

ence materials containing course content such as lecture notes, video lectures, or weekly readings provide resources to support the discourse that is the foundation of the community.

Most virtual learning communities are text-based. Access to these learning communities is gained via a software interface, which runs over the Internet. Students can use their personal computer to type messages and contribute or "post" them to ongoing asynchronous discussions that are maintained on a host server (Augar & Zhou, 2003).

Deakin University runs an e-learning environment called Deakin Studies Online (DSO). DSO uses WebCT Vista software, which has been customized especially for Deakin University. Figure 2 shows a screen shot of the DSO asynchronous discussion tool. This tool is used regularly by students, both to communicate with their peers informally and to participate in structured learning activities, such as online tutorials.

Synchronous text-based chat systems can also facilitate virtual learning communities. IRC, MSN

Figure 2. DSO's discussion tool

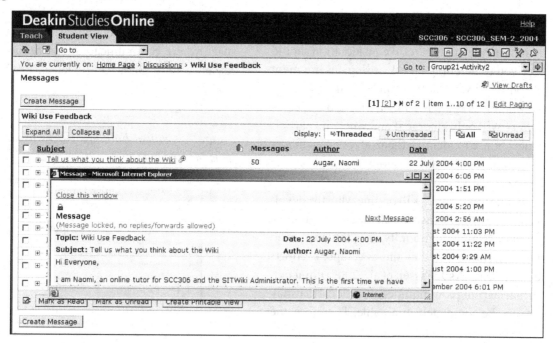

Messenger, and ICQ provide simple examples of software interfaces that allow learners from around the world to participate in real-time discussions. Each user can compose messages, which can be immediately viewed by other participants who in turn have the opportunity to respond. MSN Messenger and ICQ differ from asynchronous technologies in that each "chat" session is initiated by individual users and is not hosted on a designated central server. Unless a participant chooses to "log" a chat session (keep a transcript), there is no ongoing record of discourse between users (Augar & Zhou, 2003).

Deakin University's DSO system has an integrated chat facility for learners. Instructors may add this facility to their subject's learning area for students to access as part of learning activities. The interface of the DSO chat facility is depicted in Figure 3.

The advent of cheap, accessible multimedia technology has allowed virtual learning communities to evolve and thus include video and audio content. Previously, video conferencing and streamed video placed a huge load on telecommunication networks. Consequently, video was an expensive and cumbersome medium for use in virtual learning communities. However, as the telecommunications network bandwidth has increased and the price of services such as broadband Internet has decreased, video has been adopted by some community builders. This trend has been encouraged further by the reduced cost of audio and video capture devices, and the increased speed and memory of personal computers (Augar & Zhou, 2003).

Computer-mounted video cameras (Web cams) can be used in conjunction with programs that support video such as MSN Messenger or Microsoft NetMeeting to establish video conferences with groups. Shareware such as CU-SeeMe allows larger groups of people to conduct video conferences in video chat rooms that can be supported with text-based chat facilities (Jonassen et al., 2003).

Facilitation

Facilitation plays a key role in the successful development of a virtual learning community (Augar et al., 2004a; Carlsen, 2003; Stacey, 2001). The

Figure 3. DSO's chat integrated facility

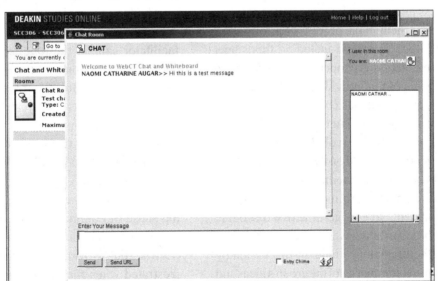

facilitation of virtual learning communities occurs when instructors begin interacting with learners in the e-learning environment. The process of guiding the learners in their development of social context and shared learning goals is critical to building the virtual learning community.

Salmon (2003) proposes a five-stage model of teaching and learning online that was developed as a result of action research undertaken at Open University in the United Kingdom. The model charts the changing needs of students and the role of the facilitator throughout the online learning process:

1. **Access and motivation:** Students focus on gaining access to and becoming familiar with the system. Facilitation at this stage is based on welcoming students, solving access issues, and encouraging participation.

2. **Online socialisation:** Students develop their online identity and begin to interact with the group. Facilitation focuses on helping individuals create their own social presence and encouraging social interaction amongst the group.

3. **Information exchange:** Participants exchange course-related information. Facilitation at this stage focuses on guiding students through the learning task, helping them to access appropriate learning materials, and guiding them in the process of information exchange. Up to and including this stage, the interaction is cooperative and supports the goals of the individual. At Stage 4, the interaction becomes collaborative.

4. **Knowledge construction:** At this stage, interaction becomes collaborative and communication is based on the common culture of the group. The facilitator adopts a more passive approach to moderation, allowing the students to engage in active discourse and broaden and develop their knowledge. The facilitator may guide the discussion by providing summaries of the group's ideas and relating them back to the central learning goals of the course.

5. **Development:** Individuals look for ways to benefit from the system and achieve their learning goals. The facilitator takes on a supportive role at this stage and responds to queries posed by the group. The learners are active and confident in learning through discourse in the online environment.

This model documents the critical and changing role the facilitator plays in the community-building process. They must teach the students how to interact and learn online, facilitate appropriate social interaction, guide their learning, and be responsive to and supportive of the needs of the learning group.

Participation in a virtual learning community requires students to review and understand the input of others, and formulate and contribute appropriate responses so they can have meaningful participation in online discourse. However, students may be more familiar with memorizing course content than they are with evaluating information and forming their own opinions about it. Consequently, the instructor may need to teach students how to communicate online, and provide ongoing monitoring to support active discourse (Jonassen et al., 2003).

The facilitator plays a critical role in modeling social presence and identity for students. The facilitator can set the tone for the community, and aid the development of trust and social bonds among learners. Building trust among learners is critical. Students can create a shared history and develop a sense of trust by sharing their experiences and knowledge within the virtual environment (Augar et al., 2004a; Daniel et al., 2002; Rovai, 2002).

The instructor needs to encourage the emerging sense of community among students while ensuring that the learning task is being completed (Lewis, 2002; Rovai, 2002). Students can become frustrated when they do not receive timely and clear advice in an online environment. By identifying and being responsive to student needs, facilitators can provide added motivation for students to participate (Augar et al., 2004a; Blunt, 2001; Hara & Kling, 1999). Another important aspect of establishing and facilitating appropriate social interaction in a virtual learning community is the implementation of a set of usage policies that are clearly and simply communicated in the e-learning environment, and enforced when necessary (Augar, Raitman, & Zhou, 2004b; Augar et al., 2005; Powazek, 2002).

Social Context

Social context defines the way social interactions are carried out within a virtual learning community. It is the sum of the identity and behaviour of individual participants and helps to define the communities' social identity (Jonassen et al., 2003). Over time, virtual communities develop unwritten rules on how to behave in the online environment. These rules allow participants to expect a certain standard of behaviour and help to develop a level of trust between community members (Haythornthwaite et al., 2000).

Virtual learning communities require students to develop social bonds in a short period of time so they can interact freely and focus on the course content. The process of developing and sustaining social context depends on the ability of learners to interact socially for enough time to develop a level of trust among the group (Augar et al., 2004a; Daniel et al., 2002).

In virtual learning communities, students are largely restricted to text-based communication, which has inherent limitations. Face-to-face communication is regulated by visual and audible cues that indicate someone has finished speaking and another person may start to talk. These cues include for example, finishing a sentence, body language, and vocalizations. Students new to learning in a virtual environment can be frustrated by their inability to detect these cues (Augar & Zhou, 2003; Hiltz & Turoff, 1993).

The absence of audible and visual cues may result in people being ruder than normal because they cannot see the recipients' reaction or gauge non-verbal cues (Baym, 1995). However, the absence of contextual cues can also be helpful as authors must take more care to ensure they communicate clearly (Jonassen et al., 2003). Consequently, the facilitator's role in modelling appropriate social interactions during the founding stages of a virtual learning community is critical to its ongoing success (Augar & Zhou, 2003; Stacey, 2001).

In a virtual learning community, each student's online identity is based on what he or she tells other community members about him or herself. Tools such as profiles (text-based biographies with an optional photograph posted within the e-learning environment) can help new students introduce themselves to the learning group in a non-threatening way (Augar & Zhou, 2003; Blunt, 2001). An interactive extension of this idea is an icebreaker exercise where groups of learners answer sets of socially oriented questions as a group in a discussion forum, introducing themselves to the other group members in the process. The facilitator can model appropriate social presence by taking part in the icebreaker exercise and constructing a profile of his or her own for the students to mimic (Augar et al., 2004b, 2005).

Shared Learning Goal

Virtual learning communities develop when participants can share knowledge about common interests and work to achieve shared learning goals (Daniel et al., 2002; Jonassen et al., 2003). Students may have their own learning goals, including attaining a degree or passing a subject. However, they may not consider participation in a discussion group or a virtual learning community to be a part of achieving those goals. Consequently, the development of a shared learning goal in a group of online learners can be very difficult to achieve (Augar et al., 2004a; Lewis, 2002).

Students can be motivated to participate through assessment that evaluates whether their contributions to group discussions were on time, relevant, and of a high quality (Rovai, 2002). However, Carlsen (2003) feels that for community to emerge, participation should be at least partially voluntary. A student's motivation for participation plays a critical role in the development of a shared learning goal. If students cannot see the benefits of participating in terms of their own goals, they may have a negative perception of the experience. Encouraging participation through assessment may be effective, but it may not result in an authentic virtual learning community.

Certain student groups may be more predisposed to participating in virtual learning communities. The work of Haythornthwaite et al. (2000) demonstrates the benefits virtual learning communities have for distance learners who experienced a reduced sense of isolation by belonging to the learning community. Reduced isolation and the support offered by the community influence a student's motivation to interact socially with other students, who would otherwise be strangers online.

Finally, the goal of any virtual learning community should always be communicated clearly to students (Blunt, 2001). Simple, unambiguous explanations about the aim of the exercise or discourse can reduce student frustration and help them focus on the learning task, rather than questioning why they have to participate. Continued prompt feedback and guidance from facilitators throughout the learning process can help students move toward the development of a shared learning goal.

The interrelated nature of the four criteria outlined here—technology, facilitation, social context, and shared learning goal—means that while all must be present, aspects of the criteria overlap. For example, by guiding the students in the completion of tasks, the facilitator aids in the process of developing the students' shared learning goal. This process highlights the relationship between effective facilitation and the development of a shared learning goal in the community. Likewise, facilitation is critical in the process of building social context. By modelling appropriate online behaviour, the facilitator helps the student establish an online identity and develop social bonds with other members of the learning group. Finally, effective facilitation can only occur if the enabling technology is usable by both the teacher and the students alike.

THE PEDAGOGY OF VIRTUAL LEARNING COMMUNITIES

This section looks at the theory of teaching and learning that provides the basis for using virtual learning communities as a teaching tool. Specifically, the areas of computer-supported collaborative learning (CSCL), constructivism, and constructionism are discussed. These areas lay the foundation for the central theme of learning communities: students working together and supporting one another in building knowledge that meets the learning objectives of the group (Jonassen et al., 2003).

Computer-Supported Collaborative Learning

The study of virtual learning communities encompasses the research areas of collaborative learning and CSCL. Collaborative learning can be achieved when students work together and share the responsibility for building on their existing knowledge (Myers, 1991). CSCL is a process where students work together on learning tasks using technology to facilitate their collaboration. CSCL can support and enhance peer interaction while enabling the sharing and distribution of knowledge and expertise among community members (Augar et al., 2004b; Lipponen, 2002; Raitman, Augar, & Zhou, 2004).

Constructivism and Constructionism

Constructivism is a process whereby the learner plays an active role in the learning process. The learner constructs new knowledge by building on his or her past and current experience (Brook & Oliver, 2003). Phillips (2000) identifies two different perceptions of constructivism. The first idea promotes constructivism as the shared body of knowledge built up through history. The second promotes the idea that knowledge is made as a result of learners constructing their own internal meaning and understanding of information (Duffy & Jonassen, 1992; Phillips, 2000).

Social interaction among learners plays a key role in the construction of knowledge. It provides students with a means to explore knowledge and achieve understanding of theory and concepts transmitted in the learning environment (Vygotsky, 1978, as cited by Stacey, 1999, 2001). In virtual learning communities, students can use discussion boards to discuss course content, question each other about subject matter, and through this process enhance their understanding of the material (Augar & Zhou, 2003).

Constructionism is similar to constructivism in that individuals create artefacts and in the process of doing so construct a greater understanding of subject matter (Dougimas & Taylor, 2002; Papert & Harel, 1991). Papert and Harel (1991) differentiate constructionism from constructivism by pointing out that constructionism occurs when learners construct real-world objects and enhance their knowledge in the process.

Bruckman (2002) contends that the true power of learning using the Internet lies not in the delivery of content to students who receive it passively. Rather, students should be active learners, gathering information resources and sharing them with their peers in an online environment supported by innovative collaborative tools. CSCL, constructivism, and constructionism all highlight the importance of learners interacting and collaborating to construct knowledge and artefacts that reflect their understanding of course materials. Research in these areas provides strong support and motivation for building virtual learning communities.

BUILDING CULTURALLY INCLUSIVE VIRTUAL LEARNING COMMUNITIES

Over that past five years, the number of international students studying at Deakin University has increased. This trend is predicted to continue over the next five years. These international students are from different cultural backgrounds and therefore have different approaches to learning. This increase is not limited to Deakin University. International student enrolments have also been on the increase over recent years at other Australian tertiary institutions, and this trend is expected to continue.

Dr. Brendan Nelson (2004) stated in a media release that Australia's international student enrolments reached an estimated 303,324 in 2003. This translated to a 17% growth in the higher education sector. The media release also indicated that Asia continues to remain the major source of international students, representing more than three-quarters of Australia's overseas students market (Lanham & Zhou, 2004a, 2004b).

An Australian Trade Commission report (2004) stated that in the year 2000, there were 182,000 international students studying at Australian institutions (150,000 onshore and 32,000 offshore). Fifty-six percent of these figures specifically related to University enrolments. The Australia-wide figures correlate with those collected by Deakin University.

During the period 2000 to 2002, there was an increase in the number of international students from Asian countries enrolling for study at Deakin. A significant increase in the number of students from China and Hong Kong was noted, showing an increase from 154 and 325 respectively in 2001, to 276 and 427 respectively in 2002 (Deakin University, 2003).

It has been indicated in several publications (Chin, Chang, & Bauer, 2000; Conlan, 1996; Lanham & Zhou, 2003a; Munro-Smith, 2002) that students with different cultural background have different learning styles. The figures above represent a diverse student body, with a majority of those international students from the Asian culture. Therefore, issues relating to virtual learning environment design for international audiences need to be addressed. Before a virtual learning community is created, an environment where this diverse student body can feel comfortable must be developed. In order to establish such an environment, the developers must focus on the issues relating to the design of virtual environments for international use.

When dealing with international or culturally diverse audiences, it is important to consider the design and layout of the interface. Nielsen (1996) suggests that the developer should ensure that the interface contains culturally neutral icons that will not cause offence to a culturally diverse audience. Metaphors and visual puns are not universally understood. For example, using a coffee cup as a visual icon representing a cyber café may provide a useful visual cue to some Western computer users. However, the developer should not assume that such an icon will be universally understood by a culturally diverse audience. Finally, where content is translated into multiple languages, developers should ensure that content is translated in its entirety so that all students have access to the same materials (Lanham & Zhou, 2003a, 2003b). Following these guidelines can aid in the construction of a culturally unbiased virtual learning environment.

Developers should also consider the design of learning materials when creating a culturally inclusive virtual learning environment. The following guidelines can aid this process:

- Avoid using colloquial language and cultural slang that can be misinterpreted by an audience from a diverse cultural background.

- Review all content and language to ensure it is not offensive to other cultures.
- Identify how different cultures approach learning, and factor this into the learning outcomes of the subject.
- Try to tailor the learning environment so that all students can understand the content provided (Lanham & Zhou, 2003a, 2003b).

These points are a sample of the techniques that can be employed in an attempt to reduce the barriers between cultures in an online learning environment. Providing a culturally inclusive environment can allow students from diverse backgrounds to feel as though they are valued participants within a virtual learning community.

Using Wikis to Build Virtual Learning Communities

"Wiki" is a Hawaiian word meaning "quick" or "fast" in English. In 1994, Ward Cunningham used the word "wiki" as the name for a fully editable Web site that he invented (Leuf & Cunningham, 2001). In their book *The Wiki Way*, Leuf and Cunningham (2001) present wikis as an ideal technology for building virtual communities. Ongoing research at Deakin University is exploring this contention by attempting to use wikis to build virtual learning communities. This section introduces wikis, explains how they work, and describes a wiki pilot study undertaken at Deakin University.

Wikis

Wikis are Web sites that allow users to collaborate to create new documents (Web pages), edit the content of existing Web pages (text and pictures), or edit the structure of the whole site. All a user needs to edit, re-organize and read a wiki is a Web browser. Many wiki clones (versions of wiki scripts written in various programming languages) are available free of charge on the

Internet. Most wiki clones are relatively easy to install on a Web server for immediate use. Consequently, wikis have the potential to provide an efficient, flexible, user-friendly, and cost-effective interface for collaboration, knowledge creation and archiving, and student interaction (Augar et al., 2004b; Leuf & Cunningham, 2001).

Wikis can be used in *document mode* or *thread mode*. Wikis that are used in *document mode* act as knowledge repositories. Multiple users update the wiki content and over a period of time the wiki content grows to reflect the shared knowledge of the contributors, who remain anonymous. Wikis can also be used in *thread mode* to facilitate discussion amongst wiki users who each sign their posts (the content or message they added to the wiki) (Augar et al., 2004b, 2005; Leuf & Cunningham, 2001; Raitman et al., 2004).

To edit a wiki, users need to learn a set of basic mark-up rules, known as *wiki syntax,* that format wiki content in a manner similar to HTML. An example of using *wiki syntax* is enclosing a word in double apostrophes to make the word appear as bold text. However, many variations of *wiki syntax* exist. Some wikis provide an editing toolbar so the user can type in his or her content and format it by selecting the required text with a mouse and clicking on the appropriate formatting button in the toolbar. MediaWiki (http://wikipedia.sourceforge.net) has toolbar functionality, which is depicted in Figure 4 (MediaWiki, 2004). Examples of wiki syntax including square brackets and double apostrophes can also be seen in the text area shown in Figure 4 (Augar et al., 2004b, 2005; Leuf & Cunningham, 2001).

Background to the Wiki Pilot Study

Deakin University Australia offers a third-year computing subject "Computers, Society and Professional Ethics" that is taught entirely online. Students use DSO (introduced in the Technology section of this chapter) to participate in online discussion groups of ten students about subject matter over a 13-week semester. In addition to engaging in discourse, students produce collaborative documents that reflect their understanding of the subject matter as a result of their discussions (Augar et al., 2004a; 2004b; 2005). This mode of e-learning reflects the constructivist and constructionist approaches to learning outlined in the Pedagogy section of this chapter.

In the 2003 delivery of this subject, students were encouraged to develop a social presence in the first week of semester by publishing a single-page biography within their designated DSO discussion forum. It was envisaged that group members would read all of the biographies and use them as a means to get to know their fellow group members. However, very little social interaction occurred, and students did not engage in true discussion about the subject matter. Most students simply added their thoughts close to the deadline for contributions and did not comment about the contributions of others (Augar et al., 2004a; 2004b; 2005).

Survey research results indicated that students also experienced technology problems during the semester that impacted negatively upon their motivation to participate. Many students also felt that

Figure 4. MediaWiki provides editing toolbar instead of using wiki syntax

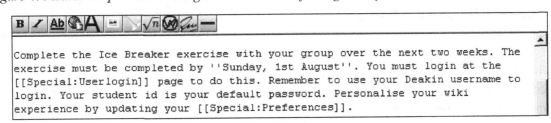

facilitators did not provide feedback and guidance in a prompt and clear manner. Students expressed general dissatisfaction about participating in the online discussion forums at the end of the semester (Augar et al., 2004a; 2004b; 2005).

Subsequent research has focused on improving the collaborative aspects of the delivery technology by introducing wikis. An icebreaker exercise was developed for use on the wiki that aimed to help learners construct their online identity and enable each learning group to develop social context. Students were surveyed at the end of the 2004 semester to gauge their response to the wiki and the icebreaker exercise.

Which Wiki?

MediaWiki was selected for use in this study because of its toolbar, tracking, and authentication capability. The toolbar functionality was judged to be a critical feature as it meant students would not need to be familiar with *wiki syntax* to use the wiki. Tracking and authentication was required to enable marking of student contributions and to minimise the possibility of intentional misuse of the wiki. Authentication also allowed students to create personal profiles and sign their contributions, contributing to their development of social presence. Finally, MediaWiki is the wiki clone used to power a well-known online collaborative encyclopaedia, Wikipedia (http://en.wikipedia.org/wiki/Main_Page). Consequently, it was judged to be robust enough to support the 450 students who would use it as part of the study. The wiki was known as the Science and Information Technology wiki, SITWiki (Augar et al., 2004b; 2005).

The Wiki Icebreaker Exercise

Each discussion group (comprising 10 students) had its own icebreaker document on the wiki to complete as a group. Eighteen statements were included in the icebreaker exercise. Each statement prompted the students to add their name below the statement if it applied to them. Students could elaborate on the statement and in doing so tell the group a little about themselves. An example of a statement is "Members who have lived overseas." This example prompted students who had lived outside of Australia to post a signed message underneath the statement that detailed the country where they had lived.

Each group had two weeks to update the icebreaker document so that every statement had at least one group member's signed response underneath it. A partially completed example is shown in Figure 5.

Prior to commencing the exercise, instructors seeded icebreaker with information about themselves. They did this to introduce themselves to the group whilst modelling appropriate social presence and setting the tone for the exercise. Instructors signed their posts and in doing so created a hyperlink (as shown in Figure 5) to their wiki user page which contained a photo and a brief biography about themselves (Augar et al., 2004b, 2005).

Results

Prior to the icebreaker, many students had not used a wiki before. Some had not even heard of a wiki. The only training students received was in the form of e-mail-based technical support (to respond to specific queries) and an FAQ page provided on the wiki that contained simple instructions on how to edit and perform other required tasks. However, all students who used the wiki were able to satisfactorily complete the icebreaker exercise and introduce themselves to the other students in their discussion group (Augar et al., 2004b; 2005).

A usage policy was developed and displayed on every page of the wiki. The policy consisted of four guidelines that were written in a positive simple manner to encourage a wiki culture of cooperative, respectful usage. Across the 50 groups who used

Figure 5. SITWiki icebreaker exercise

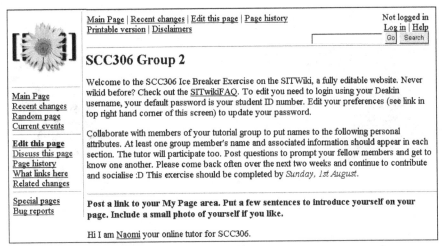

the wiki, there were no incidences of intentional misuse or deletions of wiki content. Sixty-seven percent of students reported that they enjoyed participating in the wiki environment. These positive results were mirrored in the students' overall rating of the wiki experience, as can be seen in Figure 6 (Augar et al., 2004b; 2005).

Technology

MediaWiki proved itself to be a reliable collaboration platform, supporting over 450 users with no system failures during the two-week icebreaker exercise. Students viewed the wiki between one-to two-thousand times per day and, on average, edited the wiki 150 times per day. When the SITWiki was installed and all the exercises and associated pages were uploaded, the wiki contained approximately 100 pages. Throughout the two-week duration of the exercise, the number of pages increased steadily each day to a final tally of over 1000 pages (Augar et al., 2004b).

Seventy-three percent of students surveyed found the wiki easy to use. Part of the survey asked students to identify what they felt were the positive characteristics of the wiki. Many students felt that the ability to interact with the wiki from anywhere at any time was a valuable feature. This

response may be due to the fact that 31% of total enrolments for the subject comprised distance education students, for whom time differences and flexibility are key issues. This anywhere-anytime aspect of wiki functionality positions the wiki as an accessible and inclusive platform for building virtual learning communities (Augar et al., 2005).

Some students felt that the user interface lacked simplicity and could benefit from more colour and icons. They indicated that they would appreciate more control in the final presentation of their work via greater support for HTML formatting. However, they did appreciate the fast download speeds that resulted from the basic HTML format of page content (Augar et al., 2005).

Students also recommended a feature they felt would enhance the wiki—a tool that would highlight the modifications that were made since their last access. Some students found it difficult to keep track of what they had or had not read on the wiki due to the unstructured nature of the editing process. Such a feature may include e-mail alerts that may help inspire students to revisit the wiki in order to make further contributions or read and comment on the contributions of others.

The final technical feature that students disliked was the possibility that inconsistencies

Figure 6. Students rate the wiki experience

Figure 7. Students rate whether the icebreaker helped them get to know their instructor

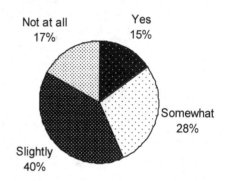

could occur through simultaneous page editing. For example, if Student A started to edit at 2:00 p.m., Student B started at 2:01 p.m. and finished at 2:03 p.m., when Student A completed his or her editing at 2:06 p.m., this final edition may not contain any of Student B's modifications (MediaWiki does include merge function that can handle this problem in certain situations). Although there was no report of this occurring in this exercise, students felt insecure about losing their wiki additions should this situation arise (Augar et al., 2005).

In fact, it can be noted that the two main concerns of content deletion and simultaneous editing were well highlighted by the students in the feedback, but in reality, there was not one incident that occurred to validate their anxieties. Leuf and Cunningham (2001) call this phenomenon the *open-edit issue*. The fear of losing work or having to create a backup of their input dissuaded students from believing the wiki environment was secure.

Facilitation

The wiki icebreaker exercise had a dual purpose of introducing the students to the other members of their group and to their instructor. Eighty-three percent of students surveyed felt that they got to know their instructor a little better through

completing the icebreaker exercise as shown in Figure 7 (Augar et al., 2005).

The icebreaker focused on providing an interactive way of promoting online socialisation, which constitutes the second phase of Salmon's five-stage model of facilitation presented earlier in this chapter (Salmon, 2003). Facilitators not only introduced themselves by participating in the exercise, they modelled appropriate social presence and encouraged group interaction (Augar et al., 2004b; 2005).

In parallel to this exercise, technical support was provided to students via e-mail and FAQ by wiki administrators. This ensured that students could access the wiki quickly and easily. Student user accounts were created prior to the start of the semester, however, there were ongoing enrolments throughout the duration of the wiki icebreaker exercise. This made quick administrative responses to student requests for account creation imperative to ensuring that phase one of Salmon's (2003) model involving access and motivation was not jeopardised.

Social Context

The goal of the icebreaker exercise was to encourage students to socialise with their online group members. Eighty-seven percent of students surveyed felt that the wiki exercise helped them get to know their group members a little better as shown in Figure 8 (Augar et al., 2005).

Observation indicated that students contributed actively to most questions in the icebreaker exercise. The most popular questions (gaining responses from virtually every group member) were those that asked if students spoke another language and in what suburb or country they resided. In addition, 68% of students placed some text or pictures on their user page to introduce themselves to the group (Augar et al., 2004b; 2005).

All students signed their posts; most used the hyperlinked signature tool supported by the SIT-Wiki toolbar. Over half the students changed their hyperlinked signature to their preferred name; a third left it as their default wiki username; and less than 10% of students chose not to use the signature tool (Augar et al., 2005).

Some interesting trends were observed among the groups of students who did not use the signature tool to sign their posts. One group commenced each individual post by including their preferred name plain text and a colon; their post would follow this signature (this format is common in synchronous chat programs). Another group hyperlinked signatures to introduce themselves under the first icebreaker statement and then signed the rest of their posts using plain text. In these instances, it was noted that rather than adopting the format

modelled by their instructor, students used the format modelled by the first student to make a post. This trend can be perceived as indicating the emergence of a group culture (Augar et al., 2005).

Shared Learning Goal

The icebreaker exercise focused on online socialisation and introducing students to online learning in a fun and informal manner. Consequently, the development of a shared learning goal relating to the subject matter did not occur. However, some students felt that the socialisation did enhance (if only slightly) their ability to communicate with their group throughout the semester, as shown in Figure 9.

Wikis in Review

The wiki icebreaker exercise showed that MediaWiki is a reliable and usable technology for supporting collaboration among large groups of students. However, research indicates that the SITWiki technology should be improved for future use.

Students were not comfortable with the possibility of losing work. Developing a short-

Figure 9. Students rate whether the icebreaker enhanced group communication throughout semester

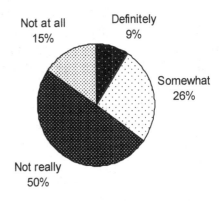

Figure 8. Students rate whether the icebreaker helped them get to know other group members

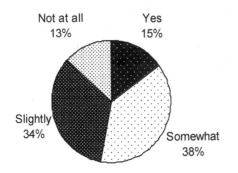

streamed multimedia training video (supported by text- and graphics-based explanations) that explains the backup and security procedures in place may make students feel more secure. Similar training resources about what a wiki is and how to use it effectively may also make the wiki easier to use.

In addition, resolving the possibility of data loss through inadvertent synchronous editing could further enhance the perceived security of the wiki. This issue could be addressed by providing either alerts to the user that a page is being edited, or by locking a page while it is being edited to ensure no data can be lost via synchronous editing.

Future research aims to further explore the community building potential of wikis by using them to facilitate student creation of collaborative knowledge repositories. Research will explore whether using a wiki in document mode empowers students with a sense of ownership that fosters a sense of community in the learning group.

USING ONLINE LECTURES TO SUPPORT VIRTUAL LEARNING COMMUNITIES

This section introduces online lectures. It explains how they work and describes a pilot study involving online lectures recently completed at Deakin University. This pilot study explores the use of video and audio lectures to enhance the delivery of distance education. A long-term aim of this ongoing research is to explore whether the inclusion of audio and video lectures enhances the sense of community felt by distance education students (DES). Another goal of this study is to determine whether or not the students' ability to "see" the lecture theatre and lecturer and to "feel" the experience as if they are a part of the lecture enhances the development of a community spirit.

Online Lectures

Video lectures are the display of lecture material in a visual context. Video lectures can be delivered in several different formats, such as recorded video files available for download, broadcast or streamed real-time video lectures, and video conferences. Video lectures can be stand-alone, individual video files, or they can be teamed with other media applications such as PowerPoint presentations.

Audio lectures convey on-campus lectures using text-based lecture materials with the addition of audio files. The audio lectures can consist of purely audio recordings or they can also include other media applications such as PowerPoint presentations or static video. The audio recordings can also be provided in several different formats such as audio cassette tapes, downloadable digital audio recordings (e.g., wave files or mp3 files), and online audio streaming.

Enhancing Distance Education at Deakin University

Distance education students at Deakin University have in the past received a hardcopy of text-based lecture notes, study guides, and readers via the postal service to help them complete their studies. Video and audio lectures have been used on occasion in the delivery of distance education units at Deakin University. However, they were made available to students via video tapes and CD-ROMs. The current pilot study extends this idea by exploring the provision of video and audio lectures online for students to access.

The provision of video and audio lectures can benefit students in many ways. It can allow students to:

- review lecture material they did not understand at the time of the first delivery;
- add to, or amend the notes they had taken in the lecture;

- catch up and take lecture notes from any lectures they had missed;
- revise the lecture at times more suited to their life style; and
- allow DES access to material which was previously unavailable to them (Lanham & Zhou, 2004b; McCrohon, Lo, Dang, & Johnston, 2001).

The learning styles and approaches of individual students can vary widely (McCrohon et al., 2001). The use of video lectures caters to the needs of students with a visual learning style, just as the use of text-based lecture notes caters to students with a preference for learning from text-based materials.

It is apparent that an increase in the use of visual material would be beneficial to English as second language (ESL) students. Studies support this contention and acknowledge that Korean, Chinese, Arab, and Filipino students are more oriented toward visual learning styles than Anglo students (Park, 1997; Reid, 1987) cited in (Park, 2002).

Students from non-English speaking backgrounds may find lectures easier to understand when the visual and verbal cues are combined in video streaming (McCrohon et al., 2001). When static images are used in conjunction with text, it attracts the learner's attention, aids knowledge retention and recall, and acts as a clarification tool when verbal forms are insufficient (Duchastel & Waller, 1979, as cited in Asensio & Young, 2002). These studies all indicate that the inclusion of video and audio lecture materials can enhance the learning experience of ESL and international students.

As discussed in an earlier section of this chapter, Deakin University has a culturally diverse student body with a large number of international students from Asian countries. It is envisaged that providing these students with visual alternatives to text-based learning materials will create a more culturally inclusive learning environment, thus

enhancing the delivery of distance education at Deakin University.

The Online Lecture Pilot Study

This pilot study involved the participation of students studying a tertiary subject as part of an Information Technology Master's Degree. Students can study this subject in either on-campus or off-campus study modes. Previously, text-based lectures notes for this subject were provided to all students online using DSO. The goal of introducing online lectures was to provide all students with access to the "physical" lectures via the Internet, and to document their interaction with the lectures provided.

The pilot study was conducted in two stages. The first stage dealt with the creation and implementation of the video and audio lectures and the provision of student access. The lectures were created in both video and audio formats in order to determine which format would suit the students' learning requirements.

The second stage of this pilot study was the completion of an anonymous survey, in which students recorded their experiences and opinions regarding the online lectures. This pilot study was primarily concerned with discovering the most efficient and usable technologies for the delivery of lectures online. Future detailed studies will explore the effects that video and audio lectures have on building culturally inclusive learning environments and supporting virtual learning communities.

Producing Online Lectures

Several lectures were recorded (via audio and video devices) during the second semester in 2004. These recorded lectures were then made available to students in streaming format via the Internet, and the Deakin intranet. Providing the video and audio lectures in streaming format meant that the students did not have to download the files to their personal computers. They could simply view the information as it streamed from the University's server.

The audio lectures were recorded using an audio recording device such as Mini-disk player. The files were then transferred from the audio device to a PC where they were edited and then converted into either a wave or mp3 file. Once transferred, the complete audio files (approximately 45 minutes in length) were edited and then modularized into smaller files (approximately 1 to 5 minutes in length). The modularized files are then linked to their corresponding topics contained in the lecture material (Lanham & Zhou, 2004b). The unit lectures were delivered on-campus by lecturers using a PowerPoint presentation. The synchronized audio files and PowerPoint slides were then transferred to DSO where they could be accessed by students.

Streaming video lectures were also provided in conjunction with a PowerPoint presentation to enhance the delivery and clarity of the lecture content. The video files were captured by using a Mini-DV (digital video) camcorder, and the files were then transferred to a PC via a Firewire cable (IEEE 1394). The files were imported from a camcorder into Microsoft Windows Movie Maker and then encoded into MPEG-2 movie files.

Once the MPEG-2 file was encoded, it was transferred into sofTV© (XStream Software, http://www.softv.net/Public/index.asp) so that the PowerPoint slides could be synchronised with the corresponding video content. This synchronisation process ensured that the slide show could run independently without user involvement, which enabled the students to avoid having to familiarise themselves with the sofTV© program.

Results

Results were gathered immediately after the first online lecture was made public. At that time, a brief survey was conducted focusing on the student's ability to access and interact with the online lectures. The questions covered issues that included accessibility, usability, quality, and usefulness to their studies. The majority of students who responded to the preliminary survey were enrolled in an on-campus mode and were male, international students aged between 20 and 25. There were no female respondents to the survey.

The students were able to access the online lectures at their convenience and as frequently as they required. It is interesting to note that, of the students that responded to the survey, only one student stated that he had not used the online lectures more than once. The other participants indicated that they had used the online lectures on several occasions.

All of the students who completed the survey indicated that they would use the online lectures again, that they found the online lectures helpful in their studies, and that they thought the inclusion of video materials in the future would be worthwhile.

The pilot study indicated that students would appreciate the use of online lectures in the future. The high level of use exhibited by on-campus international students indicates that off-campus, international, and DES might also benefit from the use of online lectures in the future.

Online Lectures in Review

The predominantly text-based existence of DES has often led to feelings of isolation, solitude, and the absence of connection with other students. The use of video can put a face to the name, and give a voice and actions to otherwise static text. These features combine to help create a virtual lecture environment for the DES and off-campus students.

The importance of actually seeing who is responsible for the delivery of the subject content can help to promote a sense of physically being in the lecture. Further exploration into the role that video may play in the support of virtual learning communities is planned for implementation in the first semester 2005. This research will explore the benefits that online lectures provide to students, how they support different learning styles, and their impact on learning for students from diverse cultural backgrounds.

Future Directions for Virtual Learning Communities

The two studies outlined in this chapter use wikis and online lectures to support the creation of virtual learning communities. As technology evolves, many more affordable and accessible means of community building will become available to developers. The focus of future learning communities will be in bringing the community to the student and providing enhanced learning materials that take advantage of the latest technology and support the range of learning styles that exist within the learning community.

The research presented in the wiki case study outlined the possibility of providing e-mail alerts to students to notify them of recent activity and encourage them to return and contribute to the learning exercise. In the future, Short Message Service (SMS) may be the preferred technology. While enthusiastic students may check their e-mail every day to keep abreast of updates, e-mail cannot provide the instantaneous real-time alerts to students that SMS can. SMS can provide students with a sense of connection to their community, reminding them of important deadlines, and studies indicate that students appreciate the use of SMS as a means of communicating with their instructors (Horstmanshof, 2004).

As bandwidth increases and Internet access costs decrease, the provision of multimedia and streamed resources to support diverse learning styles has become a viable option. Virtual learning communities based on discourse about subject matter can be daunting for some students who have difficulty absorbing information provided in a text-based format. The provision of alternatives such as video or audio lectures, animations, and the like can make learning more accessible and enjoyable for students.

Additionally, where time differences are not an issue, some virtual learning communities are already moving away from text-based discussion forums. Real-time video and audio conferences between students and instructors have the potential to further enhance the social presence and sense of belonging felt by community members. Using video and audio in teaching materials and forums provides students with a more personalised and authentic learning experience. Putting a face and a voice to their instructors and peers can help them to feel less isolated and provide a richer learning experience, enhancing the sense of community and inclusion provided by the e-learning environment.

CONCLUSION

This chapter has introduced virtual learning communities and discussed their key criteria: social context, facilitation, technology, and shared learning goal. Essential theory relating to the pedagogy of virtual learning communities clearly supports the validity of such communities and their benefits to the e-learning arena and to distance education in particular. The focus of the chapter was, however, building virtual learning communities. Research results and case studies, such as DSO and SITWiki, were presented and analysed to show practical examples of how e-learning environments can be developed into virtual learning communities.

Having read this introduction to virtual learning communities, it is now left to the developer to innovate and create the virtual learning communities of the future.

REFERENCES

Asensio, M. & Young, C. (2002). Section 2 —A learning and teaching perspective. In S. Thornhill, M. Asensio, & C. Young (Eds.), *Video streaming: A guide for educational development* (Vol. 1, pp. 10-19). Manchester, UK: The JISC Click and Go Video Project.

Augar, N., Raitman, R., & Zhou, W. (2004a). From e-learning to virtual learning community: Bridging the gap. Paper presented at *ICWL'04*, Beijing, China.

Augar, N., Raitman, R., & Zhou, W. (2004b). Teaching and learning online with wikis. Paper presented at *ASCILITE*, Perth, Australia.

Augar, N., Raitman, R., & Zhou, W. (2005). Towards building Web-based learning communities with Wikis. Paper presented at *IADIS International Conference on Web-Based Communities 2005*, February 23-25, Algarve, Portugal (pp. 207-214).

Augar, N., & Zhou, W. (2003). *Virtual communities: Literature survey.* Technical Report No. TRC04/03. Geelong, Australia: Deakin University.

Australian Trade Commission. (2004). *Education capability overview.* Retrieved August 30, 2004, from *http://www.austrade.gov.au/overseas/layout/0,,0_S3-1_3zo-2_-3_PWB1153530-4_-5_-6_0-7_,00.html.I*

Baym, N. K. (1995). The emergence of community in computer-mediated communication. In S.G. Jones (Ed.), *Cybersociety computer-mediated communication and community* (pp. 138-163). Thousand Oaks, CA: Sage Publications.

Blunt, R. (2001). *How to build an e-learning community.* Retrieved January 19, 2004, from *http://www.elearningmag.com/ltimagazine/article/articleDetail.jsp?id=5040*

Brook, C. & Oliver, R. (2003). Online learning communities: Investigating a design framework. *Australian Journal of Educational Technology, 19*(2), 139-160. Retrieved June 28, 2005, from *http://www.ascilite.org.au/ajet/ajet19/brook.html*

Bruckman, A. (2002). The future of e-learning communities: The learning potential of Internet technology can come from the most familiar sources—peers and elders. *Communications of the ACM, 45*(4), 60-63.

Carlsen, R. (2003). Building productive online learning communities: Investigating and interacting with Internet educational genres. Paper presented at *Quality Education @ a Distance*, Geelong, Australia (pp. 137-144). Kluwer.

Chin, K.L., Chang, V., & Bauer, C. (2000). The use of Web-based learning in culturally diverse learning environments. Paper presented at the *Sixth Australian World Wide Web Conference*, Cairns, Australia.

Conlan, F. (1996). Can the different learning expectations of Australian and Asian students be reconciled in one teaching strategy? In J. Abbott & L. Willcoxson (Eds.), *Proceedings of the 5th Annual Teaching and Learning Forum* (pp. 41-45). Perth, Australia: Murdoch University. Retrieved June 28, 2005, from *http://lsn.curtin.edu.au/tlf/tlf1996/conlan.html*

Daniel, B., McCalla, G., & Schwier, R. (2002). A process model for building social capital in virtual learning communities. Paper presented at the *International Conference on Computers in Education*, Aukland, New Zealand (pp. 574-575).

Deakin University. (2003). *FactBook 2002.* Victoria, Australia: Deakin University.

Dougimas, M. & Taylor, P. C. (2002). Interpretive analysis of an Internet-based course constructed using a new courseware tool called Moodle. Paper presented at the *Annual International Confer-*

ence of the Higher Education Research and Development Society of Australasia (HERDSA), Perth, Australia. Retrieved June 28, 2005, from *http://www.ecu.edu.au/conferences/herdsa/main/ papers/nonref/pdf/MartinDougiamas.pdf*

Dourish, P. & Bly, S. (1992). Portholes: Supporting awareness in a distributed work group. Paper presented at *SIGCHI Conference on Human Factors in Computing Systems*, Monterey, CA. Retrieved June 28, 2005, from *http://pages.cpsc.ucalgary. ca/~saul/601.13/readings/portholes.pdf*

Duchastel, P. C. & Waller, R. (1979). Pictorial illustration in instructional texts. *Educational Technology,* (November), 20-25.

Duffy, T. M. & Jonassen, D. H. (1992). Constructivism: New implications for instructional technology. In T. M. Duffy & D. H. Jonassen (Eds.), *Constructivism and the technology of instruction: A conversation* (pp. 1-15). Hillsdale, NJ: Lawrence Erlbaum Associates.

Ellis, J. B. & Bruckman, A. (2001). Designing Palaver Tree online: Supporting social roles in a community of oral history. Paper presented at *CHI01*, Seattle. Retrieved June 28, 2005, from *http://www.cc.gatech.edu/elc/palaver/papers/pt-chi01.pdf*

Hara, N. & Kling, R. (1999). Students' frustrations with a Web-based distance education course. *First Monday, 4*(12). Retrieved June 28, 2005, from *http://www.firstmonday.dk/issues/issue4_12/hara/*

Haythornthwaite, C., Kazmer, M. M., Robins, J., & Shoemaker, S. (2000). Community development among distance learners: Temporal and technological dimensions. *Journal of Computer-Mediated Communication, 6*(1). Retrieved June 28, 2005, from *http://www.ascusc.org/jcmc/vol6/ issue1/haythornthwaite.html*

Hiltz, S. R. & Turoff, M. (1993). *The network nation: Human communication by computer* (revised ed.). Cambridge, MA: MIT Press.

Horstmanshof, L. (2004). Using SMS as a way of providing connection and community for first-year students. Paper presented at *ASCILITE*, Perth, Australia (pp. 432-427).

Jonassen, D. H., Howland, J., Moore, J., & Marra, R. M. (2003). *Learning to solve problems with technology: A constructivist perspective* (2nd ed.). Upper Saddle River, NJ: Pearson Education.

Jones, Q. (1997). Virtual-communities, virtual settlements & cyber-archaeology: A theoretical outline. *Journal of Computer Mediated Communication, 3*(3). Retrieved July 20, 2004, from *http://www.ascusc.org/jcmc/vol3/issue3/jones. html*

Lanham, E. & Zhou, W. (2002). *E-learning: Literature survey.* Technical Report No. TR C 02/20. Geelong, Australia: Deakin University.

Lanham, E. & Zhou, W. (2003a). Cultural issues in online learning: Is blended learning a possible solution. *International Journal of Computer Processing of Oriental Languages, 16*(4), 275-292.

Lanham, E. & Zhou, W. (2003b). Cultural issues relating to teaching IT professional ethics online: Lessons learned. Paper presented at *Advances in Web-Based Learning ICWL 2003*, Melbourne, Australia (pp. 134-144). Springer.

Lanham, E. & Zhou, W. (2004a). Giving lectures a voice for a cross-cultural audience. Paper presented at *ASCILITE*, Perth, Australia. Retrieved June 28, 2005, from *http://www.ASCILITE.org. au/conferences/perth04/procs/lanham-poster. html*

Lanham, E. & Zhou, W. (2004b). Video lectures for cross-cultural use: A three phase model. Paper presented at *World Conference on E-Learning in Corp., Govt., Health., & Higher Ed.*, Washington, DC (pp. 2368-2373). AACE.

Leuf, B. & Cunningham, W. (2001). *The Wiki way: Quick collaboration on the Web.* Upper Saddle River, NJ: Addison Wesley.

Lewis, R. (2002). Learning communities: Old and new. Paper presented at *International conference on Computers in Education*, Auckland, New Zealand (pp. 6-13). IEEE Computer Society.

Lipponen, L. (2002). *Exploring foundations for computer-supported collaborative learning*. Finland: University of Helsinki. Retrieved June 28, 2005, from *http://newmedia.colorado. edu/cscl/31.pdf*

McCrohon, M., Lo, V., Dang, J., & Johnston, C. (2001). Video streaming of lectures via the Internet: An experience. Paper presented at *ASCILITE*, Melbourne, Australia (pp. 397-406).

Munro-Smith, N. (2002). A tale of two cities: Computer-mediated teaching & learning in Melbourne and Singapore. Paper presented at *ASCILITE*, Auckland, New Zealand (pp. 861-864).

Myers, J. (1991). Cooperative learning in heterogeneous classes. *Cooperative Learning, 11*(4).

Nelson, B. (2004). International student numbers. Retrieved August 30, 2004, from *www.dest.gov. au/Ministers/Media/Nelson/2004/03/n638040 304.asp*

Nielsen, J. (1996). International Web usability. Retrieved June 15, 2003, from *http://www.useit. com/alertbox/9608.html*

Oren, A., Nachmias, R., Mioduser, D., & Lahav, O. (1998). *LEARNET: A model for virtual learning communities in the World Wide Web* (Research Report No. 52). Tel-Aviv, Israel: Tel-Aviv University. Retrieved March 15, 2004, from *http://muse. tau.ac.il/publications/learnets.html*

Papert, S. & Harel, I. (1991). *Constructionism*. Norwood, NJ: Ablex Publishing Company. Retrieved June 28, 2005, from *http://www.papert. org/articles/situatingconstructionism.html*

Park, C. C. (1997). Learning style preferences of Asian American (Chinese, Filipino, Korean, and

Vietnamese) students in secondary schools. *Equity & Excellence in Education, 30*(2), 68-77.

Park, C. C. (2002). Cross-cultural differences in learning styles of secondary English learners. *Bilingual Research Journal, 26*(2), 213-229.

Phillips, D. C. (2000). An opinionated account of the constructivist landscape. In D. C. Phillips (Ed.), *Constructivism in education*. Chicago, IL: The National Society for the Study of Education.

Powazek, D. M. (2002). *Design for community. The art of connecting real people in virtual places*. Indianapolis, IN: New Riders Publishing.

Raitman, R., Augar, N., & Zhou, W. (2004). Constructing wikis as a platform for online collaboration in an e-learning environment. Paper presented at the *International Conference on Computers in Education*, Melbourne, Australia.

Reid, J. (1987). The learning style preferences of ESL students. *TESOL Quarterly, 21*(1), 87-111.

Rheingold, H. (1994). *The virtual community: Finding connection in a computerized world*. London: Secker & Warbur.

Rovai, A. P. (2002). Building a sense of community at a distance. Retrieved February 19, 2004, from *http://www.irrodl.org/content/v3.1/rovai.html*

Salmon, G. (2003). *E-moderating: The key to teaching and learning online* (2nd ed.). London: RoutledgeFalmer.

Saragina, P. (1999). Creating a virtual learning community. Retrieved March 15, 2004, from *http://leahi.kcc.hawaii.edu/org/tcon99/papers/ saragina.html*

Schraefel, M. C., Ho, J., Chignell, M., & Milton, M. (2000). Building virtual communities for research collaboration. Paper presented at *Academia/Industry Working Conference on Research Challenges (AIWORC'00)*, Buffalo, NY (pp. 27-32). Retrieved June 28, 2005, *http://www.dgp. toronto.edu/~mc/papers/virtualOrgPaper.pdf*

Stacey, E. (1999). *Collaborative learning in an online environment, 14*(2), 14-33. Retrieved June 27, 2005, from *http://cade.icaap.org/vol14.2/stacey.html*

Stacey, E. (2001). Social presence online: Networking learners at a distance. Paper presented at the *Seventh IFIP World Conference on Computers in Education,* Copenhagen, Denmark.

Vygotsky, L. S. (1978). Mind in society: The development of higher psychological processes. In M. Cole, V. John-Steiner, S. Scribner, & E. Souberman (Eds.). Cambridge, MA: Harvard University Press.

Wenger, E. (1998). *Communities of practice: Learning, meaning, and identity.* Cambridge, UK: Cambridge University Press.

Wikipedia. (2004). *Wikipedia.* Retrieved August 9, 2004, from *http://en.wikipedia.org/wiki/Main_Page*

Wood, A. F. & Smith, M. J. (2001). *Online communication: Linking technology, identity, and culture.* Hillsdale, NJ: Lawrence Erlbaum Associates, Inc.

This work was previously published in Web-Based Intelligent E-Learning Systems: Technologies and Applications, edited by Z. Ma, pp. 72-100, copyright 2006 by Information Science Publishing (an imprint of IGI Global).

Chapter XVI
Support Networks for Rural and Regional Communities

Tom Denison
Monash University, Australia

ABSTRACT

Using a case study approach, this chapter examines the role of organizational networks in the success and failure of information and communications technology projects. Within a framework informed by the literature of information systems failure, the diffusion of innovation and social network analysis, it argues that information systems projects must take into account the social context in which they are implemented. To be successful such networks require a mix of extended and locally based support networks, because they provide access to much needed resources, including innovations, strategic advice, training, and support at the appropriate level. It further argues that the people who are working in a regional setting felt themselves to be in an extremely disadvantageous situation because they typically lacked support from similar networks. The author hopes that highlighting the importance of such support networks will lead to a better understanding of systems failure and success, and will contribute to improved policy formulation and practice.

INTRODUCTION

Quite often it is assumed that the mere implementation of technology and some initial guidance and training in its use will result in successful projects and their ongoing effective use. Time after time this has been found to be insufficient.

The literature on information systems failure deals with the multiple causes of this phenomenon, but the intention of this chapter is to focus on one aspect that is particularly important in the context of rural and regional development: the role and type of support networks that are needed to properly plan, implement, and sustain information and communications technology (ICT) projects.

The starting point will be a brief overview of the literature on information systems failure, highlighting recent research that seeks to emphasise the importance of understanding the social context in which systems are implemented and the impact that can have on their success or failure. This will be followed by an introduction to the literature on the diffusion of innovation and social network analysis. Then it will provide a broad theoretical background that can be used to examine the characteristics of organisations as nodes in broader networks, the nature of the relationships they establish within those networks and the importance of those relationships in providing access to information, skills, and resources. These theoretical concerns will then be illustrated by drawing upon a selection of case studies available in the literature, as well as practical experience the author gained when implementing information systems in Vietnam.

The case studies have been chosen because they provide examples of the theoretical issues in rural or regional settings. While some, such as the attempt to implement geographic information systems in India (Barratt, Sahay & Walsham, 2001), serve to illustrate the extent of the problems that can arise when a lack of local knowledge and infrastructure is not addressed, most of the studies illustrate more positive outcomes and act to reinforce insights derived from the theory. As a whole, they demonstrate that network relationships are essential for development in rural and regional areas because they provide access to new ideas and innovations, strategic advice, training and support, as well as a host of other necessary resources. They also demonstrate that some resources, such as access to new ideas, should typically continue to be provided through extended networks, but successful and sustainable projects require the development of a localised infrastructure capable of harnessing resources in a trusted environment.

INFORMATION SYSTEMS FAILURE

There is a significant body of literature that has been found discussing the causes of information systems failure from a project management perspective, for example, the work of Lyytinen and Hirschheim (1987), Keil, Cule, Lyytinen, and Schmidt (1998), and Schmidt, Lyytinen, Keil, and Cule (2001). These have tended to focus on management issues, such as the lack of top management commitment to the project, failure to gain user commitment, misunderstanding the requirements, lack of adequate user involvement, lack of required knowledge/skills in the project personel and lack of frozen requirements (Schmidt et al., 2001) although recently there has been significant interest in concepts such as learning organizations (Lyytinen & Robey, 1999) and their role in nurturing projects. The main thrust of the literature, however, relates to the ability of large organisations to successfully undertake new systems development.

Given its importance, the focus of this chapter is to assist those who seek to implement information systems in regional areas, specifically in the creation of the infrastructure or framework necessary for the successful diffusion and sustainability of technology. It complements the work of others such as Kling (2000) and Orlikowski (2000) who, having recognised that technology is not socially neutral, have attempted to broaden the understanding of the factors that contribute to systems failure by considering the social context in which information systems are implemented. The importance of such an approach has clearly been recognised by the United Nations Development Program (UNDP) Evaluation Office which identified six generic challenges that critically affect ICT for development initiatives: awareness; politics; access; relevancy and meaningful use; sustainability; and coordination (UNDP, 2001).

The work of Heeks (2002) is also important in this context, as he has attempted to model the implementation of information systems in developing countries in such a way as to identify the potential for failure, including what he terms "sustainability failure." He identified "design-actuality differences" as a powerful contributor to systems failure and suggested that systems which allow "contingent improvisation" – that is the ability to accommodate design changes and adapt to local needs – are more likely to be successful, and proved to be sustainable. As he notes, however, the success of this approach is based on environments in which the necessary skills and resources to adapt and successfully implement systems are available locally. This raises the question, then, of just what skills and resources are required, and how access to them can be provided. In this respect, this chapter provides significant insights relating to the diffusion of innovation and to network analysis.

DIFFUSION OF INNOVATION AND NETWORK ANALYSIS

The literature on the diffusion of innovation is dominated by Rogers (2003), who defines innovation as "an idea, practice, or object that is perceived as new by an individual or other unit of adoption" (p. 12). He describes five attributes of innovations: relative advantage, compatibility, complexity, trialability, and observability. According to Rogers, the way in which these attributes are perceived by those who are the beneficiaries of the innovation determines both the speed of adaptation and the degree to which a specific innovation is adopted, modified or ignored. This framework has been successfully used to model the diffusion of innovation in a wide range of studies, for example, Grover and Teng's (1992) study on the take-up of database technology, and Garrison's (2001) study on the adoption of online technology by news organisations.

Studies on the diffusion of innovation have been enriched by adding insights derived from social network analysis which, as Wellman (1988) explains, is based on the relationships between units, rather than the categorisation of those units into predefined categories, and on interpreting behavior in terms of structural constraints on activity rather than in terms of inner forces. In this theory, networks structure collaborative and competitive activities in order to secure scarce resources including information, support, and power. So, to understand the behavior and capabilities of those units it is necessary to consider the relationships between all groups and individuals in their immediate environment. These relationships are important to innovation, because it is through them that many of Rogers' five attributes are realised.

A highly influential work in this field is that of Granovetter (1973), whose work centered on the strength of weak ties, defined as a casual or infrequent connections between two people or organisations. He emphasised the importance of social networks in the distribution of information and resources, arguing that those with networks of weak ties are best placed to receive new information and resources, since they can act as bridges to the broader community. He also found that the longer linked the network – that is the more links required to establish a connection between two people or units – the less effective it is.

In contrast, Coleman (1988) studied dense closed networks—those with multiple strong internal links but few weak links—finding them to be important for the enforcement of social norms, obligations, and expectations. These, he argued, are important in facilitating effective action. He further argued that those with limited ties to external communities have structural holes that, if they are not closed, can result in a lack of access to the information and resources necessary to facilitate action, particularly innovation. Burt (2000), building on this, argued that all networks can have structural holes and that those who can arrange relationships spanning across those holes may achieve a competitive advantage because they are best placed to obtain new ideas, information, support, and other resources. In this view, network closure is about maintaining the status quo while brokerage is about change. However, a number of researchers (Aldrich & Zimmer, 1986; Kadushin, 2002) have found that both brokerage and cohesion networks are required for the successful diffusion and exploitation of resources.

Considering the issues relating to brokerage and cohesion networks in more detail, Aldrich and Zimmer (1986) emphasised that the maintenance of effective networks requires the continual creation of weak ties so as to prevent a few strong ties from closing them to opportunities and alternatives, while Kadushin (2002) argued that "safety drivers," which act against change, are common when the costs of interaction are low, visibility is high, and moral obligations are more salient—a situation typical of rural and regional networks. And, in work of special significance for the diffusion of innovation, Valente (1995, 2005) found that a significant difference between effectiveness (brokerage) networks and safety (cohesive) networks is the location of trust, which is an important factor in the realisation of Rogers' (2003) five attributes.

Others have attempted to identify issues that relate to the development and success of regional groupings, and their work has obvious implications for developments in rural and regional areas. For instance, Hakansson (1990) suggested that networks are a new organisational form necessary to supplement internal competencies and that this implied a mutual dependence between government and business, particularly in regional areas where location has a strong impact on the availability of resources. Steward and Conway (2000) examined the conflicting goals and cultural variations that are likely to exist between organizations with extended supply chains, and identified that differences in culture, language, and business practices at the levels of individuals and organizations are potential sources of tension.

Finally, Furst, Schubert, Rudolph, and Spieckermann (2001) related the concepts of cohesion and brokerage to the complementary categories of stationary and mobile social capital. In their view, regional networks need a high degree of stationary capital to ensure self governance but also need to be able to lock in mobile social capital in order to bring in new ideas and the flexibility needed for development. Bebbington (1997) provided a clear example of this in the author's study on communities in the Ecuadorian and Bolivian Andes that had managed to improve their local economies, reversing trends in both migration and environmental protection, via a program of agricultural intensification based on the use of new technology. He demonstrated that this could not have been achieved without a broadening of support networks and the access to ideas, contacts, and resources they bring, nor without the involvement of strong local community groups that helped create the pre conditions to take advantage of those networks and opportunities when they were presented.

In summary, the successful diffusion of technology, particularly in rural and regional areas, is in large part dependent on the flow of resources and the capacity for local improvisation. Organizations and communities seeking to implement technologically based change, require both brokerage and cohesion networks: brokerage networks because they provide access to opportunities, innovation, strategic advice, new skills and support; cohesion networks because they provide a trusted environment in which to operate, harness local capacity and manage "contingent improvisation."

CASE STUDIES

There are a significant number of case studies in the literature that explore these issues, but for the purposes of this chapter it will be sufficient to highlight five. The first, a study by Sherry (1998), illustrates a straightforward analysis of a technology diffusion program, using Rogers' (1995) framework to evaluate IT training programs in regional school districts in the United States. In the second, an ambitious, three year longitudinal study by Barratt, Sahay, and Walsham (2001), the efforts of the Indian Ministry of Environment and Forests (MoEF) to apply geographic information systems (GIS) technology to forestry management and wasteland reclamation are examined. Issues of trust are explored in some depth, as are the types of problems can arise when local conditions and expertise are not adequately acknowledged, themes that are further developed in an Australian study by Terziovski and Howell (2001). They examine network linkages connecting multiple stakeholders, demonstrating that interaction between government, business, and the community is important in facilitating new initiatives, particularly if trusted local connections can be harnessed.

An extended examination of the author's experiences in implementing a series of information systems in regional Vietnamese university libraries is then provided. This is a prime example of a project that was struggling to succeed because the technology was implemented without regard to the local context, but which was revitalised when gaps in local infrastructure were identified and the need to establish local support networks recognized (Johanson, Denison & Otis, 2004). This is complemented by the final case study, that of Gibb and Adkihary (2000) on the work of non-government organisations (NGOs) in South Africa. They explore the nature and role of NGOs as network brokers capable of supporting external interventions by using their relationships to assist in the development of local stakeholder networks.

Training and the Diffusion of Skills: Boulder Valley Internet Project

Sherry (1998) used Rogers' (1995) framework for studying the diffusion of technology to evaluate the Boulder Valley Internet Project (BVIP), a five-year collaborative venture between the University of Colorado at Boulder and the Boulder Valley School District (BVSD). The project was funded by the National Science Foundation (NSF) and aimed to incorporate Internet-based technologies and strategies into the teaching program of the District, by developing training programs and integrated telecommunications throughout.

Commencing in 1992, the project used a trainer-of-trainers model to create a core group of 26 teachers. Their mission was to become proficient in the use of e-mail and in investigating Internet resources, and experienced in integrating these into school curricula, so as to pass on their skills to other teachers within the district. Using a participatory design model, the bulk of the training concentrated on the needs of classroom teachers. Workshops and classes were given in BSVD classrooms, using the very platforms that the teachers would use once their classrooms were connected. Sherry found that the program achieved considerable success and that, as of January 1996, there were 435 teachers on the BSVD network who logged in regularly. However, she also reported that the project later lost much of its momentum when it lost the support of the school administrators and key policy makers at the district level.

She made the following points with respect to the level of success that was achieved:

- Rogers' (1995) framework emphasises the role of change agents in influencing their clients' behavior, and their ability to help them realise change. In this case, the project used BSVD teachers drawn from the district as change agents rather than relying on outside experts that could have been drawn from the project's partner organizations. This ensured a significant level of client/agent empathy.

- By focusing on providing an authentic context (dealing with real issues in an actual work environment) in which situated learning could take place, the project presented the opportunity for clients to observe the benefits of the technology firsthand, another critical factor in Rogers' (1995) model.

- The self-reflection involved in the participatory design process ensured that trainers and trainees explored the issues, dealt with conflicts and solved problems together, contributing substantially to the success of the training program.

- At least in its initial stages, the district as an organization ensured that the effort was aligned with district-wide visions and policies and integrated into the established telecommunications channels. As a result, the project had strong grassroots support from the local teachers who were the primary participants in the training program.

As Sherry (1998) noted, however, the project was not a complete success. The reason for this was that, as the project evolved, the attitudes of the policy makers became more conservative and the project gradually ceased to address the needs of all stakeholders, specifically the school administration and the district's policy making bodies. As a result, it received a lower priority and stalled. Sherry concluded that "If there was a single lesson to be learned from the BVIP experiment it is ... [that] information technology interventions cannot be separated from their ecological contexts or from the educational activities that they enhance" (p. 141).

Rogers' (1995) model postulates five stages that a successful intervention must pass through. They are: (a) seeking information about the innovation's existence and some understanding of how it functions; (b) forming a favourable or unfavourable attitude towards it; (c) engaging in activities that lead to a choice to either adopt or reject the innovation; (d) putting the innovation to use; and (e) seeking reinforcement of an innovation decision that has already been made (Sherry, 1998). In the case of the BVIP project, it can be seen that external linkages (brokerage networks) were used to successfully introduce new technology as in step (a), while the strong peer-to-peer (cohesive networks) represented by the teachers within the district assisted steps (b) to (d). However, the ultimate failure of the project was due to the poor management of its broader internal stakeholder network, allowing Kadushin's (2002) "safety drivers" to take affect, thereby cutting off access to the required resources and external support needed to reinforce the innovation as in step (e).

The Role of Trust in Local Adaptation: GIS Systems in India

Barratt et al. (2001) also undertook an in depth case study of a technology diffusion program. It was a three-year longitudinal study of the efforts of the Indian Ministry of Environment and Forests (MoEF) to apply geographic information systems (GIS) technology in the areas of forestry management and wasteland reclamation. For their analysis they used a framework strongly influenced by both Giddens (1990, 1991) and Kling (2000) to explore the types of problems that can arise when local conditions and expertise are not adequately acknowledged and utilised during the introduction of new systems.

The project commenced in 1991, initiated by the U.S. Agency for International Development (USAID), which also provided seed money, training, and software. Phase 1 of the project aimed to establish the technical feasibility of using GIS in eight scientific institutions. Phase 2 envisaged the subsequent transfer of those systems to local district offices. Although Phase 1 was completed in 1993, by the end of the research period only minimal progress had been made in transferring the technology to district level and it is this failure that the analysis focuses on.

While acknowledging variable management support that affected the enthusiasm with which the project was undertaken in different districts, Barratt et al. (2001) identified a number of specific issues that contributed strongly to the failure of Phase 2:

- There was no work culture based around the use of IT because there was no history of access to technology. At the same time, the social structure, organizational forms, and existing work arrangements were not taken into consideration. The pressure for change had come from external sources—governmental agencies and international bodies such as the World Bank and the United Nations (UN). These pressures confronted strong existing traditions and systems of work, but while the process of technology transfer was useful in providing know how, technology, and funding, it promoted western values and management techniques that were often incompatible within the context of a developing country. The difficulties caused by these unresolved tensions hampered the development of the restructured and standardised work practices required to introduce GIS at the local level.

- Compounding the problems mentioned in the first point, the technology itself was not neutral. GIS systems were built on western notions of rationality and coordination, while the depiction of space as an objective was a value-free reality. Assuming the widespread use of maps and knowledge of spatial planning concepts, the new systems required a reorientation from planning based on non-spatial parameters such as development schemes and households, as was the existing practice, to planning based on spatial criteria, such as "watershed units" and "wasteland distributions." These concepts were in conflict with local practice and, as a consequence, the system was perceived to be less relevant to local need.

- There was a lack of relevant professional skills. The effect of the first two points may have been ameliorated had more attention been given to providing support and building local expertise and capacity. Forestry officials needed to develop new conceptual skills to translate their forestry related problems into the spatial terms required by the GIS models, but they also needed the skills to adapt those models to local conditions in order to facilitate contingent improvisation. The professional skills that were locally available enabled the achievement of success in Phase 1, but not in Phase 2. However, the models developed in Phase 1 reflected the view of the institutes as scientific research and development centers by placing little emphasis on other important socioeconomic variables in the context of the districts, for example population and livestock data.

- Regarding professional skills requirements, it was recognized by a number of the institutes that there would be problems in transferring the technology to the districts, because they considered that their technical resources and the skills of institute staff were inadequate to provide sustained support in the field. They lacked a core group of people with GIS expertise who could nurture the projects over time and, in any case, many scientists considered that their institutional mandate was limited to developing the technology, not its transfer to the district level.

As can be seen, this was an intervention that required significant changes in professional culture, technical skills, and work practices. Remote organizations were encouraging the take up of the technology, and although the project provided support networks sufficient to ensure implementation by the scientific institutions, the networks that were provided were inadequate to ensure the transfer of skills and the conditions required to effectively exploit the technology at the local level.

The analysis by Barratt et al. (2001) is also of interest because of the way in which it uses Giddens' (1990, 1991) theories to explore notions of trust, the lack of which they consider contributed to the problems that arose. Giddens identified two types of trust, distinguishing between situations in which the actors are face-to-face and those in which they are not. In this case, a typical situation in which information systems are implemented for the first time, it is a prime example of the latter, and required reconciliation between traditional and new knowledge systems and the development of new trust systems. However, the effectiveness of these processes depended on the manner in which the technology was introduced and the nature of support provided and, in this case, these were inadequate to the task. As a result, the disembedding of traditional practices of forestry management did not occur, and made it difficult for standard methodologies to be modelled, codified, and applied.

The introduction of GIS technology also exposed workers at all levels to new networks of people, required to introduce and support the technology. For the project to be successful, they needed to develop trust in these new networks. But this could not happen in conditions where an unresolved tension existed between local requirements and the introduced system.

Barratt et al. (2001) argued that the project was not successful because it attempted to impose a new professional and technological framework without taking local conditions into account. There seems to have been little provision for local contingency in design, and little recognition of the types of support and support networks that would be required to implement and sustain the new environment. Significantly, there seems to

have been little recognition of the need to develop trust in this new environment or the impact that that might have on the success of the project. Their final comment, noting that "the entry of the private sector into government GIS projects is one factor that can potentially lead to more rapid changes in the future" (2001, p. 15), clearly indicated an important issue. This comment is significant because it recognises that the private sector represents a means of providing additional expertise and support, localised in a way that enhances trust.

The Role of Trust in Technology Diffusion: E-Commerce in Regional Australia

The issue of trust also arises, albeit in a slightly different form, in an Australian study by Terziovski and Howell (2001). Reviewing a series of e-commerce projects undertaken by local government in regional Victoria, they found that while network linkages connecting external stakeholders were important to drive new initiatives, trusted local connections were also essential for their proper implementation and ongoing exploitation.

The scheme in question, VEEM (Victorian E-Commerce Early Movers) Scheme, was funded by the state government with the aim of identifying linkages that could aid and support local government usage of e-commerce and its subsequent take up by local industry and the wider community. A number of local government areas were funded to develop a range of projects, including promotional events such as e-commerce business planning workshops and regional expos, and more specific activities such as the development of regional business portals and the development of business plans to enable local businesses to adopt online fulfilment and procurement.

Feedback from participants confirmed that the scheme was a success, with e-commerce being embraced by business and communities alike.

They also noted that, as the project progressed, many of the activities had been customised to better fit community and private sector expectations, reflecting the flexibility that had been built into the scheme, and the willingness of the responsible government agency to work with local government in a meaningful way.

Terziovski and Howell's (2001) report highlighted several strategies that were critical to this success, but noted that to achieve sustainability it was necessary for participants to develop their own expertise, and it was important that strategies had been framed with that end goal in mind. Specifically, they commented that:

- Participants recognized that the projects would not have been undertaken without the stimulus provided by the state government, nor would they have been seen as a high priority for local government without that support, which provided credibility, resources, and a secure working environment.

- While participants acknowledged the important role of the state government, they also understood that, in order to ensure meaningful participation, it was essential to devolve decision making to local government and communities. In this context, local government saw its role as seeding community or industry based networks, and providing infrastructure support and training.

- As local small businesses were intensely focused on their own immediate needs, it was considered far more effective to use local experts to talk to local people, maintaining the focus on their needs rather than those identified by external stakeholders. These grassroots champions were seen as important because they could provide examples of success and act as marketing agents for uptake of technology. These are important factors in reducing local indifference. It

was also considered more effective to have a number of champions, drawn from different business sectors, who had existing relationships with other local centers of influence such as banks, accountants, and community business groups. For example, one local government office sponsored six business champions from three targeted industry sectors – transport/distribution, manufacturing, and services industries – and was instrumental in connecting them to the economic development in the region by providing better access to its networks.

- While it was recognized that external expertise was essential to the success of the diffusion process, and that that expertise would be required on an ongoing basis, it was also recognized that much expertise could, and should, be localised. To facilitate this, the report recommended that the state government should fund an ICT Center in each regional area, using a local body such as part of the council or a university or the local e-commerce association, to deliver information, training, and so forth. These centres could not only provide trusted support, but could also strengthen the relationship between the State Government, local councils, and the community, thereby providing a sound foundation for future programs.

- Finally, it was recognized that something as simple as a database of service providers could be invaluable in assisting both local government and local businesses, by preventing duplication of time and resources when identifying and evaluating existing service providers.

Reflecting these considerations, the report proposed a model of best practice based on a tripartite relationship between state and local government, and local government and the community. In this model, the state government provides the vision, policies, initiatives, and funding, while local government provides a leadership role to facilitate e-commerce diffusion, working with local businesses and the community to address real needs.

All of the strategies adopted by the project built on existing networks and relationships to facilitate the successful diffusion of e-ommerce, using them to establish and reinforce existing trust systems and to develop strong relationships on a regional, business and individual basis. The creation of support (brokerage) networks that facilitate a flow of information, skills and resources was absolutely essential, but it was recognised that these would only be useful if they were combined with the strengths and resources of the local community (cohesion networks). As in the MoEF project (Barratt et al., 2001), trust in the ability of those managing the project to understand local needs and conditions was identified as a significant factor, but unlike the MoEF project, trust was harnessed and the project achieved its goals.

Building Support Networks: University Library Systems in Vietnam

Many of the themes and issues raised in this chapter found practical application in a series of projects in which the author participated, involving the diffusion of new technology among regional universities in Vietnam. In this case, which has been documented by Johanson et al. (2004), the NGOs managing the project not only brokered networks to support the initial diffusion of technology and distribution of resources, but also assisted in the development of more localized networks capable of exploiting the technology on an ongoing basis.

The first of these projects began in 1999, after Atlantic Philanthropies (AP), a US based NGO, decided to contribute to the educational infrastructure of Vietnam by developing a series of Learning Resource Centers (LRCs) in collaboration with regional universities in Da Nang, Hue,

Can Tho, and Thai Nguyen. Each project involved the design and construction of a modern library facility based on western models and standards of information service, together with the provision of state of the art technology, and high quality teaching and learning facilities.

The initial project, the Da Nang University Information Resource Center (IRC), was completed in 2001 with high expectations. Staff had received training in the form of a short study tour to Australia and an introduction to the use of library management systems. The initial collection included 10,000 monograph and serial titles, in both English and Vietnamese, and access to a range of electronic resources. A Vietnamese company was contracted to provide both a local area network and an integrated library management system (ILMS) to manage housekeeping and public access functions. Although well resourced in comparison with other university libraries, it quickly became apparent that it was under utilized. Management decided not to circulate material and, partly in consequence of that decision, staff used only a fraction of the functionality of the ILMS. Further, without a support contract for either the communications infrastructure or the ILMS, there were ongoing problems with the stability of the technology.

AP was surprised by this result and delayed work on the remaining LRCs while a review was conducted. That review, undertaken by RMIT University Vietnam, found that strong and committed management had been provided and, although there were a number of resourcing issues, the most significant problems related to the fact that the IRC was operating without the supportive infrastructure that its western counterparts take for granted:

- The proposed operating environment of the IRC was essentially new to academic libraries within Vietnam and, although there was a training program for staff, it was both limited in scope and had no provision for ongoing support. There were only a few librarians with whom they could discuss ideas and share experience. The library schools were not producing appropriate graduates and the limited number of similar libraries were scattered throughout the country. Somehow, with little advice from the scanty professional infrastructure, traditional tasks such as cataloguing fared well, but new areas such as circulation, the use of IT, and the identification, acquisition, and use of electronic resources, did not.

- Also, apart from the inability to obtain immediate practical advice at a local level, the overall professional library infrastructure within the country was underdeveloped. There was little support for activities such as the adoption and promotion of national standards, the nurture of a national professional association or the encouragement of local systems vendors. That made it difficult for management to obtain strategic advice.
- Neither staff nor vendors had the experience to develop procedures that would allow them to incorporate the automated system into the new style of operation, nor to identify problems with the system that would allow them to recommend appropriate modifications. There was little capacity for local adaptation.
- Modern western libraries make intense use of IT, relying on a shared infrastructure that allows them to reduce the real costs of that technology as well as the resources required to manage it. Typically, that infrastructure includes consortia to support the purchase of electronic resources, the shared development of IT strategies and applications, interlibrary loan networks, and shared cataloguing. None of this was available to the IRC.
- The decision on how to proceed with acquiring an ILMS was crucial to the successful operation of the IRC. At that time the available choices were limited to importing

an international system or developing one locally. Importing one had the advantage that it could be expected to be fully functional and would comply with the relevant standards, but there would also be several disadvantages: none had a Vietnamese language version; none provided local support; and none provided support in Vietnamese. Furthermore, the cost of the initial purchase and of ongoing maintenance was unaffordable. Eventually, a Vietnamese company was commissioned to develop an ILMS for the IRC. The chosen company was new to libraries and although it learnt quickly, the system it initially delivered had a number of serious problems.

- There were, and there still are, serious limitations in the national infrastructure with regard to the availability of trained IT staff, particularly in the regions where, although the number of IT staff is growing, there remains a shortage because there is an increasing demand for their services from other developing industries.

AP had come to realise that developing a sustainable service required a significantly broader perspective than that was at first apprehended. One other thing they recognised was that the LRCs not only had to be effective in themselves, but also they had to be integrated within the broader educational and professional communities. To advance their interests it was necessary to work within the already established framework in the country, putting emphasis on those aspects that had been identified as being important to the LRC projects and their further development. The profession within Vietnam had already instigated work on a program of modernization but had been hampered by lack of funds. AP sponsored a workshop to discuss further on the adoption of standards at a national level. That workshop also explored issues of cooperative and collaborative activity, including the possibility of developing a national organisation of professional librarians and library educators, as well as recommending a national strategy for the development and acquisition of library management systems within the country. Working closely with the profession, AP subsequently initiated projects in a number of these areas.

From the view point on the diffusion of innovation and Rogers' (2003) framework, this intervention was strong enough in terms of relative advantage, but at the same time was weak in terms of compatibility, complexity, trialability, and observability. It became obvious that the success of the first IRC was dependent on the broader national infrastructure and it could not be considered successful if it was treated as self-contained. It could only be considered successful if it was treated as a first stage in the overall development of services within the country. In their analysis, Johanson et al. (2004) argued that support networks were essential to the success of these projects because they provided access to strategic advice, skills transfer, and an ongoing professional culture. Hence, the LRCs could not achieve their full potential until stakeholder communities had themselves progressed to the stage where they could provide the required additional support. In network terms, the first IRC had been created with numerous structural holes that could not be effectively closed until a shorter linked brokerage network and a stronger internal (cohesive) network had been established. Therefore, the other elements of Rogers' (2003) framework could come into play until that had been done.

The project is also of interest from the point of view of developing local capacity in order to support local adaptation or contingent improvisation. As mentioned earlier, the library management system was plagued with problems and the resolution of these problems was beyond the reach of the staff of the IRC and the vendor. An outside expert was called in to evaluate the system and to work with both parties to recommend improve-

ments so that the resultant system would at least provide the necessary core functionality and meet international standards. This strategy resonates well with the views of Heeks (2002) because it allowed the staff of the local vendor and the IRC to build up the expertise required to take future development of the system under their own control. In this case, even though the need for local adaptation had been recognized, the capacity to undertake it was only achieved when the relevant support networks had been established.

Concluding their analysis, Johanson et al. (2004) reported that these issues were addressed directly in the development of the subsequent LRCs. They found that not only were the subsequent projects more successful, but that their success contributed to a revitalization of the Da Nang IRC.

Using NGOs to Build Support Networks: The CEFE Network in South Africa

A common question running through these case studies is the question of how best to maximise the effectiveness of external interventions. The work of Barratt et al. (2001) highlights some of the problems that can occur, and although Terziovski and Howell (2001) describe a more successful case, they are clearly considering a technically potent and culturally homogenous environment. The projects documented by Johanson et al. (2004) are useful in that they provide examples of a successful intervention in a developing country, but a more general consideration of the issues is provided by Gibb and Adkihary (2000) who examine the role of NGOs in this process. In their view, NGOs can provide a useful mechanism for promoting the diffusion of innovation and development because they are more likely to be embedded in their communities and, as a consequence of that, are more likely to be capable of helping to develop the networks of trusted stakeholders that lead to sustainable outcomes.

They studied the Competency-based Economies through the Formation of Enterprise (CEFE) Network, an alliance of six NGOs in South Africa. In South Africa, the role of small business is seen as critical in supporting government policy, in meeting targets for new job creation, and as an effective means of redistributing income and opportunity to the indigenous population. NGOs, such as those of the CEFE Network, are important because they are seen as a means of delivering financial and business development services, including training and consultancy, and establishing the necessary support structure for small businesses to thrive. CEFE is important because it forms part of a national grouping of NGOs operating with a broader stakeholder group comprising major national players, including government organizations and public funding sources, national and international, private businesses (large and small), professional service companies, local and regional government, business representative organisations, and the media. Thus, it is in a position to broker a wide range of services.

Gibb and Adkihary (2000) chose the CEFE Network to study because, since its inception in 1995, it had successfully met a number of challenges, including the need to deliver services over a broad geographic area by focusing on local need and underpinning sustainability. As a result, it had been successful in helping its member NGOs to distribute resources and provide training, while developing a more standardised range of services that allowed them to mesh better with national priorities. By studying their experience, Gibb and Adkihary aimed to identify and promote new forms of partnerships and governance that could be used to assist the development of small and medium enterprises (SMEs) more generally.

They found that NGOs can play an important role in this type of activity because they are essentially bottom-up organizations which are more likely to be embedded in their communities and are thereby more likely to reflect local needs. Not only that, but they also have the ability to act as

brokers, capable of connecting those communities to the support networks that can provide them with the access to external expertise and the resources they require to meet their needs. In this way, they can act to identify the local needs and close structural holes.

Gibb and Adkihary also recognised that NGOs are not without potential problems, though they are intrinsically connected with their strengths. For example, NGOs often have a weak resource base, and as a result, can fall into the trap of expending their energies on chasing funding to ensure their continued existence rather than on fulfilling local needs. By focusing more on the requirements of their funding bodies, they react more to supplier needs rather than those of the community they seek to serve. Another potential problem is that, because of their commitment to meeting local needs, they may find it difficult to standardize service delivery by harming their ability to fit into national networks and to align with national priorities.

Gibb and Adkihary observed that, to be successful in helping their communities, NGOs must develop strategies to neutralise those problems. To that end, they proposed a Stakeholder Assessment Model (SAM) of NGO effectiveness, based on a series of key evaluation questions, including:

- To what degree the overall focus of the NGO on meeting the needs of the stakeholders?
- How well is the NGO known by the stakeholders?
- How clear is the mission/objectives of the NGO to the stakeholders?
- How well is the NGO perceived by the stakeholders to be meeting its objectives?
- To what extent does the NGO undertake joint ventures in partnership with stakeholders?
- Are these initiatives perceived as being successful? (Gibb & Adkihary, 2000, p. 145)

The model as developed, focuses on the requirements of NGOs as organizations at the center of stakeholder networks that need a clear understanding of their own missions and the needs of their various stakeholders. Gibb and Adkihary observed further that, if used correctly, the model can not only ensure a focus on client needs, but also can help in setting management objectives by contributing to NGO sustainability.

The study concluded by reporting that the CEFE Network was continuing to deliver successful programs and gain greater acceptance from government. By increasing its range of strategic alliances, it was also improving its ability to broker new services. Gibb and Adkihary's (2000) examination of the CEFE network demonstrates that, despite the potential problems, NGOs that focus on the issues identified in their SAM model can successfully act to facilitate network development and achieve the mutual support that derives from bringing local groups and external stakeholder communities together.

FUTURE TRENDS

International agencies that are involved in development projects, for example the World Bank, are including social capital measurements in their analyses and are starting to acknowledge the role of social factors in their strategies for systems development (UNDP, 2001). Significant research is being undertaken in the areas of technology diffusion, social capital and network analysis. However, despite the examples provided in this chapter, much of it relates to the role of business and the corporate world, which are generally seen as the most important drivers of economic growth. Furthermore, much of the work in regional areas is actually undertaken through the agency of NGOs, and therefore, there needs to be more intensive research into characteristics, role, and operating culture of NGOs.

This is particularly important in developing countries and there are a growing number of organizations working to explore those issues, for example, the research being undertaken by the Institute for Development Policy and Management at Manchester University, which focuses on policy formulation and implementation, and organisational design (Baark & Heeks, 1998; Madon, 2000). The emergent field of community informatics is also making a strong contribution in this context. For example, two recent conferences focusing on technology for development, and framing the issues in terms of sustainability and the social appropriation of technology, are of special relevance to the issues raised in this chapter (Erwin, Taylor, Bytheway, & Strumpfer, 2005; Johanson & Stillman, 2004).

CONCLUSION

The projects discussed in this chapter demonstrate that an over-emphasis on technology and technology-based services, and their development in isolation from the communities that they are intended to serve, will not lead to successful and sustainable outcomes. Successful, sustainable projects are the result of a careful interplay of controlled variables, many of which may need to go through a complex iterative process based on changing stages of organizational culture. Projects targeted at rural and regional communities must address the real needs of the communities they aim to serve. That requires not only long term commitment and strategic funding, but also, meaningful participation and proper consideration of all influences within and between the affected communities.

This chapter has used a framework provided by the diffusion of innovation within a network environment to highlight how necessary resources can be provided to make such developments a sustainable reality. Successful, sustainable projects require access to a complex infrastructure maintained by a range of stakeholders. Network relationships are essential in both the development and maintenance of such infrastructure because they provide access to new ideas and innovations, strategic advice, training, technical support, and a host of other resources. While some of these resources, such as access to new ideas, typically should continue to be provided through extended networks, successful and sustainable projects require a localized infrastructure capable of localizing and harnessing resources in a trusted environment. Specifically, it is important to recognise this sort of support network in rural and regional areas, and even more so in developing countries, because it is precisely these network structures that they lack.

The case studies examined, particularly those of Johanson et al. (2004) and Gibb and Adkihary (2000), highlight the fact that those networks are often brokered through the agency of NGOs, who provide access to contacts and resources that would otherwise be inaccessible to local communities. And while it could be argued that broad networks could be established without NGOs, the case studies emphasise that their importance derives from the fact that they are more often embedded within their communities, so that they can make use of existing trust systems and local links to identify and close structural holes which would otherwise deny those communities access to much needed resources and expertise.

ACKNOWLEDGMENT

This chapter is based on research supported by the Australian Research Council.

REFERENCES

Aldrich, H., & Zimmer, C. (1986). Entrepreneurship through social networks. In D. Sexton & R. Smilor (Eds.), *Art and science of entrepreneurship*, 3-23. Cambridge, MA: Ballinger,

Baark, E., & Heeks, R. (1998). Evaluation of donor-funded information technology projects in China: A lifecycle approach. *Development informatics working chapter series*. Manchester: Institute for Development Policy and Management, University of Manchester.

Barratt, M., Sahay, S., & Walsham, G. (2001) Information technology and social transformation: GIS for forestry management in India. *The Information Society, 17*, 5-20.

Bebbington, A. (1997). Social capital and rural intensification: Local organizations and islands of sustainability in the rural Andes. *The Geographical Journal, 163*(2), 189-197.

Burt. R. (2000). The network structure of social capital. *Research in Organizational Behavior, 22*, 345-423.

Coleman, J. (1988). Social capital in the creation of human capital. *American Journal of Sociology, 94,* S95-S120.

Erwin, G., Taylor, W., Bytheway, A., & Strumpfer, C. (Eds.). (2005, August 23-26). CIRN2005: *The Second Annual Conference of the Community Informatics Research Network, Cape Town, South Africa.*

Furst, D., Schubert, H., Rudolph, A., & Spieckermann, H. (2001). Regional actor networks between social capital and regional governance. *Connections, 24*(1), 42-67.

Garrison, B. (2001). Diffusion of online information technologies in newschapter newsrooms. *Journalism, 2*(2), 221-239.

Gibb, A., & Adhikary, D. (2000). Strategies for local and regional NGO development: Combining sustainable outcomes with sustainable organizations. *Entrepreneurship & Regional Development, 12*, 137-161.

Giddens, A. (1990). *The consequences of modernity*. Cambridge: Polity Press.

Giddens, A. (1991). *Modernity and self-identity: Self and society in the late modern age.* Cambridge: Polity Press.

Granovetter, S. (1973). The strength of weak ties. *The American Journal of Sociology, 78*(6), 1360-1380.

Grover, V., & Teng, J. (1992) An examination of DBMS adoption and success in American organizations. *Information Management, 23*(5), 239-248.

Hakansson, H. (1990). Technological collaboration in industrial networks. *European Management Journal, 8*(3), 371-379.

Heeks, R. (2002) Information systems and developing countries: Failure, success, and local improvisations. *The Information Society, 18*(2), 101-112.

Johanson, G., Denison, T., & Otis, N. (2004, September 29-October 1). Building sustainable learning communities in Vietnam. In G. Johanson & L. Stillman (Eds.), *Sustainability and community technology: What does this mean for community informatics?* Monash Prato Colloqium, Prato, Italy. Available at http://www.ccnr.net/?q=node/5. Accessed Jan. 30, 2006

Johanson, G., & Stillman, L. (Eds.). (2004, September 29-October 1). *Sustainability and community technology: What does this mean for community informatics?* Monash Prato Colloqium, Prato, Italy.

Kadushin, C. (2002) The motivational foundation of social networks. *Social Networks,* 24, 77-91.

Keil, M., Cule, P., Lyytinen, K., & Schmidt, R. (1998). A framework for identifying software project risks. *Communications of the ACM, 41*(11), 76-83.

Kling, R. (2000) Learning about information technologies and social change: The contribution of social informatics. *The Information Society,* 16, 217-232.

Lyytinen, K., & Hirschheim, R. (1987). Information Systems failures – A survey and classification of the empirical literature. *Oxford Surveys in Information Technology,* 4, 257-309.

Lyytinen, K., & Robey, D. (1999). Learning failure in information systems development. *Information Systems Journal, 9*(2), 85-101.

Madon, S. (2000). International NGOs: Networking, information flows and learning. *Development informatics working chapter series.* Manchester: Institute for Development Policy and Management, University of Manchester.

Orlikowski, W. (2000). Using technology and constituting structures: A practice lens for studying technology in organisations. *Organization Science, 11*(4), 404-428.

Rogers, E. (1995). *Diffusion of innovations* (4th ed.). New York: The Free Press.

Rogers, E. (2003). *Diffusion of innovations* (5th ed.). New York: The Free Press.

Schmidt, R., Lyytinen, K., Keil, M., & Cule, P. (2001) Identifying software project risks: An international Delphi study. *Journal of Management Information Systems, 17*(4), 5-36.

Sherry, L. (1998). An integrated technology adoption and diffusion model. *International Journal of Educational Telecommunications, 4*(2/3), 113-145.

Steward, F., & Conway, S. (2000). Building networks for innovation diffusion in Europe: Learning from the SPRINT Programme. *Enterprise and Innovation Management Studies, 1*(3), 281-301.

Terziovski, M., & Howell, A. (2001). *e-Commerce best practice: A review of the Victorian e-Commerce early movers* (VEEM) scheme in Victorian local councils. Report prepared for Multimedia Victoria, State and Regional Development.

UNDP. (2001). Information communications technology for development. *Essentials,* 5. Available at http://www.undp.org/eo/documents/essentials_5.PDF. Accessed Jan. 30, 2006.

Valente, T. (1995). *Network models of the diffusion of innovations*. Cresskill, NJ: Hampton Press.

Valente, T. (2005). Models and methods for innovation diffusion. In P. Carrington, J. Scott, & S. Wasserman (Eds.), *Models and methods in social network analysis*. Cambridge: Cambridge University Press.

Wellman, B. (1988). Structural analysis: From method and metaphor to theory and substance. In B. Wellman & S. Berkowitz (Eds.), *Social structures: A network approach* (pp. 19-61). Cambridge: Cambridge University Press.

This work was previously published in Information and Communication Technologies for Economic and Regional Developments, edited by H. Rahman, pp. 102-120, copyright 2007 by IGI Publishing, formerly known as Idea Group Publishing (an imprint of IGI Global).

Chapter XVII
Building Virtual Communities through a De–Marginalized View of Knowledge Networking

Kam Hou Vat
University of Macau, Macau

ABSTRACT

The chapter investigates an actionable context of knowledge networking, from the perspective of sustainable development which should accommodate the building of communities in cyberspace so much exemplified in today's Internet and World Wide Web. The premise of this exploration is that members, or participants, in any community are engaged in learning that is critical to the survival and reproduction of that community. Through community participation, learners find and acquire models and have the opportunity themselves to become models and apprentices of others. This investigation provides a basis for thinking about the possibilities of a virtual community and the dynamics of its construction across a variety of computer-based contexts. The design and refinement of technology as the conduit for extending and enhancing the possibilities of virtual community building is an essential issue, but the role of the individuals as participants in such a community is as important. The idea of sustainable knowledge networking is to bring about continual learning and change for the community in need. The emergent challenge of such a mission is to de-marginalize many of the non-technical issues of building virtual communities for knowledge transfer and learning. The chapter concludes by reiterating the challenge of expositing what it means to create an appropriate context of knowledge networking through which purposeful actions can be supported with the elaboration of suitable information technologies.

INTRODUCTION

The term *virtual community* today mostly refers to many types of Internet-based social interaction. In fact, the term *community*, according to Williams (1973), in the English language referred primarily to a geographically localized group of people until approximately the 17th century, and it expanded somewhere between the 17th and the 19th centuries to include the idea of a group of people who hold something in common, or who share a common sense of identity even if they do not live in a single locale. Interestingly, the term *virtual* came into the English language from Latin by way of French at about the same time as did *community*, around the 14th century. Initially, it referred to things that had special and effective physical capacities, linking it closely to our ideas of virtuous. Yet, its meaning underwent changes in the 17th and the 18th centuries to refer to something that seems almost completely real to the people in so far as the effect or result is concerned, although not formally or actually real in the physical sense, according to *The Complete Oxford English Dictionary* (1971).

Rheingold (1994), who appears to have coined the term *virtual community* in the first place, provides a definition that accords reasonably well with the context of being virtual: namely, people in virtual communities do just about everything people do in real life (meet one another and exchange ideas and information), but we leave our bodies behind. We cannot kiss anybody and nobody can punch us in the nose, but a lot can happen within those boundaries (Rheingold, 1994, pp. 57-58).

In the virtual community, relationship is typically defined not by proximity but by contents of individual interest — classes of objects, ideas, or events about which participants have differing levels of both stored knowledge and stored values (Renninger, 2000). Participants' connections to the community are often based on cognition and

affection rather than simply spatial and temporal. Such a connection is also supported by affordances (Gibson, 1966) that invoke imagination about and identification with a site, such as autonomy, support, and depth of content. Besides, the learning that is undertaken as participants work with a site has an opportunity for changed understanding of our self. Thereby, it is important to consider what a virtual community means, what it offers, what it affords its participants, and what its boundaries are at the advent of the Internet that has undoubtedly created numerous possibilities for interaction that people did not have before (Cherny, 1999; Davis & Brewer, 1997; Herring, 1996).

THE BACKGROUND OF KNOWLEDGE NETWORKING

The last decade of the twentieth century saw explosive growth in discussions about knowledge — knowledge work, knowledge management, knowledge-based organizations, and the knowledge economy (Cortada & Woods, 2000). Against this backdrop, enterprises including educational institutes are challenged to do things more collaboratively in order to remain vital in an increasingly global environment of knowledge networking (Stalk, Evans, & Shulman, 1992). By knowledge networking, it means there is a strong need to share knowledge in a way that makes it easier for individuals, teams, and enterprises to work together to effectively contribute to an organization's success.

This idea of knowledge sharing has well been exemplified in Rheingold's (1994) description of the WELL project (Whole Earth 'Lectronic Link), which is one of the first virtual communities, still going strong today. Rooted in the San Francisco Bay Area, the WELL (http://www.well.com) is an open-ended and self-governing community that started in 1985. Attracting people from a wide diversity of backgrounds, many of them professionals, it hosted computer conferences on a wide range of topics — education, arts, recreation, computers, and entertainment. It went on to the Internet in 1992 where over 200 separate conferences are hosted.

Its introductory Web pages emphasize that it is not just another Web site or collection of Web pages: "More than just another 'site' or 'home page' the WELL has a sense of place that is palpable." One spin-off of the WELL was the Global Business Network (GBN; http://www.gbn.com), created in 1986, that drew together planners and strategists from companies like ABB, AT&T, Volvo, BP, and Bell South. This group used a mix of face-to-face meetings and online conferences to develop scenarios of the future. Through GBN, company executives and leading thinkers in a variety of fields would openly share their knowledge and insights. This interplay of knowledge generated new thinking about the future. It also led to increased collaboration among GBN members.

Interestingly, the WELL and the GBN could both be considered as instances of the notion of learning organizations (Senge, 1990; Garvin, 1993; King, 1996; Levine, 2001). Essentially, a learning organization could be considered as an organization that focuses on developing and using its information and knowledge capabilities in order to create higher-value information and knowledge, to modify behaviors to reflect new knowledge and insights, and to improve bottom-line results. Practically, there are many possible instances of a learning organization that could be incorporated into the daily experiences.

An obvious example as mentioned earlier is the concept of community of practice, which according to Wenger, McDermott, and Snyder (2002, p. 4), refers to groups of people who share a common concern, a set of problems, or a passion about a topic, and who deepen their knowledge and expertise by interacting on an ongoing basis. As people in the community spend time together, they typically share information, insight, and advice. They help one another to solve problems; they ponder common issues, explore ideas, and accumulate knowledge. Often, they become informally bound by the value that they find in learning together. This value is not merely instrumental for their work. Over time, they develop a unique perspective on their topic as well as a body of common knowledge, practices, and approaches. They also develop personal relationships, a common sense of identity, and established ways of interacting.

Indeed, communities of practice are not a new idea (Wenger, 1998). They were the first knowledge-based social structures, back when humans lived in caves and gathered around the fire to discuss strategies for cornering prey, the shape of arrowheads, or which roots were edible. They have captured the attention today because with the advent of the Internet, especially the World Wide Web, it has been realized that knowledge sharing, coupled with the possibilities of technological advances, is the key to the sustainable development regardless of the temporal and spatial boundaries. Undeniably, in the emerging knowledge society, people are expected to continually improvise and invent new methods to deal with unexpected difficulties and to solve immediate problems, and share these innovations or lessons learned with others through some effective channels. In this regard, the idea of the virtual community has inspired many an organization to initiate their collective learning based not so much on delineated learning paths, but rather on experience sharing, the identification of best practices, and reciprocal support for tackling day-to-day problems in the workplace. Importantly, cultivating virtual communities in strategic areas is considered as a practical way to manage knowledge in terms of critical knowledge domains. Organizations need to identify the people and the specific knowledge needed for their growth, and explore how they connect them into suitable virtual communities of practice so that together they could steward the necessary knowledge.

A DEFINABLE CONTEXT FOR VIRTUAL COMMUNITIES

Literally, the term virtual community is not hard to understand, yet it is slippery to define owing to its multi-disciplinary nature. In order to develop virtual communities — a complex practical activity — a disciplinary definition is needed to guide the practices. According to Preece (2000, p. 10), an online community consists of four important elements: the people, who interact socially as they strive to satisfy their own needs, or perform special roles, such as leading or moderating; a shared purpose, such as an interest, need, information exchange, or service that provides a reason for the community; policies, in the form of tacit assumptions, rituals, protocols, rules, and laws that guide people's interactions; and computer systems, to support and mediate social interaction and facilitate a sense of togetherness. Indeed, this definition is sufficiently general to apply to a range of different communities, including physical communities that have become networked and those that are embedded in Web sites (Lazar & Preece, 1998).

Undeniably, the idea of virtual community has somehow become a blanket term to describe any collection of people who communicate online, as exemplified by the networked communities (Cohill & Kavanaugh, 1997), also known as the community networks (Schuler, 1996) to which citizens can link through the Internet to discuss typical community issues. For better or worse, people are shaped by the communities to which they belong. As more people gain Internet access, they are increasingly empowered to organize themselves across local, national, and international boundaries. A call to action, a warning message, a cheer of encouragement, and the inspiring words of a leader can be distributed to members at lightning speed and at almost no cost, with just the click of a few keys.

Yet, developing successful virtual communities is not trivial. Successful virtual communities

satisfy their members' needs and contribute to the well-being of society. The role of a community developer is to work with community members to plan and guide the community's social evolution. Putting basic policies in place helps members know how to behave, what to expect from each other, and provides a framework for social growth. As the community develops and forms its own character, its social policies and structure also evolve. Sociability is concerned with planning and developing social policies that are understandable and acceptable to members, to support the community's purpose.

The software that supports the continuous evolution of a community must be dynamically designed and adapted to its growth. More importantly, the software must be designed with good usability so that people can interact and perform their tasks intuitively and easily. Software with good usability supports rapid learning and high skill retention. Understanding a community's needs is essential for developing virtual communities with good sociability and usability: the former focuses on social interaction, and the latter focuses on human-computer interaction. Developers and users have the responsibility to plan, guide, and mold communities to support the people in them. Like contemporary town planners and architects, the researchers can profoundly shape the virtual community landscape, paying particular attention to the issues of usability and sociability therewith to support the activities of knowledge networking.

VIRTUALIZATION OF KNOWLEDGE NETWORKING ACTIVITIES

The move to virtualization has been developing rapidly over the last decade, and has attracted a corresponding vocabulary, such as *virtual communities* (Rheingold, 1994). A virtual community, like its local counterpart, gives people a sense of identity and belonging, except that instead of being rooted in a physical place, it is a locality in cyberspace. Such communities emerged in the 1980s based around bulletin board systems. Today, they exist on the Internet in newsgroups, e-mail discussion lists, and conferences, and on company intranets or groupware systems.

Virtual communities come in many shapes and sizes. Some are open to anyone who cares to join, attracted by the topic of interest. Others are closed, in that they can join by invitation or subscription. In practice, people in such communities may or may not work together on a day-to-day basis, but they do value the learning that takes place when they spend time together. What they know may seem trivial or of great value, but their interactions with one another are crucial to their ability to do what they can do. What these groups or communities have in common is that engaging with each other around issues of common interest, sharing insights and information, helping each other, or discussing new ideas together are all part of belonging to the group. Interestingly, this is also the community's process of stewarding knowledge, which can hardly be separated from the communities that own it.

Today, many organizations have realized that unless knowledge is owned by people to whom it matters, it will not be developed, used, and kept up to date optimally. Knowledge is not a thing that can be managed at a distance like in an inventory. It is part of the shared practice of communities that need it, create it, use it, debate it, distribute it, adapt it, and transform it. As the property of a community, knowledge is not static; it involves interactions, conversations, actions, and inventions. Thereby, networking knowledge in a virtual community is not primarily a technological challenge, but one of community development.

Addressing this kind of dynamic knowing that makes a difference in practice requires the participation of people who are fully engaged in the process of creating, refining, communicating, and using knowledge. The thrust to develop, organize, and communicate knowledge must

come from those who will use it. What matters is not how much knowledge can be captured, but how documenting can support people's abilities to know and to learn when the community itself becomes the living repository of people's knowledge. In the following discussion, the author examined a case study of community development through looking into the design considerations and strategies for creating online learning communities in order to facilitate the transformation and sharing of resources to support integrated understanding within the communities of teachers and students.

The Case of WISE

WISE, short for the Web-based Integrated Science Environment (Slotta & Linn, 2000; http://wise.berkeley.edu), is used to scaffold teacher and student communities as they exchange resources, develop coherent ideas, and support individual understanding in scientific investigations. From a community-building perspective, WISE defines learning communities as supporting networks of personal relationships that enable the exchange of resources and the development of a common framework for analysis of these resources. WISE also defines resources as a collection of ideas or interactions that are accessible to community members and can be incorporated into their practice. Besides, members of the community are expected to jointly analyze resources and develop a common set of criteria for evaluating those resources. However, it is important to discuss how different strategies can progressively involve individual members by helping them become resources for other community members.

The WISE Rationale

WISE is informed by a scaffolded knowledge integration (SKI) framework, which emphasizes coherent understanding by supporting participants as they compare, contrast, sort out, and organize their ideas. The SKI framework is inspired by cognitive apprenticeship (Tudge & Rogdoff, 1989) and the work of Vygotsky (1978). The framework has four design tenets that jointly encourage students to link and connect their ideas so that they develop more integrated and cohesive ideas. These tenets are: (1) to make the process of thinking visible, (2) to make science accessible, (3) to encourage students to learn from each other, and (4) to foster lifelong learning. WISE stresses the coordination and integration of ideas as well as encouraging different paths for learning.

By mixing hands-on learning with online discussions and modeling tools, WISE helps create a repertoire of experience representations that aid students as they become part of a community of learners. Such representations also provide support for teachers and curriculum designers as they collect resources for constructing learning projects. In many WISE projects, the presence of a shared resource (mostly from Internet sites) is used as evidence to support theories and to ground discussions, creating the potential for negotiation, clarification, justification, synthesis, and other processes that contribute to knowledge integration. Learning to use WISE requires teachers to adopt a new stance toward teaching where they serve more as a guide-on-the-side than as a sage-on-the-stage, transmitting knowledge.

By designing resources to scaffold and support interactions, WISE provides models of constructive engagement, as well as offering community tools for connecting people working on shared projects. Examples include: seeding discussions with comments to illustrate how evidence is used to support different theories; using video clips of student-teacher interactions to anchor discussions about pedagogy; and developing templates for activities to guide project authors as they create projects involving theory debate, critique, and design. The WISE software lets teachers and researchers track how resources circulate through communities, providing insights into the processes of community development. In addition, by mak-

ing the process of critique visible, it encourages students to reflect upon the credibility, reliability, and usefulness of those resources.

Design Strategies for Teacher Communities

WISE involves teachers in communities for teaching WISE projects, customizing projects, and authoring new projects. Many teachers use curriculum units as they exist in the project library. As they begin to localize and customize projects, they interact with other teachers who have used the project as well as with the project designers (Linn & Slotta, 2000). Eventually, some teachers join or form partnerships with other community members to author new projects (Linn, 2000). In practice, curriculum design is the arrangement of parts, assembling conceptual, strategic, and material components in a pattern that functions to support specific goals (Mollison, 1990, p. 36).

The WISE NetCourse introduces teachers to the pedagogical framework and the technical supports for WISE through which individual teachers can move from peripheral participation to more sophisticated involvement over time (Lave & Wenger, 1992). In particular, WISE makes authoring accessible in a number of important ways, for example, through project templates for critique, theory debate, and design of projects. It enables community members to learn from one another with collaborative tools such as shared white boards, resource libraries, and task lists.

Indeed, community exists only in the sense of teachers having access to a collection of online discussions about their teaching experiences and strategies. As these teachers reflect on their own practice and begin to customize projects with WISE, they contribute to the community by exchanging ideas with other teachers using similar projects. Therefore, recognizing the need to support teachers' actual practice as a way of involving them in a broader community is a crucial step in the design of self-sustaining communities.

Design Strategies for Student Communities

The instructional designers and teachers need to ask how they can structure relationships within learning communities so that the community members share resources and help refine each other's ideas. WISE offers innovative strategies for creating personalized electronic discussions that help elicit self-explanation and clarification from students (Cuthbert, Clark, Slotta, & Jorde, 2000). In fact, WISE projects have made advances in supporting students to share ideas in online learning communities, by investigating reflection and knowledge integration through scientific inquiry (Hoadley & Linn, 2000; Linn & Hsi, 2000).

Two of the most successful approaches involve personally seeded discussions and peer review discussions. In personally seeded discussions, WISE uses students' scientific explanations as initial comments in the discussion. Students work to clarify and justify their own scientific principles, comparing and contrasting them with other students' principles. Thinking is made visible for students as they elaborate upon and justify their ideas. By having students explain and defend their own principles, WISE gets students not only to take an interest in their own ideas, but also to take interest in responding to and critiquing the other ideas in the discussion. In peer review discussions, WISE uses students' shared research findings in an online question-and-answer session, creating resources that are accessible to the entire community of learners through such peer review activities as making comments, asking questions, and offering suggestions. In either case, the overarching design is for students to begin to adopt an orientation toward discourse that is based on comparison, critique, and justification, and the critical resources are the community members and their ideas. The common goal is the refinement of the community members' ideas.

Accordingly, the WISE strategies employed typically involve contrasting students' perspectives on a given topic of interest, and increasing students' personal relevance by making them responsible for pursuing specific areas of knowledge. Indeed, contrasting one's perspectives about a given topic can encourage an individual student to clarify his or her own formulation while considering the relevance of other students' opinions (Chi, Lewis, Reimann, & Glaser, 1989; DiSessa & Minstrell, 1998). Besides, by increasing personal relevance around the process of contrasting different students' understanding, WISE helps elicit community members' collaborative thinking (a valuable resource itself) to refine the community's ideas.

Design Considerations for WISE

According to Cuthhert, Clark, and Linn (2002), there are four main design considerations behind the design of WISE which serve as general guidelines for creating effective online learning communities: (1) support the actual practices and daily tasks of the participants, (2) collect experiences and represent them in an accessible and equitable manner, (3) provide a framework to guide the learning process, and (4) represent the identities of the community members. It is worthwhile to examine some of the strategies related to the four design considerations aimed at creating effective online communities.

- **Support the actual practices and daily tasks of the participants:** WISE communities support the actual practices and daily tasks of teachers by helping them guide students' learning process through the creation of a visible history of student work. For students, WISE communities support learning practices and tasks by making the thinking of their peers visible, and by illustrating the process of group inquiry. Moreover, WISE elicits teachers' ideas and helps them develop curricula through its authoring communities.

From a knowledge integration perspective, the practice of teaching and learning involves developing a repertoire of models for explaining situations. The scaffolded knowledge integration framework mentioned earlier can help students and teachers in their daily practice by illustrating the repertoire of models which provides general guidelines for designing projects and serves as an inspiration for creating design considerations for online communities.

- **Collect experiences and represent them in an accessible and equitable manner:** WISE communities collect experiences and represent them in an accessible and equitable manner to promote the process of connecting ideas so that participants (students and teachers) can use them in consequential tasks such as during arguments and debates. Communities, if viewed as a network of relationships and resources, can be structured to elicit ideas, develop shared understanding, and promote the integration of a diverse set of ideas. It is important to investigate the potential of structuring discussions in different ways based on the type of discussion and the associated pedagogical goals.

Linking different types of pedagogical goals to design strategies is a challenging task because most community members are not accustomed to reflecting on the nature of their contributions. For instance, there are important differences between discussions depending on whether the purpose of the discussion is debate, brainstorming, or peer review. Each of these discussion types has a distinct structure and format, and hence demands different requirements for setting up, running, and assessing the discussion.

- **Provide a framework to guide the learning process:** WISE requires participants to support their ideas with evidence (e.g., Internet sites, references to laboratory work, scientific principles, or everyday experiences). This creates a culture where people ask each other for justification and clarification (Linn & Hsi, 2000). It is essential to investigate how participants adjust their behavior as their peers prompt them to support their ideas with evidence (Cuthbert et al., 2000).

One strategy is to create commonly agreed-upon criteria, and examine how these criteria are adopted and transformed by community members as they interact with one another. For communities to maintain coherence and develop a sense of what is appropriate behavior, it is important that a strong community culture be established with a common set of values and criteria for making contributions (Brown, 1992). Communities need a general framework to help define the mission and vision for the learning process.

In WISE, the knowledge integration framework characterizes the learning and curriculum design processes. This framework lends a shared focus to teacher professional development discussions, creating the potential to view instruction as a design problem that is interpreted to have multiple solutions and can be improved by selecting appropriate solutions and testing them in context. For example, it is important to understand how the WISE strategy off-loads the procedural guidance for students onto the learning environment, so as to free teachers to engage students individually, elicit their ideas, and encourage them to reformulate their ideas by considering other alternatives and supporting their ideas with evidence.

- **Represent the identities of community members:** Socially relevant information helps participants recognize the coherence of an individual's comments (Hoadley, 1999). WISE provides ways to represent the identities of community members, to illustrate the refinement of ideas, and to mark departures from past views. One common strategy is to link identities to resources based on who contributed or accessed a resource. Another is to display the identities separately in the profiles section of the community site. Representing people's backgrounds and interests can help develop personal relationships, especially when face-to-face interaction may be limited. However, entering profile information needs to be part of an ongoing process linked to the use of the community system (WISE) so that the task of entering descriptors (say, background, area of expertise, and instructional topics) does not deter members. The idea of mutually revealing information (not being able to see other members' pictures until someone submits) is another way to motivate people to complete their profiles.

Knowledge Networking for Learning Communities

As the WISE story indicates, it is often necessary to coordinate in joint action — more precisely, collaborate — to achieve tasks larger than any one person could accomplish alone. Through the processes of acculturation in learning communities, knowledge and culture are perpetuated and transformed as people interact, define new problems, and take on new challenges. The primary question for any learning community is how they can learn from one another so as to increase their knowledge together. One term for this type of learning community is a *knowledge-building community* (Scardamalia & Bereiter, 1994), where individuals are committed to share information for the purpose of building understanding (knowledge) in all the participants.

When attempting to design technology in support of such learning communities, it is important to remember the triad of components (Bedny'i & Meister, 1997; Kuutti & Bannon, 1993) which involves in every situation the interdependence of tools, activities, and people; namely, a change in

one element affects the others. When a new tool is introduced, people and their activities change to accommodate it. Over time, people begin to change, learning the new possibilities of the new tool, and adapting their practices (activities) to take advantage of its benefits and work around its shortcomings.

Thereby, in contrast to typical information and knowledge management tools, where the focus is on helping to route information, knowledge networking tools should help foster the constituent activities that increase knowledge building. Hence, these activities include not only information capture and transmission, but also the establishment of social relationships in which people can collaboratively construct understanding.

FUTURE TRENDS OF A DE-MARGINALIZED CONTEXT FOR KNOWLEDGE NETWORKING

The development of virtual communities for knowledge networking is a complex and multifaceted endeavor. If the goal is to help solve the puzzle of how to nurture such communities, there are quite a number of issues to be examined according to Hoadley and Pea (2002, pp. 345-351):

...defining learning communities, examining existing practices, identifying potential changes to improve practices, finding ways that technology might effect these changes, designing and building the technology, cultivating a community of use, understanding the consequences of the technology, and evaluating the community with respect to the original goal.

The investigation of these issues constitutes an important de-marginalized context to understand the intricacies behind the building of such virtual communities for the purpose of knowledge building and learning. In practice, each of the eight types of inquiry mentioned draws on a different research paradigm, demonstrating the multi-disciplinary nature of virtual communities. Here the term *de-marginalized* is used to emphasize the holistic nature of these issues. Oftentimes, the issues of technology seem to have marginalized the other issues in the discussion of virtualizing learning communities.

In the following discussion, some of the issues have been elaborated that must be de-marginalized in the study of building virtual communities. This is followed by some reflective recommendations on the value of community networks on knowledge sharing.

Defining Learning Communities

Loosely, almost any group of individuals who interact might be called a community, and certainly people change and learn in some fashion as a result of every life experience. Yet, it is often not easy to answer the question of what defines a learning or knowledge-building community. There have been a number of important efforts to offer such definitions.

Organizational behaviorists identify the learning organization as the important proponent (Garratt, 1987) that offers a few concrete measures of learning as a community. Woodruff (1999) describes some features that distinguish learning communities in terms of cohesion. Hsi (1997), following Pea (1993), defined learning communities as communities in which participants construct productive discussions (defined in terms of inclusiveness and knowledge integration processes). Research inquiry is still needed to examine the possible spectrum of communities which may be characterized as learning or knowledge building.

Finding Ways Technology Can Help

Oftentimes, technology is thrown at problems with an attitude that it can solve any problem. The study of human-computer interaction tells a different story. A user is unlikely to adopt tools that do not support his or her goals at least, as well as other alternatives. Since technology affects the community only through its impact on individual people, supporting a community often means encouraging individuals to behave in a group-oriented fashion through the use of enhanced technology which minimizes costs to the individual users. The idea of participatory design (Bodker, 1991; Ehn, 1989), coupled with the research findings from human-computer interaction, should predict the impact of different technologies on various human activities in the learning communities.

Cultivating a Community of Use

In the process of virtualization, community-oriented tools need nurturing for adoption (or appropriation) to take place, as do the communities they are intended to help (Newman, Griffin, & Cole, 1989; Pea, 1992). Typically, community users come to appropriate a tool by establishing its fitness with their work practices, or changing their work practices to accommodate special properties of the tool as they come to perceive them. The proponents of the technology must help users overcome initial hurdles to appropriation.

They must also help the community and the tool to reach a productive equilibrium, which may include the development of very new practices or ways of working. In fact, creating this culture of use is an important person-to-person task that goes beyond simply taking a technology and throwing it over to the intended user community.

Use is a design issue which does not end with what the technical designers have created, but continues in ways the user community makes out of it in context. It is a form of reciprocal evolution of technology, work practice, and basic research (Allen, 1993), whose action-oriented nature should be understood by technology coordinators, community facilitators, and reformers who help advocate the use of the tool and its participation in the community.

Evaluating the Growth of a Virtual Community

Obviously, the growth of a virtual community depends on the goals against which it used to measure whether the technology, the community, and the individuals are successful. In the case of learning communities, individuals might be assessed for learning, or groups of students might be assessed on their group skills for problem solving in the learning domain. Entire communities might be evaluated on the amount of participation, the degree to which members of the community help other members, or the net quality of the community's output.

A tool's success could be measured by changes in the individual's or group measures, or by looking at the tool's direct use, for example by investigating whether the tool is appropriated, by asking users how they use the tool and whether they find it helpful, or by documenting stories of how the tool changes the community and individuals (Gay & Bennington, 1999).

Reflecting on Community Networks for Knowledge Sharing

The idea of a networked community dates back to 1984 when Tom Grundner in Cleveland, Ohio, USA (Bajjaly, 1999), using a small computer and a single modem line, established an online bulletin board dubbed *St. Silicon's Hospital and Information dispensary*. His goal was to test the effectiveness of online access as a way to deliver health information to the general public. Local citizens there were able to dial into St. Silicon's, leave medically related questions, and receive an answer from a board-certified physician within a day.

This experiment proved so successful that Grundner secured enough funding to start a full-scale *community computer system* to provide free e-mail to the people around Cleveland and electronic information in areas as diverse as law, medicine, education, the arts, science, and government.

In July 1986, this system, called the Cleveland Free-Net, went online. Over the following three years, that system registered more than 7,000 users and handled between 500 and 600 calls per day. A second system, the Youngstown Free-Net, began operation in July 1987. Over the next couple of years, three more systems became operational: Tri-State Online in Cincinnati, Ohio; the Heartland Free-Net in Peoria, Illinois; and the first rural system, the Medina County Free-Net in Medina, Ohio.

In 1989, the concept of a community computer system was expanded and formalized and the National Public Tele-computing Network (NPTN) was born. Its goal was to help new systems come online and to support them afterward with services and information resources. Today, well over 200 communities in the U.S. and Canada host their own community networks.

Although Grundner is now no longer a visible part of the community networking movement and NPTN is no longer a functioning organization, his insights remain true today even though much in the world of computing has changed. Firstly, it is clear that these community computers represent the leading edge of what can only be described as a new telecommunications medium. Secondly, it is clear that a critical mass of people now exists who are prepared to utilize this new medium. Thirdly, there is a certain sense of inevitability to the development of community computing.

Simply stated, people find themselves unable to imagine a century in which they do not have community computer systems, just as the last century had the free public library. Moreover, it is believed that the community network, as a resource, will have at least as much impact on this century just as the public library has had on the society in the last century, such as to satisfy basic information needs of the physical community, to improve community collaboration through joint efforts and resource sharing, to promote and encourage individual lifelong education, to expand the knowledge base of the citizens of the community, and many others to be thought of.

CONCLUSION

For the past few decades, it has been witnessed that many cities and towns all over the world have established their respective community computer systems, more appropriately called community networks (or virtual communities) based on the discussion of knowledge networking so far. Such community networks help people and organizations to experience the transition from the face-to-face world they know so well to the online, electronic, networked world of the future.

Today, every community can easily connect to the Internet so that distant people and locals alike can tap into the repertoires of local information, communicate with one another, and experience almost firsthand the benefits a particular community has to offer. With this worldwide connectivity, even the smallest, most rural community can become an important part of the burgeoning *global village*.

Hence, every community can make its appearance in the global platform, telling its own story of growth, and relating why it is a good community to experience. Indeed, as people move into an electronically driven world, the story of each virtual community needs to be told online in terms of its various information or knowledge services offered to its physical members. Thereby, the author has examined in this chapter a specific story in the WISE community, and presented some

perspectives on the de-marginalized aspects of building virtual communities.

In closing the discussion, it is essential to articulate the challenge of knowledge networking in virtual communities. In the broadest sense, the major theme of knowledge networking in and among virtual communities could be understood from the perspective of effectively applying information and communications technologies (ICTs) to improve the lives of local people in different locales, in terms of getting knowledge to those of a community who need it in the right amount of time.

Of much concern here is an effort to theorize the social dimensions of ICT-based knowledge networking. In the words of David Hakken (2002, p. 362), it has to be asked: "What kinds of theorizations make sense in analyzing what happens when a concerted effort is made to introduce a technology supportive of knowledge networking in a *holistic* way — that is, to try to anticipate and address the social context/consequences of the interventions?" In simpler terms, it can be said, while a community network is based upon technology, its success rests with its people — organizers, information and knowledge providers, sponsors, users, volunteers — who support the virtual community in a variety of ways.

Most importantly, it must be ensured that a level playing field exists between the *haves* and the *have-nots*: those who have access to technology and those who do not. These underserved members of the community include those who are poor, uneducated, members of minority groups, elderly, or those with disabilities. But providing access to technology to these groups is not sufficient. It must be ensured further that no discrepancy exists between those who are computer literate and those who are not: the so-called *cans* and *cannots*. This is especially important as more and more information goes online and may not be available in any other format.

REFERENCES

Allen, C. (1993). Reciprocal evolution as a strategy for integrating basic research, design, and studies of work practices. In D. Shuler & A. Namioka (Eds.), *Participatory design* (pp. 239-253). Hillsdale, NJ: Lawrence Erlbaum.

Bajjaly, S. T. (1999). *The community networking handbook*. Chicago and London: American Library Association.

Bedny'i, G. Z., & Meister, D. (1997). *The Russian theory of activity: Current applications to design and learning*. Mahwah, NJ: Lawrence Erlbaum.

Bodker, S. (1991). *Through the interface: A human activity approach to user interface design*. Hillsdale, NJ: Lawrence Erlbaum.

Brown, A. L. (1992). Design experiments: Theoretical and methodological challenges in creating complex interventions in classroom settings. *The Journal of the Learning Sciences, 2*(2), 141-178.

Cherny, L. (1999). *Conversation and community: Chat in a virtual world*. Stanford, CA: CSLI Publications.

Chi, M. T. H., Lewis, M. W., Reimann, P., & Glaser, R. (1989). Self-explanations: How students study and use examples in learning to solve problems. *Cognitive Science, 13*, 145-182.

Cohill, A. M., & Kavanaugh, A. L. (1997). *Community networks: Lessons from Blacksburg, Virginia*. Norwood, MA: Artech House.

Cortada, J. W., & Woods, J. A. (Eds.). (2000). *The knowledge management yearbook 2000-2001*. Butterworth-Heinemann.

Cuthbert, A., Clark, D., & Linn, M. C. (2002). WISE learning communities: Design considerations. In K. A. Renninger & W. Shumar (Eds.), *Building virtual communities: Learning and change in Cyberspace* (pp. 215-246). Cambridge, UK: Cambridge University Press.

Cuthbert, A., Clark, D., Slotta, J., & Jorde, D. (2000). Helping elicit self-explanation and clarification through personalized electronic discussions. In *Proceedings of the Annual Meeting of the America Research Association (AERA)*. New Orleans.

Davis, B. H., & Brewer, J. (1997). *Electronic discourse: Linguistic individuals in virtual space*. Albany, NY: State University of New York Press.

DiSessa, A. A., & Minstrell, J. (1998). Cultivating conceptual change with benchmark lessons. In J. G. Greeno & S. Goldman (Eds.), *Thinking practices* (pp. 155-187). Mahwah, NJ: Lawrence Erlbaum.

Ehn, P. (1989). *Work-oriented design of computer artifacts*. Stockholm: Arbetslivscentrum.

Garratt, B. (1987). *The learning organization: And the need for directors who think*. Aldershot, Hampshire, England: Ashgate.

Gay, G., & Bennigton, T. L. (Eds.). (1999). *Information technologies in evaluation: Social, moral, epistemological, and practical implications. New Directions for Evaluations #84*. San Francisco: Jossey-Bass.

Gibson, J. J. (1966). *The senses considered as perceptual systems*. Boston: Houghton Mifflin.

Hakken, D. (2002). Building our knowledge of virtual community: Some responses. In K.A. Renninger & W. Shumar (Eds.), *Building virtual communities: Learning and change in cyberspace* (pp. 355-367). Cambridge, UK: Cambridge University Press

Herring, S. (1996). Posting in a different voice: Gender and ethics in computer-mediated communication. In C. Ess (Ed.), *Philosophical approaches to computer-mediated communication* (pp. 115-145). Albany, NY: State University of New York Press.

Hoadley, C., & Pea, R. D. (2002). Finding the ties that bind: Tools in support of a knowledge-building community. In K. A. Renninger & W. Shumar (Eds.), *Building virtual communities: Learning and change in cyberspace* (pp. 321-354). Cambridge, UK: Cambridge University Press.

Hoadley, C. (1999). *Scaffolding scientific discussion using socially relevant representations in networked multimedia.* Unpublished doctoral dissertation, University of California, Berkeley.

Hoadley, C., & Linn, M. C. (2000). Teaching science through online peer discussions: Speak-Easy in the knowledge integration environment. *International Journal of Science Education, 22*(8), 839-858.

Hsi, S. H. (1997). *Facilitating knowledge integration in science through electronic discussion: The multimedia forum kiosk.* Unpublished doctoral dissertation, University of California, Berkeley.

Kuutti, K., & Bannon, L. J. (1993). Searching for unity among diversity: Exploring the "interface" concept. In *Proceedings of the International Computer Human Interaction Conference (Inter CHI '93)* (pp. 263-268). New York: ACM Press.

Lave, J., & Wenger, E. (1992). *Situated learning: Legitimate peripheral participation.* Cambridge, UK: Cambridge University Press.

Lazar, J., & Preece, J. (1998). Classification schema for online communities. In *Proceedings of the 1998 Association for Information Systems, Americas Conference.*

Levine, L. (2001, Winter). Integrating knowledge and processes in a learning organization. *Information Systems Management,* 21-32.

Linn, M. C. (2000). Designing the knowledge integration environment: The partnership inquiry process. *International Journal of Science Education, 22*(8), 781-796.

Linn, M. C., & Hsi, S. (2000). *Computers, teachers, peers: Science learning partners.* Mahwah, NJ: Lawrence Erlbaum.

Linn, M. C., & Slotta, J. D. (2000). WISE curriculum projects: Bridging the gap between educational research and classroom customization. *Educational Leadership, 58*(2), 29-33.

Mollison, B. (1990). *Permaculture: A practical guide for a sustainable future.* Washington, DC: Island Press.

Newman, D., Griffin, P., & Cole, M. (1989). *The construction zone: Working for cognitive change in school.* New York: Cambridge University Press.

Pea, R. D. (1992). Augmenting the discourse of learning with computer-based learning environments In E. De Corte, M. Linn, H. Mandl, & L. Verschaffel (Eds.), *Computer-based learning environments and problem solving* (pp. 313-343). New York: Springer-Verlag.

Pea, R. D. (1993). Seeing what we build together: Distributed multimedia learning environments for transformative communications. *Journal of the Learning Sciences, 3*(3), 285-299.

Preece, J. (2000). *Online communities: Designing usability, supporting sociability.* Chichester: John Wiley & Sons.

Renninger, K. A. (2000). Individual interest and its implications for understanding intrinsic motivation. In C. Sansone & J.M. Harackiewicz (Eds.), *Intrinsic and extrinsic motivation: The search for optimal motivation and performance* (pp. 373-404). New York: Academic.

Rheingold, H. (1994). The virtual community. Retrieved December 31, 2004, from http://www.rheingold.com/vc/book/

Scardamalia, M., & Bereiter, C. (1994). Computer support for knowledge-building communities.

Journal of the Learning Sciences, 3(3), 265-283.

Schuler, D. (1996). *New community networks: Wired for change.* Reading, MA: ACM Press and Addison-Wesley.

Senge, P. (1990). *The fifth discipline: The art and practice of the learning organization.* London: Currency Doubleday.

Slotta, J., & Linn, M. C. (2000). How do students make sense of Internet resources in the science classroom? In M. J. Jacobson & R. Kozma (Eds.), *Learning the sciences of the 21ˢᵗ century* (pp. 193-226). Mahwah, NJ: Lawrence Erlbaum.

Stalk, G., Jr., Evans, E., & Shulman, L. E. (1992, March-April). Competing on capabilities: The new rules of corporate strategy. *Harvard Business Review.*

The Complete Oxford English Dictionary. (1971). Oxford: Oxford University Press.

Tudge, J., & Rogdoff, B. (1989). Peer influences on cognitive development: Piagetian and Vygotskian perspectives. In M. H. Bornstein & J. S. Bruner (Eds.), *Interaction in human development* (pp. 17-40). Hillsdale, NJ: Lawrence Erlbaum.

Vygotsky, L. S. (1978). *Mind in society: The development of higher psychological processes* (M. Cole, V. John-Stenier, S. Scribner, & E. Souberman, Trans.). Cambridge, MA: Harvard University Press.

Wenger, E. (1998). *Communities of practice: Learning, meaning, and identity.* Cambridge, MA: Cambridge University Press.

Wenger, E., McDermott, R., & Snyder, W. M. (2002). *Cultivating communities of practice: A guide to managing knowledge.* Boston: Harvard Business School Press.

Williams, R. (1973). *Keywords.* Oxford: Oxford University Press.

Woodruff, E. E. (1999). Concerning the cohesive nature of CSCL communities. In C. M. Hoadley & J. Roschelle (Eds.), *Proceedings of Computer Supported Collaborative Learning '99 Conference* (pp. 677-680). Mahwah, NJ: Lawrence Erlbaum.

KEY TERMS

Community Network: A term often used to refer to a networked community of people (or a virtual community), with subsequent emphasis on three more elements of concerns besides the people: (1) a shared purpose, such as an interest, need, information exchange, or service that provides a reason for the community; (2) policies, in the form of tacit assumptions, rituals, protocols, rules, and laws that guide people's interactions; (3) computer systems, to support and mediate social interaction and facilitate a sense of togetherness.

De-Marginalization: A term often used to squarely offset the idea of marginalization, which often means the minimal effect rendered to influence the whole, given the marginal position of the issue in consideration.

Knowledge Networking: An emergent activity of people or an organization to share knowledge in a way that makes it easier for individuals, teams, and enterprises to work together (or collaborate) to effectively contribute to one another's success in today's Internet-based knowledge society.

Virtual Community: A group of people — be they geographically localized or dispersed — who hold something in common, or who share a common sense of identity, through maintaining some types of social interaction over some electronic medium, such as the Internet and the World Wide Web.

Virtualization: A term often used to describe the electronic transformation of some organization in today's Internet era, such as in the context of people's transitioning from a physical bricks-and-mortar village to an electronic clicks-and-mortar experience.

This work was previously published in Empowering Marginal Communities with Information Networking, edited by H. Rahman, pp. 278-299, copyright 2006 by IGI Publishing, formerly known as Idea Group Publishing (an imprint of IGI Global).

Chapter XVIII
A Basis for the Semantic Web and E-Business:
Efficient Organization of Ontology Languages and Ontologies

Changqing Li
National University of Singapore, Singapore

Tok Wang Ling
National University of Singapore, Singapore

ABSTRACT

This chapter introduces how to effectively organize ontology languages and ontologies and how to efficiently process semantic information based on ontologies. In this chapter we propose the hierarchies to organize ontology languages and ontologies. Based on the hierarchy of ontology languages, the ontology designers need not bear in mind which ontology language the primitives exactly come from, also we can automatically and seamlessly use the ontologies defined with different ontology languages in an integrated environment. Based on the hierarchy of ontologies, the conflicts in different ontologies are resolved, thus the semantics in different ontologies are clear without ambiguities. Also, these semantic-clear ontologies can be used to efficiently process the semantic information in Semantic Web and e-business.

INTRODUCTION

The Extensible Markup Language (XML) (Bray et al., 2004) developed by the World Wide Web Consortium (W3C) has recently emerged as a new standard for data representation and exchange on the Internet. However, the information exchange based on XML is at the syntactic level (Garshol & Moore, 2004). Nowadays, how to process and exchange semantic information becomes very important. Semantic Web and e-business are two important applications which need to process the semantic information. *Semantic Web* (Lee, 1999) means that the Web pages are annotated with the *concepts* (terms and relationships) from sharing ontologies; because Web information refers to the sharing ontologies, computers can automatically understand and process the semantic information. Similarly, when different partners (agents) of e-business refer to the sharing concepts in ontologies, they can semantically communicate with each other. This is a *semantic e-business* which is different from the traditional e-business. To process the semantic information, the traditional e-business is a person-to-person communication; now with ontologies the semantic communication of e-business partners is an agent-to-agent communication.

It can be seen that ontologies play a core role in processing semantic information. An *ontology* defines the basic terms and relationships comprising the vocabulary of a topic area, as well as the rules for combining terms and relationships to define extensions to the vocabulary (Gruber, 1993). How to organize ontologies and clearly define the semantics in ontologies are very important. Presently, the ontologies are built by different organizations for their own purposes, therefore we need to effectively organize different ontologies together with hierarchies, then the concepts of the ontologies can be efficiently used to annotate Web pages and e-business agents, and semantic information can be efficiently processed based on the well-organized ontologies.

To define ontologies, *ontology languages* are required. Ontolingua (Gruber, 1992) is an ontology interchange language which was proposed to support the design of ontologies. Loom (MacGregor, 1991), a knowledge representation system, is used to provide deductive support. We will further introduce the XML-based ontology languages in the "Background" section.

In this chapter, we propose hierarchies to effectively organize ontology languages and ontologies and discuss how to efficiently process semantic information in Semantic Web and e-business.

The rest of this chapter is organized as follows. In the "Background" section, we introduce the background and the motivation of this chapter. In the "Ontology Language Organization" section, the hierarchy to organize ontology languages is proposed. We propose the hierarchy to organize ontologies and discuss how to resolve the conflicts in the ontology hierarchy in the "Building Ontology System" section. How to efficiently process the semantic information in the Semantic Web and e-business is discussed in the "Semantic Information Processing in the Semantic Web and E-Business" section. In the "Conclusion" section, we summarize this chapter.

BACKGROUND

Some comparisons have been done to compare different ontology languages. Although XML(S) has no semantics, it may help bootstrap the development of content and tools for the Semantic Web (Gil & Ratnakar, 2002). Another comparison (Gomez-Perez & Corcho, 2002) about ontology languages is from three aspects, that is, (1) general issues (partitions and documentation), (2) attributes (instance attributes, class attributes, local scope, and global scope), and (3) facets (default value, type constraints, cardinality constraints, and documentation). The existing works are mainly about comparing different ontology languages, then choosing the best ontology language to use. Different from the existing works, this chapter is mainly about how to organize ontology languages and ontologies with hierarchies, therefore we mainly compare the changes of primitives in different ontology languages. From these changes, we can find the change trends of ontology languages, then it is motivated, that is, it is very important to effectively organize different ontology languages.

The Simple HTML Ontological Extensions (SHOE) (Luke & Heflin, 2000) extends HTML with machine-readable knowledge annotated, thus the implicit semantic information can be discovered by a computer. Although SHOE has the XML version, it is not based on the Resource Description Framework (RDF) (Lassila & Swick, 2004) and RDF Schema (RDFS) (Brickley & Guha, 2004).

RDF (Lassila & Swick, 2004) is a standard language of W3C for defining ontologies. RDF defines a simple model for describing relationships among resources in terms of properties and values. A resource represents anything specified by a uniform resource identifier (URI) (Lee, Fielding, & Masinter, 1998). Properties are the attributes of resources, which have either atomic entities (strings, numbers, etc.) or other resources as their values. For a person to understand the semantics of a sentence, a sentence is organized in a subject-verb-object (SVO) form. Similarly, the fundamental design pattern of RDF is to structure data as resource-property-resource triples. Here, resource can represent both subject and object in the SVO form, while property (relationship between resources) represents the verb in the SVO form. Thus, the RDF files can be processed semantically. An RDF model can be represented in three ways, namely, graph syntax, triple syntax, and RDF/XML syntax. In this chapter, we focus on the XML representation of RDF.

RDF organizes information in the SVO form, but it does not define the many standard *primitives* (see Table 1) required to construct ontologies. Thus, RDFS (Brickley & Guha, 2004) is created to provide some more basic primitives, such as "subClassOf" and "subPropertyOf" (to represent the relationships between classes or properties).

More semantic-rich primitives are added into the successors of RDFS, namely, U.S. Defense Advanced Research Projects (DARPA) DARPA Agent Markup Language (DAML) (Popp, 2000), Ontology Inference Layer (OIL) (Horrocks et al., 2001), DAML+OIL (Connolly et al., 2001a), and Web Ontology Language (OWL) (Harmelen et al., 2004).

DAML (Popp, 2000), which is funded by DARPA aims at developing a language to facilitate the semantic concepts and relationships understood by machines. The DAML language is based on RDF and RDFS.

OIL (Horrocks et al., 2001), from the On-To-Knowledge Project, is an ontology representation language that extends RDF and RDFS with additional language primitives not yet presented in RDF and RDFS.

Now the latest extension of DAML is DAML+OIL (Connolly et al., 2001b), which has some important features of OIL imported into DAML. Presently, DAML+OIL is evolving as OWL (Harmelen et al., 2004), and OWL is being promoted as the Web ontology language of W3C. OWL is almost same as DAML+OIL, but some primitives of DAML+OIL are renamed in OWL for more easily understanding.

In the "Hierarchy and Primitives of RDF and RDFS-Based Ontology Languages" section, we illustrate the hierarchies of the RDF-based ontology languages, and we compare the primitive differences among different ontology languages. Note that a primitive is a basic term in ontology languages that is used to define ontologies. In the "Motivation" section, we introduce the motivation of this chapter.

Hierarchy and Primitives of RDF and RDFS-Based Ontology Languages

RDF and RDFS are the ground of DAML, OIL, DAML+OIL, and OWL. In Table 1, we list some primitives of RDF and RDFS.

RDF and RDFS define some basic primitives, and these primitives are not capable of describing many other important concepts and relationships, for example, equivalentClass, therefore DAML, OIL, DAML+OIL, and OWL extend RDF and RDFS by adding some new primitives. In Table 2, we compare the primitive differences among DAML, OIL, DAML+OIL, and OWL. We summarize the differences into several cases, and for

Table 1. Some primitives of RDF and RDFS

Category	Primitives	Comment
RDF	rdf:ID	Used to identify a class or property or any other resources
	rdf:resource	Used to refer to a resource; a resource represents anything specified by a URI
	rdf:Property	To define a property; the first letter of a property ID is in lower case
	rdf:Bag	An unordered collection (set) of members
	rdf:Seq	An ordered collection (set) of members
	rdf:Alt	A collection (set) of alternatives of members
RDFS	rdfs:Class	To define a Class; the first letter of a class ID is in capital
	rdfs:label	To provide a human-readable version of a resource name
	rdfs:comment	To provide a human-readable description
	rdfs:domain	To restrict the domain of a property
	rdfs:range	To restrict the range of a property
	rdfs:subClassOf	To indicate the specialization of a class
	rdfs:subPropertyOf	To indicate the specialization of a property
	rdfs:Container	Super class of rdf:Bag, rdf:Seq and rdf:Alt

Table 2. Primitive differences among DAML, OIL, DAML+OIL, and OWL

OIL	DAML	DAML+OIL	OWL	Comment
(1) Primitives included in all the four languages				
Class	Class	Class	Class	used to define class
inverseRelationOf	inverseOf	inverseOf	inverseOf	if P1(x,y) then P2(y,x)
FunctionalProperty	UniqueProperty	UniqueProperty	FunctionalProperty	if P(x,y) and P(x,z) then y=z
(2) Primitives not included in OIL, but included in the other three languages				
	sameClassAs	sameClassAs	equivalentClass	C1 = C2
	samePropertyAs	samePropertyAs	equivalentProperty	P1 = P2
(3) New primitives added in DAML+OIL, used by OWL				
		ObjectProperty	ObjectProperty	relates Resource to Resource
		DatatypeProperty	DatatypeProperty	relates Resource to Literal or data type
(4) OIL primitives not used by DAML+OIL, but used by OWL				
SymmetricProperty			SymmetricProperty	if P(x, y), then P(y, x)

each case, we only list a few primitives which satisfy this case. Cases: (1) primitives included in all the four languages; (2) primitives not included in OIL, but included in the other three languages; (3) new primitives added in DAML+OIL, used by OWL; and (4) OIL primitives not used by DAML+OIL, but used by OWL. The four different cases indicate the primitive relationships among different ontology languages.

Now we discuss how to define an ontology based on ontology languages.

Example 1. Consider a simple Person ontology shown in Figure 2. The start tag "<rdf:RDF>" at line 1 and the end tag "</rdf:RDF>" at line 16 show that this ontology complies with the RDF syntax. Lines 1-4 specify some XML namespace declarations (Bray, Hollander, & Layman, 1999), then we can use "rdf" to refer to the primitives defined in the URL "http://www.w3.org/1999/02/22-rdf-syntax-ns#" (similarly for other namespaces). The namespace "xsd" at line 4 is used to refer to XML Schema in which some data types are defined. Lines 5-8 define a class "Person" using the primitive of OWL, "owl:Class". Also we can see from lines 6 and 7 that primitives "label" and "comment" are from RDFS, therefore there is a namespace "rdfs" before "label" and "comment", that is, "rdfs:label" and "rdfs:comment". Lines 9-12 define a data type property ("owl: DatatypeProperty") "office_phone"; similarly we can define other properties for person, for example, "name", and so forth. Lines 13-15 define a property "contact_number" which is equivalent to the "home_phone".

Remark 1. The "Person" at line 5 is an original definition, while the "Person" at line 10 has a hash mark "#" before which means the "Person" at line 10 is a reference. There is no namespace (URL) before "#Person" at line 10 because "Person" is defined in the same file as "office_phone". Because the "string" data type is defined in XML Schema (not in the same file as "Person") and the

Figure 1. The hierarchy of the RDF-based ontology languages

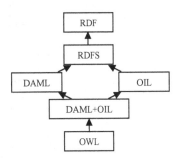

namespace of XML Schema is "xsd", there is an "xsd" before "#string" at line 11.

Remark 2. The first character of a class name is in uppercase, for example, the "P" in "Person" is in uppercase. The first character of a property name is in lowercase, for example, the first "o" in "office_phone" is in lowercase.

A *concept* is a term defined in ontologies which includes both the resources (entities) and the properties (relationships). For example, the "Person," "office_phone," and "contact_number" after the "rdf:ID" in Figure 2 are all called concepts.

Motivation

Figure 1 shows the hierarchy of different ontology languages, and from Example 1, we know that the primitives of RDF, RDFS, and OWL are used together to define an ontology. OWL is a replacement of DAML, OIL, and DAML+OIL, therefore the primitives of DAML, OIL, and DAML+OIL do not appear in the definition of an ontology which is defined with OWL. However, this is only an example which is defined now with the OWL. In practice, before OWL appears, a lot of ontologies have already been defined with ontology languages DAML, OIL, and DAML+OIL. Can we still use those ontologies defined with DAML, OIL, and DAML+OIL in the current OWL environment? The answer is yes, in this chapter, we clearly define the hierarchy and the

Figure 2. A Person_Ontology represented using OWL language

```
<rdf:RDF  xmlns:rdf ="http://www.w3.org/1999/02/22-rdf-syntax-ns#"
          xmlns:rdfs="http://www.w3.org/2000/01/rdf-schema#"
          xmlns:owl="http://www.w3.org/2002/07/owl#"
             xmlns:xsd="http://www.w3.org/2000/10/XMLSchema#">
   <owl:Class rdf:ID="Person">
     <rdfs:label>Person</rdfs:label>
     <rdfs:comment>Person is a specific kind of animal.</rdfs:comment>
   </owl:Class>
   <owl:DatatypeProperty rdf:ID="office_phone">
     <rdfs:domain rdf:resource="#Person"/>
     <rdfs:range rdf:resource="xsd#string"/>
   </owl:DatatypeProperty>
   <owl:DatatypeProperty rdf:ID="contact_number">
     <owl:euqivalentProperty rdf:resource="#office_phone"/>
   </owl:DatatypeProperty>
   ...
   ...
</rdf:RDF>
```

relationships among different ontology languages, and this hierarchy enables us to automatically use the previous ontologies defined with DAML, OIL, and DAML+OIL.

The second problem about the ontology language is that the primitives from different ontology languages should be used together to define the ontology. For example, from Example 1 and Figure 2, we can see that "rdf:ID", "rdfs:label", and "owl:Class" are used together to define the concepts in ontologies. However, it will be a burden for the ontology designer to bear in mind which ontology language the primitives are exactly from. Can we just use single namespace to refer to all the primitives, and the system can automatically translate the namespace to the proper namespaces, for example, the ontology designer can use "owl" as the namespace to refer to all the primitives, that is, "owl:ID", "owl:ID", and "owl:Class", and the system can automatically translate them back to "rdf:ID", "rdfs:label", and "owl:Class"? The answer is yes. In this chapter, we clearly define the relationships of the primitives in different ontology languages, and this will help to translate the single namespace to the proper namespaces. In this way, the efficiency of the ontology design can be improved.

Moreover, the ontologies are presently designed by different organizations for their own purposes. If we can organize all of these ontologies in an integrated environment, we can improve the usability of ontologies, and the semantic information in the Semantic Web and e-business can be processed more efficiently.

ONTOLOGY LANGUAGE ORGANIZATION

In this chapter, we mainly focus on the theoretical analysis of organizing ontology languages and ontologies with hierarchies, so that this method can be widely used to organize different ontology languages and ontologies, though we implement a prototype tool to organize ontology languages and ontologies in the "Architecture" section.

There already exist practical tools, for example, Daml2owl (Amin & Morbach, 2005), and so forth, that allow the translation from one language to another, but these tools are not general ones. They can only be used to translate between two specific ontology languages; however, our method is a general one, which can be used to organize all the existing ontology languages as well as the future coming ontology languages. This is the most important benefit of our approach over prior works.

In the "Operations to Organize Ontologies" section, we define some operations which can be used to describe the relationships among the primitives in different ontology languages. Based on these operations, in the "Easy Use of Ontology Languages" section, we show how to automatically use the existing ontologies defined with DAML, OIL, and DAML+OIL and show how to automatically translate the namespace to the proper namespaces.

Operations to Organize Ontologies

We use the following operations to describe the relationships among the ontology languages and the primitives in ontology languages, that is, inheritance, block, atavism, and mutation.

We use "gmoe" as the namespace before each operation. "gmoe" represents "Genetic Model for Ontology (language) Engineering", because these operations are borrowed from genetics.

Inheritance

The inheritance relationships of ontology languages can be seen in Figure 1. RDFS inherits RDF; DAML and OIL inherit RDFS; DAML+OIL

inherits both DAML and OIL; and OWL inherits DAML+OIL. The following example shows how to use the inheritance operation to define the relationships between two ontology languages.

Example 2. As we know, DAML+OIL inherits both DAML and OIL. We use the inheritance operation shown in Figure 3 to indicate the inheritance relationship. With the inheritance operation, we need not copy the primitives in DAML and OIL into DAML+OIL. In DAML+OIL we only need to define the new primitives which can not be inherited from DAML and OIL.

Block

It is not enough to indicate the relationships among ontology languages with the inheritance operation only. Some primitives in previous ontology languages are not used by later ontology languages. We need to use the block operation to reflect this relationship. The following example shows how to use the block operation.

Example 3. From Figure 1, we know that DAML+OIL inherits the primitives in both DAML and OIL, but the primitive "SymmetricProperty" of OIL is not used by DAML+OIL (see Table 2). We can use the block operation to indicate that this primitive is not used by DAML+OIL.

Figure 3. Definition of DAML+OIL based on inheritance operation

```
<rdf:RDF  xmlns:daml="http://www.daml.org/2000/10/daml-ont.daml#"
          xmlns:oil="http://www.ontoknowledge.org/oil/rdf-schema/2000/11/10-oil-standard#"
          gmoe:inheritance="daml, oil">
   ...
   ...
</rdf:RDF>
```

Figure 4. The use of block operation in DAML+OIL

```
<gmoe:block rdf:resource="oil#SymmetricProperty"/>
```

Atavism

We found that some primitives blocked by the child ontology languages are reused by the descendant ontology languages. To process this kind of relationships we borrow the atavism mechanism in genetics. *Atavism* means that the characteristics of the grandparent do not appear at the child generation, but appear at the grandchild generation or the offspring of grandchild. We use an example to show how to use the atavism operation to process the relationships of the primitives in ontology languages.

Example 4. The "SymmetricProperty" of OIL is blocked by its child DAML+OIL, but the grandchild OWL again includes this primitive (see Table 2). Without our atavism operation, the definition of "SymmetricProperty" of OIL has to be copied into OWL, but with our atavism operation we only need to indicate in OWL that the "SymmetricProperty" in OWL is an atavism of the "SymmetricProperty" in OIL which is shown in Figure 5.

Mutation or Override or Redefine

Furthermore, we use the mutation operation to describe the relationship that two primitives have the same name, but they have different semantics. See the following example.

Example 5. RDFS defines primitive "Class", and OWL also defines primitive "Class". Though the two "Classes" have the same name, they have different semantics; the "Class" in OWL permits greater expressiveness than the "Class" in RDFS. Thus the primitive "Class" in OWL mutates the "Class" in RDFS (see Figure 6).

Easy Use of Ontology Languages

In the "Operations to Organize Ontologies" section, we discuss how to describe the relationships among the primitives in different ontology languages based on different operations. Based on the relationship description in "Operations to Organize Ontologies," we can process the following two problems efficiently: (1) automatically use the existing ontologies defined with ontology languages DAML, OIL, and DAML+OIL; and (2) automatically translate single namespace to proper namespaces.

1. Using ontologies defined with ontology languages DAML, OIL, and DAML+OIL

Before OWL appeared many ontologies have been defined based on the ontology languages DAML, OIL, and DAML+OIL. Now DAML, OIL, and DAML+OIL are being replaced by OWL, but if we can automatically translate all the ontologies defined with DAML, OIL, and DAML+OIL to the ontologies defined with OWL,

Figure 5. Definition of "SymmetricProperty" in OWL based on atavism

```
<gmoe:atavism rdf:resource="oil#SymmetricProperty"/>
```

Figure 6. Definition of "Class" in OWL based on mutation operation

```
<gmoe:mutation rdf:resource="rdfs#Class"/>
```

we can save a lot of time in building new ontologies based on OWL.

Because we have described the relationships among different primitives in different ontology languages, we can automatically build a mapping between different primitives, thus the ontologies defined with DAML, OIL, and DAML+OIL can be automatically translated to the ontologies defined with OWL. We use the following example for illustration.

Example 6. Suppose that there is an ontology in which a concept is defined using the primitive "daml:inverseOf" in DAML. Because OWL *inherits* DAML, and there are no changes for this primitive in DAML and OWL (see Table 2), we can directly translate "daml:inverseOf" to "owl: inverseOf". Furthermore, if a concept is defined with the primitive "oil:SymmetricProperty" in OIL, we can translate it to "owl:SymmetricProperty" because the "SymmetricProperty" in OWL is an atavism of the "SymmetricProperty" in OIL. There are no primitives in DAML, OIL, and DAML+OIL, which are blocked or overrided in OWL, therefore we need not consider these two operations in translating the ontologies defined with DAML, OIL, and DAML+OIL to ontologies defined with OWL.

With this technique, we can automatically use all the existing ontologies which are defined using the ontology languages DAML, OIL, and DAML+OIL. Therefore less effort will be paid to build new ontologies based on OWL.

2. Using single namespace to refer to all primitives in different ontologies

From Example 1 and Figure 2, we know that the primitives in RDF, RDFS, and OWL should be used together to define an ontology. It will be a burden for the ontology designer to bear in mind where each primitive exactly comes from. Based on the organization of ontology languages in the "Operations to Organize Ontologies" section,

we can use single namespace to refer to all the primitives defined in different ontology languages, and we can automatically translate the single namespace to the proper namespaces.

Example 7. For the primitives "ID", "label", and "Class", the ontology designer can use them with the same namespace "owl", that is, "owl:ID", "owl:label", and "owl:Class". As we know from Figure 1, OWL inherits RDF and RDFS, thus we can search the "ID" primitive bottom up, that is, search OWL firstly, then RDFS, and then RDF. The "ID" primitive is found in RDF, therefore we change the "owl:ID" to "rdf:ID". Similarly the "owl:label" will be translated to "rdfs:label" when searching the ontology languages bottom up. For the primitive "Class", it is defined in both RDFS and OWL, and the "Class" in OWL is a mutation of the "Class" in RDFS. We will use the "owl: Class" rather than the "rdfs:Class", because the "Class" in OWL is an mutation and it is the latest one, and actually, all the ontologies are defined with "owl:Class" rather than "rdfs:Class".

The number of primitives in ontology languages is limited and their relationships are fixed, therefore based on the organization and relationship descriptions of ontology languages in the "Operations to Organize Ontologies" section, the translations in "Easy Use of Ontology Languages" section can be done without ambiguities.

BUILDING ONTOLOGY SYSTEM

In the "Ontology Language Organization" section, we describe the hierarchy of different ontology languages based on the inheritance, block, atavism, and mutation operations. These operations can also be applied to the ontology building.

As we know, the ontologies are now built by different organizations for their own purposes. It is important to organize these ontologies together in an integrated environment, then the semantic information in one domain is more complete. Only when the semantics in one domain are all defined clearly, it is true that the semantic information in Semantic Web and e-business can be processed correctly.

In this section, we firstly discuss how to organize ontologies based on the operations discussed in "Ontology Language Organization." Also we summarize the guidelines for organizing ontologies, that is, different information should be put at different hierarchies of ontologies. Furthermore, different from primitives in ontology languages, which will not change, the concepts in ontologies will change. When inserting or deleting a concept in ontologies, we should keep the ontologies consistent, otherwise it will hurt the ontologies to provide sharing information. Hence, we also discuss how to resolve the conflicts in ontology organizations.

Architecture

To make easy the use of inheritance, block, atavism, and mutation operations discussed in the "Ontology Language Organization" section, we build a graphical tool to implement these operations in ontology building. This tool can be applied to ontologies as well as ontology languages.

Example 8. Figure 7 shows that, there exists a Person_Ontology, and we need to build a Student_Ontology. Then in the "Parent Ontologies" frame, we select the "Person_Ontology", and in the "Child or grandchild Ontologies" frame, we input the ontology name "Student" and the namespace "stu" for this Student_Ontology. When clicking the "Inheritance" button, a simple Student_Ontology is automatically created which will be shown in the right "Codes" frame. In addition, as we select the "Person_Ontology" in the "Parent Ontologies" frame, all the concepts of "Person_Ontology" will be listed in the "Select Concepts" combo in the "Parent Ontologies" frame (some concepts of "Person_Ontology" are defined in Figure 2), then we can select one concept, and by clicking the "Block" button, a certain concept of the parent ontology is blocked in the child ontology. Also, after selecting a concept from the parent ontology and clicking the "Mutation" button, we can indicate that certain concept of the parent ontology is mutated in the child ontology. From the right "Codes" frame of Figure 7, we can see that "office_phone" is blocked by Student_Ontology, and "contact_no" is mutated in Student_Ontology. If we click the "Save" button, the new Student_Ontology will be saved in a file; but if there are problems, we can roll back

Figure 7. A graphical tool for ontology language and ontology organization

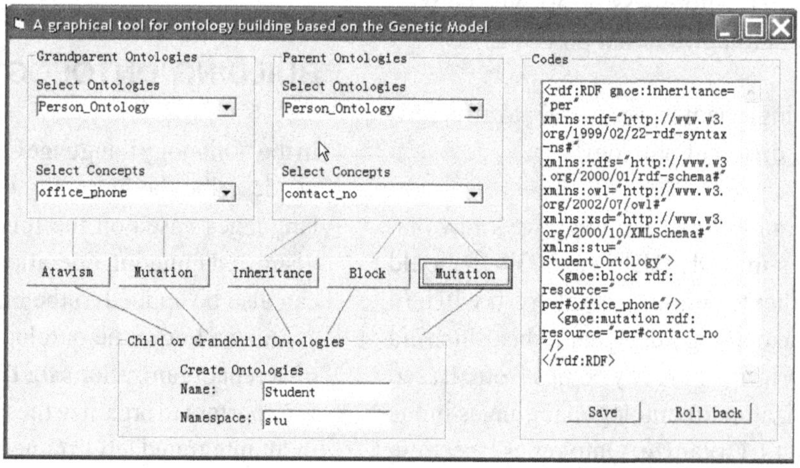

10 steps. When a new ontology is created, it will be automatically listed in the "Select Ontologies" combos of "Grandparent Ontologies" and "Parent Ontologies" frames. Similarly, we can use the atavism operation to indicate that some concepts of the grandparent ontology are atavismed in the grandchild ontology or in the offspring ontologies of the grandchild ontologies. Note that the "gmoe" in Figure 7 indicates that the operations in the "Ontology Language Organization" section are a genetic model.

This tool is a prototype to indicate that the inheritance, block, atavism, and mutation operations really work in organize ontology language and ontologies. This prototype tool can be further improved for commercial use.

Next we summarize the guidelines of how to organize information in ontologies, that is, different information should be put at different hierarchies of ontologies.

The general concepts in a domain should be put in the highest level ontologies, for example, O1 in Figure 8. Here O represents Ontologies. If some concepts are specific, they should be put in the lower level ontologies, for example, O2 and O3 in Figure 8. When some concepts are more specific, they should be put in even lower ontologies, for example, O4-O9 in Figure 8. Figure 8 shows the hierarchy of ontologies. We allow multiple inheritance in ontology organizations, for

example, O6 inherits both O2 and O3. In practice, the hierarchies can be more than three levels.

The hierarchy of ontologies is similar to the hierarchy of ontology languages. However, because the concepts in ontologies will change (add in, move out, and update), next we mainly discuss how to resolve the conflicts in ontology organizations.

Resolve Conflicts in Ontology Organization

Kalfoglou and Schorlemmer (2003) survey the related works on ontology mapping and indicate that most of the previous works are about finding the similarities and differences among ontologies, then the ontologies can be accessed from a common layer. There are no related works on resolving the conflicts in design ontologies. Here we discuss some techniques to resolve conflicts in designing ontologies with hierarchies.

When designing ontologies with hierarchies, it is important to keep the ontologies consistent. A concept is specified in an ontology if it is either defined or redefined for the ontology. A redefined concept overloads a similar concept in some ancestor ontologies. Figure 9 shows the hierarchies of ontologies. The O in Figure 9 represents ontologies which are displayed as rounded rectangles, and the C in Figure 9 rep-

Figure 8. Architecture of building ontology systems

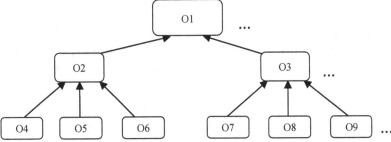

Figure 9. Conflicts in ontology design

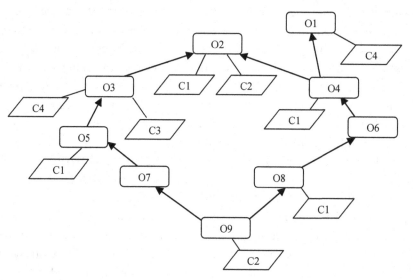

resents concepts defined in ontologies which are displayed as parallelograms.

In this section, we discuss how to resolve the conflicts. An inherited concept is well defined if it is specified in one and only one ancestor ontology, possibly indirect. A conflict situation exists when an inherited concept is not well defined, that is, two or more ancestor ontologies specify the same concept. For example, from Figure 9, we can see that concept C1 of ontology O2 is redefined in ontologies O4, O5, and O8. C1 contributes to a conflict situation in O9, but C3 is well defined in O9.

We have the following methods to solve the conflict problem.

Redefining (or Overriding)

The C2 in O9 and O2 in Figure 9 have the same name, thus it may be a conflict. However, if C2 in O9 is defined to override the C2 in O2, and redefined C2 with different meaning, then there are no conflicts.

Explicitly Selecting or Renaming

We use an example to show how to use explicitly selecting or renaming to solve conflicts.

Example 9. If the two C4 in O3 and O1 of Figure 9 have the different semantics, there will be a conflict in O9. To solve this conflict, we have two options. The first option has the ontology designer explicitly mention that the C4 in O9 is inherited from the C4 in O3. However, explicitly selecting has a problem, that is, some information will be lost. If O9 explicitly mentions that O9 uses the C4 in O3, the information of the C4 in O1 can not be inherited by O9, which is a loss of information. The second option to process this conflict is rename the C4 in either O3 or O9 or both; in this way, all the information can be kept without lost.

Redesigning the Organizations of Ontologies (e.g. Factoring)

We use the ontology hierarchies shown in Figure 10 to introduce this conflict resolving approach. The two Cs in ontologies O2 and O3 have the

Figure 10. Resolve conflicts by redesigning the organizations of ontologies

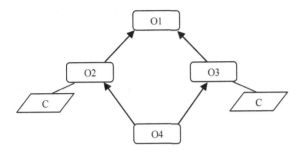

Figure 11. Factor to parent ontology

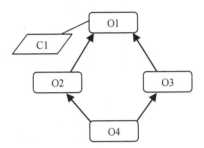

Figure 12. Factor to an intermediate level of ontology

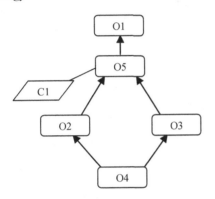

O5. Figure 12 shows this approach. In this way, the conflict can be resolved, and the C is at an appropriate level.

Algorithm to Resolve Conflicts

Figure 13 shows the algorithm to resolve conflicts, which is a formal summary of the cases in the "Resolve Conflicts in Ontology Organization" section.

With these conflict processing approaches, when inserting concepts into or deleting concepts from ontologies, we should be careful to make the ontologies consistent without conflicts (Ling & Teo, 1993).

SEMANTIC INFORMATION PROCESSING IN THE SEMANTIC WEB AND E-BUSINESS

The present Web exists in the HTML and XML formats for persons to browse. Recently there is a trend towards the Semantic Web where the information can be processed and understood by a computer. The present e-business also requires that the semantic information can be automatically exchanged among different agents of the e-business partners.

When the concepts in different ontologies are defined with *clear semantics* and *without conflicts*,

same semantics, and they have the same name. Obviously, there will be confusion when O4 inherits C from O2 and O3. In ontology design, the semantics of each concept in the ontology should be clear without any ambiguities because the concepts are shared by the Semantic Web or e-business applications for semantic information processing.

To process this conflict, there are two cases to consider.

1. If O1= O2 ∪ O3, Figure 11. shows that we can factor C to the parent ontology of Q2 and O3, that is, O1. In this way, O4 inherits concept C from a single ancestor ontology, therefore there are no conflicts.
2. If O1 ⊃ O2 ∪ O3, then we create ontology O5 such that O5 = O2 ∪ O3, and factor C to

Figure 13. Algorithm to resolve conflicts

```
Given ontologies with hierarchies
FOR each conflict situation in the hierarchy DO
        Let the conflict situation be ontologies A, B1, ..., Bn (n > 1) where B1, ..., Bn are
        the nearest ancestor ontologies of A that specify a property p.
        /* Note that a ancestor ontology of some Bi may itself specify a property p. */
        /* Check the semantics of p in B1, ..., Bn */
        IF semantics of p is the same in B1, ..., Bn THEN
                IF intersection of B1, ..., Bn is empty THEN
                    ***Design error, since ontology A (which is the intersection of B1, ..., Bn) is empty
                ELSE
                    ******/* same semantics (Factoring) */
                        IF there exists a more general ontology K which is UNION of B1, ..., Bn THEN
                            Factor p to ontology K
                        ELSE
                            Resolve the conflict by either:
                            (a) creating a general ontology K that is the UNION of B1, ..., Bn and
                                factoring p to K.
                            OR
                            (b) Explicitly choosing one parent ontology to inherit the property.
                        ENDIF
                ENDIF
        ELSE
                /* different semantics */
                Let G1, G2, ..., Gm be sets of mutually exclusive ontologies from B1, ..., Bn such
                that ontologies in a group share the same semantics for p. Resolve the conflict in A
                by adopting one of the following:
                (a) redefine p in ontology A, /* not a good solution */ or
                (b) Rename p in Gj to, say, p_Gj for j = 1, ..., m to reflect their different semantics.
                    To conform to the unique name assumption. Each p in the schema that has the
                    same semantics as P_Gj must be renamed to p_Gj.
                    FOR each group Gj (j = 1, ..., m) with 2 or more ontolgoies having property
                    p_Gj DO
                        /* An conflict situation exists between ontology A and the ontologies in Gj;*/
                        /* p_Gj has the same semantics in the ontologies of Gj */
                        Resolve the conflict in ontology A using the method described in *** and
                        ******.
                    ENDFOR
        ENDIF
ENDFOR
```

the sharing concepts in ontologies can be used to annotate the Semantic Web pages or the agents of the e-business partners. If the information in two different Semantic Web pages refers to the same concept from the same ontology, the information has the same semantics, otherwise the information is different in the two Semantic Web pages. This can be automatically recognized by the computer. It is similar for the semantic information processing in e-business.

We use an example to show how to achieve the automatically and semantically exchange of information.

Example 10. Figure 14 shows how to process the semantic information in Semantic Web and e-business applications based on the ontology hierarchy introduced in the "Building Ontology System" section. We consider the Semantic Web pages firstly. Semantic Webpage1 refers to ontologies O4, O5, and O7. Semantic Webpage2 refers to ontologies O5 and O3. If some information in Semantic Webpage1 is annotated with the concepts from O4, obviously Semantic Webpage2 has no such information corresponding to Semantic Webpage1, that is, Semantic Webpage1 is semantically different from Semantic Webpage2 for such information. If some information in Semantic Webpage1 is annotated by the concepts

Figure 14. Semantic information processing in Semantic Web and e-business

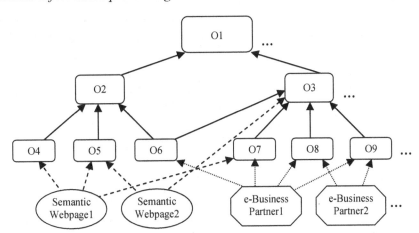

from O5, it is possible that Semantic Webpage1 and Semantic Webpage2 have the same semantic information because Semantic Webpage2 is also annotated with concepts from O5; they can exchange the semantic information. Semantic Webpage1 is annotated with the concepts from O7, Semantic Webpage2 is annotated with the concepts from O3, and we can see that O7 inherits O3. Therefore if Semantic Webpage1 is annotated with the concepts newly defined in O7, Semantic Webpage1 and Semantic Webpage2 do not have the same semantic information about the concepts in O7. If Semantic Webpage1 is annotated with the concepts in O7 which are inherited from O3, Semantic Webpage1 and Semantic Webpage2 may have the same semantic information about the concepts in O3. It is similar for the semantic information exchange among the e-business partners.

Because we organize ontologies with hierarchies, it is easy to find the appropriate concepts in ontologies (based on classifications and levels) to annotate the Semantic Web pages and the agents for e-business partners. Also, because of the hierarchy of ontologies, it is faster to process the semantic information, that is, it is faster to search and map the concepts in ontologies based on hierarchies; the search is only at several related

(related to the semantic information in semantic Web or e-business) paths of the ontology hierarchy, but not all the paths.

CONCLUSION

In this chapter, we discuss how to effectively organize ontology languages and ontologies and discuss how to efficiently process semantic information in Semantic Web and e-business. Figure 15 shows the whole framework to organize ontology languages, ontologies, and semantic applications (Semantic Web and e-business). The primitives in ontology languages organized with hierarchies are used to define ontologies, and the concepts in ontologies organized with hierarchies are used to annotate and process semantic information in Semantic Web pages and e-business.

More concretely, because we organize ontology language with hierarchies, we can automatically use the existing ontologies defined with ontology languages DAML, OIL, and DAML+OIL. Our architecture can help to translate the existing ontologies to ontologies defined with the latest ontology language—OWL. Furthermore, we can use single namespace to refer to all the primitives from different ontology languages, and our on-

Figure 15. Framework to organize ontology languages, ontologies and semantic applications

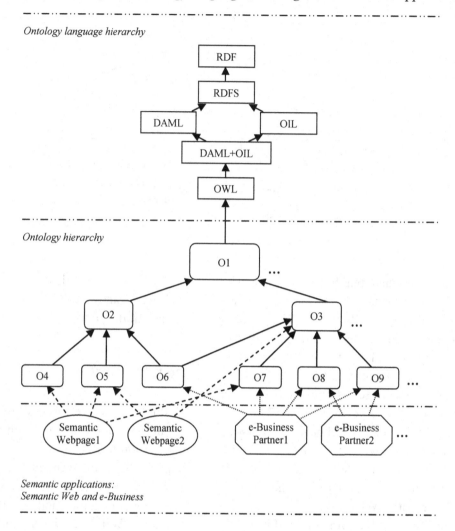

tology language hierarchies can help to translate the namespace to the proper namespaces. The ontology designer need not bear in mind which ontology language the primitive exactly comes from. With these techniques, the efficiency of ontology building will be improved.

We also organize ontologies with hierarchies and we discuss some techniques to process the conflicts in ontology design. Consistent and semantic clear ontologies are very important to semantic information processing. The integrated environment of ontology organizations makes the semantics in a domain clear.

Based on the hierarchy of ontologies, the Web pages of Semantic Web and the agents for e-business partners can be easily annotated, and the semantic information processing can be processed efficiently.

REFERENCES

Amin, M. A., & Morbach, J. (2005). *The DAML+OIL to OWL converter.* Retrieved July 10, 2005, from http://www.lpt.rwth-aachen.de/ Research/OntoCAPE/daml2owl.php

Bray, T., Hollander, D., & Layman, A. (1999). *Namespaces in XML*. World Wide Web Consortium. Retrieved January 14, 1999, from http://www.w3.org/TR/REC-xml-names/

Bray, T., Paoli, J., Sperberg-McQueen, C. M., Maler, E., Yergeau, F., & Cowan, J. (2004). *Extensible markup language (XML) 1.1*. W3C recommendation. Retrieved February 4, 2004, from http://www.w3.org/TR/2004/REC-xml11-20040204/

Brickley, D., & Guha, R. V. (2004). *Resource description framework schema (RDFS) specification 1.0*. W3C Recommendation. Retrieved February 10, 2004, from http://www.w3.org/TR/rdf-schema/

Connolly, D., Harmelen, F. V., Horrocks, I., McGuinness, D., Patel-Schneider, P. F., & Stein, L. A. (2001a). *Annotated DAML+OIL ontology markup*. W3C note. Retrieved December 18, 2001, from http://www.w3.org/TR/daml+oil-walkthru/

Connolly, D., Harmelen, F. V., Horrocks, I., McGuinness, D., Patel-Schneider, P. F., & Stein, L. A. (2001b, March). *DAML+OIL reference description*. W3C Note. Retrieved April 11, 2001, from http://www.daml.org/2001/03/reference.html

Garshol, L. M., & Moore, G. (2004). *Topic maps—XML syntax*. Retrieved March 16, 2004, from http://www.jtc1sc34.org/repository/0495.htm

Gil, Y., & Ratnakar, V. (2002). *A comparison of (semantic) markup languages*. In M. S. Haller & G. Simmons (Eds.), *Proceedings of the 15th International FLAIRS Conference, Special Track on Semantic Web*, Pensacola, FL (pp. 413-418). AAAI Press.

Gomez-Perez, A., & Corcho, O. (2002). *Ontology languages for the Semantic Web. Intelligent Systems, IEEE, 17*(1), 54- 60.

Gruber, T. R. (1992). *Ontolingua: A mechanism to support portable ontologies* (Tech. Rep. No.

KSL-91-66). Standford Knowledge Systems Laboratory.

Gruber, T. R. (1993). *A translation approach to portable ontologies. Knowledge Acquisition, 5*(2), 199-220.

Harmelen, F. V., Hendler, J., Horrocks, I., McGuinness, D. L., Patel-Schneider, P. F., & Stein., L. A. (2004). *OWL Web ontology language reference*. W3C Recommendation. Retrieved February 10, 2004, from http://www.w3.org/TR/owl-ref/

Horrocks, I., Fensel, D., Broekstra, J., Decker, S., Erdmann, M., Goble, C., et al. (2001). *The ontology inference layer OIL*. Retrieved December 31, 2001, from http://www.ontoknowledge.org/oil/

Kalfoglou, Y., & Schorlemmer, M. (2003). *Ontology mapping: The state of the art. The Knowledge Engineering Review, 18*(1), 1-31.

Lassila, D. O., & Swick, R. (1999). *Resource description framework (RDF) model and syntax specification*. W3C Recommendation. Retrieved January 5, 1999, from http://www.w3.org/TR/PR-rdf-syntax/

Lee, T. B. (1999). *The SemanticWeb homepage*. Retrieved December 31, 1999, from http://www.semanticweb.org

Lee, T. B., Fielding, R., & Masinter, L. (1998, August). *Uniform resource identifiers (URI): Generic syntax*. IETF Draft Standard (RFC 2396). Retrieved August 31, 1998, from http://www.ietf.org/rfc/rfc2396.txt

Ling, T. W., & Teo, P. K. (1993). *Inheritance conflicts in object-oriented systems*. In V. Marík, J. Lazanský, & R. Wagner (Eds.), *Proceedings of Database and Expert Systems Applications* (LNCS 720, pp. 189-200). Prague, Czech Republic: Springer.

Luke, S., & Heflin, J. (2000, April 28). *SHOE specification 1.01*. Retrieved April 28, 2000, from

http://www.cs.umd.edu/projects/plus/SHOE/spec.
html

MacGregor, R. (1991). *Inside the LOOM description classifier. SIGART Bulletin, 2*(3), 88-92.

Popp, B. (2000). *The DARPA agent markup language homepage*. Retrieved September 1, 2000,
from http://daml.semanticweb.org/

*This work was previously published in Semantic Web Technologies and E-Business: Toward the Integrated Virtual Organiza-
tion and Business Process Automation, edited by A. Salam and J. Stevens, pp. 212-235, copyright 2007 by IGI Publishing,
formerly known as Idea Group Publishing (an imprint of IGI Global).*

Chapter XIX
User–Centered Design Principles for Online Learning Communities:
A Sociotechnical Approach for the Design of a Distributed Community of Practice

Ben K. Daniel
University of Saskatchewan, Canada

David O'Brien
University of Saskatchewan, Canada

Asit Sarkar
University of Saskatchewan, Canada

ABSTRACT

This chapter examines current research on online learning communities (OLCs), with the aim of identifying user-centered design (UCD) principles critical to the emergence and sustainability of distributed communities of practice (DCoPs), a kind of OLC. This research synthesis is motivated by the authors' involvement in constructing a DCoP dedicated to improving awareness, research, and sharing data and knowledge in the field of governance and international development. It argues that the sociotechnical research program offers useable insights on questions of constructability. Its attention in particular to participatory design and human-computer interaction are germane to designing user-centered online learning communities. Aside from these insights, research has yet to probe in any systematic fashion the factors affecting the performance and sustainability of DCoP. The chapter concludes with a discussion of UCD principles for online learning community to support the construction and deployment of online learning communities.

INTRODUCTION

Increasingly, distributed communities of practice (DCoPs) are attracting attention for their potential to enhance learning, to facilitate information exchange, and to stimulate knowledge creation across cultural, geographical, and organizational boundaries. Research shows the utility of DCoP on their members is positive (Daniel, Sarkar, & O'Brien, 2004a; Daniel, Poon, & Sarkar, 2005; Schwier & Daniel, Chapter II, this volume). Their allure aside, experience indicates that they may not emerge or flourish even in the presence of demand from users. In fact the process of constructing DCoP is not well understood, and factors influencing sustainability merit further research attention.

This chapter introduces the authors' involvement in the development of a DCoP. The DCoP in question is the Governance Knowledge Network (GKN). This project began in 2001 with the aim of assessing the interest of academics and practitioners in Canada to develop an online learning community (OLC) for systematizing the exchange of information at the intersection of governance and international development (Daniel et al., 2004a). The surveys of key Canadian stakeholders in the project indicated considerable data existed, and recommended the proposed GKN to: actively engage in dissemination and archiving of data not widely accessible in the public sphere, profile community members, promote social network building and collaboration, and inform members of current events and opportunities.

Following the identification of the demand and interest, the second stage of our research involved the development of a GKN prototype. In this unchartered course, we were guided by enabling technology and other DCoP models (World Bank, UNDP).[1] We also turned to research to inform our efforts on how to effectively sustain the project. Our synthesis of research in the area identified promising insights from studies we refer to as the sociotechnical approach. As applied to DCoP,

the sociotechnical approach aims at understanding people's interaction with technology and the ensuing communication, feedback, and control mechanisms necessary for people to take ownership of the design and implementation process.

This chapter focuses on this interaction, as it is germane to the development and sustainability of the GKN, in particular, and DCoP more generally. The chapter is divided into the following sections. The next section outlines relevant research on DCoPs and the sociotechnical approach. We next provide an overview of the GKN OLC project and present key results from the research that informed the design of the GKN. A discussion of various human and technology elements we consider critical to the initiation, development, growth, and sustainability of the GKN follows, and in the next section, we revisit the key human and technology design issues. Finally, we conclude the chapter and present UCD principles for OLCs drawn from the sociotechnical approach.

RELATED WORK

Daniel, Schwier, and McCalla (2003b) observe that online learning communities have attracted diverse disciplinary interest, but that it is possible to identify two dominant perspectives—technological determinism and social constructivism. The basic tenet of the technology determinism research is that technology shapes cultural values, social structure, and knowledge. In technology-related fields, such as computer science and information systems, significant attention has been given to understanding technological developments and how these changes influence social structures.

The social constructivism perspective, on the other hand, posits that knowledge and world views are created through social interaction. Social constructivism theories have inspired research on knowledge construction within communities of practice. Lave and Wenger (1991) assert that a society's practical knowledge is situated in relations among practitioners, their practice, and the social organization and political economy of communities of practice. For this reason, learning should involve such knowledge and practice (Lave & Wenger, 1991). Between these heuristic poles there are cross-disciplinary perspectives, of which it is possible to further discern them into four subcategories:

1. **Applied Technology Perspective:** Much of the work on OLC by computer scientists and information systems researchers is driven by a desire to understand and improve computational approaches. Studies in computer science, information systems, and educational technologies are mainly aimed at understanding technology to develop tools and systems that support learning environments (Daniel, Zapata-Rivera, & McCalla, 2003a; Preece, 2002; Schwier, 2001). Findings have been utilized for building technologies that support OLC. For instance, a growing number of developers and researchers in industry and universities are investigating ways to create software packages that add new functionality to systems supporting interaction, collaboration, and leaning in online learning communities (Kim, 2000; McCalla, 2000; Preece, 2000; Resnick, 2002; Schraefel, Ho, Milton, & Chignell, 2000).

2. **Ethno-Narrative Perspective:** Ethno-narrative research is devoted to revealing personal experiences of being a member of an OLC. Most studies adopt a narrative approach, similar to participant observation inquiry used in anthropology. Researchers in this tradition have undertaken comparative analysis of both online learning and temporal communities (Schwier, 2001). Critics have disparaged ethno-narrative studies on the grounds that findings tend to be anecdotal and lack external validity; their conclusions are tentative and limited to the groups under study (cf. Downes, 2001; Rhiengold, 1993,

1999, 2002). Stolterman, Croon, and Argren (2000) argue that although the generalization and validity of such studies is limited, understanding personal perceptions of learning in OLC is essential. It is difficult to imagine how one can improve the learning environment of OLC without the subjective feedback of the learners.

3. **Cultural Studies Perspective:** Cultural studies have contributed enormously to understanding online learning communities. For instance, research by Brook and Boal (1995), Dery (1994), and Hershman and Leason (1996) investigate the relationship between the virtual and the physical, and they fall within the context of cultural interpretation research. Approaches employed in this category include experimental studies, with an emphasis on cultural events in online environments. The background disciplines of this group are diverse, including social psychology, philosophy, psychology, and fine arts.

4. **Sociotechnical Perspective:** The sociotechnical research tradition argues for a balanced approach to integrating cognitive and technical dimensions of OLC. This approach emerged from the extension of sociology, anthropology, and psychology to the study of HCI. Subsequently this research informed disciplines, including computer science and information systems (Heylighten, 1999). Research in sociotechnical areas addresses issues such as:

    •   **User-Centered Design:** Moving the focus of interest to learners and away from technology in the design of online learning (Norman, 1996).

    •   **Contextual Enquiry:** Understanding the user's context and its potential influence on the use of technology (Preece, 2000).

    •   **Sociability:** Appreciating the importance of community policies for interactions, governance, and social protocols in OLC (Preece, 2000).

- **Participatory Design:** Involving user participation in the design of OLC and the effects on learning outcomes (Mumford, 1987; Nguyen-Ngoc, Rekik, & Gillet, Chapter XIII, this volume).

- **Direct-Manipulation:** Creating tools for users to create their online learning environment and exploring the effects of functional options such as menu-driven and graphical interfaces (Shneiderman, 1998).

Common to this growing body of research issues is the need for the interplay of human and technology factors to guide the design, development, deployment, and evaluation of online learning communities.

Formal and Informal Online Learning Communities

There are numerous computational tools that support social learning across time and place (Laghos & Zaphiris, Chapter XI, this volume). New tools and patterns of communication have enabled social engagement, information, and knowledge sharing within social systems now referred to as OLC. Unlike a temporal community that resides in a fixed locale and whose members often know each other well enough to carry effective interactions, OLCs exist in cyberspace and may or may not be aware of each other (Daniel, Schwier, & McCalla, 2003). The character of an OLC is influenced by structural features, which may include: community size, duration of interaction and anticipated lifespan, location or distribution of the community, the homogeneity/heterogeneity of members, and breadth or narrowness of subject area. Variation of these features gives rise to diverse OLCs.

In Table 1, we simplify this diversity by distinguishing between formal and informal online learning communities. Formal online learning communities have explicit learning goals and evaluation criteria. Examples would include courses/programs offered by education institutions or companies (McCalla, 2000; Schwier, 2001). In contrast, informal OLCs achieve learning outcomes through social learning. Examples would include distributed communities of practice (Daniel, O'Brien, & Sarkar 2004b). A unique feature of DCoPs is the absence of a teacher or instructor; rather, in a DCoP, the learners are also teachers, as members collectively determine the content and support each other throughout the learning process. Further differences are contrasted in Table 1.

A growing body of research identifies the contribution of DCoPs to facilitating information exchange and knowledge creation, thereby enriching the work of the collective (Brown & Duguid, 1991; Hildreth, Kimble, & Wright, 1998; Lesser & Prusak, 2000). These positive outcomes have caught the interest of scholars and knowledge managers. And yet, there is little comparative research on the correlates of DCoP performance or sustainability. We find this surprising, given the fact that OLCs emerged and proliferated with the advent of the Internet and then World Wide Web over a decade ago. The case-study foundations for comparative research are certainly present, however (Kalaitzakis, Dafoulas, & Macaulay, 2003; Hartnell-Young, McGuinness, & Cuttance, Chapter XII, this volume).

Germane to the topic of DCoP emergence and sustainability is the question of "constructability". Can the DCoP features listed in Table 1 be built, or have DCoPs simply migrated from the temporal to the online world? If we return to the literature review briefly touched on earlier, perhaps not surprisingly we would find a different answer to this question depending on the literature consulted. For example, the sociology and cultural studies literature tends to be skeptical

Table 1. Features of online learning communities and distributed communities of practice (adapted from Daniel et al., 2003b)

Formal: Online Learning Communities (OLCs)	Informal: Distributed Communities of Practice (DCoPs)
• Membership is explicit and identities are generally known	• Membership may or may not be made explicit
• Participation is often required	• Participation is mainly voluntary
• High degree of individual awareness (who is who, who is where)	• Low degree of individual awareness
• Explicit set of social protocols for interaction	• Implicit and implied set of social protocols for interactions
• Formal learning goals	• Informal learning goals
• Possibly diverse backgrounds	• Common subject matter
• Low shared understanding of domain	• High shared understanding of domain
• Loose sense of identity	• Strong sense of identity
• Strict distribution of responsibilities	• No formal distribution of responsibilities
• Easily disbanded once established	• Less easily disbanded once established
• Low level of trust	• Reasonable level of trust
• Lifespan determined by extent in which goals are achieved	• Lifespan determined by the instrumental/expressive value the community provides to its members
• Pre-planned enterprise and fixed goals	• A joint enterprise as understood and continually renegotiated by its members

of the view that DCoPs can be constructed (Kollock & Smith, 1996). By contrast, the computer science and information systems research, on the whole, seem more optimistic that robust DCoPs can be constructed (Preece, 2000; Daniel et al., 2003b; McCalla, 2000).

Further, informed by user-centered design principles, Preece formulated the community-centered development (CCD) framework to guide practitioners in the field (Preece, 2000). CCD provides a blueprint for building a DCoP. The framework encourages designers to: (1) assess members' interests, (2) identify community norms and appropriate technology, (3) involve stakeholders in prototype design and testing, (4) correct for poor usability, and (5) foster community network building and identity. Literature informed by this approach draws attention to the interaction between human and technology dimensions in setting the context for the development and sustainability of DCoPs.

CCD integrates a sociotechnical perspective and pays attention to HCI. On the human dimension side, attention has been drawn to understanding participants' goals, motivations, and perceptions of the learning environment (Daniel et al., 2003b); trust (Preece, 2002); and culture and learning needs (Daniel et al., 2004a). On the technology side, issues include privacy and security, usability, scalability, and authenticity (Daniel et al., 2003a; Preece, 2000).

The attention paid by a sociotechnical approach to HCI makes this framework particularly well suited to understanding the development and sustainability of DCoPs. In particular, the relevance of a sociotechnical approach to the evolution of the GKN project results from the attention to, and monitoring of, feedback loops to inform design and subsequent operation. For example, a sociotechnical approach cautions against a "build it and wait till they come" approach, and favors a co-design process that enables potential users to define their goals and areas of concerns. Joint construction can be regarded as fostering a shared identity and building networks necessary for the development of trust and effective ICT-mediated interaction.

OUR CURRENT RESEARCH

The GKN project was launched to address a perceived need to span geography and cross-organizational boundaries to enhance the scholarship on, and the practice of, governance and its role in advancing international development. The underlying challenge of praxis is not unique to this particular subject area. A consultation document issued by the Social Science and Humanities Research Council of Canada, for example, re-stated the networking challenge for advancing collaboration and innovation in the humanities and the social sciences in the following terms:

Canada is a will against geography. It has a relatively small population, mostly scattered across more than 5,000 kilometres. It has no centres equivalent to Paris or London that naturally draw the best minds and greatest talents...to meet and interact on a regular basis. It does not have the numerous institutions...the Americans have to move people and ideas around. The net result...is that it is hard for people to know each other well, to trust each other and to work together over time and distance. (SSHRC, 2004)

With the emergence of ICTs, these obstacles to the exchange of information and collaboration were no longer permanent fixtures, though they have tended to endure.

Research Approach to the Design of User-Centered Online Learning Communities

We began our effort to overcome these obstacles through a participatory design approach (PDA). Key to PDA is an iterative process that seeks to address users' needs and promotes their involve-

ment in project development (Schuler & Namioka, 1993). A PDA, also known as a cooperative design approach, shares numerous similarities with Preece's (2000) community-centered approach.

The first step identified potential technologies capable of spanning geography and nurturing collaboration in a DCoP. Working on the human dimension, the project team created a profile of key stakeholders of 200 individuals from academia, government, and the non- and for-profit sectors. This list represented our target population for the survey of potential users' views on knowledge sharing in the field and interest in participating in the development of a DCoP.

The users' assessment was divided into three sections:

- an assessment of existing communication/ networking mechanisms among potential community users,
- an assessment of the level of awareness of work undertaken by users and their affiliated organizations, and
- users' perceived value of a DCoP and what services would contribute to its potential value.

The goal of the users' assessment was to identify a target group's interests, perceived knowledge gaps, thematic content, and potential design models for the proposed GKN portal.

Following the analysis of the assessment, we identified design features that matched identified services together with appropriate technological requirements. We further contacted those who had completed the survey by telephone for a follow-up interview. The goal of the interview was to elicit further information regarding individuals' preferences for content and portal design. These steps also served the equally important objective of engaging potential community participants. In addition, we were able to gauge the reaction to the objectives of the GKN project and method of development and implementation. In addition, the telephone follow-up was an opportunity to initiate informal connections among various individuals working in the same area of research.

RESULTS AND DISCUSSION

The target population for the survey was close to 200 organizations identified as working in the field of international development and governance. The response rate to the survey was 25%. Of those responding, 38% were university based, 23% were from provincial and federal government institutions, 30% were from non-governmental and research organizations, and 9% were from private consulting firms. The respondents were distributed across Canada: 45% from western Canada, 53% from central Canada, and only 2% from the eastern part of the country. These figures reflect the geographical and sectoral diversity of our sample. Four out of five respondents were interested in applied research and technical assistance in this area, and a similar proportion were interested in influencing, contributing, or participating in the policy-making process. In addition, over 80% of respondents revealed that it is important for them to keep current on new developments in research and practice. Depending on their organizational affiliation, 50% to 80% of the respondents were interested in building collaborative partnerships for research and technical assistance

We also asked respondents what kind of research (applied vs. basic research) they were interested in, and if they were willing to share a range of potential outputs with potential GKN members. The majority (90%) responded that they were interested in applied research. They were also willing to contribute to, and participate in, policymaking processes. Participants identified the potential for the GKN to support their interest in keeping abreast of current research and practice in their fields. In terms of collaboration, a large number of the respondents viewed the GKN as a potential mechanism to facilitate information ex-

change and knowledge sharing among members. These findings were encouraging for, as Lave and Wenger (1991) suggest, CoP development when individuals realize the potential to benefit by sharing knowledge, insights, and experiences with each other, and enhance their practices and performances.

Survey data and follow-up interviews revealed low levels of awareness of contemporary research and practice in the field. At the same time informants commented on the specialized nature of their work and the limited number of organizations active in the field, they also reported that they were largely unaware of contemporary contributions to knowledge and action that their counterparts have made. Though establishing a benchmark of awareness is problematic, our results indicated a considerable lack of awareness among researchers and practitioners working on governance and international development in Canada. The majority of the participants described current knowledge on governance and development as fragmented, and said that there was a serious lack of awareness among people working on similar issues across provinces and between organizations. Similarly, it was observed that a considerable amount of publicly funded research, reports, and policy documents are not exchanged in a systematic manner. Respondents identified the potential of a GKN initiative to facilitate relations among public, private, non-governmental organizations and academia.

Though overall results revealed that information sharing and knowledge awareness were fragmented, there was a pattern to the responses. First, organizations within a sector were more knowledgeable of current work undertaken by their counterparts within the same sector than organizations in different sectors. Second, there were marked differences in the level of awareness among counterparts within provinces compared to those operating outside their provinces. Although there was a high utilization of information and communication technologies as means to exchange information and data, they were not used systematically to break down the information barriers across organizations and across geographic jurisdictions.

Consistent with previous findings (Wenger, McDermott, & Snyder, 2000), geographic distance is considered an obstacle to knowledge sharing and utilization, even by those who are active users of ICTs. Moving from geographic to language barriers, several respondents underscored the importance of Canada's two official languages as a potential barrier. Language is critical to any community, since it is deemed as a part of a community identity: identity fosters collaboration and shared understanding within a community (McCalla, 2000). Turning to services, the following list identifies the top four stakeholder recommendations:

- Design a DCoP to facilitate information exchange and knowledge sharing.
- Provide a platform for sharing lessons, experiences, and best practices.
- Identify and nurture collaboration among government, research community, academia, NGOs, and development practitioners.
- Build linkages and partnerships with other international research communities to advance policy and practice.

Following the analysis of the data and feedback to respondents, we identified and profiled different technologies capable of supporting a DCoP that would perform to stakeholder expectations. Once the technological elements were identified, feedback was sought again from participants on the relevance of these models. This feedback was integrated in the prototype development of the GKN portal, which is currently in its formative stages. As the GKN project moved from a needs assessment to co-development with interested partners, human and technology interaction issues are gaining more importance.

At present, the GKN team has implemented a beta version of the system, while at the same time pursuing research into social and technical means to nurture and support an evolving community. Currently, we are experimenting with the use of blended strategies of face-to-face workshops and videoconferencing as additional avenues to encourage integration of human and technology factors. We are also developing an evaluation plan to assess the importance of the factors identified earlier to developing and sustaining the GKN project. In the following section, we describe the dimensions of HCI that have the potential to affect the viability and robustness of the GKN project.

EMERGENT HUMAN AND TECHNOLOGY ISSUES

There are multiple factors affecting the emergence and sustainability of a DCoP. Drawing from the GKN experience and insights from the sociotechnical approach outlined previously, we maintain that the following set of factors are important to HCI. Their influence and relative importance to the emergence and sustainability of a DCoP is introduced briefly in the following:

- **Didactics:** Learning is a shared experience, and by extension DCoPs are learning communities. Some OLCs have explicit learning goals (e.g., formal OLCs created around WebCT courses), while others have more implicit goals of sharing ideas, practices, and knowledge (e.g., DCoPs among corporate-oriented/professional communities). The technology must therefore enable learning, and perceptions of learning feedback would likely affect participation.
- **Trust:** Stakeholder surveys revealed that a key attraction of the proposed GKN online community would be the ability to share and retrieve archived data that was not widely

available. The creation of this shared resource would depend on the willingness of these stakeholders to contribute their data. Their decision to share data would likely be influenced by their trust in others in the community as well as the environment in which they interact, for instance, questions such as: How would community members treat my data? Would my research be reproduced without my permission or quoted out of context? Creating generalized trust within a DCoP is difficult to "engineer", but likely a pre-requisite condition for the sharing and accumulation of data.

- **Privacy and Security:** Privacy and security tools address individual perceptions of safety in the community. In an environment where a person feels their privacy threatened, declining participation is anticipated. In this regard, computational tools that protect the privacy and security of individuals must be provided.

- **Scalability and Authenticity:** Scalability expresses the ability of a system to accommodate multiple users, and authenticity refers to the ability of a system to protect individuals in a community from outsiders. A DCoP must encourage entrants and their participation. This dimension is critical to the growth of the DCoP, whereas authenticity appears more important to sustainability. For example, an open system that does not protect users (e.g., from hackers) is susceptible to negative feedback and eventual decline of member participation.

- **Sociability:** Sociability relates to the protocols in use for communication and interaction in the community (Preece, 2000). These protocols may be imposed in the first instance, but will likely shift in response to community dynamics. Sociability is of particular importance to "constructed" online communities that do not inherit protocols

in use, as would temporal communities that have migrated to an ICT-mediated environment. This dimension is likely critical to the sustainability of a DCoP, as protocols in use will need to reflect members' preferences and practices. As new protocols emerge, technology must accommodate such changes.

- **Usability:** Our research indicated that interest in the GKN initiative centered on the promise of instrumental outcomes (e.g., access to information, new insights, and expanded contacts). Here, technology and human interaction are clearly linked, as relevant content is dependent on member input and its ease of retrieval is dependent on technology. User-centered interface design and continuous involvement of users are critical to both the emergence and sustainability of the GKN project.

- **Culture:** An explicit objective of the GKN project was to bridge organizational and linguistic boundaries. As organizational theory suggests that organizations inculcate and perpetuate cultures that may promote or discourage inter-organizational information sharing and/or collaboration. Once organizational or individual participation is present (a human, not a technical issue), we are uncertain of how technology may shape or accommodate different culture(s). Though others suggest that the viability of DCoPs depends on the development of a shared culture, our project is not sufficiently far advanced to comment on this hypothesis.

- **Awareness:** The ability of ICT tools to provide awareness among its members is predicted to have a powerful impact on members' interactions in the community. More specifically, awareness (e.g., awareness about who is who, and who does and knows what) can have a significant positive feedback that would in turn promote participation and contribute to sustainability.

These elements highlighted exert different forces on technology and human interaction. For reasons stated, we anticipate that each will have a bearing on the emergence and sustainability of the GKN initiative and DCoP more generally.

DISCUSSION

The sociotechnical approach to the development of a DCoP suggests that human and technical factors are interlinked and they co-determine the emergence, evolution, growth, and sustainability of DCoPs. For practitioners involved in designing or developing a DCoP, the variables outlined previously will likely provide a useful starting point for guiding implementation and identifying key relationships. For researchers, our preliminary exploration of these relationships creates a number of hypotheses for future investigation. As these relationships have a bearing on both practice and research, we intend to track these relationships through user evaluations and internal monitoring. We anticipate that these findings will work toward a framework for comparative research on factors affecting the emergence and sustainability of a DCoP.

By way of conclusion, we offer the following general UCD principles for designing and sustaining online learning communities based on the sociotechnical approach.

Design Principles

- Assessing needs of actual or potential users/learners.
- Identifying the gap between what is and what needs to be.
- Understanding users and usage contexts.
- Profiling learning styles.
- Benchmarking existing community models.
- Identifying existing technological tools.

- Maintaining an iterative design and development processes that keep users/learners informed.
- Providing appropriate tools to support and mediate learning, social interaction and facilitate a sense of togetherness.
- Exploring navigation tools to enable members to gather information about others and have access to community interactions traces of activities.

Didactic Principles

- Nurturing open and informal discourse as members interact to satisfy their own personal and community learning needs.
- Encouraging learners to become active users and contributors of content.
- Supporting different learning styles.
- Encouraging participation and discourse around central themes, ideas, or purposes.
- Guiding participants throughout the interaction process, and providing them with clear directions to attainment of learning goals.
- Understanding unique individual learning needs differences, and encouraging participants to construct their own meaning based on unique individual experiences.

Sociability Principles

- Establishing a clear set of social protocols for interactions.
- Encouraging informal interaction and an environment conducive to learner/user interaction so that members have opportunities to test the trustworthiness of others.
- Supporting shared objectives—which creates a rationale for belonging to the community.
- Maintaining relevant content and context for interaction throughout the lifespan of the community.

- Encouraging ongoing active dialogue among members.
- Maintaining different forms of awareness (who is who, who knows what, who knows who knows what, etc.) in the community to lubricate effective interaction.

ACKNOWLEDGMENT

The research reported in this chapter has been supported financially by the Policy Branch of the Canadian International Development Agency (CIDA), the Social Sciences and Humanities Research Council of Canada (SSHRC), and the International Center for Governance and Development at the University of Saskatchewan.

REFERENCES

Brook, J., & Boal, I. A. (Eds.). (1995). *Resisting the virtual life: The culture and politics of information.* San Francisco: City Lights Books.

Brown, J. S., & Duguid, P. (1991). Organizational learning and communities of practice: Towards a unified view of working, learning and innovating. *Organization Science, 2,* 40-57.

Cothrel, J. (1999). Virtual community today. *The Journal of AGSI, 7,* 52-55.

Daniel, B. K., O'Brien, D., & Sarkar, A. (2004b, July 21-25). The cybernetics of distributed communities of practice. *Proceedings of the Joint International Conference on Education and Information Systems, Technologies and Applications* (EISTA 2004) *and the International Conference on Cybernetics and Information Technologies, Systems and Applications* (CITSA 2004), Orlando, FL.

Daniel, B. K., Poon, N., & Sarkar, A. (2005, June 27-July 2). Analysis of patterns of interactions in video-chat supported virtual communities to model social capital. *Proceedings of the World Conference on Educational Multimedia, Hypermedia and Telecommunications* (ED-MEDIA 2005), Montreal, Canada.

Daniel, B. K., Sarkar, A., & O'Brien, D. (2004a, June 21-26). A participatory design approach for a distributed community of practice on governance and international development. *Proceedings of the World Conference on Educational Multimedia, Hypermedia and Educational Telecommunications* (pp. 4606-4613), Lugano, Switzerland.

Daniel, B. K., Schwier, R. A., & McCalla, G. I. (2003b). Social capital in virtual learning communities and distributed communities of practice. *Canadian Journal of Learning and Technology, 29*(3), 113-139.

Daniel, B. K., Zapata-Rivera, D. J., & McCalla, G. I. (2003a). A Bayesian computational model of social capital. In M. Huysman, E. Wenger, & V. Wulf (Eds.), *Communities and technologies.* London: Kluwer.

Downes, S. (2001). *Learning communities.* Retrieved May 1, 2003, from http//www.atl.ualberta. ca/downes/future/communities.htm

Gutwin, C., & Greenberg, S. (1998). Design for individuals, design for groups: Tradeoffs between power and workspace awareness. *Proceedings of the ACM Conference on Computer-Supported Cooperative Work* (pp. 207-216).

Heylighten, F. (1999). *What are socio-technical approaches and systems science? Principia socio-technical approach Web.* Retrieved from http://pespmc1.vub.ac.be/CYBSWHAT.html

Hildreth, P., Kimble, C., & Wright, P. (1998). Computer-mediated communications and international communities of practice. *Proceedings of the 4ᵗʰ International Conference on Ethical Issues of Information Technology* (Ethicomp98), Rotterdam, Holland.

Kalaitzakis, E., Dafoulas, G., & Macaulay, L. (2003, June 22-27). Designing online communities: Community-centered development for intensively focused user groups. *Proceedings of the 10th HCI International Conference*, Greece.

Kim, A. J. (2000). *Community building on the Web: Secret strategies for successful online communities.* Berkeley, CA: Peachpit Press.

Kim, E.E. (2003). *An introduction to open source communities.* Retrieved May 1, 2003, from http://www.blueoxen.org/research/00007/

Kollock, P., & Smith, M. (1996). Managing the virtual commons: Cooperation and conflict in computer communities. In S. Herring (Ed.), *Computer-mediated communication: Linguistic, social, and cross-cultural perspectives.* Amsterdam: John Benjamins.

Krippendorf, K. (1984). Epistemological foundation for communication. *Journal of Communication, 84.*

Lave, J., & Wenger, E. (1991). *Situated learning: Legitimate peripheral participation.* New York: Cambridge University Press.

Lesser, E. L., & Prusak, L. (2000). Communities of practice, social capital and organizational knowledge. In E. L. Lesser, M. A. Fontaine, & J. A. Slusher (Eds.), *Knowledge and communities.* Boston: Butterworth Heinemann.

Lesser, E., & Storck, J. (2001). Communities of practice and organizational performance. *IBM Systems Journal, 40*(4).

McCalla, G. (2000). The fragmentation of culture, learning, teaching and technology: Implications for artificial intelligence in education research. *International Journal of Artificial Intelligence, 11*(2), 177-196.

Mumford, E. (1987). Socio-technical systems design: Evolving theory and practice. In P. Ehn & M. Kyng (Eds.), *Computers and democracy: A Scandinavian challenge* (pp. 59-76). London: Avebury.

Norman, D.A. (1996). Cognitive engineering. In D. A. Norman & S. W. Draper (Eds.), *User-centered systems design: New perspectives on human-computer interaction* (pp. 31-61). Hillsdale, NJ: Lawrence Erlbaum.

Preece, J. (2000). *Online communities: Designing usability and supporting sociability.* New York: John Wiley & Sons.

Preece, J. (2002). Supporting community and building social capital. *Communications of the ACM, 45*(4), 37-39.

Resnick, P. (2002). Beyond bowling together: Socio-technical capital. In J.M. Carroll (Ed.), *HCI in the new millennium* (pp. 247-272). New York: Addison-Wesley.

Rheingold, H. (1993). *The virtual community: Homesteading on the virtual frontier.* New York: Addison-Wesley.

Riedl, M. O. (2001, January 14-17). A computational model and classification framework for social navigation. *Proceedings of the International Conference on Intelligent User Interfaces 2001* (pp. 137-144), Santa Fe, NM.

Schraefel, M. C., Ho, J., Chignell, M., & Milton, M. (2000). Building virtual communities for research. *Proceedings of the International Working Conference and Industrial Expo on New Advances and Emerging Trends in Next Generation Enterprises,* Buffalo, NY.

Schuler, D., & Namioka, A. (Eds.). (1993). *Participatory design: Principles and practices.* Hillsdale, NJ: Lawrence Erlbaum.

Schwier, R. A. (2001). Catalysts, emphases, and elements of virtual learning communities. Implication for research. *The Quarterly Review of Distance Education, 2*(1), 5-18.

Sclove, R. E. (1995). *Democracy and technology.* New York: The Guildford Press.

Shneiderman, B. (1998). *Designing the user interface. Strategies for effective human-computer interaction.* Boston: Addison-Wesley.

Smith, M. (1992). *Voices from the WELL: The logic of the virtual commons.* Master's thesis, Department of Sociology, UCLA, USA.

SSHRC. (2004). *From a granting to a knowledge council.* Ottawa: Social Sciences and Humanities Research Council of Canada.

Stolterman, E., Croon, A., & Argren, P.-O. (2000). *Virtual communities: Why and how they are studied.* Working paper, Department of Informatics, Umeå University, Sweden.

Wenger, E., McDermott, R., & Snyder, W. M. (2002). *Cultivating communities of practice: A guide to managing knowledge.* Boston: Harvard Business School Press.

Wickre, K. (1995). *Virtual communities: Are they real? Are they real enough?* Retrieved May 1, 2003, from http://www.thenet-usa.com/mag/back/0995/community.html

ENDNOTE

[1] Presenters at the *1st GKN Workshop on Building Distributed Communities of Practice for Enhanced Research-Policy Interface,* May 28-31, 2004. Presentations available at http://www.icgd.usask.ca/workshopPlan. html

This work was previously published in User-Centered Design of Online Learning Communities, edited by N. Lambropoulos and P. Zaphiris, pp. 54-70, copyright 2007 by Information Science Publishing, formerly known as Idea Group Publishing (an imprint of IGI Global).

Compilation of References

7th European Conference on e-Learning (2008). Retrieved June 27, 2008 from http://academic-conferences.org/ecel/ecel2008/ecel08-abstracts.htm

Acquisti, A., & Gross, R. (2006). *Imagined communities: Awareness, information sharing, and privacy on the facebook.* In G. Danezis, & P. Golle (Eds.), (pp. 36-58). Berlin Heidelberg: Springer-Verlag.

Adams, J. M., & Carfagna, A. (2006). *Coming of Age in a Globalized World: The Next Generation Kumarian Press* (See especially the section titled: Global Education: Schooling World Citizen).

Adida, B., & Birbeck, M. (2008). *RDFa Primer.* Technical Report, W3C Working Draft.

Ahanotu N. D. (1998). Empowerment and production workers: a knowledge-based perspective. *Empowerment in Organizations, 6*(7), 177-18.

Ainley, P., & Rainbird, H. (Eds) (1999). *Apprenticeship: towards a new paradigm for learning* (p. 58). London: Kogan Page.

Alavi, M., & Leidner, D. E. (2001). Review: Knowledge management and knowledge management systems: Conceptual foundations and research issues. *MIS Quarterly, 25*(1), 107-136.

Aldrich, H., & Zimmer, C. (1986). Entrepreneurship through social networks. In D. Sexton & R. Smilor (Eds.), *Art and science of entrepreneurship,* 3-23. Cambridge, MA: Ballinger,

Allen, C. (1993). Reciprocal evolution as a strategy for integrating basic research, design, and studies of work practices. In D. Shuler & A. Namioka (Eds.), *Participatory design* (pp. 239-253). Hillsdale, NJ: Lawrence Erlbaum.

Alley, L. R. (1999). Diverting a crisis in global human and economic development: A new transnational model for lifelong continuous learning and personal knowledge management. *Higher Education in Europe, 24*(2), 187-195.

Amin, M. A., & Morbach, J. (2005). *The DAML+OIL to OWL converter.* Retrieved July 10, 2005, from http://www.lpt.rwth-aachen.de/Research/OntoCAPE/daml2owl.php

Anonymous. (2007). Business: Social graph-iti; internet companies. *The Economist, 385*(8551), 90.

Anonymous. (2007, Nov 21). Facebook time with recruits. *National Post,* (pp. WK.1).

Anonymous. (2007). Serena software adopts facebook as corporate intranet. *Canada NewsWire,, 1.*

Anonymous. (2008). Branded apps on facebook fail to attract users. *New Media Age, 2.*

Anonymous. (2008). CellSpin launches the first MySpace and facebook instant mobile posting application for audio, video, photos and text on 300+ phones worldwide. *Canada NewsWire.*

Anonymous. (2008). CIO and LinkedIn share common goals. *MIN's B 2 B, 11*(16).

Anonymous. (2008). Healthplan provider HSA launches unique facebook personal planner. *PR Newswire Europe Including UK Disclose.*

Anonymous. (2008). MySpace india launches. *Wireless News.*

Anonymous. (2008). Myspace mobile launches on verizon wireless. *Telephone IP News, 19*(5).

Anonymous. (2008). Nissan launches "N-square" for staff. *Strategic Communication Management, 12*(1), 9.

Anonymous. (2008h). Quick study: Moms drive word of mouth; getting hired through social networks; greenbacks versus green initiatives. *PR News, 64*(17).

Anonymous. (2008). Workers naive over online presence. *Strategic Communication Management, 12*(1), 9.

Anonymous. (2008). How to...use LinkedIn as an effective business tool. (2008). *PR News, 64*(16)

Antoniou, G., & Harmelen, F. (2004). *A Semantic Web prime.* Cambridge, MA: MIT Press.

Arjan, R., Pfeil, U., & Zaphiris, P. (2008). Age differences in online social networking. *CHI '08: CHI '08 Extended Abstracts on Human Factors in Computing Systems,* Florence, Italy. (pp. 2739-2744).

Armsby, P., Costley, C., Garnett, J. (2006). The legitimisation of knowledge: a work-based learning perspective of APEL. *Lifelong Learning and Education, 25*(4), 369-83. Retrieved June 27, 2008, from www.emeraldinsight.com/.../published/emeraldfulltextarticle/pdf/0860190301_ref.html

Arndt, H-K., & Günther, O. (Eds.). (2000). Environmental Markup Language (EML). *First Workshop, Berlin 1999.* Metropolis: Marburg.

Arthur, D., Sherman, C., Appel, D., & Moore, L. (2006). Why young consumers adopt interactive technologies. *Young Consumers, 7*(3), 33.

Artilium (2008). Educational technology—a long look back. *BJET, 39*(4), 234-236. Published online.

Asensio, M. & Young, C. (2002). Section 2—A learning and teaching perspective. In S. Thornhill, M. Asensio, & C. Young (Eds.), *Video streaming: A guide for educational development* (Vol. 1, pp. 10-19). Manchester, UK: The JISC Click and Go Video Project.

Association of Chartered Certified Accountants (ACCA). (1998). *Making Values Count: Contemporary Experience in Social and Ethical Accounting, Auditing, and Reporting.* London: The Certified Accountants Educational Trust.

Association of Chartered Certified Accountants (ACCA). (2001). *Environmental, Social and Sustainability Reporting on the World Wide Web: A Guide to Best Practice.* London: ACCA, (pp. 18-21).

Association of Chartered Certified Accountants (ACCA). (2004). *Towards Transparency: Progress on Global Sustainability Reporting 2004.* London: Certified Accountants Educational Trust.

Augar, N., & Zhou, W. (2003). *Virtual communities: Literature survey.* Technical Report No. TRC04/03. Geelong, Australia: Deakin University.

Augar, N., Raitman, R., & Zhou, W. (2004). From e-learning to virtual learning community: Bridging the gap. Paper presented at *ICWL'04*, Beijing, China.

Augar, N., Raitman, R., & Zhou, W. (2004). Teaching and learning online with wikis. Paper presented at *ASCILITE*, Perth, Australia.

Augar, N., Raitman, R., & Zhou, W. (2005). Towards building Web-based learning communities with Wikis. Paper presented at *IADIS International Conference on Web-Based Communities 2005*, February 23-25, Algarve, Portugal (pp. 207-214).

Australian Government Department of the Environment and Heritage. (2003). *Corporate Sustainability – An Investor Perspective. The Mays Report.* Canberra: Environmental Protection Branch. Department of the Environment and Heritage. http://deh.gov.au/industry/finance/publications/index.html [22 March 2004].

Australian Trade Commission. (2004). *Education capability overview*. Retrieved August 30, 2004, from *http://www.austrade.gov.au/overseas/layout/0,,0_S3-1_3zo-2_-3_PWB1153530-4_-5_-6_0-7_,00.html.1*

Baark, E., & Heeks, R. (1998). Evaluation of donor-funded information technology projects in China: A lifecycle approach. *Development informatics working chapter series*. Manchester: Institute for Development Policy and Management, University of Manchester.

Bagozzi, R. P., Gopinath, M., & Nyer, P. U. (1999). The role of emotions in marketing. *Journal of the Academy of Marketing Science, 27*(2), 184-206.

Bajjaly, S. T. (1999). *The community networking handbook*. Chicago and London: American Library Association.

Barabási, A.-L., & Albert, R. (1999). Emergence of scaling in random networks. *Science, 286*.

Barnes, D. (1992). The significance of teachers' frames for teaching. In T. Russell & H. Munby (Eds.), *Teachers and teaching: from classroom to reflection* (pp. 9-32). London: The Falmer Press.

Barratt, M., Sahay, S., & Walsham, G. (2001) Information technology and social transformation: GIS for forestry management in India. *The Information Society, 17*, 5-20.

Basiel (1999). Retrieved June 27, 2008. *Paper*: http://www.elearning.mdx.ac.uk/research/pushpull/pushpull/Push&Pull.htm. *Toolkit*: http://www.elearning.mdx.ac.uk/research/pushpull/pushpull/PROFILE.HTM

Basiel A., Commins R., & Howarth M. (2008). Retrieved June 27, 2008 from http://www.elearning.mdx.ac.uk/research/index.htm.#digital_literacy

Baym, N. K. (1995). The emergence of community in computer-mediated communication. In S.G. Jones (Ed.), *Cybersociety computer-mediated communication and community* (pp. 138-163). Thousand Oaks, CA: Sage Publications.

BBC (British Broadcasting Corporation). (2004). "Plagiarist" to sue university. *BBC News World Edition,* (May 27). Retrieved December 5, 2005, from http://news.bbc.co.uk/2/hi/uk_news/education/3753065.stm

Beamsley, T. (1999). Securing digital image assets in museums and libraries: A risk management approach. *Library Trends, 48*(2), 358-378.

Beattie, V., & Pratt, K. (2003). Issues concerning web-based business reporting: An analysis of the views of interested parties. *The British Accounting Review, 35*(2), 155-187.

Bebbington, A. (1997). Social capital and rural intensification: Local organizations and islands of sustainability in the rural Andes. *The Geographical Journal, 163*(2), 189-197.

Bedny'i, G. Z., & Meister, D. (1997). *The Russian theory of activity: Current applications to design and learning*. Mahwah, NJ: Lawrence Erlbaum.

Beer, D. (2008). Social network(ing) sites... revisiting the story so far: A response to danah boyd & nicole ellison. *Journal of Computer-Mediated Communication, 13*(2), 516-529.

Beniger, J. R. (1986). *The Control Revolution. Technological and Economic Origins of the Information Society*. Harvard University Press

Beniger, J. R. (1988). Information Society and Global Science. In Telescience: Scientific Communication in the Information Age. *Annals of the American Academy of Political and Social Science, 1*, 14-28. The study was republished in Dunlop and Kling (1991)

Berners-Lee et al. (2001). The Semantic Web. *Scientific American*. Retrieved from http://www-personal.si.umich.edu/~rfrost/courses/SI110/readings/In_Out_and_Beyond/Semantic_Web.pdf

Berners-Lee, T. et al, (2006). Tabulator: Exploring and Analyzing linked data on the Semantic Web. *Proceedings of the 3rd International Semantic Web User Interaction Workshop (SWUI06) workshop*, Athens, Georgia.

Berners-Lee, T. (2006). *Linked Data Design Issues*. Available at http://www.w3.org/DesignIssues/LinkedData.html

Berners-Lee, T., Hendler, J., & Lassila, O. (2001). The Semantic Web. *Scientific American, 284*(5), 34-43.

Bernoff, J., & Li, C. (2008). Harnessing the power of the oh-so-social web. *MIT Sloan Management Review, 49*(3), 36.

Berolazzi, P., Krusich, C., & Missikoff, M. (2001). *An Approach to the Definition of a Core Enterprise Ontology: CEO,* http://cersi.luiss.it/oesseo2001/papers/9.pdf

Berrueta, D. et al, (2008). *Best practice recipes for publishing RDF vocabularies.* Technical Report, W3C Note.

Berrueta, D., Fernández, S., & Shi, L. (2007). Bootstrapping the Semantic Web of Social Online Communities. *In Proceedings of workshop on Social Web Search and Mining (SWSM2008), co-located with WWW2008,* Beijing, China.

Besser, H. (2002). The Next Stage: Moving from Isolated Digital Collections to Interoperable Digital Libraries. *First Monday,* 7(6), http://firstmonday.org/issues/issue7_6/besser

Birchall, J. (2008, Mar 14). Amazon taps facebook potential. *Financial Times,* (p. 18).

Bloom, N., & Stout, C. (2005). Using digitised primary source materials in the classroom: A Colorado case study. *First Monday,* 10(6), http://firstmonday.org/issues/issue10_6/bloom/index.html.

Blunt, R. (2001). *How to build an e-learning community.* Retrieved January 19, 2004, from *http://www.elearningmag.com/ltimagazine/article/articleDetail.jsp?id=5040*

Bodker, S. (1991). *Through the interface: A human activity approach to user interface design.* Hillsdale, NJ: Lawrence Erlbaum.

Bojārs, U. & Breslin, J. (2007). *SIOC Core Ontology Specification.* Available at http://rdfs.org/sioc/spec/.

Bonniface, L., & Green, L. (2007). Finding a new kind of knowledge on the HeartNET website. *Health Information and Libraries Journal, 24*(1), 67-76.

Borgman, C. L. (1999). What are digital libraries? Competing visions. *Information Processing and Management, 35*(3), 227-243. http://portal.acm.org/citation.cfm?id=779042.779051&dl=GUIDE&dl=ACM

BOS (2007). Retrieved June 27, 2008 from http://oasisplus.mdx.ac.uk/webct/urw/lc4831306002.tp4831347002/CourseContentDispatch.dowebct?tab=view&displayinfo=47723305021

Bothman, B. (2002). The past that archives keep: Memory, history, and the preservation of archival records, *Archivaria, 51,* 48–80.

Boucouvalas, A. C. (2002). Real time text-to-emotion engine for expressive internet communications. In G. Riva & F. Davide (Eds.), *Emerging Communication: Studies on New Technologies and Practices in Communication.* IOS Press.

Boulos, M., Kame, N., Maramba, I., & Wheeler, S. (2006). Wikis, blogs and podcasts: a new generation of *Web*-based tools for virtual collaborative clinical practice and education. *BMC Medical Education, 6,* 41.

Bouthillier, F., & Shearer, K. (2002). Understanding knowledge management and information management: The need for an empirical perspective. *Information Research, 8*(1), No. 141, http://InformationR.net/ir/8-1/paper141.html

Boyd, D. (2006). In Heer J. (Ed.), *Profiles as conversation: Networked identity performance on friendster.*

boyd, d. m., & Ellison, N. B. (2007). Social network sites: Definition, history, and scholarship. *Journal of Computer-Mediated Communication, 13*(1), 210-230.

Brandtzeg, P. B., & Heim, J. (2007). User loyalty and online communities: Why members of online communities are not faithful. *INTETAIN '08: Proceedings of the 2nd International Conference on INtelligent TEchnologies for Interactive enterTAINment,* Cancun, Mexico. (pp. 1-10).

Brauchli, K., Killingback, T., & Doebeli, M. (1999). Evolution of cooperation in spatially structured populations. *Journal of Theoretical Biology.*

Bray, T., Hollander, D., & Layman, A. (1999). *Namespaces in XML*. World Wide Web Consortium. Retrieved January 14, 1999, from http://www.w3.org/TR/REC-xml-names/

Bray, T., Paoli, J., Sperberg-McQueen, C. M., Maler, E., Yergeau, F., & Cowan, J. (2004). *Extensible markup language (XML) 1.1*. W3C recommendation. Retrieved February 4, 2004, from http://www.w3.org/TR/2004/REC-xml11-20040204/

Breslin, J. et al (2005). Towards Semantically-Interlinked Online Communities. *Proceedings of the 2nd European Semantic Web Conference, ESWC 2005*, Heraklion, Crete, Greece.

Breslin, J. et al (2006). SIOC: an approach to connect web-based communities. *International Journal of Web Based Communities, 2*(2), 133-142.

Brewer, M., & Kramer, R. (1986). Choice behavior in social dilemmas. *Journal of Personality and Social Psychology, 50*, 543-549.

Brickley, D. (2006). *Basic geo (WGS84 lat/long) vocabulary*. Technical report, W3C Informal Note.

Brickley, D., & Guha, R. V. (2004). *Resource description framework schema (RDFS) specification 1.0*. W3C Recommendation. Retrieved February 10, 2004, from http://www.w3.org/TR/rdf-schema/

Brickley, D., & Miller, L. (2005). *FOAF Vocabulary Specification*. Technical report.

Brockett, J. (2007). Face to face with social networking. *People Management, 13*(16), 15.

Broekstra, J. et al (2002) Sesame: A generic architecture for storing and querying RDF and RDF Schema. In *Springer Lecture Notes in Computer Science, 2342*, 54–68.

Brook, C. & Oliver, R. (2003). Online learning communities: Investigating a design framework. *Australian Journal of Educational Technology, 19*(2), 139-160. Retrieved June 28, 2005, from *http://www.ascilite.org.au/ajet/ajet19/brook.html*

Brook, J., & Boal, I. A. (Eds.). (1995). *Resisting the virtual life: The culture and politics of information*. San Francisco: City Lights Books.

Brown, A. L. (1992). Design experiments: Theoretical and methodological challenges in creating complex interventions in classroom settings. *The Journal of the Learning Sciences, 2*(2), 141-178.

Brown, J. S., & Duguid, P. (1991). Organizational learning and communities of practice: Towards a unified view of working, learning and innovating. *Organization Science, 2*, 40-57.

Bruckman, A. (2002). The future of e-learning communities: The learning potential of Internet technology can come from the most familiar sources—peers and elders. *Communications of the ACM, 45*(4), 60-63.

Buckland, M. K. (1997). What is a "document"? *Journal of the American Society of Information Science, 48*(9), 804-809, http://www.interscience.wiley.com/

Burt. R. (2000). The network structure of social capital. *Research in Organizational Behavior, 22*, 345-423.

Bussler, C. (2008). Is Semantic Web Technology Taking the Wrong Turn? *IEEE Internet Computing, 12*(1), 75-79.

Cabrales, A. (2000). Stochastic replicator dynamics. *International Economic Review, 41*(2).

Cabrera, A., & Cabrera, E. F. (2002). Knowledge-sharing dilemmas. *Organization Studies, 23*(5), 687-710.

Cain, J. (2008). Online social networking issues within academia and pharmacy education. *American Journal of Pharmaceutical Education, 72*(1), 1.

Cardew, B., & Emanuel, H. (2008). Merlin enters MySpace talks. *Music Week, 1*.

Cardoso, J. (2004). Semantic Web processes and ontologies for the travel industry. *AIS SIGSEMIS Bulletin, 1*(3), 25-28.

Carlsen, R. (2003). Building productive online learning communities: Investigating and interacting with Internet educational genres. Paper presented at *Quality*

Education @ a Distance, Geelong, Australia (pp. 137-144). Kluwer.

Carneiro, A. (2000). How does knowledge management influence innovation and competitiveness? *Journal of Knowledge Management, 4*, 87-98.

CastleWorks. (2005). *Resources by topic: Cheating.* Retrieved December 5, 2005, from http://pbskids.org/itsmylife/parents/resources/cheating.html

Cayzer, S. (2004). Semantic blogging and decentralized KM. *Communications of the ACM, 47*(12), 47-52.

Celma, O. (2006). FOAFing the music: Bridging the semantic gap in music recommendation. *Proceedings of the 5th International Semantic Web Conference*, Athens, USA.

Cervini (2005). Semantic networks and social networks. *The Learning Organization, 12*(5).

Chandler, R. L. (2002). Museums in the Online Archive of California (MOAC): Building Digital Collections Across Libraries and Museums. *First Monday, 7*(5), http://firstmonday.org/issues/issue7_5/chandler/index.html

Chapman, C. N., & Lahav, M. (2008). International ethnographic observation of social networking sites. *CHI '08: CHI '08 Extended Abstracts on Human Factors in Computing Systems,* Florence, Italy. (pp. 3123-3128).

Chen, A. (2004, July 5). Semantic Web is 2 steps closer. *eWeek,* p. 46.

Chen, H., & Finin, T. (2004). An ontology for context aware pervasive computing environments. *Knowledge Engineering, 18*(3), 197-207.

Chen, J. T. (2003). *A study on feasible strategies and impeditive factors for elementary teachers' application of knowledge management in Tainan County.* Master dissertation, National Kaohsiung Teachers University.

Chen, M. Y. (2002). The future development of personal knowledge management on teacher professional. *Secondary Education, 53*(3), 84-93.

Chen, M. Y. (2005). Teachers college students' personal knowledge management and it's impact on professional learning and development. *Journal of National Taiwan Normal University, 50*(2), 181-202.

Chen, M. Y. (2006). Application research of teacher personal knowledge management in the professional development: Nine-year curriculum as an example. *Curriculum and Teaching, 9*(1), 99-122.

Cherny, L. (1999). *Conversation and community: Chat in a virtual world.* Stanford, CA: CSLI Publications.

Chi, M. T. H., Lewis, M. W., Reimann, P., & Glaser, R. (1989). Self-explanations: How students study and use examples in learning to solve problems. *Cognitive Science, 13*, 145-182.

Chin, K.L., Chang, V., & Bauer, C. (2000). The use of Web-based learning in culturally diverse learning environments. Paper presented at the *Sixth Australian World Wide Web Conference*, Cairns, Australia.

Chin, Y. J. (2002). *Teachers' knowledge management in elementary schools: Analyses at individual and organisational levels.* Master dissertation, National Taipei Teachers' College.

Choo, C. (1998). *The Knowing Organization: How Organizations Use Information to Create Meaning, Create Knowledge, and Make Decisions,* Oxford University Press, Oxford, UK.

Clark, K. G. (2008). *SPARQL protocol for RDF.* Technical report, W3C Recommendation.

Clarke, T. (2001). Balancing the triple bottom line: Financial, social and environmental performance. *Journal of General Management, 26*(4), 16-27.

Clausen, J., Loew, T., Klaffke, K., Raupach, M., & Schoenheit, I. (2001). *The INEM Sustainability Reporting Guide – A Manual on Practical and Convincing Communication for Future-Oriented Companies.* International Network for Environmental Management (INEM): Hamburg. http://www.inem.org/free_downloads [22 March 2002].

Clemons, E. K., Barnett, S., & Appadurai, A. (2007). The future of advertising and the value of social network websites: Some preliminary examinations. *ICEC '07: Proceedings of the Ninth International Conference on Electronic Commerce*, Minneapolis, MN, USA. (pp. 267-276).

Cohen, D. (2004). History and the second decade of the web. *Rethinking History, 8*(2), 293-301. http://chnm.gmu.edu/resources/essays/essay.php?id=34.

Cohill, A. M., & Kavanaugh, A. L. (1997). *Community networks: Lessons from Blacksburg, Virginia.* Norwood, MA: Artech House.

Coleman, J. (1988). Social capital in the creation of human capital. *American Journal of Sociology, 94*, S95-S120.

Conlan, F. (1996). Can the different learning expectations of Australian and Asian students be reconciled in one teaching strategy? In J. Abbott & L. Willcoxson (Eds.), *Proceedings of the 5th Annual Teaching and Learning Forum* (pp. 41-45). Perth, Australia: Murdoch University. Retrieved June 28, 2005, from *http://lsn.curtin.edu.au/tlf/tlf1996/conlan.html*

Connolly, D. (2007). *Gleaning Resource Descriptions from Dialects of Languages (GRDDL).* Technical report, W3C Candidate Recommendation.

Connolly, D., Harmelen, F. V., Horrocks, I., McGuinness, D., Patel-Schneider, P. F., & Stein, L. A. (2001). *Annotated DAML+OIL ontology markup.* W3C note. Retrieved December 18, 2001, from http://www.w3.org/TR/daml+oil-walkthru/

Connolly, D., Harmelen, F. V., Horrocks, I., McGuinness, D., Patel-Schneider, P. F., & Stein, L. A. (2001, March). *DAML+OIL reference description.* W3C Note. Retrieved April 11, 2001, from http://www.daml.org/2001/03/reference.html

Connor, E. (2007) Medical librarian 2.0. *Medical Reference Services Quarterly, 26*(1), 1-15.

Cope, M. (2000). *Know your value? Value what you know.* Essex: Financial Times Prentice Hall Prentice Hall.

Corporate Social Responsibility (CSR) Europe. (2000). *Communicating Corporate Social Responsibility. Trans-*

parency, Reporting and Accountability. Recommendations for CSR Reporting. CSR Europe: Brussels.

Cortada, J. W., & Woods, J. A. (Eds.). (2000). *The knowledge management yearbook 2000-2001.* Butterworth-Heinemann.

Cothrel, J. (1999). Virtual community today. *The Journal of AGSI, 7*, 52-55.

Counts, S. (2008). In K. E.Fisher (Ed.), *Mobile social networking: An information grounds perspective.*

Cross et al. (2004). *An informal history of eLearning.* Retrieved from http://www.emeraldinsight.com/Insight/viewContentItem.do?contentType=Article&hdAction=lnkpdf&contentId=839895

Cuthbert, A., Clark, D., & Linn, M. C. (2002). WISE learning communities: Design considerations. In K. A. Renninger & W. Shumar (Eds.), *Building virtual communities: Learning and change in Cyberspace* (pp. 215-246). Cambridge, UK: Cambridge University Press.

Cuthbert, A., Clark, D., Slotta, J., & Jorde, D. (2000). Helping elicit self-explanation and clarification through personalized electronic discussions. In *Proceedings of the Annual Meeting of the America Research Association (AERA).* New Orleans.

D'Aquin, M., Bouthier, C., Brachais, S., Lieber, J., & Napoli, A. (2005). Knowledge editing and maintenance tools for a semantic portal in oncology. *International Journal of Human-Computer Studies, 62*(5), 619-638.

d'Artigues, A., & Vignolo, T. (2003). Why global integration may lead to terrorism: An evolutionary theory of mimetic rivalry. *Economics Bulletin, 6*(11).

Dalbello, M. (2004). Institutional Shaping of Cultural Memory: Digital Library as Environment for Textual Transmission. *Library Quarterly, 74*(3), 265-29. http://64.233.183.104/search?q=cache:qlBn7-HYNMgJ:www.scils.rutgers.edu/~dalbello/research/Dalbello%2520(LQ74_2004).pdf+Tefko+Saracevic,+Marija+Dalbello-+article&hl=el&ie=UTF-8&inlang=el

Daniel, B. K., O'Brien, D., & Sarkar, A. (2004b, July 21-25). The cybernetics of distributed communities of practice. *Proceedings of the Joint International Conference on Education and Information Systems, Technologies and Applications* (EISTA 2004) *and the International Conference on Cybernetics and Information Technologies, Systems and Applications* (CITSA 2004), Orlando, FL.

Daniel, B. K., Poon, N., & Sarkar, A. (2005, June 27-July 2). Analysis of patterns of interactions in video-chat supported virtual communities to model social capital. *Proceedings of the World Conference on Educational Multimedia, Hypermedia and Telecommunications* (ED-MEDIA 2005), Montreal, Canada.

Daniel, B. K., Sarkar, A., & O'Brien, D. (2004, June 21-26). A participatory design approach for a distributed community of practice on governance and international development. *Proceedings of the World Conference on Educational Multimedia, Hypermedia and Educational Telecommunications* (pp. 4606-4613), Lugano, Switzerland.

Daniel, B. K., Schwier, R. A., & McCalla, G. I. (2003). Social capital in virtual learning communities and distributed communities of practice. *Canadian Journal of Learning and Technology, 29*(3), 113-139.

Daniel, B. K., Zapata-Rivera, D. J., & McCalla, G. I. (2003). A Bayesian computational model of social capital. In M. Huysman, E. Wenger, & V. Wulf (Eds.), *Communities and technologies*. London: Kluwer.

Daniel, B., McCalla, G., & Schwier, R. (2002). A process model for building social capital in virtual learning communities. Paper presented at the *International Conference on Computers in Education*, Aukland, New Zealand (pp. 574-575).

Dasgupta, P., & David, P. A. (1994). Toward a New Economy of Science. *Research Policy, 23,* 487-521.

Davenport, T. H., & Prusak, L. (2000). *Working knowledge: How organizations manage what they know*. Boston, MA: Harvard Business School Press.

Davenport, T. H., De Long, D. W., & Beers, M. C. (1998). Successful knowledge management projects. *Sloan Management Review, 39*(2), 43-57.

David Skyrme Associates (1999). *Knowledge management assessment: A practical tool from David Skyrme Associates*, December 15, 2000, http://www.skyme.com/tools/index.htm

Davies, N. J., Fensel, D., & Harmelen, F. V. (Eds.). (2003). *Toward the Semantic Web: Ontology-based knowledge management*. Hoboken, NJ: John Wiley & Sons.

Davis, B. H., & Brewer, J. (1997). *Electronic discourse: Linguistic individuals in virtual space*. Albany, NY: State University of New York Press.

Deakin University. (2003). *FactBook 2002*. Victoria, Australia: Deakin University.

DeJean, D. (2008). Social networking gets moving. *Computerworld, 42*(15), 30.

Dell'Erba, M. (2004). Exploiting Semantic Web technologies for data interoperability. *AIS SIGSEMIS Bulletin, 1*(3), 48-52.

Deloitte Touche Tohmatsu International (DTTI). International Institute for Sustainable Development (IISD), SustainAbility Ltd. (1993). *Coming Clean - Corporate Environmental Reporting, Opening up for Sustainable Development*. DTTI: London.

Diederich, J., & Kindermann, J. (2003). Authorship Attribution with Support Vector Machines. *Applied Intelligence, 19*(1/2), 109–123.

DiMicco, J. M., & Millen, D. R. (2007). Identity management: Multiple presentations of self in facebook. *GROUP '07: Proceedings of the 2007 International ACM Conference on Supporting Group Work*, Sanibel Island, Florida, USA. (pp. 383-386).

DiPiazza, S. A., & Eccles, R.G. (2002). *Building Corporate Trust. The Future of Corporate Reporting*. Wiley: New York, (p. 127).

DiSessa, A. A., & Minstrell, J. (1998). Cultivating conceptual change with benchmark lessons. In J. G. Greeno

& S. Goldman (Eds.), *Thinking practices* (pp. 155-187). Mahwah, NJ: Lawrence Erlbaum.

Dornan, T., Hadfield, J., Brown, M., Boshuizen, H., & Scherpbier, A. (2005). How can medical students learn in a self-directed way in the clinical environment? Design-based research. *Medical Education, 39*, 356–64.

Dornan, T., Scherpbier, A., King, N., & Boshuizen, H. (2005). Clinical teachers and problem-based learning: A phenomenological study. *Medical Education, 39*, 163–70.

Dougimas, M. & Taylor, P. C. (2002). Interpretive analysis of an Internet-based course constructed using a new courseware tool called Moodle. Paper presented at the *Annual International Conference of the Higher Education Research and Development Society of Australasia (HERDSA)*, Perth, Australia. Retrieved June 28, 2005, from *http://www.ecu.edu.au/conferences/herdsa/main/papers/nonref/pdf/MartinDougiamas.pdf*

Douglis, F. (2008). *On social networking and communication paradigms.*

Dourish, P. & Bly, S. (1992). Portholes: Supporting awareness in a distributed work group. Paper presented at *SIGCHI Conference on Human Factors in Computing Systems*, Monterey, CA. Retrieved June 28, 2005, from *http://pages.cpsc.ucalgary.ca/~saul/601.13/readings/portholes.pdf*

Downes, S. (2001). *Learning communities.* Retrieved May 1, 2003, from http//www.atl.ualberta.ca/downes/future/communities.htm

Downs S. (2006). E-Learning 2.0. *National Research Council of Canada.* Retrieved from, www.elearningmag.org/subpage.cmf?section=articles&article=29-1

Duchastel, P. C. & Waller, R. (1979). Pictorial illustration in instructional texts. *Educational Technology,* (November), 20-25.

Duffy, T. M. & Jonassen, D. H. (1992). Constructivism: New implications for instructional technology. In T. M. Duffy & D. H. Jonassen (Eds.), *Constructivism and the*

technology of instruction: A conversation (pp. 1-15). Hillsdale, NJ: Lawrence Erlbaum Associates.

Dumbill, E. (2002). *Finding Friends with XML and RDF, XMLWatch.* Retrieved June 27, 2008 from http://www-106.ibm.com/developerworks/xml/library/x-foaf.html

Dunlop, C., & Kling, R. (Eds) (1991). *Computerization and Controversy: Value Conflicts and Social Choices.* San Diego: Academic Press

Dwyer, C. (2007). *Digital relationships in the "MySpace" generation: Results from a qualitative study.*

Dwyer, C. (2008). In S. R.Hiltz (Ed.), *Understanding development and usage of social networking sites: The social software performance model.*

Dwyer, C., Hiltz, S. R., & Passerini, K. (2007). Trust and privacy concern within social networking sites: A comparison of facebook and MySpace. *Proceedings of the Thirteenth Americas Conference on Information Systems,* Keystone, Colorado.

Eberhardt, D. M. (2007). Facing up to facebook. *About Campus, 12*(4), 18-26.

EBLIDA (2001). Why is lifelong learning important for archives and libraries? *EBLIDA statements in response to European Commission memorandum on lifelong learning.* www.eblida.org/topics/lifelong/lifelonglearning.htm

Echarte, F., Astrain, J. J., Córdoba, A., & Villadangos, J. (2007). Ontology of Folksonomy: A New Modeling Method. In S. Handschuh, N. Collier, T. Groza, R. Dieng-Kuntz, M. Sintek, & A. de Waard, (Ed.), *Semantic Authoring, Annotation and Knowledge Markup - SAAKM 2007-* (pp. 63-70), Sun SITE Central Europe: RWTH Aachen University.

Edgington, T., Choi, B., Henson, K., Raghu, T. S., & Vinze, A. (2004). Adopting ontology to facilitate knowledge sharing. *Communications of the ACM, 47*(11), 85-90.

Eduards, R., & Usher, R. (2000). *Globalization and pedagogy: Space, place, identity* (p. 83). London: Routeldge.

Edvinsson, L., & Malone, M. S. (1997). *Intellectual capital: Realizing your company's true value by finding its hidden brainpower.* New York: Harper Collins.

Ehn, P. (1989). *Work-oriented design of computer artifacts.* Stockholm: Arbetslivscentrum.

Eikelmann, S., Hajj, J., & Peterson, M. (2008). Opinion piece: Web 2.0: Profiting from the threat. *Journal of Direct, Data and Digital Marketing Practice, 9*(3), 293–295.

Ekman, P. (1972). Universals and Cultural Differences in Facial Expressions of Emotion, In, J. Cole (Ed.), *Nebraska Symposium on motivation,* (pp. 207-283).

Ekman, P. (1984). Expression and the nature of emotion. In K. Scherer & P. Ekman (Eds.), *Approaches to emotion.* Hillsdale, NJ: Erlbaum.

Elkington, J. (1997). *Cannibals With Forks: The Triple Bottom Line of 21st Century Business.* Capstone: Oxford.

Ellis, J. B. & Bruckman, A. (2001). Designing Palaver Tree online: Supporting social roles in a community of oral history. Paper presented at *CHI01,* Seattle. Retrieved June 28, 2005, from *http://www.cc.gatech.edu/elc/palaver/papers/pt-chi01.pdf*

Ellison, N. B., Steinfield, C., & Lampe, C. (2007). The benefits of facebook "Friends:" social capital and college students' use of online social network sites. *Journal of Computer-Mediated Communication, 12*(4), 1143-1168.

Ellison, N., Steinfield, C., & Lampe, C. A. C. (2006). Spatially bounded online social networks and social capital: The role of facebook. *Annual Conference of the International Communication Association (ICA),* Dresden, Germany.

Emerald InTouch (2008). Retrieved June 27, 2008 from http://info.emeraldinsight.com/products/intouch/index.htm

Erwin, G., Taylor, W., Bytheway, A., & Strumpfer, C. (Eds.). (2005, August 23-26). CIRN2005: *The Second Annual Conference of the Community Informatics Research Network, Cape Town, South Africa.*

Esuli, A., & Sebastiani, F. (2006). SentiWordNet: A Publicly Available Lexical Resource for Opinion Mining. *Proceedings of LREC 2006 - 5th Conference on Language Resources and Evaluation,* 22-28/5/2006, Genova (IT).

Everest, K. (2008) *Business drivers for social networking* (Presentation May 2, 2008. Queen's University.

Facebook (2008). Retrieved June 27, 2008 from http://www.facebook.com/

Fahey, R. (2005). *Knowledge management. The impact of rewards within communities of practice. A case study.* Unpublished master's thesis, Sheffield Hallam University, UK.

Fernández, S., Berrueta, D., & Labra, J. E. (2008). A Semantic Web Approach to Publish and Consume Mailing Lists. *IADIS International Journal on WWW/Internet, 6,* 90-102.

Fernándrez, S. (2008). *RDFohloh, a RDF Wrapper of Ohloh. Proceedings of 1st workshop on Social Data on the Web (SDoW2008), collocated with 7th International Semantic Web Conference,* Karlsruhe, Germany.

Fikes, R., Hayes, P., & Horrocks, I. (2004). OWL-QL: A language for deductive query answering on the Semantic Web. *Web Semantics: Science, Service and Agents on the World Wide Web, 2*(1), 19-29.

Flatz, A. (2003). Screening for sustainability. A case study of the Dow Jones Sustainability Index. In S. Waage (Ed.), *Ants, Galileo, and Gandhi. Designing the Future of Business Through Nature, Genius, and Compassion* (pp. 144-168). Greenleaf: Sheffield.

Fodor, O., & Werthner, H. (2004). Harmonise: A step toward an interoperable e-tourism marketplace. *International Journal of Electronic Commerce, 9*(2), 11-39.

Foster, D. (2003). Test piracy: The darker side of certification. *Certification Magazine,* (January). Retrieved

December 5, 2005, from http://www.certmag.com/articles/templates/cmag_feature.asp?articleid=2

FP7 (2008). Retrieved June 27, 2008 from http://www.elearning.mdx.ac.uk/research/index.htm.#4_April_

FP7 European Commission (2008). Retrieved June 27, 2008 from http://cordis.europa.eu/fp7/

Francisco, V., Gervás, P., & Peinado. F. (2007). Ontological reasoning to configure emotional voice synthesis. In M. Marchiori, J. Z. Pan, & C. de Sainte Marie (Eds.), *Web Reasoning and Rule Systems, 1st Int. Conf., RR 2007*, (pp. 88–102).

Frand, J., & Hixon, C. (1999). *Personal knowledge management: Who, what, why, when, where, how*. Retrieved June 25,2007. http://www.anderson.ucla.edu/faculty/jason.frand/researcher/speeches/PKM.htm.

Frey, B. S., & Luechinger, S. (2002). Terrorism: Deterrence may backfire. *European Journal of Political Economy, 20*(2).

Fröchlich, G. (1996). The (Surplus) Values of Scientific Communication. *Review of Information Science, 2.* http://www.inf-wiss.uni-konstanz.de/RIS/1996iss02_01/articles01/02.html

Furst, D., Schubert, H., Rudolph, A., & Spieckermann, H. (2001). Regional actor networks between social capital and regional governance. *Connections, 24*(1), 42-67.

Galbraith, J. R., & Lawler, E. E. (1993). *Organizing for the Future*. San Francisco, CA Jossey-Bass Publishers.

Galbreath, J.(2000). Knowledge management technology in education: An overview. *Educational Technology, 40*(5), 28-33.

Gamon, M. (2004). Sentiment Classification on Customer Feedback Data: noisy data, large feature vectors, and the role of linguistic analysis. *Proceedings of the 20th international conference on Computational Linguistics*, Geneva, Switzerland. Article No. 841.

Garratt, B. (1987). *The learning organization: And the need for directors who think*. Aldershot, Hampshire, England: Ashgate.

Garrison, B. (2001). Diffusion of online information technologies in newschapter newsrooms. *Journalism, 2*(2), 221-239.

Garshol, L. M., & Moore, G. (2004). *Topic maps—XML syntax*. Retrieved March 16, 2004, from http://www.jtc1sc34.org/repository/0495.htm

Gay, G., & Bennigton, T. L. (Eds.). (1999). *Information technologies in evaluation: Social, moral, epistemological, and practical implications. New Directions for Evaluations #84*. San Francisco: Jossey-Bass.

Gerald, S. E., & Rob, P. (2002). Creating shared knowledge: Instructional knowledge management systems. *Educational Technology & Society, 5*(1), 100-104.

Giachetti, R. E. (2004). A framework to review the information integration of the enterprise. *International Journal of Production Research, 42*(6), 1147-1166.

Gibb, A., & Adhikary, D. (2000). Strategies for local and regional NGO development: Combining sustainable outcomes with sustainable organizations. *Entrepreneurship & Regional Development, 12*, 137-161.

Gibson, J.J.(1966). *The senses considered as perceptual systems*. Boston: Houghton Mifflin.

Giddens, A. (1990). *The consequences of modernity*. Cambridge: Polity Press.

Giddens, A. (1991). *Modernity and self-identity: Self and society in the late modern age*. Cambridge: Polity Press.

Gil, Y., & Ratnakar, V. (2002). *A comparison of (semantic) markup languages*. In M. S. Haller & G. Simmons (Eds.), *Proceedings of the 15th International FLAIRS Conference, Special Track on Semantic Web*, Pensacola, FL (pp. 413-418). AAAI Press.

Gilliland-Swetland, A. J.(2000). Setting the stage: Defining metadata. In M. Baca (Ed.), *Introduction to Metadata: Pathways to Digital Information.* 2nd ed. Los Angeles: Getty Information Institute, http://www.getty.edu/research/institute/standards/intrometadata/index.html

Global Reporting Initiative (GRI) (2006). *G3 Sustainability Reporting Guidelines*. Amsterdam: GRI

Glushko, R. J., & McGrath, T. (2005). *Document Engineering. Analyzing and Designing Documents for Business Informatics and Web Services*. MIT: Cambridge, London.

Golder, S. A., & Huberman, B. A. (2005). The Structure of Collaborative Tagging Systems. *Journal of Information Science, 32*(2), 198-208.

Gomez-Perez, A., & Corcho, O. (2002). *Ontology languages for the Semantic Web. Intelligent Systems, IEEE, 17*(1), 54- 60.

Gonzalez, R. C., & Thomason, M. G. (1978). *Syntactic Pattern Recognition. An Introduction*. Reading: Addison-Wesley.

Gooding, J. (2008). Web 2.0: A Vehicle for Transforming Education. *International Journal of Information and Communication Technology Education, 4*(2), 44-53.

Goth, G. (2008). *Are social networking sites growing up?*

Gountas, J., & Gountas, S. (2007), Personality orientations, emotional states, customer satisfaction, and intention to repurchase. *Journal of Business Research, 60*(1), 72-75.

Govani, T., & Pashley, H. (2005). Student awareness of the privacy implications when using facebook. *Student Poster*, Pittsburgh, PA: Carnegie Mellon University.

GPMG (2003) *XHTML Friends Network (XFN)*. Retrieved from, http://gmpg.org/xfn/ and http://www.downes.ca/cgi-bin/page.cgi?post=31624 and http://www.emeraldinsight.com/Insight/ViewContentServlet;jsessionid=0672AB01BCFD4DC910E9F3D12B123297?Filename=Published/EmeraldFullTextArticle/Pdf/1190120502_ref.html

Granovetter, S. (1973). The strength of weak ties. *The American Journal of Sociology, 78*(6), 1360-1380.

Green, H. (2007). The water cooler is now on the web. *Business Week,* (4052), 78.

Green, H. (2008). One place for your many online lives. *Business Week,* (4080), 54.

GRI (2006). *G3 - Leitfaden zur Nachhaltigkeitsberichterstattung*. Amsterdam: Global Reporting Initiative.

Grier, D. A. (2005). *When computers were human*. Princeton University Press

Gross, R., Acquisti, A., & Heinz, H. J.,III. (2005). Information revelation and privacy in online social networks. *WPES '05: Proceedings of the 2005 ACM Workshop on Privacy in the Electronic Society,* Alexandria, VA, USA. (pp. 71-80).

Grover, V., & Teng, J. (1992) An examination of DBMS adoption and success in American organizations. *Information Management, 23*(5), 239-248.

Gruber, T. (1993). A Translation Approach to Portable Ontology Specifications. *Knowledge Acquisition, 5*(2), 199-220.

Gruber, T. R. (1992). *Ontolingua: A mechanism to support portable ontologies* (Tech. Rep. No. KSL-91-66). Standford Knowledge Systems Laboratory.

Gruber, T. R. (1993). A translation approach to portable ontologies. *Knowledge Acquisition, 5*(2), 199-220.

Gutwin, C., & Greenberg, S. (1998). Design for individuals, design for groups: Tradeoffs between power and workspace awareness. *Proceedings of the ACM Conference on Computer-Supported Cooperative Work* (pp. 207-216).

Guy, M., & Tonkin, E. (2006). Folksonomies - Tidying up Tags? *DLib Magazine, 12*(1).

Hakansson, H. (1990). Technological collaboration in industrial networks. *European Management Journal, 8*(3), 371-379.

Hakken, D. (2002). Building our knowledge of virtual community: Some responses. In K.A. Renninger & W.

Shumar (Eds.), *Building virtual communities: Learning and change in cyberspace* (pp. 355-367). Cambridge, UK: Cambridge University Press

Hall, E. (2005). *RFC 4155 - the application/mbox media type*. Technical report, The Internet Society.

Hamming, R. W. (1950). Error Detecting and Error Correcting Codes. *Bell System Technical Journal, 26*(2), 147-160.

Handal, G., & Lauvas, P. (1987). *Promoting reflective teaching: Supervision in practice.* London: Open University Press.

Hansen, M. T. (1999). The Search- Transfer Problem: The Role of Weak Ties in Sharing Knowledge Across Organization Subunits. *Administrative Science Quarterly, 44*(1), 82-111.

Hansen, M. T. (2002). Knowledge networks: Explaining effective knowledge sharing in multiunit companies. *Organization Science, 13*(3), 232-48.

Hara, N. & Kling, R. (1999). Students' frustrations with a Web-based distance education course. *First Monday, 4*(12). Retrieved June 28, 2005, from *http://www.first-monday.dk/issues/issue4_12/hara/*

Hargittai, E. (2007). Whose space? differences among users and non-users of social network sites. *Journal of Computer-Mediated Communication, 13*(1), 276-297.

Hargreaves, D. H. (2000). The knowledge creating school. *British Journal of Education Studies, 47*(2), 122-144.

Harmelen, F. V., Hendler, J., Horrocks, I., McGuinness, D. L., Patel-Schneider, P. F., & Stein., L. A. (2004). *OWL Web ontology language reference.* W3C Recommendation. Retrieved February 10, 2004, from http://www.w3.org/TR/owl-ref/

Harré, R. (1986). *The social construction of emotions.* Oxford: Blackwell.

Harvard's Open Collections Programs, *Immigration to the United States, 1789-1930.* http://ocp.hul.harvard.edu/ei

Harvard's Open Collections Programs, *Women Working, 1800-1930.* http://ocp.hul.harvard.edu/ww

Hathi, S. (2008). Billions lost from social networking. *Strategic Communication Management, 12*(2), 9.

Hausenblas, M., & Rehatschek, H. (2007). mle: Enhancing the Exploration of Mailing List Archives Through Making Semantics Explicit. *Semantic Web Challenge 07*, Busan, South Korea.

Haythornthwaite, C., Kazmer, M. M., Robins, J., & Shoemaker, S. (2000). Community development among distance learners: Temporal and technological dimensions. *Journal of Computer-Mediated Communication, 6*(1). Retrieved June 28, 2005, from *http://www.ascusc.org/jcmc/vol6/issue1/haythornthwaite.html*

Hedstrom M. (2002). Archives, memory, and interfaces with the past. *Archival Science, 2*, 21–43.

Heeks, R. (2002) Information systems and developing countries: Failure, success, and local improvisations. *The Information Society, 18*(2), 101-112.

Helleloid, D., & Simonin, B. (1994). Organizational learning and a firm's core competence. In G. Hamel & A. Heene (Eds.), *Competence-Based Competitive*, Wiley, New York (pp. 213-239).

Hepburn, G. A. (2004). Seeking an educational commons: The promise of open source development models. *First Monday, 9*(8), http://www.firstmonday.org/issues/issue9_8/hepburn/

Herring, S. (1996). Posting in a different voice: Gender and ethics in computer-mediated communication. In C. Ess (Ed.), *Philosophical approaches to computer-mediated communication* (pp. 115-145). Albany, NY: State University of New York Press.

Hesseldahl, A. (2008). In browsers, flock may lead the flock. *Business Week (Online).*

Hevner, A. R., March, S. T., Park, J., & Ram, S. (2004). Design science in information systems research. *MIS Quarterly, 28*(1), 75-105.

Hewitt, A., & Forte, A. (2006). Crossing boundaries: Identity management and Student/Faculty relationships on the facebook. Paper presented at the *CSCW '06 Poster*, Banff, Alberta, Canada.

Heylighten, F. (1999). *What are socio-technical approaches and systems science? Principia socio-technical approach Web.* Retrieved from http://pespmc1.vub.ac.be/CYBSWHAT.html

Hildreth, P., Kimble, C., & Wright, P. (1998). Computer-mediated communications and international communities of practice. *Proceedings of the 4th International Conference on Ethical Issues of Information Technology* (Ethicomp98), Rotterdam, Holland.

Hiltz, S. R. & Turoff, M. (1993). *The network nation: Human communication by computer* (revised ed.). Cambridge, MA: MIT Press.

Hiroshi, K., & Tetsuya, N. (2004). Deeper Sentiment Analysis Using Machine Translation Technology. *Proceedings of International Conference on Computational Linguistics (COLING2004)*, August 23 - 27, University of Geneva, Switzerland.

Hoadley, C. (1999). *Scaffolding scientific discussion using socially relevant representations in networked multimedia.* Unpublished doctoral dissertation, University of California, Berkeley.

Hoadley, C., & Linn, M. C. (2000). Teaching science through online peer discussions: SpeakEasy in the knowledge integration environment. *International Journal of Science Education, 22*(8), 839-858.

Hoadley, C., & Pea, R. D. (2002). Finding the ties that bind: Tools in support of a knowledge-building community. In K. A. Renninger & W. Shumar (Eds.), *Building virtual communities: Learning and change in cyberspace* (pp. 321-354). Cambridge, UK: Cambridge University Press.

Hodge, M. J. (2006-2007). Fourth amendment and privacy issues on the new internet: Facebook.com and myspace.com, the. *Southern Illinois University Law Journal, 31*, 95-123.

Hofbauer, J., & Sigmund, K. (2003). Evolutionary game dynamics. *Bulletin of the American Mathematical Society, 40*(4).

Horrocks, I., Fensel, D., Broekstra, J., Decker, S., Erdmann, M., Goble, C., et al. (2001). *The ontology inference layer OIL.* Retrieved December 31, 2001, from http://www.ontoknowledge.org/oil/

Horstmanshof, L. (2004). Using SMS as a way of providing connection and community for first-year students. Paper presented at *ASCILITE*, Perth, Australia (pp. 432-427).

Houle, C. O. (1961). *The Inquiring Mind. A study of the adult who continues to learn* (pp. 34-36), Madison, Wisconsin: University of Wisconsin Press.

Howarth, L. C. (2001). Designing a Metadata-Enabled Namespace for Enhancing Resource Discovery in Knowledge Bases [Version presented at the International Conference]. In M. Guerrini & S. Gambari, & L. Sardo (Eds.), *Proceedings International Conference Electronic Resources: Definition, Selection and Cataloguing*, Rome, 2001, http://66.249.93.104/search?q=cache:a8QFjPNp_p0J:eprints.rclis.org/archive/00000174/ ca,+Murtha+what:+Introduction+to+Metadata:+Pathways+to+Digital+Information+&hl=el&ie=UTF-8&inlang=el

HR-XML Consortium (2005). Retrieved from, http://www.hrcertify.org/index.php

Hsi, S. H. (1997). *Facilitating knowledge integration in science through electronic discussion: The multimedia forum kiosk.* Unpublished doctoral dissertation, University of California, Berkeley.

Hu, Y-W., & Chen, M-F. (2008). A knowledge management method which based on Web 2.0 distributed toolkit. *Modern Educational Technology, 16*(6), 98-101.

Huang, M. H. (2001). The Theory of Emotions in Marketing. *Journal of Business and Psychology, 16*(2), 239-247.

Huang, N. S. (2008). A study on elementary school teachers' knowledge management and teachers' professionalism in Kaohsiung city. *NPUE.* Thesys, http://etd.npue.edu.tw/ETD-db/ETD-search-c/view_etd?URN=etd-0118108-084133

Huang, S. Y. (2005). The Relationships among Professional Growth, Organizational Enablers, and Knowledge Management for Primary School Teachers. *MCU Thesys,* http://ethesys.lib.mcu.edu.tw/ETD-db/ETD-search/view_etd?URN=etd-0822105-041457, pp. 27-57.

Hund, G., Engel-Cox, J., & Fowler, K. (2004). *A Communications Guide for Sustainable Development. How Interested Parties Become Partners.* Battelle: Columbus.

ICS-FORTH. (2005). *The RDF query language (RQL).* Retrieved January 24, 2006, from http://139.91.183.30:9090/RDF/RQL/

IDEF- (2001). *A What is.com definitions.* http://64.233.183.04/search?q=cache:syss28wuqsoJ:cersi.luiss.it/oesseo2001/papers/9.pdf+IDEF5+(integrated+definition)+&hl=el&ie=UTF-8&inlang=el

Illich, I. (1970). *Deschooling Society.* New York: Harper and Row

IMS Global Learning Consortium. (2005). *IMS Learner Information Package Specification.* Available at: www.imsglobal.org/profiles/

Ingram H. (1997). Performance management: processes, quality and team working. *International Journal of Contemporary Hospitality Management, 9*(7), 295-303.

International Institute for Sustainable Development (IISD). Deloitte & Touche, Business Council for Sustainable Development. (1992). *Business Strategy for Sustainable Development. Leadership and Accountability for the 90'.* IISD: Winnipeg.

InTouch (2008). Retrieved June 27, 2008 from http://intouch.emeraldinsight.com/

Irvine, M. (2008, Apr 28). Social networking applications can pose security risks. *Telegraph-Journal,* (p. B.5).

Irwin, A. (1995) *Citizen Science: A Study of People, Expertise and Sustainable Development (Environment and Society).*

Isenmann, R., & Kim, K. (2006). Interactive sustainability reporting. Developing clear target group tailoring and stimulating stakeholder dialogue. In S. Schaltegger, M.

Bennett, & R. Burritt (Eds.), *Sustainability Accounting and Reporting* (pp. 533-555). Springer: Berlin.

Isenmann, R., & Marx Gómez, J. (2004). How to provide customized environmental reports properly. In A. Scharl (Ed.), *Environmental Online Communication* (pp. 173-182). Springer: London.

Iyamu, E. O. S., & Ukadike, J. O. (2007). Perception of Self-Directed Cooperative Learning Among Undergraduate Students in Selected Nigerian Universities. *International Journal of Information and Communication Technology Education, 3*(4), 13-20.

Izard, C. E. (1977). *Human Emotions.* New York: Plenum Press.

J2SDK. (2006). *Sun developer network.* Retrieved February 24, 2006, from http://java.sun.com/j2se/1.4.2/download.html

Jánossy F. (1975). *A gazdasági fejlödés trendvonaláról* (On the trendline of economic development) (2. enlarged edition, Magvető, Budapest. (English version: The end of the economic miracle; Appearance and reality in economic development International Arts and Sciences Press (1971)

Jena. (n.d.). A Semantic Web framework (Version 2.4) [Computer software]. Retrieved January 24, 2006, from http://jena.sourceforge.net/

Jensen, R. E., & Xiao, J. Z. (2001). Customized financial reporting, networked databases, and distributed file sharing. *Accounting Horizons, 15*(3), 209-222.

JISC (2008). Retrieved June 27, 2008 from www.jisc.ac.uk/

Johanson, G., & Stillman, L. (Eds.). (2004, September 29-October 1). *Sustainability and community technology: What does this mean for community informatics?* Monash Prato Colloqium, Prato, Italy.

Johanson, G., Denison, T., & Otis, N. (2004, September 29-October 1). Building sustainable learning communities in Vietnam. In G. Johanson & L. Stillman (Eds.), *Sustainability and community technology: What does this mean for community informatics?* Monash Prato

Colloqium, Prato, Italy. Available at http://www.ccnr. net/?q=node/5. Accessed Jan. 30, 2006

Johnson, G. N. Y., & Scholes, K. (1997). *An Integrated Approach.* Boston: Houghton Mifflin Company. *Exploring Corporate Strategy*, London: Prentice Hall.

Jonassen, D. H., Howland, J., Moore, J., & Marra, R. M. (2003). *Learning to solve problems with technology: A constructivist perspective* (2nd ed.). Upper Saddle River, NJ: Pearson Education.

Jones, K. (a.k.a. "handy vandal"). (2003). Student logs teacher's keystrokes. *Slashdot,* (February 5). Retrieved December 5, 2005, from http://yro.slashdot.org/article. pl?sid=05/02/03/0156243

Jones, Q. (1997). Virtual-communities, virtual settlements & cyber-archaeology: A theoretical outline. *Journal of Computer Mediated Communication, 3*(3). Retrieved July 20, 2004, from *http://www.ascusc.org/ jcmc/vol3/issue3/jones.html*

Jonhson-Laird, P. N., & Oatley, K. (1989). The language of emotions: an analysis of a semantic field. *Cognition and Emotion, 3*, 81-123.

Joo, J. (2002). A business model and its development strategies for electronic tourism markets. *Information Systems Management, 19*(3), 58-69.

Joo, J., & Jeong, Y. (2004). *An implementation of the semantic search system based on the ontology for global knowledge management in tourism business domain.* Paper presented KMIS Conference, Seoul, 448-454.

Kadushin, C. (2002) The motivational foundation of social networks. *Social Networks,* 24, 77-91.

Kalaitzakis, E., Dafoulas, G., & Macaulay, L. (2003, June 22-27). Designing online communities: Community-centered development for intensively focused user groups. *Proceedings of the 10th HCI International Conference,* Greece.

Kalfoglou, Y., & Schorlemmer, M. (2003). *Ontology mapping: The state of the art. The Knowledge Engineering Review, 18*(1), 1-31.

Kamel, B., Maged, N., & Wheeler, S. (2007). The emerging Web 2.0 social software: an enabling suite of sociable technologies in health and health care education. *Health Information and Libraries Journal, 24*(1), 2-23.

Kao, Y. J. (2002). A study of the Relation of Teachers' Knowledge Management, Learning Style, Professional Growth and Professional Performance in the Elementary Schools. *Electronic Theses and Dissertations System,* http://etds.ncl.edu.tw/theabs/site/sh/detail_result.jsp?id =090NKNU0332047,pp.122-136.

Keil, M., Cule, P., Lyytinen, K., & Schmidt, R. (1998). A framework for identifying software project risks. *Communications of the ACM, 41*(11), 76-83.

Kerr, N. L. (1996). Does my contribution really matter? *European Review of Social Psychology, 7,* 209-240.

Key, E. (1900). *The Century of the Child.* In English it was first published in 1909, following the German translation of 1902.

Killingback, T., & Doebeli, M. (1996). Spatial evolutionary game theory: Hawks and doves revisited. In *Proceedings of The Royal Society (Biological Sciences).*

Kim, A. J. (2000). *Community building on the Web: Secret strategies for successful online communities.* Berkeley, CA: Peachpit Press.

Kim, D., Cameron, S., & Quinn, R. E. (1998). *Diagnosing and Changing Organizational Culture: Based on the Competing Values Framework.* (Addison-Wesley Series on Organization Development) by Addison-Wesley Pub Co.

Kim, E.E. (2003). *An introduction to open source communities.* Retrieved May 1, 2003, from http://www. blueoxen.org/research/00007/

Kim, K., & Yun, H. (2007). *Cying* for me, *cying* for us: Relational dialectics in a korean social network site. *Journal of Computer-Mediated Communication, 13*(1), 298-318.

Klaassen, A. (2008). Actions louder than words on social nets. *Advertising Age, 79*(14), 3.

Kleinginna, P. R., & Kleinginna, A. M. (1981). A categorized list of emotion definitions, with suggestions for a consensual definition. *Motivation and Emotion, 5*(4), 263-291.

Kling, R. (2000) Learning about information technologies and social change: The contribution of social informatics. *The Information Society, 16*, 217-232.

Klyne, G., & Carroll, J. J. (2004). *Resource Description Framework (RDF): Concepts and abstract syntax*. Technical report, W3C Recommendation.

Kolk, A. (2004). A decade of sustainability reporting: developments and significance. *International Journal of Environment and Sustainable Development, 3*(1), 51–64.

Kollock, P. (1999). The economies of online cooperation: Gifts and public goods in cyberspace. In M.A. Smith & P. Kollock (Eds.), *Communities in cyberspace* (pp. 220-239). London/New York: Routledge.

Kollock, P., & Smith, M. (1996). Managing the virtual commons: Cooperation and conflict in computer communities. In S. Herring (Ed.), *Computer-mediated communication: Linguistic, social, and cross-cultural perspectives*. Amsterdam: John Benjamins.

Kourtoumi, Tr. (2004). 'Intelligent' Cultural Heritage & Archival Applications: A Case Study of Usefulness of Semantic Indexing in a Collection Level Description. In J. Hemsley (Ed.), *Conference Proceedings, EVA 2004*. London: The London Institute of Archaeology, University College London, July 26-30, 29.1-29.11.

Kourtoumi, Tr. (2005). Knowledge management technology: Facing the challenge of managing archives. *International Journal of Knowledge, Culture and Change Management, 5*(4), 25-30, http://ijm.cgpublisher.com/product/pub.28/prod.259

KPMG. (2000). *Beyond the Numbers: How Leading Organisations are Linking Values with Value to Gain Competitive Advantage*. KPMG's Assurance & Advisory Services Center (AASC): KPMG.

KPMG. (2005). *KPMG International Survey of Corporate Responsibility Reporting 2005*. University of Amsterdam (The Netherlands), KPMG global sustainability service. KPMG: Amsterdam.

Krippendorf, K. (1984). Epistemological foundation for communication. *Journal of Communication, 84*.

Kuutti, K., & Bannon, L. J. (1993). Searching for unity among diversity: Exploring the "interface" concept. In *Proceedings of the International Computer Human Interaction Conference (Inter CHI '93)* (pp. 263-268). New York: ACM Press.

Kyriazopoulos, P. (2000). The Modern firm in the starting of the 21st century. In S. Ekdotiki (Ed.), *E-Commerce* (pp. 284-323) Athens.

Lampe, C. A. C., Ellison, N., & Steinfield, C. (2007). A familiar face(book): Profile elements as signals in an online social network. *CHI '07: Proceedings of the SIGCHI Conference on Human Factors in Computing Systems,* San Jose, California, USA. (pp. 435-444).

Lanham, E. & Zhou, W. (2002). *E-learning: Literature survey*. Technical Report No. TR C 02/20. Geelong, Australia: Deakin University.

Lanham, E. & Zhou, W. (2003). Cultural issues in online learning: Is blended learning a possible solution. *International Journal of Computer Processing of Oriental Languages, 16*(4), 275-292.

Lanham, E. & Zhou, W. (2003). Cultural issues relating to teaching IT professional ethics online: Lessons learned. Paper presented at *Advances in Web-Based Learning ICWL 2003*, Melbourne, Australia (pp. 134-144). Springer.

Lanham, E. & Zhou, W. (2004). Giving lectures a voice for a cross-cultural audience. Paper presented at *ASCILITE*, Perth, Australia. Retrieved June 28, 2005, from *http://www.ASCILITE.org.au/conferences/perth04/procs/lanham-poster.html*

Lanham, E. & Zhou, W. (2004b). Video lectures for cross-cultural use: A three phase model. Paper presented at *World Conference on E-Learning in Corp., Govt., Health., & Higher Ed.*, Washington, DC (pp. 2368-2373). AACE.

Laros, F. J. M., & Steenkamp, J. B. E. M. (2005). Emotions in consumer behavior: A hierarchical approach. *Journal of Business Research, 58*(10), 1437-1445.

Lassila, D. O., & Swick, R. (1999). *Resource description framework (RDF) model and syntax specification*. W3C Recommendation. Retrieved January 5, 1999, from http://www.w3.org/TR/PR-rdf-syntax/

Latham, R. P., Butzer, C. C., & Brown, J. T. (2008). Legal implications of user-generated content: YouTube, MySpace, facebook. *Intellectual Property & Technology Law Journal, 20*(5), 1.

Lau, A., & Tsui, E. (2009). Knowledge Management Perspective on E-learning Effectiveness. *Knowledge-based Systems* (in print).

Lave, J., & Wenger, E. (1991). *Situated learning: Legitimate peripheral participation*. New York: Cambridge University Press.

Lazar, J., & Preece, J. (1998). Classification schema for online communities. In *Proceedings of the 1998 Association for Information Systems, Americas Conference.*

Lee, H., Tsui, E., & Garner, B. J. (2008). Leveraging Web 2.0 concepts to create an open and adaptive approach to Corporate Learning. *Cutter IT Journal, 21*(1), January, 2008, 14-20.

Lee, K. H. (2003). *Text Categorization with a Small Number of Labeled Training Examples*. Ph.D. thesis, School of Information Technologies, University of Sydney.

Lee, T. B. (1999). *The Semantic Web homepage*. Retrieved December 31, 1999, from http://www.semanticweb.org

Lee, T. B., Fielding, R., & Masinter, L. (1998, August). *Uniform resource identifiers (URI): Generic syntax*. IETF Draft Standard (RFC 2396). Retrieved August 31, 1998, from http://www.ietf.org/rfc/rfc2396.txt

LEGO Group. (1999-2001). *LEGO.com MINDSTORMS Hall of Fame*. Retrieved December 5, 2005, from http://mindstorms.lego.com/eng/community/halloffame/default.asp

LEGO Group. (2005). *LEGO.com Educational Division—MINDSTORMS for schools*. Retrieved December 5, 2005, from http://www.lego.com/eng/education/mindstorms/home.asp?menu=community&pagename=community

Lenz, Ch. (2003). *Empfängerorientierte Unternehmenskommunikation. – Einsatz der Internet-Technologie am Beispiel der Umweltberichterstattung*. Eul: KölnEul, J. (p. 212).

Lesser, E. L., & Prusak, L. (2000). Communities of practice, social capital and organizational knowledge. In E. L. Lesser, M. A. Fontaine, & J. A. Slusher (Eds.), *Knowledge and communities*. Boston: Butterworth Heinemann.

Lesser, E., & Storck, J. (2001). Communities of practice and organizational performance. *IBM Systems Journal, 40*(4).

Lessig, L. (1999). *Code: And other laws of cyberspace*. New York: Basic Books.

Leuf, B. & Cunningham, W. (2001). *The Wiki way: Quick collaboration on the Web*. Upper Saddle River, NJ: Addison Wesley.

Levenshtein, V. I. (1966). Binary codes capable of correcting deletions, insertions, and reversals. *Soviet Physics Doklady, 10*(8), 707-710.

Levine, L. (2001, Winter). Integrating knowledge and processes in a learning organization. *Information Systems Management*, 21-32.

Levy, R. I. (1984). The emotions in comparative perspective. In K. Scherer & P. Ekman (Eds.), *Approaches to emotion*. Hillsdale, NJ: Erlbaum.

Lewis, R. (2002). Learning communities: Old and new. Paper presented at *International conference on Computers in Education*, Auckland, New Zealand (pp. 6-13). IEEE Computer Society.

Li, Q. (2005). Teacher professional growth and knowledge management in the age of information. *Zhejiang Education Science, 5*, 23-24.

Library of Congress (2000). *Digitizing the collection: American Memory.* http://lcweb2.loc.gov/ammem/daghtml/dagtech.html

Lin, Y-H-K. (2007). *Teachers' Personal Knowledge Management: Theoretical Foundations and Building Blocks,* May 18, 2008, http://www.atee2007.org.uk/docs/LinYHK.doc

Ling, K., Beenen, G., Ludford, P., Wang, X., Chang, K., Li, X., et al. (2005). Using social psychology to motivate contributions to online communities. *Journal of Computer-Mediated Communication, 10*(4).

Ling, T. W., & Teo, P. K. (1993). *Inheritance conflicts in object-oriented systems.* In V. Marík, J. Lazanský, & R. Wagner (Eds.), *Proceedings of Database and Expert Systems Applications* (LNCS 720, pp. 189-200). Prague, Czech Republic: Springer.

Linn, M. C. (2000). Designing the knowledge integration environment: The partnership inquiry process. *International Journal of Science Education, 22*(8), 781-796.

Linn, M. C., & Hsi, S. (2000). *Computers, teachers, peers: Science learning partners.* Mahwah, NJ: Lawrence Erlbaum.

Linn, M. C., & Slotta, J. D. (2000). WISE curriculum projects: Bridging the gap between educational research and classroom customization. *Educational Leadership, 58*(2), 29-33.

Lipponen, L. (2002). *Exploring foundations for computer-supported collaborative learning.* Finland: University of Helsinki. Retrieved June 28, 2005, from *http://newmedia. colorado.edu/cscl/31.pdf*

Lisbon European Council (2000). *Resolution on lifelong learning.* http://europa.eu.int/eurlex/pri/en/oj/dat/2002/c_163/c_16320020709en00010003.pdf

Liu, H. (2007). Social network profiles as taste performances. *Journal of Computer-Mediated Communication, 13*(1), 252-275.

López, J. M, Gil, R., García, R., Cearreta I., & Garay, N. (2008). Towards an Ontology for Describing Emotions. *In Proceedings of the 1st World Summit on the Knowledge Society. LNCS/LNAI , 5288*, 96-104. Springer.

Luke, S., & Heflin, J. (2000, April 28). *SHOE specification 1.01.* Retrieved April 28, 2000, from http://www.cs.umd.edu/projects/plus/SHOE/spec.html

Lynch, C. A. (2002). Digital Collections, Digital Libraries and the Digitization of Culture Heritage Information. *First Monday, 7*(5). http://www.firstmonday.org/issues/issue7_5/lynch/author

Lyytinen, K., & Hirschheim, R. (1987). Information Systems failures – A survey and classification of the empirical literature. *Oxford Surveys in Information Technology, 4*, 257-309.

Lyytinen, K., & Robey, D. (1999). Learning failure in information systems development. *Information Systems Journal, 9*(2), 85-101.

MacGregor, R. (1991). *Inside the LOOM description classifier. SIGART Bulletin, 2*(3), 88-92.

MacLeod, E. (2008, Apr 17). Facing our past on facebook; when long-lost 'friends' reach out it's best just to slam the electronic door, experts advise. *Toronto Star,* (p. L.4).

Madon, S. (2000). International NGOs: Networking, information flows and learning. *Development informatics working chapter series.* Manchester: Institute for Development Policy and Management, University of Manchester.

Maedche, A., Motik, B. Stojanovic, L., Studer, R., & Voltz, R. (2003). Ontologies for enterprise knowledge management. *IEEE Intelligent Systems, 18*(2), 26-33.

Manyika, J. M., Roberts, R. P., & Sprague, K. L. (2007). Eight business technology trends to watch. *The McKinsey Quarterly.* December 2007. Available http://www.mckinseyquarterly.com/PDFDownload. aspx?L2=13&L3=0&ar=2080 (last verified: 29 December, 2008)

Marshall, S. R., & Brown, D. (2003). Corporate environmental reporting: What's in a metric? *Business Strategy and the Environment, 12*(2), 87-106.

Martin, J. (2006). *The Meaning of the 21st Century. A vital blueprint for ensuring our future.* Riverhead Books

Martin, J. (2007). How businesses are using web 2.0: A McKinsey global survey. *The McKinsey Quarterly,* (March), May 8, 2008. Retrieved from http://www.mckinseyquarterly.com/home.aspx.

Mathes, A. (2004). Folksonomies - Cooperative Classification and Communication Through Shared Metadata. *Computer Mediated Communication – LIS590CMC,* University of Illinois Urbana-Champaign. Retrieved Jan. 30th, 2007, from http://www.adammathes.com/academic/computer-mediated-communication/folksonomies.html

Mathieu, Y. (2005) Annotation of emotions and Feelings in texts. In J. Tao, T. Tan, & R.W. Picard (Eds). ASCII 2005, *LNCS 3784*, 350-357.

May, C. (2000). The Information Society as Mega-Machine. The Continuing Relevance of Lewis Mumford. *Information, Communication and Society, 2,* 241-265.

Mazer, J. P., Murphy, R. E., & Simonds, C. J. (2007). I'll see you on "Facebook": The effects of computer-mediated teacher self-disclosure on student motivation, affective learning, and classroom climate. *Communication Education, 56*(1), 1.

McCalla, G. (2000). The fragmentation of culture, learning, teaching and technology: Implications for artificial intelligence in education research. *International Journal of Artificial Intelligence, 11*(2), 177-196.

McCrohon, M., Lo, V., Dang, J., & Johnston, C. (2001). Video streaming of lectures via the Internet: An experience. Paper presented at *ASCILITE*, Melbourne, Australia (pp. 397-406).

McGee, J. B., & Begg, M. (2008). What medical educators need to know about "Web 2.0". *Medical Teacher,* (2), 164-9.

McKay, S. (2003). Research Library, Getty Research Institute, "Digitization in an Archival Environment. *Electronic Journal of Academic and Special Librarianship, 4*(1). http://64.233.183.104/search?q=cache:C80VfM-VXulcJ:southernlibrarianship.icaap.org/content/v04n01/Mckay_s01.htm+content-+archival+collection-+digital&hl=el&ie=UTF-8&inlang=el

McKinsey (2007). How businesses are using Web 2.0: A McKinsey Global Survey. *The McKinsey Quarterly,* March 2007. Available http://www.mckinseyquarterly.com/PDFDownload.aspx?L2=16&L3=16&ar=1913&gp=0 (last verified: 29 December, 2008)

McLean, R., Brian, H. R., & Janet, I. W. (2007). The effect of Web 2.0 on the future of medical practice and education: Darwikinian evolution or folksonomic revolution? *The Medical Journal of Australia, 187*(3), 174-7.

Mencke, M. (2007). *Benchmarking a Text Classification Technique.* M.Sc. Thesis, School of Computer Science and Statistics, Trinity College Dublin, Ireland.

Mercier, L., & Wykoff, L. (2005). Engaging the public with digital primary sources: A tri–state online history database and learning center. *First Monday, 10*(6), http://firstmonday.org/issues/issue10_6/mercier/index.html

Meskó, B., & Dubecz, A. (2007). New possibilities provided by the internet in medicine. *Orvosi hetilap, 148*(44), 2095-9.

MessageLabs. (2005). *Monthly report: June 2005.* Retrieved December 5, 2005, from http://www.messagelabs.com/publishedcontent/publish/threat_watch_dotcom_en/intelligence_reports/june_2005/DA_118149.chp.html

Meyer, P. (1998, January-March). Killer applications. *Business & Economic Review, 44* (2)13-17.

Middleton, C. A. (2003). What if there is no killer application? An exploration of a user-centric perspective on broadband. *Journal of Information Technology, 18,* 231-245.

Millen, D. R., & Feinberg, J. (2006). Using Social Tagging to Improve Social Navigation. In: *Workshop on the*

Social Navigation and Community based Adaptation Technologies. In Conjunction with *Adaptive Hypermedia and Adaptive Web-Based Systems.*

Mischo, W. H. (2005). Digital Libraries: Challenges and Influential Work. *D-Lib Magazine, 11*(7/8), http://66.249.93.104/search?q=cache:37XAKs6S7JAJ: www.dlib.org/ William+H.+Mischo,+%26%238220%3 BDigital+Libraries:+Challenges+and+Influential+Wor k%26%238221%3B,+D-Lib+Magazine,+Vol+11,+No+7/ 8,+July/August+2005&hl=el&ie=UTF-8&inlang=el

Mollison, B. (1990). *Permaculture: A practical guide for a sustainable future.* Washington, DC: Island Press.

Mullen, T., & Malouf, R. (2006). A preliminary investigation into sentiment analysis of informal political discourse. *Proceedings of the AAAI-2006 Spring Symposium on Computational Approaches to Analyzing Weblogs.*

Mumford, E. (1987). Socio-technical systems design: Evolving theory and practice. In P. Ehn & M. Kyng (Eds.), *Computers and democracy: A Scandinavian challenge* (pp. 59-76). London: Avebury.

Mumford, L. (1967). *The Myth of the Machine, 1: Technics and Human Development.* New York: Harcourt Brace Jovanovich. The Myth of the Machine, vol. 2: The Pentagon of Power. New York: Harcourt Brace Jovanovich, 1970.

Munro, K. (2008, Apr 30). Simple rules that make social networking safer. *Financial Times,* (p. 4).

Munro-Smith, N. (2002). A tale of two cities: Computer-mediated teaching & learning in Melbourne and Singapore. Paper presented at *ASCILITE,* Auckland, New Zealand (pp. 861-864).

Myers, J. (1991). Cooperative learning in heterogeneous classes. *Cooperative Learning, 11*(4).

n.a. (2003). *Institutional Repositories: Essential Infrastructure for Scholarship in the Digital Age, ARL, 226,* 1-7. http://www.arl.org/newsltr/226/ir.html

Navarro, G. (2001). A Guided Tour to Approximate String Matching, *ACM Computing Surveys, 33*(1), 31-88.

NCH. (2005). *Putting U in the picture—Mobile bullying survey 2005.* Retrieved December 5, 2005, from http://www.nch.org.uk/uploads/documents/Mobile_bullying_%20report.pdf

Nelson, B. (2004). International student numbers. Retrieved August 30, 2004, from *www.dest.gov.au/Ministers/Media/Nelson/2004/03/n638040 304.asp*

Nemertes Research (2007). *Supporting mobile worker networks: components for effective workplaces.* Retrieved June 27, 2008 from http://www.emeraldinsight.com/Insight/ViewContentServlet?Filename=Published/EmeraldFullTextArticle/Articles/3120090303.html

Nentwich, M. (2005). Cyberscience: modelling ICT-induced changes of the scholarly communication system. *Information, Communication and Society, 4,* 542-560.

Newman, D., Griffin, P., & Cole, M. (1989). *The construction zone: Working for cognitive change in school.* New York: Cambridge University Press.

Nielsen, J. (1996). International Web usability. Retrieved June 15, 2003, from *http://www.useit.com/alertbox/9608.html*

Nonaka, I. (1994). The dynamic theory of organizational knowledge creation. *Organization Science, 5*(1), 14-37.

Nonaka, I., & Takeuchi, H. (1995). *The Knowledge Creating Company: How Japanese Companies Create the Dynamics of Innovation.* New York: Oxford University Press.

Norman, D.A. (1996). Cognitive engineering. In D. A. Norman & S. W. Draper (Eds.), *User-centered systems design: New perspectives on human-computer interaction* (pp. 31-61). Hillsdale, NJ: Lawrence Erlbaum.

Norton, O (2004). Planet Ice. Mars revisited. *National Geographic, 1*(9).

Nowak, M., & May, R. (1993). The spatial dilemmas of evolution. *International Journal of Bifurcation and Chaos, 3.*

Noy, N. F., & Musen, M. A. (2004). Ontology versioning in an ontology management framework. *IEEE Intelligent Systems, 19*(4), 6-13.

Noy, N. F., Doan, A., & Halevy, A. Y. (2005). Semantic integration. *AI Magazine, 26*(1), 7-9.

Noy, N. F., Sintek, M., Decker, S., Crubezy, M., Ferferson, R. W., & Musen, M. A. (2001). Creating Semantic Web contents with Protégé-2000. *IEEE Intelligent Systems, 16* (2) 60-71.

O'Brien L. (2005). E-Research: An Imperative for Strengthening Institutional Partnerships. EDUCAUSE, 40(6), http://www.educause.edu/apps/er/erm05/erm0563.asp

O'Neill, P.A., Willis, S. C., & Jones, A. (2002). A model of how students link problem-based learning with clinical experience through 'elaboration'. *Academy of Medicine, 77*, 552–61.

O'Reilly, T. (2005). *What Is Web 2.0. Design Patterns And Business Models For The Next Generation Of Software.* 30 September 2005. http://www.oreillynet.com/pub/a/oreilly/tim/news/2005/09/30/what-is-web-20.html (last verified: 29 December, 2008)

O'Reilly, T. (2007). What is Web 2.0: Design Patterns and Business Models for the Next Generation of Software. *Communications & Strategies, 1*, 17

OASIS (2005). *Customer Information Quality TC*, available at: www.oasis-open.org/committees/ciq/charter.php

Oberle, D., Staab, S., Studer, R., & Volz, R. (2005). Supporting application development in the Semantic Web. *ACM Transactions on Internet Technology, 5*(2), 328-358.

O'Dell, C., & Grayson, C. J. (1998). If only we knew what we know: Identification and transfer of internal best practice. *California Management Review, 40*(3), 154-174.

OECD (1996). *The knowledge-based economy report.* Paris.

OED Definition (2008). Retrieved June 27, 2008 from http://www.oed.com/

Oluic-Vukovic, V. (2001). From information to knowledge: some reflections on the origin of the current shifting towards knowledge processing and further perspective. *Journal of the American Society for Information Science and Technology, 52*, 54-61.

OntoEdit. (n.d.). (Version 0.6) [Computer Software]. AIFB, University of Karlsruhe. Retrieved 2005, from http://www.ontoknowledge.org/tools/ontoedit.shtml

Oommen, B. J., & Loke, R. K. S. (1997). Pattern recognition of strings with substitutions, insertions, deletions, and generalized transpositions. *Pattern Recognition, 30*(5), 789-800.

Oren, A., Nachmias, R., Mioduser, D., & Lahav, O. (1998). *LEARNET: A model for virtual learning communities in the World Wide Web* (Research Report No. 52). Tel-Aviv, Israel: Tel-Aviv University. Retrieved March 15, 2004, from *http://muse.tau.ac.il/publications/learnets.html*

Orlikowski, W. (2000). Using technology and constituting structures: A practice lens for studying technology in organisations. *Organization Science, 11*(4), 404-428.

Orlikowski, W. J. (2002). Knowing in practice: enacting a collective capability in distributed organizing. *Organization Science, 13*(3), 249-273.

Orlikowski, W. J., & Iacono, C. S. (2001). Research commentary: Desperately seeking the "IT" in IT research. A call to theorizing the IT artifact. *Information Systems Research, 12*(2), 121-134.

Ortony, A., & Turner, T. J. (1990). What's basic about basic emotions? *Psychological Review, 97*, 315-331.

Pan, Z. et al (2006). *An investigation into the feasibility of the semantic web.* Technical Report LU-CSE-06-025, Dept. of Computer Science and Engineering, Lehigh University.

Pang, B., Lee, L., & Vaithyanathan, S. (2002). Thumbs Up? Sentiment Classification Using Machine Learning Techniques. *Proceedings of EMNLP 2002*, (pp. 79–86).

Papert, S. & Harel, I. (1991). *Constructionism.* Norwood, NJ: Ablex Publishing Company. Retrieved June 28, 2005, from *http://www.papert.org/articles/situatingconstructionism.html*

Park, C. C. (1997). Learning style preferences of Asian American (Chinese, Filipino, Korean, and Vietnamese) students in secondary schools. *Equity & Excellence in Education, 30*(2), 68-77.

Park, C. C. (2002). Cross-cultural differences in learning styles of secondary English learners. *Bilingual Research Journal, 26*(2), 213-229.

Park, P., Brydon-Miller, M., Hall, B., & Jackson, T. (1993) *Voices of Change: Participatory Research in the United States and Canada.*

Parrott, W. (2001). *Emotions in Social Psychology.* Philadelphia: Psychology Press.

Patel-Schneider, P. F., Hayes, P., & Horrocks, I. (2004). *OWL Web Ontology Language: Semantics and Abstract Syntax.* Recommendation, W3C, February.

Pea, R. D. (1992). Augmenting the discourse of learning with computer-based learning environments In E. De Corte, M. Linn, H. Mandl, & L. Verschaffel (Eds.), *Computer-based learning environments and problem solving* (pp. 313-343). New York: Springer-Verlag.

Pea, R. D. (1993). Seeing what we build together: Distributed multimedia learning environments for transformative communications. *Journal of the Learning Sciences, 3*(3), 285-299.

Phillips, D. C. (2000). An opinionated account of the constructivist landscape. In D. C. Phillips (Ed.), *Constructivism in education.* Chicago, IL: The National Society for the Study of Education.

Plutchik, R. (1962). *The emotions: Facts, theories and a new model.* Nueva York: Random House.

Popp, B. (2000). *The DARPA agent markup language homepage.* Retrieved September 1, 2000, from http://daml.semanticweb.org/

Porter (1990). Retrieved June 27, 2008 from http://books.google.co.uk/books?hl=en&lr=&id=TT596zcGF0oC&oi=fnd&pg=PT454&dq=Porter,+1990&ots=Wl4aMVx-NL&sig=MAonDDTcOBsSLJR31MnGmXxGTu8

Powazek, D. M. (2002). *Design for community. The art of connecting real people in virtual places.* Indianapolis, IN: New Riders Publishing.

Prahalad C. K., & Krishnan, M. S. (2008) *The New Age of Innovation: Driving Co-created Value through Global Networks.* McGraw-Hill.

Preece, J. (2000). *Online communities: Designing usability and supporting sociability.* New York: John Wiley & Sons.

Preece, J. (2002). Supporting community and building social capital. *Communications of the ACM, 45*(4), 37-39.

Protégé. (n.d.). (Version 3.1.1) [Computer software]. Stanford Medical Informatics. Retrieved 2005, from http://protege.stanford.edu/

Prud'hommeaux, E., & Seaborne, A. (2008). *SPARQL Query Language for RDF.* Technical report, W3C recommendation.

Raar, J. (2002). Environmental initiatives: Towards triple-bottom line reporting. *Corporate Communications, 7*(3), 169-183.

Raitman, R., Augar, N., & Zhou, W. (2004). Constructing wikis as a platform for online collaboration in an e-learning environment. Paper presented at the *International Conference on Computers in Education*, Melbourne, Australia.

Rapoza, J. (2008). Social Engineering. *eWeek, 25*(3), 39-45.

Raskin, R. (2006). Facebook faces its future. *Young Consumers, 7*(2), 56.

Ratto, M., Shapiro, R. B., Truong, T. M., & Griswold, W. G. (2003). The ActiveClass project: Experiments in encouraging classroom participation. In B. Wasson, S. Ludvigsen, & U. Hopper (Eds.), *Computer support for collaborative learning 2003* (pp. 477-486). Dordect: Kluwer.

Reid, E. (1994). *Cultural formations in text-based virtual realities.* Unpublished master's thesis, University of Melbourne, Australia.

Reid, J. (1987). The learning style preferences of ESL students. *TESOL Quarterly, 21*(1), 87-111.

Renninger, K. A. (2000). Individual interest and its implications for understanding intrinsic motivation. In C. Sansone & J.M. Harackiewicz (Eds.), *Intrinsic and extrinsic motivation: The search for optimal motivation and performance* (pp. 373-404). New York: Academic.

Resnick, P. (2001). *RFC 2822 - internet message format*, Technical report, The Internet Society.

Resnick, P. (2002). Beyond bowling together: Socio-technical capital. In J.M. Carroll (Ed.), *HCI in the new millennium* (pp. 247-272). New York: Addison-Wesley.

Resnick, P., Zeckhauser, R., Swanson, J., & Lockwood, K. (2002). *The value of reputation on eBay: A controlled experiment*. Working Paper Series No. RWP03-007, John F. Kennedy School of Government, Harvard University, USA.

Rheingold, H. (1993). *The virtual community: Homesteading on the virtual frontier*. New York: Addison-Wesley.

Rheingold, H. (1994). *The virtual community: Finding connection in a computerized world*. London: Secker & Warbur.

Rheingold, H. (1998). *The art of hosting good conversations online*. Retrieved December 5, 2005, from http://www.rheingold.com/texts/artonlinehost.html

Ricket, D. (2006). Google Maps and Google Earth integration using KML. In *American Geophysical Union 2006 Fall Meeting*.

Riedl, M. O. (2001, January 14-17). A computational model and classification framework for social navigation. *Proceedings of the International Conference on Intelligent User Interfaces 2001* (pp. 137-144), Santa Fe, NM.

Roach, R. (2006). Prospective college students receptive to electronic social networking recruitment methods, survey finds. *Diverse Issues in Higher Education, 23*(23), 40.

Rocha, R. (2007, Sep 1). Even the CIA is recruiting using facebook. *Calgary Herald*, (p. D.6).

Rogers, E. (1995). *Diffusion of innovations* (4th ed.). New York: The Free Press.

Rogers, E. (2003). *Diffusion of innovations* (5th ed.). New York: The Free Press.

Rosenblum, D. (2007). *What anyone can know: The privacy risks of social networking sites*.

Rosenfeld, E. (2008). Expanding your professional network with nings. *Teacher Librarian, 35*(3), 60.

Rovai, A. P. (2002). Building a sense of community at a distance. Retrieved February 19, 2004, from *http://www.irrodl.org/content/v3.1/rovai.html*

Rushkoff, D. (1996). *Playing the Future. What We Can Learn from Digital Kids*. Riverhead Books, New York

Russell, J. (2007). Social networking: Applications for health care recruitment. *Nursing Economics, 25*(5), 299.

Russell, J. A. (1991). Culture and the categorization of emotions. *Psychological Bulletin, 110*(3), 426-450.

Salmon, G. (2003). *E-moderating: The key to teaching and learning online* (2nd ed.). London: RoutledgeFalmer.

Sandars, J., & Schroter, S. (2007). Web 2.0 technologies for undergraduate and postgraduate medical education: an online survey. *Postgraduate Medical Journal, 83*(986), 759-62.

Santoro, E. (2007). Podcasts, wikis and blogs: the web 2.0 tools for medical and health education. *Recenti progressi in medicina, 98*(10), 484-94.

Saragina, P. (1999). Creating a virtual learning community. Retrieved March 15, 2004, from *http://leahi.kcc.hawaii.edu/org/tcon99/papers/saragina.html*

Scardamalia, M., & Bereiter, C. (1994). Computer support for knowledge-building communities. *Journal of the Learning Sciences, 3*(3), 265-283.

Schafer, I. (2008). An open letter to CEOs of social-network sites: Get a relationship point person. *Advertising Age, 79*(15), 38.

Schmidt, R., Lyytinen, K., Keil, M., & Cule, P. (2001) Identifying software project risks: An international Delphi study. *Journal of Management Information Systems, 17*(4), 5-36.

Schneider, M., Lim, H., & Shoaff, W. (1992). The utilization of fuzzy sets in the recognition of imperfect strings. *Fuzzy Sets and Systems, 49*(5), 331-337.

Schoefer, K., & Diamantopoulos, A. (2008). Measuring experienced emotions during service recovery encounters: construction and assessment of the ESRE scale. *Service Business, 2*(1), 65-81.

Schraefel, M. C., Ho, J., Chignell, M., & Milton, M. (2000). Building virtual communities for research. *Proceedings of the International Working Conference and Industrial Expo on New Advances and Emerging Trends in Next Generation Enterprises*, Buffalo, NY.

Schreiber, T., & Harbo, K. (2004). Information literacy and personal knowledge management. Paper presented at the *Nord I&D, Knowledge and Change, 12th Nordic Conference on Information and Documentation*, Aalborg, Denmark, (pp. 106-114).

Schuler, D. (1996). *New community networks: Wired for change.* Reading, MA: ACM Press and Addison-Wesley.

Schuler, D., & Namioka, A. (Eds.). (1993). *Participatory design: Principles and practices.* Hillsdale, NJ: Lawrence Erlbaum.

Schwier, R. A. (2001). Catalysts, emphases, and elements of virtual learning communities. Implication for research. *The Quarterly Review of Distance Education, 2*(1), 5-18.

Sclove, R. E. (1995). *Democracy and technology.* New York: The Guildford Press.

Sebastiani, F. (2002). Machine Learning in Automated Text Categorization. *ACM Computing Surveys, 34*(1), 1–47.

Selwyn, N. (2007). *Screw blackboard... do it on facebook!': An investigation of students' educational use of facebook'.* Unpublished manuscript.

Senge, P. (1990). *The fifth discipline: The art and practice of the learning organization.* London: Currency Doubleday.

Sherry, L. (1998). An integrated technology adoption and diffusion model. *International Journal of Educational Telecommunications, 4*(2/3), 113-145.

Shi, L., Berrueta, D., Fernández, S., Polo, L., & Fernández, S. (2008). Smushing RDF instances: Are Alice and Bob the same open source developer? *Proceedings of 3rd ExpertFinder workshop on Personal Identification and Collaborations: Knowledge Mediation and Extraction (PICKME 2008), collocated with 7th International Semantic Web Conference*, Karlsruhe, Germany.

Shneiderman, B. (1998). *Designing the user interface. Strategies for effective human-computer interaction.* Boston: Addison-Wesley.

Shulman, S. (1987). Knowledge and teaching: Foundations of the new reform. *Harvard Educational Review, 57*(1), 1-22.

Simon, B. (2008, Apr 14). Campaigning investors turn to facebook the networking site helped activists get a hearing, says bernard simon. *Financial Times,* (p. 14).

Sinnema, J. (2008). Facebook could help save health care: Expert. *CanWest News.*

Skiba, D. J. (2007). Nursing education 2.0: Poke me. where's your face in space? *Nursing Education Perspectives, 28*(4), 214.

Skyrme, D. J. (1999). *Knowledge Networking: Creating the Collaborative Enterprise.* Oxford: Oxford University Press.

Slotta, J., & Linn, M. C. (2000). How do students make sense of Internet resources in the science classroom? In M. J. Jacobson & R. Kozma (Eds.), *Learning the sciences of the 21st century* (pp. 193-226). Mahwah, NJ: Lawrence Erlbaum.

Smith, Carl (1998). Can you do serious history on the Web? *AHA Perspectives, 36*(5), http://chnm.gmu.edu/resources/essays/serioushistory.php

Smith, M. (1992). *Voices from the WELL: The logic of the virtual commons.* Master's thesis, Department of Sociology, UCLA, USA.

Sociaal Economische Raad (SER). (2001). *Corporate Social Responsibility. A Dutch Approach.* Koninklijke: Assen.

Solomon, R. C. (1976). *The passions.* Garden City, NJ: Anchor Press.

Specia, L., & Motta, E. (2007). Integrating Folksonomies with the Semantic Web. In: *European Semantic Web Conference -ESWC 2007-. LNCS Vol. 4519. The Semantic Web: Research and Applications.* (pp. 503-517), Springer. Heidelberg.

Sproull, L., & Kiesler, S. (1991). Computers, networks and work. *Scientific American, 265,* 116-123.

SSHRC. (2004). *From a granting to a knowledge council.* Ottawa: Social Sciences and Humanities Research Council of Canada.

Stacey, E. (1999). *Collaborative learning in an online environment, 14*(2), 14-33. Retrieved June 27, 2005, from *http://cade.icaap.org/vol14.2/stacey.html*

Stacey, E. (2001). Social presence online: Networking learners at a distance. Paper presented at the *Seventh IFIP World Conference on Computers in Education,* Copenhagen, Denmark.

Stalk, G., Jr., Evans, E., & Shulman, L. E. (1992, March-April). Competing on capabilities: The new rules of corporate strategy. *Harvard Business Review.*

Stephenson, J. & Young, D. (2007) *The Use of an Interactive Learning Environment to Support Learning Through Work, in Work-based Learning Futures.* Young D & Garnett, J, University Vocational Awards Council, Bolton. June 27, 2008 from http://www.johnstephenson.net/jsfullcv.htm

Steward, F., & Conway, S. (2000). Building networks for innovation diffusion in Europe: Learning from the SPRINT Programme. *Enterprise and Innovation Management Studies, 1*(3), 281-301.

Stojanovic, L., Schneider, J., Maedche, A., Libischer, S., Studer, R., Lumpp, Th. Abecker, A., Breiter, G., & Dinger, J. (2004). *The role of ontologies in autonomic computing systems, IBM Systems Journal, 43*(3). http://www.research.ibm.com/journal/sj/433/stojanovic.html

Stolterman, E., Croon, A., & Argren, P.-O. (2000). *Virtual communities: Why and how they are studied.* Working paper, Department of Informatics, Umeå University, Sweden.

Storm, C., & Storm, T. (1987). A taxonomic study of the vocabulary of emotions. *Journal of Personality and Social Psychology, 53,* 805-816.

Subasic, P., & Huettner, A. (2001). Affect Analysis of Text Using Fuzzy Semantic Typing. *IEEE Transactions on Fuzzy Systems, 9*(4), 483–496.

Süpke, D., Marx Gómez, J., & Isenmann, R. (2008). Concept and implementation of a flexible and differentiated shopping cart functionality for creating personalised sustainability report. *IEEE Proceedings 3rd International Conference on Information & Communication Technologies: from Theory to Applications (ICTTA-2008) – Section Very Large Business Applications,* Damascus, (pp. 963-964).

SustainAbility Ltd, United Nations Environment Programme (UNEP). (1999). *Engaging Stakeholders 1999. The Internet Reporting Report.* Beacon Press: London.

Sycara, K., Scerri, P., & Chechetka, A. (2006). Evolutionary games and social networks in adversary reasoning. In *Proceedings of the international conference on complex systems.* Boston.

Szeto, E. (2000). Innovation capacity: working towards a mechanism for improving innovation within an inter-organizational network. *The TQM Magazine, 12*(2), 149-158.

Tarlow, M. (2003, January 30). Paper presented at HP Laboratories, Palo Alto, CA.

Taylor, P., & Jonker, L. (1978). Evolutionary stable strategies and game dynamics. *Mathematical Biosciences, 40.*

Teo, H-H., Oh, L. B., Liu, C., & Wei, K. K. (2003). An empirical study of the effects of interactivity on web user attitude. *International Journal of Human-Computer Studies, 58*(3), 281-305.

Terziovski, M., & Howell, A. (2001). *e-Commerce best practice: A review of the Victorian e-Commerce early movers* (VEEM) scheme in Victorian local councils. Report prepared for Multimedia Victoria, State and Regional Development.

The Complete Oxford English Dictionary. (1971). Oxford: Oxford University Press.

Thomond P., & Lettice F. (2002). Disruptive Innovation Explored. *9th IPSE International Conference on Concurrent Engineering: Research and Applications* (CE2002).

Tidd, J., & Bessant, J., & Pavitt, K. (2001). *Managing Innovation, Integrating Technological, Market and Organizational Change.* John Wiley.

Times Newspapers. (2004). The Sunday Times university guide 2004. *Sunday Times* (London), (September 12), supplement.

Tiwana, A., & Ramesh, B. (2001). Integrating knowledge on the Web. *IEEE Internet Computing,* 5(3), 32-39.

Tomkins, S. S. (1984). Affect theory. In K. R. Scherer & P. Ekman (Eds.), *Approaches to emotion.* Hillsdale, NJ: Lawrence Erlbaum Associates.

Tong, S. T., Van Der Heide, B., Langwell, L., & Walther, J. B. (2008). Too much of a good thing? the relationship between number of friends and interpersonal impressions on facebook. *Journal of Computer-Mediated Communication, 13*(3), 531-549.

Travers, J., & Milgram, S. (1969). An experimental study of the small world problem. *Sociometry, 32,* 425-443.

Tudge, J., & Rogdoff, B. (1989). Peer influences on cognitive development: Piagetian and Vygotskian perspectives. In M. H. Bornstein & J. S. Bruner (Eds.), *Interaction in human development* (pp. 17-40). Hillsdale, NJ: Lawrence Erlbaum.

UNDP. (2001). Information communications technology for development. *Essentials,* 5. Available at http;//www.undp.org/eo/documents/essentials_5.PDF. Accessed Jan. 30, 2006.

Unerman, J., & Bennett, M. (2004). Increased stakeholder dialogue and the internet: Towards greater corporate accountability or reinforcing capitalist hegemony? *Accounting, Organziations and Society, 29*(7), 685-707.

United Nations Environment Programme Industry and Environment (UNEP), Sustainability Ltd. (1994). *Company Environmental Reporting. A Measure of the Progress of Business and Industry Towards Sustainable Development.* Technical Report 24. UNEP: Paris.

University College London (2006). Retrieved June 27, 2008 from http://www.publishing.ucl.ac.uk/events.html

Valente, T. (1995). *Network models of the diffusion of innovations.* Cresskill, NJ: Hampton Press.

Valente, T. (2005). Models and methods for innovation diffusion. In P. Carrington, J. Scott, & S. Wasserman (Eds.), *Models and methods in social network analysis.* Cambridge: Cambridge University Press.

van Dolen, W., de Ruyter, K., & Lemmink, J. (2004). An empirical assessment of the influence of customer emotions and contact employee performance on encounter and relationship satisfaction. *Journal of Business Research, 57*(4), 437-444.

Vander Wal, T. (2008). *Folksonomy.* Retrieved October 27, 2008, from http://vanderwal.net/folksonomy.html

Vargo, S. L., & Lusch, R. F. (2004). Evolving To A New Dominant Logic For Marketing. *Journal of Marketing, 68*(1), 1-17.

Verhaart, M. (2003). Developing a system to capture knowledge based on sharable and self documenting learning objects. *International Forum of Educational Technology & Society.* http://www.ymlp.com/pubarchive_show_message.php?eLearning+138

Visser, W. (2002). Sustainability reporting in South Africa. *Corporate Environmental Strategy, 9*(1), 79-85.

Volund, E. (1993). *Grundriss der soziobiologie.* Stuttgart/Jena: G. Fischer Verlag.

Vygotsky, L. S. (1978). *Mind in society: The development of higher psychological processes* (M. Cole, V. John-Stenier, S. Scribner, & E. Souberman, Trans.). Cambridge, MA: Harvard University Press.

W3C (2001). Retrieved June 27, 2008 from www.w3.org/

Wallace, A. E. C., & Carson, M. T. (1973). *Sharing and diversity in emotion terminology. Ethos, 1,* 1-29.

Walther, J. B., Van Der Heide, B., Kim, S., Westerman, D., & Tong, S. T. (2008). The role of friends' appearance and behavior on evaluations of individuals on facebook: Are we known by the company we keep? *Human Communication Research, 34*(1), 28-49.

Wang, Y. (2008). In Kumar V. (Ed.), *Will the overseas expansion of facebook succeed?*

Watson, M. (2008). Social networking: An opportunity for health and social care? *Journal of Integrated Care, 16*(1), 41.

Watts, D. J., Dodds, P. S., & Newman, M. E. J. (2002). Identity and search in social networks. *Science, 296*(5571), 1302-1305.

Watts, D., & Strogatz, S. (1998). Collective dynamics of small-world networks. *Nature, 393.*

Weaver, A. C. (2008). In Morrison B. B. (Ed.), *Social networking.*

Webb, G. (2007). A new future for brand marketing. *The British Journal of Administrative Management*, 13.

Weibull, J. (1995). *Evolutionary game theory.* Cambridge, MA: MIT Press.

Weinberg, A. M. (1989). Science, government, and information: 1988 perspective. *Bull. Med. Libr. Assoc., 1,* 1–7.

Wellman, B. (1988). Structural analysis: From method and metaphor to theory and substance. In B. Wellman & S. Berkowitz (Eds.), *Social structures: A network approach* (pp. 19-61). Cambridge: Cambridge University Press.

Wenger, E. (1998). *Communities of practice: Learning, meaning, and identity.* Cambridge, MA: Cambridge University Press.

Wenger, E., McDermott, R., & Snyder, W. M. (2002). *Cultivating communities of practice: A guide to managing knowledge.* Boston: Harvard Business School Press.

Westerman, D. (2008). How do people really seek information about others? Information seeking across internet and traditional communication channels. *Journal of Computer-Mediated Communication, 13*(3), 751-767.

Wheeler, D., & Elkington, J. (2001). The end of the corporate environmental report? Or the advent of cybernetic sustainability reporting and communication. *Business Strategy and the Environment, 10*(1), 1-14.

Wickre, K. (1995). *Virtual communities: Are they real? Are they real enough?* Retrieved May 1, 2003, from http://www.thenet-usa.com/mag/back/0995/community.html

Wierzbicka, A. (1992). Defining emotion concepts. *Cognitive Science, 16*(4), 539 – 581.

Wikipedia. (2004). *Wikipedia.* Retrieved August 9, 2004, from *http://en.wikipedia.org/wiki/Main_Page*

Williams, R. (1973). *Keywords.* Oxford: Oxford University Press.

Wise, K., Hamman, B., & Thorson, K. (2006). Moderation, response rate, and message interactivity: Features of online communities and their effects on intent to participate. *Journal of Computer-Mediated Communication, 12*(1), 24-41.

Wood, A. F. & Smith, M. J. (2001). *Online communication: Linking technology, identity, and culture.* Hillsdale, NJ: Lawrence Erlbaum Associates, Inc.

Woodruff, E. E. (1999). Concerning the cohesive nature of CSCL communities. In C. M. Hoadley & J. Roschelle (Eds.), *Proceedings of Computer Supported Collaborative Learning '99 Conference* (pp. 677-680). Mahwah, NJ: Lawrence Erlbaum.

WordNet. http://wordnet.princeton.edu/. Last verified: 02 October, 2008.

World Business Council for Sustainable Development (WBCSD). (2002). *Communications and Stakeholder Involvement Guidebook for Cement Facilities*. Report prepared by the Battelle Memorial Institute and Environmental Resources Management. http://www.wbcsdcement.org/pdf/final_report1_2.pdf [18 September 2003].

World Wide Consortium (W3C). (1999). *Resource description framework (RDF) model and syntax specification*. Retrieved January 24, 2006, from http://www.w3.org/TR19991/REC-rdf-syntax-19990222/

World Wide Consortium (W3C). (2000, March 21). *Resource description framework (RDF) schema specification 1.0*. Retrieved January 24, 2006, from http://www.w3.org/TR/2000/CR-rdf-schema-20000327/

World Wide Consortium (W3C). (2004, February 10). *OWL Web ontology language overview*. Retrieved January 24, 2006, from http://www.w3.org/TR/2004/REC-owl-features-20040210/

World Wide Consortium (W3C). (2004, January 9). *RDQL: A query language for RDF*. Retrieved January 24, 2006, from http://www.w3.org/Submission/2004/SUBM-RDQL-20040109/

Wu, C-S., & Huang, H-C. (2006) A Study of Knowledge Management in Elementary Schools: Advantageous Situations, Difficulties, and Strategies. *Bulletin of Educational Research, 52*(2), 33-65.

Yamagishi, T., & Matsuda, M. (2002). *Improving the lemons market with a reputation system: An experimental study of Internet auctioning*. Retrieved December 5, 2005, from http://joi.ito.com/archives/papers/Yamagishi_ASQ1.pdf

Yang, I. S., Ryu, S. S., Cho, K.,J., Kim, J. K., Ong, S. H., Mitchell, W. P., Kim, B. S., Oh, H. B., & Kim, K. H. (2008). IDBD: Infectious Disease Biomarker Database. *Nucleic Acids Research, 36*(1), 455-460.

Yang, S. P. (2005). *A Study on the Relationship between Elementary School Teachers' Personal Knowledge Management and Their Professional Performance*. Institute of Education Management and Administration, National University of Tainan, unpublished Master thesis, http://lib.nutn.edu.tw, (pp. 69-74).

YouTube (2008) Retrieved June 27, 2008 from www.YouTube.co.uk

Zahner, J. (2002). Teachers explore knowledge management and e-learning as models for professional development. *TechTrends, 46*(3), 11-16.

Zeelenberg, M., & Pieters, R. (2004). Beyond valence in customer dissatisfaction A review and new findings on behavioral responses to regret and disappointment in failed services. *Journal of Business Research, 57*(4), 445-455.

Zipf, G. K. (1949). *Human Behavior and the Principle of Least-Effort*. Addison-Wesley.

Zuber-Skerritt, O. (2005). A model of values and actions for personal knowledge management. *The Journal of Workplace Learning*, 17(1/2), 49-64.

About the Contributors

Miltiadis D. Lytras is an assistant professor in the Computer Engineering and Informatics Department-CEID (University of Patras). His research focuses on semantic web, knowledge management and e-learning, with more than 100 publications in these areas. He has co-edited / co-edits, 25 special issues in International Journals (e.g. *IEEE Transaction on Knowledge and Data Engineering, IEEE Internet Computing, IEEE Transactions on Education, Computers in Human Behaviour*, etc.) and has authored/[co-]edited 12 books [e.g. *Open Source for Knowledge and Learning management, Ubiquitous and Pervasive Knowledge Management, Intelligent Learning Infrastructures for Knowledge Intensive Organizations, Semantic Based Information Systems*] . He is the founder and officer of the Semantic Web and Information Systems Special Interest Group in the Association for Information Systems (http://www.sigsemis.org). He serves as the (Co) Editor in Chief of 12 international journals [e.g. *International Journal of Knowledge and Learning, International Journal of Technology Enhanced Learning, International Journal on Social and Humanistic Computing, International Journal on Semantic Web and Information Systems, International Journal on Digital Culture and Electronic Tourism, International Journal of Electronic Democracy, International Journal of Electronic Banking, International Journal of Electronic Trade*] while he is associate editor or editorial board member in seven more.

Patricia Ordóñez de Pablos is professor in the Department of Business Administration and Accountability, at the Faculty of Economics of The University of Oviedo (Spain). Her teaching and research interests focus on the areas of strategic management, knowledge management, intellectual capital measuring and reporting, organizational learning and human resources management. She is executive editor of the *International Journal of Learning and Intellectual* and the *International Journal of Strategic Change Management* (Inderscience Publisher). She is editor of *International Journal of Asian Business and Information Technologies* (IGI-Global)

* * *

José Javier Astrain received his MS degree in telecommunications engineering from the State University of Navarra in 1999, and his PhD degree in computer science from the same university in 2004. He is currently an assistant professor of computer science at the State University of Navarra. His current research interests include pattern recognition, Semantic Web and folksonomies.

Naomi Augar completed her Bachelor's of computing (applied computing) with Honours in 2002 at Deakin University, Melbourne Australia. Presently she is a PhD candidate in the School of Information Technology at Deakin University. Her PhD research focuses on virtual learning communities. Her research interests include issues relating to constructing an online identity, virtual communication and e-learning.

Anthony 'Skip' Basiel has been researching eLearning pedagogy, and teaching, since moving from the U.S. to England to pursue his graduate education in the mid-1990s. He is a certified online tutor for the University for Industry, has published his research internationally, and has been the keynote speaker at several international eLearning conferences. In 2004, Skip was awarded the title "eTutor of the Year" by the Higher Education Academy-UK. Skip's eLearning research has enabled him to work with trans-national partners in European higher education as well as private organizations, corporate trainers, and government agencies. A prime example is the British Council—CEDEFOP study, hosted by Middlesex University in 2004.

Diego Berrueta Muñoz holds a MSc in computer science by the University of Oviedo. He was awarded with two intermediate and two final awards to the best qualifications. At the present moment, he studies for his PhD degree at the same university. He has proven experience on the development of declarative languages and compilers (Zinc Project, awarded by the Asturian Institute of Computer Engineers). He coordinates the Semantic Web Unit at the CTIC Foundation R&D department, where he is involved in national and European research projects. He has advised three students in their degree projects on the Semantic Web field. As part of his participation in the Semantic Web Deployment Working Group at W3C, he has edited a W3C technical report and reviewed the RDFa specifications.

Anton Chechetka is a doctoral student at the Robotics Institute at Carnegie Mellon University. He received his BS in applied mathematics and physics from Moscow Institute of Physics and Technology in Russia, and an MS in robotics from the Robotics Institute. His research interests are mostly in machine learning and probabilistic inference.

Ricardo Colomo-Palacios has been a faculty member of the Computer Science Department at Universidad Carlos III de Madrid since 2002. His research interests include software process improvement, software project management and information systems. He received his PhD in computer science from the Universidad Politécnica of Madrid (2005). He also holds a MBA from the Instituto de Empresa (2002). He has been working as software engineer, project manager and software engineering consultant in several companies including Spanish IT leader INDRA.

Alberto Córdoba received the MS degree in physics from the University of the Basque Country (Spain) in 1982 and the PhD degree in physics from the same university in 1991. He is currently an associate professor at the State University of Navarra. His research interests include Semantic Web, Web 2.0, distributed systems and algorithms, operating systems design, and databases. He is a member of the ACM.

Paul Coyne, with over 13 years experience in software and training systems engineering, is currently Emerald's research and development manager. He has a special interest and responsibility for developing e-learning and emerging technology propositions. Prior to joining Emerald, Paul was the senior e-learning systems architect with ICT Consultancy firm LogicaCMG where he was responsible for the design, delivery and development of e-learning content and delivery systems. In 2006 Paul was the lead designer and developer of the JISC funded ToCross project, successfully delivered to the JISC and subsequently rolled out by TALIS, Emerald and the University of Derby.

Ben K. Daniel has a broad research interest in artificial intelligence in education (AIED), currently; his active research focuses on virtual learning communities, distributed communities of practice, knowledge management, and the Bayesian Belief Network. He works with the GKN project as a research associate. He is also a member of the Virtual Learning Communities Research Laboratory in Educational Communications and Technology, and the Laboratory for Advanced Research in Intelligent Educational Systems (ARIES) in the Department of Computer Science. In the two research laboratories, he works under the supervision of Dr. Richard A. Schwier, professor of educational communications and technology, and Dr. Gordon McCalla, professor of computer science, both at the University of Saskatchewan, Canada. Mr. Daniel is currently pursuing his PhD.

Tom Denison, a doctoral candidate, is attached to the Centre for Community Networking Research at Monash University. With a background in library automation, he has worked on library automation projects in Vietnam and Australia and has experience in system design and specification. He co-founded INFORMIT Electronic Publishing and has consulted widely, specializing in the development of online services including online library services, the development of commercial publishing via the Internet, and the design and delivery of related educational materials. His research interests focus on the effective use of information and communications technology (ICT) by community sector organisations.

Francisco Echarte received his MS degree in computer science from the University of the Basque Country in 1999. He is currently a PhD student in computer science at the State University of Navarra. He is also working as IT specialist at the Healthcare Service of Navarra Government. His current research interests include Semantic Web, folksonomies and social Webs.

Sergio Fernández holds a BSc in computer science by the University of Oviedo (2006). His degree dissertation, SWAML, is a software project which uses the SIOC ontology to generate semantic representations of mailing lists. SWAML received the First Spanish University Free Software Award. Sergio co-authored the SIOC specifications and related documents, currently a W3C Member Submission. Currently, he works as junior researcher in the Semantic Web Unit at the CTIC Foundation R&D Department, whereby he takes part in several national and European projects and initiatives. After an internship in DERI NUI Galway, he continues studying his MSc in computer science at the University of Oviedo.

Angel García-Crespo is the head of the SofLab Group at the Computer Science Department in the Universidad Carlos III de Madrid and the head of the Institute for promotion of Innovation Pedro Juan de Lastanosa. He holds a PhD in industrial engineering from the Universidad Politécnica de Madrid (Award from the Instituto J.A. Artigas to the best thesis) and received an Executive MBA from the Instituto de Empresa. Professor García-Crespo has led and actively contributed to large European projects of the FP V and VI, and also in many business cooperations. He is the author of more than a hundred publications in conferences, journals and books, both Spanish and international.

Kam Hou Vat is currently a lecturer in the Department of Computer and Information Science, under the Faculty of Science and Technology, at the University of Macau, Macau SAR, China. His current research interests include learner-centered design with constructivism in Software Engineering education, architected applications developments for Internet software systems, information systems for learning organization, information technology for knowledge synthesis, and collaborative technologies for electronic organizations and virtual communities.

Ralf Isenmann read economics, business administration, and industrial engineering at the University of Kaiserslautern (Germany). Currently, he is a senior researcher at the Fraunhofer Institute for Systems and Innovation Research (ISI), Karlsruhe (Germany). Further he is an associate professor at the Faculty of Business Studies and Economics and a member of the Research Center for Sustainability (artec), University of Bremen (Germany). He teaches innovation management, corporate communications, sustainability management, and industrial ecology management. He received his venia legendi from the University of Bremen for a professional academic thesis (Habilitation) on "Internet-based sustainability reporting. Corporate communication in the information society" and his PhD from the University of Kaiserslautern for a thesis on environmental management. His research interests are in the interfaces between innovation management, sustainability management, and information management.

Yongil Jeong is an associate research engineer of Saltlux Inc. in Korea. His research areas include applications of the Semantic Web and natural language processing.

Jaehun Joo is a professor at Dongguk University (Korea). His research has appeared in *Information Systems Management, Expert Systems with Applications, International Journal of Industrial Engineering, INFORMS, Journal of MIS Research, Korean Management Reviews,* and other publications. His research interests include e-business, e-tourism, u-commerce, knowledge management, and Semantic Web. This work was supported by the research program of Dongguk University.

Laszlo Z. Karvalics, (47) Budapest, Hungary. Founding director, BME-UNESCO Information Society Research Institute (1998), associate professor, head, Department of Library and Information Science, University of Szeged (2007). Teaching and research on social impacts of information technology, comparative analysis of national information strategies, information history and education in the information age. Founding editor of the Hungarian language *Information Society Quarterly.* His best-selling books are (in Hungarian): *Introduction to Information History* (Gondolat, 2004), *Information, Society, History* (Typotex, 2003), *Searching of the Information Society* (Aula, Budapest, 2001). MA in history, literature and linguistics, PhD and Hab. in history, ELTE, Budapest.

Triantafillia Kourtoumi serves as a senior archivist at the General State Archives of Greece; as an associate lecturer at the Department of Human Studies of the Hellenic Open University; as an associate lecturer at the Department of Librarian and Information Studies, the Technological Educational Institution of Greece; as an associate lecturer at the Hellenic National Centre of Public Management. She is mainly focused on exploratory studies of knowledge management applications in the archival domain (i.e. Principal Investigator of the "Thematic Web Collections for Social Sciences and the Humanities." The Oral History Project *"Migrant Women in the Greek City of Thessaloniki, 1990s-2000s"* in progress, in open access at migrant-women.jeromeDL.org).

Jose Emilio Labra Gayo obtained his PhD in computer science engineering in 2001. Since 2004, he is the dean of the School of Computer Science Engineering at the University of Oviedo, Spain and since 2006 he coordinates the Master's on Web engineering at that school. His research areas are programming languages and Web technologies, especially XML and Semantic Web. He participates in several research projects with some companies interested in the practical application of Semantic Web technologies. He leads the research group WESO (Semantic Web Oviedo) and is member of several internacional scientific committees related with his research areas. He is also the author of numerous publications in those fields.

Elicia Lanham received her B.Computing (information management) and B.Computing (Honours) degrees from Deakin University, Melbourne, Australia in 2001 and 2002, respectively, and a Certificate II in small business management from the Vocational and Educational Training Accreditation Board (VETAB), Australia, 2000. She is currently a PhD candidate in the School of Information Technology, Deakin University, Melbourne, Australia. Her research interests include practical and cultural issues of Internet education, cross-cultural learning styles and e-learning.

Adela Lau is an assistant professor in school of nursing and serves as knowledge management specialist in the knowledge management research center at the department of industrial and systems engineering of the Hong Kong Polytechnic University. Her specialties are ontology engineering, knowledge management, health informatics and intelligence, healthcare systems and technology. She has extensive consultancy and training experience on knowledge audit, technology and strategy formulation. She is an active researcher of ontology engineering, health informatics and applications. She is the editor-in-chief of the *International Journal of Knowledge Engineering and Data Mining* and an editorial board member of the *International Journal of Electronic Healthcare*.

Sang M. Lee is the university eminent professor, Firstier bank distinguished professor, chair of the Management Department, CBA, University of Nebraska (Lincoln). He has authored or co-authored 50 books, mostly in the field of management. He has published more than 170 journal articles, and 360 original papers and has presented over 2,000 speeches. He is currently president of the Pan-Pacific Business Association. He also served as president of the Decision Sciences Institute. He has organized 26 international conferences as the program chair. He is on the editorial board of 23 journals, and has been listed in more than 50 Who's Who publications, including *Who's Who in America*.

Changqing Li is a PhD candidate in Department of Computer Science, School of Computing, National University of Singapore. He has submitted his PhD thesis. His research interests include ontology modeling, Semantic Web, data integration and data interoperability, XML query and update processing based on labeling schemes, and query of XML changes. During his PhD period, Changqing published 10 papers at different journals and conferences, including *VLDB Journal,* ICDE06, DASFAA06, CIKM05, DASFAA05, DEXA05, and ER04. In addition, he has published three papers during his MS period in Peking University, China. He is a student member of IEEE.

Tok Wang Ling is a professor in the Department of Computer Science, School of Computing at the National University of Singapore. His research interests include data modeling, entity-relationship approach, object-oriented data model, normalization theory, logic and database, integrity constraint checking, semistructured data model, and data warehousing. He has published more than 150 international journal/conference papers and chapters in books, and co-authored a book, mainly in data modeling. He also co-edited 12 conference and workshop proceedings. He organized and served as program committee co-chair of DASFAA'95, DOOD'95, ER'98, WISE 2002, and ER 2003. He organized and served/serves as conference co-chair of Human.Society@Internet conference (HSI) in 2001, 2003, and 2005, WAIM 2004, ER 2004, DASFAA 2005, SIGMOD 2007. He is the honorary conference chair of DASFAA 2006. He serves/served on the program committees of more than 100 international database conferences since 1985. He is the advisor of the steering committee of International Conference on Database Systems for Advanced Applications (DASFAA), a member of the steering committee of International Conference on Conceptual Modeling (ER), and the International Conference on Human. Society@Internet (HSI). He was chair and vice chair of the steering committee of ER conference and DASFAA conference, and was a member of the steering committee of International Conference on Deductive and Object-Oriented Databases (DOOD). He is an editor of the *Journal Data & Knowledge Engineering, International Journal of Cooperative Information Systems, Journal of Database Management, Journal of Data Semantics,* and *World Wide Web: Internet and Web Information Systems.* He is a member of ACM, IEEE, and Singapore Computer Society.

Jorge Marx Gómez studied computer engineering and industrial engineering at the University of Applied Science of Berlin (Technische Fachhochschule). He was a lecturer and researcher at the Otto-von-Guericke-Universität Magdeburg where he also obtained a PhD degree in business information systems with the work "Computer-Based Approaches to Forecast Returns of Scrapped Products to Recycling." In 2004 he received his habilitation for the work "Automated Environmental Reporting through Material Flow Networks" at the Otto-von-Guericke-Universität Magdeburg. From 2002 till 2003 he was a visiting professor for business informatics at the Technical University of Clausthal. In 2005 he became a full professor of business information systems at the Carl von Ossietzky University Oldenburg. He is the chair of the department Very Large Business Applications. His research interests include business information systems, business intelligence, e-Commerce, material flow management systems, life cycle assessment, eco-balancing, sustainability reporting, recycling program planning, disassembly planning and control, simulation and neuro-fuzzy-systems.

Juan Miguel Gomez-Berbís is a visiting professor at the Computer Science Department of the Universidad Carlos III de Madrid. He holds a PhD in Computer Science from the Digital Enterprise Research Institute (DERI) at the National University of Ireland, Galway and received his MSc in telecommunications engineering from the Universidad Politécnica de Madrid (UPM). He was involved in several EU FP V and VI research projects and was a member of the Semantic Web Services Initiative (SWSI). His research interests include semantic web, semantic web services, business process modelling, b2b integration and, recently, bioinformatics.

Myriam Mencke is a researcher in Natural Language Processing in UC3M. She holds an MSc by research in computational linguistics, M.Phil. in linguistics, and Postgraduate Diploma in statistics from Trinity College Dublin, Ireland. Her primary degree is a Bachelor of Business Studies degree with French, Waterford Institute of Technology, Waterford, Ireland. Her research interests include computational linguistics, text classification, and Semantic Web. The title of her MSc thesis is "Benchmarking a Text Classification Technique" She has researched in Digital Enterprise Research Institute (DERI), Galway, Ireland, working on the NEPOMUK Project (Networked Environment for Personal Ontology-based Management of Unified Knowledge). She has also been a team member on the projects SONAR (Buscador Financiero Corporativo Basado en Tecnologia Semantica) and GODO (Goal Oriented Discovery for Semantic Web) in UC3M.

Miranda Mowbray is a technical contributor at HP's European research laboratories in Bristol, UK. She received a PhD degree in algebra from London University. Dr. Mowbray co-authored *Online Communities: Commerce, Community Action, and the Virtual University,* published by Prentice-Hall in 2000, and she was one of the founders of e-mint, the Association of UK Online Community Professionals, which has been listed as one of the most-cited influences on the industry. She has advised many projects on the design of online communities.

David O'Brien, a PhD candidate, is the manager of international research at the University of Saskatchewan, Canada. His interest in collective action problems has led to research on communities and interest groups, and their effect on policy development and social service delivery. His interaction with his chapter co-authors has taken his research interests in the temporal world into the virtual domain. He also holds an MPhil from Sussex University, UK.

Ruth Raitman received her BSc (mathematics) and BComputing (Honours) degrees from Deakin University, Australia in 2000 and 2001, respectively, and is currently a PhD candidate in the same university, intending to complete all requirements by the end of 2005. She is the HDR representative of the Faculty of Science and Technology School of Information Technology School Board at Deakin and also acts as an online facilitator and tutor for several units. Her research interests include e-learning, online collaboration and the employment of wikis in the virtual environment.

I. Samanta is a faculty member of the Department of Business Administration, Graduate Technological Education Institute of Piraeus, she received her Bachelor's in business administration from the Graduate Technological Education Institute of Piraeus, her Master's degree from University of Paisley, UK. She is a PhD candidate from University of the West of Scotland, UK. Her current scientific research activities include e-marketing, B2B relationship, marketing communication, innovation culture. Her research has been presented in more than 16 European and global conferences with proceedings.

In addition, she has published a number of articles in scientific journals. She is member of the editorial committee in *Strategic Outsourcing*, an international journal (EMERALD Group Publishing) and responsible for suggesting acceptance or rejection of each submission.

Asit Sarkar is professor of management and marketing, and director of the International Center for Governance and Development, both at the University of Saskatchewan, Canada. Spanning a career of more than 30 years, Dr. Sarkar held a variety of academic and administrative appointments at the University of Saskatchewan and other institutions in Canada and abroad. He served as the first director of the University of Saskatchewan International (USI) and special advisor to the president of the University of Saskatchewan.

Paul Scerri is a system scientist at the Robotics Institute at Carnegie Mellon University. He holds a BS in applied science (honors) from RMIT University in Australia and a PhD from Linkoping University in Sweden. He has been a research associate at the Information Sciences Institute at the University of Southern California. His research focuses on multi-agent coordination and human interaction with intelligent systems. He has contributed to the areas of adjustable autonomy, multi-agent systems, and team work. He has authored over 70 technical publications and has made contributions to several research programs including Defense Advanced Research Projects Agency (DARPA) programs software for distributed robotics, robot-agent-person teams, and autonomous negotiating teams.

Lian Shi graduated from Guizhou University, China, 2003. After that, she majored in computer science, especially artificial intelligence, and attained her Master's degree from college of Computer Science and Technology, Jilin University in 2006. Afterward, she's continuing her PhD studies since 2006 until now in Jilin University with the main research topics of Semantic Web and description logics. Furthermore, in 2008, she won an internship as a junior researcher at CTIC Foundation in Spain. Whilst there, she bears into semantic web related projects with the main aim of developing prototypes by applying semantic web technologies.

Sandy Staples is a professor and distinguished research faculty fellow of management information systems in the School of Business at Queen's University, Kingston, Canada. His research interests include virtual work, knowledge sharing, and IS effectiveness. His current research is investigating how Web 2.0 technologies can help manage the diversity in distributed teams. Sandy has published articles in various journals and books including *Organization Science, Information & Management, Information Systems Research, Small Group Research, Information Systems Journal,* and *Research in Personnel and Human Resources Management*. He has served as an associate editor for *MIS Quarterly* and on other journal editorial boards.

Daniel Süpke studied computer science at the University Oldenburg with focus on environmental informatics. He continued his work in Oldenburg as a research assistant at the Department Very Large Business Applications. Within this, he spent one semester teaching at the Wadi German Syrian University in Syria. Currently, he is a PhD student with a scholarship endowed by the Deutsche Bundesstiftung Umwelt. His research is covering sustainability reporting in combination with Web 2.0.

Katia Sycara is a professor in the School of Computer Science at Carnegie Mellon University and the Sixth Century Chair in Computing at the University of Aberdeen. She holds a PhD in computer science from Georgia Institute of Technology and an honorary doctorate from the University of the Aegean. She has authored more than 300 technical papers on Semantic Web services, multi-agent systems, and human-agent interaction. She is a lead developer of the OWL-S language for Semantic Web services. She is a fellow of IEEE, Fellow of AAAI, and the recipient of the 2002 ACM/SIGART Agents Research Award. She is a founding editor-in-chief of the journal *Autonomous Agents and Multi Agent Systems* and on the editorial board of six additional journals.

Eric Tsui is the professor of knowledge management at The Hong Kong Polytechnic University. Prof. Tsui was formerly chief research officer, Asia Pacific, in Computer Sciences Corporation (CSC) (2000-5). He joined CSC in 1989 after years of academic research in automated knowledge acquisition, natural language processing, case-based reasoning and knowledge engineering tools. His research was supported by grants and scholarships from Arthur Young, Rank Xerox, CSC, Graphic Directions, and the Australian Research Council. He was also a gratis visitor to Microsoft Research in February, 2000. Between August 2000 and January 2005, he assumed the roles of innovation manager at Australian Mutual Provident (AMP) and Maybank, two strategic outsourcing accounts at CSC in the Asia Pacific region. Eric was responsible for strategic research, knowledge brokering (between CSC and the clients), innovation management and university-industry collaborations. During his tenure at CSC, he had made significant contributions to CSC's expert systems products, applied research, Portal community leadership, and innovation programs. Eric has designed and delivered many KM and Portals workshops for government departments including CSTDI, Health, Land Registry, OGCIO and EPD.

Jesús Villadangos received his MS degree in physics from the University of the Basque Country in 1991, and his PhD degree in computer science from the State University of Navarra in 1999. He is currently associate professor at the State University of Navarra. His current research interests include software quality, and enterprise knowledge management.

Jingyuan Zhao, postdoctoral in Business Administration Postdoctoral Center, Harbin Institute of Technology(China). Her PhD is in management science and engineering in Chinese Academy of Sciences and University Science and Technology of China. Dr. Zhao's expertise is on regional innovation management, high-tech industry cluster, knowledge management, technology diffusion, organization learning. She is an invited reviewer for China state-run newspaper West Times to provide economy comments and policy analysis.

Wanlei Zhou received the BEng and MEng degrees from Harbin Institute of Technology, Harbin, China in 1982 and 1984, respectively, and the PhD degree from The Australian National University, Canberra, Australia, in 1991. He is currently the chair professor of IT and the head in School of Information Technology, Deakin University, Melbourne, Australia. Before joining Deakin University, professor Zhou has been a programmer in Apollo/HP at Massachusetts, USA, a chief software engineer in HighTech Computers at Sydney, Australia, a lecturer in National University of Singapore, Singapore, and a lecturer in Monash University, Melbourne, Australia. His research interests include theory and practical issues of building distributed systems, Internet computing and security, and e-learning. Professor Zhou is a member of the IEEE and IEEE Computer Society.

Index